Microsoft Power Platform Up and Running

Learn to Analyze Data, Create Solutions, Automate Processes, and Develop Virtual Agents with Low Code Programming

Robert Rybaric

www.bpbonline.com

Copyright © 2023 BPB Online

All rights reserved. No part of this book may be reproduced, stored in a retrieval system, or transmitted in any form or by any means, without the prior written permission of the publisher, except in the case of brief quotations embedded in critical articles or reviews.

Every effort has been made in the preparation of this book to ensure the accuracy of the information presented. However, the information contained in this book is sold without warranty, either express or implied. Neither the author, nor BPB Online or its dealers and distributors, will be held liable for any damages caused or alleged to have been caused directly or indirectly by this book.

BPB Online has endeavored to provide trademark information about all of the companies and products mentioned in this book by the appropriate use of capitals. However, BPB Online cannot guarantee the accuracy of this information.

Group Product Manager: Marianne Conor
Publishing Product Manager: Eva Brawn
Senior Editor: Connell
Content Development Editor: Melissa Monroe
Technical Editor: Anne Stokes
Copy Editor: Joe Austin
Language Support Editor: Justin Baldwin
Project Coordinator: Tyler Horan
Proofreader: Khloe Styles
Indexer: V. Krishnamurthy
Production Designer: Malcolm D'Souza
Marketing Coordinator: Kristen Kramer

First published: 2023

Published by BPB Online
WeWork, 119 Marylebone Road
London NW1 5PU

UK | UAE | INDIA | SINGAPORE

ISBN 978-93-55512-024

www.bpbonline.com

About the Author

Robert Rybaric, author of this book, had the exceptional luck and privilege to learn Microsoft CRM back in 2005, when no one could be sure, whether this product survives the next year or two. But it did and it developed to one of the leading global cloud services for building business applications, called the Microsoft Power Platform. Robert was working in this exciting area since the mentioned 2005 until now continuously and never regrated to follow this path. During this time, he worked for some Microsoft partner companies but his longest tenure was with Microsoft itself, where he worked as a solution architect between 2008 and 2018. During this time, he had the privilege to work with many large global enterprises in presales as well as delivery capacity to help them on their way into the digital transformation with Microsoft Dynamics 365 and Microsoft Power Platform. Since 2018, he is independent, working as a solution architect and trainer for the same product lines. He is a Microsoft Certified Trainer (MCT) and holds all relevant product certifications as well.

Preface

This book represents the introduction into the exciting world of low-code / no-code business applications creation with Microsoft Power Platform. You will find everything you need to understand the low-code / no-code paradigm and learn the Microsoft Power Platform. We are covering all Power Platform components, and we do this in a very practical way. You will start very early with practical exercises since we believe, that learning by doing is the best method to learn something new.

The book is divided into **11 chapters**. They cover the fundamental knowledge of the Power Platform, Microsoft Dataverse, Power Apps, Power Automate, Power BI, Power Virtual Agents, as well as AI Builder. Following are the contents of the chapters:

Chapter 1 will introduce you into the world of the business IT in the past and today and present the challenges the IT is facing today. You will learn what the low-code / no-code paradigm is, and how can it help organizations be more agile and save costs when it comes to building business applications. You will be made familiar with the fundamentals of the Power Platform, which is the Microsoft implementation of a low-code / no-code cloud solution platform. You will get an overview of the components; the Power Platform consists of. Finally, we are presenting an overview of the licensing options and at the end you will create your own Power Platform environment for the exercises, you will be offered in the subsequent chapters.

Chapter 2 is introducing the Microsoft Dataverse as the foundation for many Power Platform cloud services. You will learn about Power Apps, and what types of Power Apps are available. In this chapter we are focusing on the model-driven Power Apps applications, which are used for building enterprise-grade business solutions. You will meet Project Wizards, Inc. – a fictitious company, interested in building a new project management solution. You will start building this solution by designing a data model in Microsoft Dataverse and creating a model-driven application, followed by importing some sample data into the data model. In this chapter you will also learn about the Microsoft Dynamics 365 applications, covering the typical CRM workloads like marketing, sales, customer service or field service.

Chapter 3 will drive our attention to the other Power Apps types – the canvas apps and the portal apps. You will learn the fundamentals of canvas apps and how to build them. Next, you will create a simple canvas app for Project Wizards, Inc. to track the project hours of their employees. In the second part of this chapter, you will make yourself familiar with the portal apps, what are they used for and how to create a portal solution. You will configure a simple portal for the customers of Project Wizards, Inc., to give them the possibility to approve the project related costs.

Chapter 4 will introduce Power Automate to you. You will learn what Power Automate is, and what are the types of Power Automate flows. We are going to focus on the cloud flows and desktop flows, which represent the technologies used for enterprise-grade cross-application automation solutions. In this chapter, you will continue with the practical exercises, you will create an approval flow, used by Project Wizards, Inc. for approving project hours of the employees. In the second part of the chapter, you will learn about the desktop flows and see a possible practical implementation of a desktop flow solution for automated vendor invoice processing.

Chapter 5 continues with Power Automate by focusing on the more interactive frontend use of Power Automate. You will learn the button flows fundamentals, what are those flows, and where they can be used. You will see a couple of practical situations, where a button flow can be used as a simple mobile application combined with the automation capabilities. In the second part of this chapter, you will learn the business process flows, used to extend the model-driven applications with guided, process-driven capabilities for the users. You will create a business process flow for the model-driven application for project management, you created in chapter 2. Finally, you will learn about the remaining automations, available in the Power Platform and implement a business rule in the project management model-driven application.

Chapter 6 will introduce the next Power Platform component – the Power BI. In this chapter you will learn the fundamentals of Power BI and the very important difference between Import and DirectQuery. You will see how a Power BI solution is created using the main tool – the Power BI Desktop. You will dive deeper into the first phase of building an analytical solution with Power BI – the connection to data sources, import of data into the Power BI Desktop and the various data transformations, available within this tool. In the practical exercise in this chapter, you will connect to Microsoft Dataverse to use the data of the project management solution to build analytics with Power BI. In an advanced part of this exercise, you will connect also to local databases to import some other data used in the next chapter to build additional visualizations. Finally, you will learn about data modeling, and you will create the final data model for Project Wizards, Inc.

Chapter 7 will continue with Power BI, presenting the second part of the creation of an analytical solution – the configuration of the visualizations, the publishing into the Power BI cloud and the integration of a Power BI solution with Power App and Power Automate. In this chapter, you will learn about the main types of visualizations, available for creation of a Power BI report. You will continue with the solution for Project Wizards, Inc, by creating a report with a whole bunch of different visualization. In the second part, you will learn how to publish a report into the cloud, and you will practice this with the report for Project Wizards, Inc. After that you will learn about creating Power BI dashboards, and you will immediately also create one practically in the next exercise. Finally, we will present the integration possibilities of Power BI with the other Power Platform components, which will be also practiced in the last exercise of this chapter.

Chapter 8 will introduce Power Virtual Agents. You will learn about chatbots, and where are they used. You will see, how easy is it to create a chatbot using the Power Virtual Agents technology. We will present the fundamentals of this products, you will learn about topics, the conversation nodes, and how to integrate a chatbot with other IT systems. In this chapter, you will create a chatbot for answering project-related questions for Project Wizards, Inc. You will learn how to test a chatbot and how to integrate it into a hosting environment. In the second exercise in this chapter, you will integrate the chatbot into the portal application you created in chapter 3.

Chapter 9 will present the last Power Platform component – the AI Builder. You will learn about AI and how it can be used within business applications. We will show you which AI models are available in the product and how can they be used. You will see how AI Builder can help you to easily create an AI model. This will be illustrated in an example on how vendor invoices, sent by email, can automatically be analyzed and the context extracted. Finally, you will learn how can an AI Builder model be integrated with model-driven apps, canvas apps and Power Automate flows, which will be demonstrated with another practical example.

Chapter 10 is dedicated to administering the Power Platform. You will learn some fundamental information about Power Platform environments and how they are administered in the Power Platform Admin Center. Next, we will introduce the solution management, which is used to deploy solutions between environments. Finally, you will learn about the application lifecycle management (ALM) when building business applications with the Power Platform as well as about the possibilities how to automate the administration and the solution management using some handy Microsoft tools and products.

Chapter 11 will present two major Power Platform capabilities – the security and the governance. You will learn about the fundamentals of the IT security and how is this implemented in the Power Platform. We will present you the security capabilities in Microsoft Dataverse, the Power Apps, Power Automate and Power BI. In the second part, you will learn about the governance and why is it important to care about it. We will present the data policies and the Center of Excellence Starter Kit as the two main governance components for the Power Platform.

Code Bundle and Coloured Images

Please follow the link to download the
Code Bundle and the *Coloured Images* of the book:

https://rebrand.ly/4e4042

The code bundle for the book is also hosted on GitHub at **https://github.com/bpbpublications/Microsoft-Power-Platform-Up-and-Running**. In case there's an update to the code, it will be updated on the existing GitHub repository.

We have code bundles from our rich catalogue of books and videos available at **https://github.com/bpbpublications**. Check them out!

Errata

We take immense pride in our work at BPB Publications and follow best practices to ensure the accuracy of our content to provide with an indulging reading experience to our subscribers. Our readers are our mirrors, and we use their inputs to reflect and improve upon human errors, if any, that may have occurred during the publishing processes involved. To let us maintain the quality and help us reach out to any readers who might be having difficulties due to any unforeseen errors, please write to us at :

errata@bpbonline.com

Your support, suggestions and feedbacks are highly appreciated by the BPB Publications' Family.

> Did you know that BPB offers eBook versions of every book published, with PDF and ePub files available? You can upgrade to the eBook version at www.bpbonline.com and as a print book customer, you are entitled to a discount on the eBook copy. Get in touch with us at :
>
> **business@bpbonline.com** for more details.
>
> At **www.bpbonline.com**, you can also read a collection of free technical articles, sign up for a range of free newsletters, and receive exclusive discounts and offers on BPB books and eBooks.

Piracy

If you come across any illegal copies of our works in any form on the internet, we would be grateful if you would provide us with the location address or website name. Please contact us at **business@bpbonline.com** with a link to the material.

If you are interested in becoming an author

If there is a topic that you have expertise in, and you are interested in either writing or contributing to a book, please visit **www.bpbonline.com**. We have worked with thousands of developers and tech professionals, just like you, to help them share their insights with the global tech community. You can make a general application, apply for a specific hot topic that we are recruiting an author for, or submit your own idea.

Reviews

Please leave a review. Once you have read and used this book, why not leave a review on the site that you purchased it from? Potential readers can then see and use your unbiased opinion to make purchase decisions. We at BPB can understand what you think about our products, and our authors can see your feedback on their book. Thank you!

For more information about BPB, please visit **www.bpbonline.com**.

Table of Contents

1. **Introducing Microsoft Power Platform** 1
    Introduction 1
    Structure 1
    Objective 2
    Business IT in the 21st century 2
    The low-code/no-code paradigm 3
    Power Platform fundamentals 5
    Power Platform components 6
        Microsoft Dataverse 7
        Power Apps 7
        Power Automate 8
        Power BI 8
        Power Virtual Agents 8
        AI Builder 9
        Data connectors 9
        On-premises data gateway 9
        The fusion development 10
    Power Platform licensing overview 10
        Microsoft 365/Office 365 licensing 11
        Power Platform standalone licensing 12
        Dynamics 365 licensing 13
        Power BI licensing 13
        Power Platform trials 14
        Power Platform developer plan 14
        Power Platform pay-as-you-go (consumption-based) licensing 14
        Summary 15
    Power Platform system requirements 15
    How to start with Power Platform 16
        Power Platform tools 16

   Power Platform admin center 17
   Maker Portal 17
   Power Automate portal 17
   Power BI Desktop 18
   Microsoft SQL Server (advanced) 18
   MySQL (advanced) 19
  Power Platform mobile 19
  Prepare Power Platform environments 19
   Provision of a Microsoft cloud tenant 20
   Activating a Power Platform developer plan license 23
 Conclusion 25
 Questions 25

2. Building Enterprise Solutions with Power Apps 27
 Introduction 27
 Structure 27
 Objective 28
 Use cases for Power Apps 28
  Introducing Project Wizards, Inc. 28
 Types of Power Apps 29
  Model-driven apps 29
  Canvas apps 31
  Portal apps 32
  Power Apps for Project Wizards, Inc. 33
 Microsoft Dataverse fundamentals 33
  Exercise 1: Creating a data model 35
   Analysis and preparations 35
   Practical implementation 36
 Model-driven apps fundamentals 50
  Exercise 2: Creating a model-driven app 51
   Analysis and preparations 51
   Practical Implementation 51

    Building enterprise-ready model-driven apps 56
        Exercise 3: Importing sample data 57
    Dynamics 365 considerations 58
        Dynamics 365 Marketing 59
        Dynamics 365 Sales 59
        Dynamics 365 Customer Service 59
        Dynamics 365 Field Service 59
        Dynamics 365 Project Operations 60
        Make or buy? 60
    Conclusion 60
    Questions 60

3. Enable Mobility and Integrate Partners with Power Apps 61
    Introduction 61
    Structure 61
    Objective 62
    Use cases for Power Apps 62
    Canvas apps fundamentals 62
    Design of the Project Tracking app 64
    Connect to data with canvas apps 65
        Exercise 4 – Create app and connect it to data 66
            Create new table views 66
            Create a new canvas app 67
    Build user interface and functionality with canvas apps 68
        Canvas apps user interface 68
        Exercise 5 – Create and design an app screen 70
            Configure the application header 70
            Configure the toggle control 71
            Configure the gallery 72
            Configure the buttons 74
        Fundamentals of Power Fx 76
        Exercise 6 – Configure app functionality 77

Enable employee mobility with canvas apps 79
    Exercise 7 — Publish, share, and test the app 79
Portal apps fundamentals 80
Design of the Project Wizards customer portal 81
Configure simple portal apps 81
    Exercise 8: Create a customer portal 82
        Create the portal application 83
        Prepare a model-driven view and model-driven form 83
        Configure the portals solution I 84
        Configure the portals solution II 86
Integrate your customers with portal apps 89
Conclusion 90
Questions 90

4. Automate Processes with Power Automate 91
Introduction 91
Structure 91
Objective 92
Use cases for Power Automate 92
Types of Power Automate automations 93
Cloud flows fundamentals 94
    Cloud flows action types 95
    Cloud flows logic 96
    Cloud flows expressions 97
Automated cloud flows 100
    Exercise 9: Create an approval flow 102
        Analysis and preparations 102
        Practical implementation 103
Scheduled cloud flows 112
Desktop flows fundamentals 113
Build hyper-automated solutions 114
    Example 1 — Create a sample vendor invoice processing solution 115
Conclusion 117
Questions 117

5. Use Power Automate on Clients 119

Introduction 119

Structure 119

Objectives 120

Use cases for Power Automate 120

Button cloud flows fundamentals 120

Use button flows for personal automation 125

    Vacation request 125

    Upload files to SharePoint or OneDrive 126

    Create an Azure Active Directory user 128

Business process flows fundamentals 129

    Exercise 10: Create a business process flow 130

        Analysis and preparations 130

        Practical implementation 131

Dataverse automations fundamentals 136

    Business Rules 136

    Exercise 11: Create a business rule 137

        Analysis and preparations 137

        Practical implementation 137

    Classic workflows 140

    Classic custom actions 140

Use cloud flows in Power Apps 140

    Event-based automations 141

    Scheduled automations 141

    On-demand automations 141

    Example 2: Create an on-demand automation 141

Use Dataverse automations in Power Apps 143

    Frontend automations 143

    On-demand automations 144

    Backend automations 145

Conclusion 146

Questions 146

6. Start with Power BI 147
Introduction 147
Structure 147
Objective 148
Use cases for Power BI 148
Power BI fundamentals 149
The difference between Import and DirectQuery 151
Power BI Desktop overview 154
Connect to data with Power BI Desktop 155
    Exercise 12: Connect to Microsoft Dataverse 157
        Advanced part 159
Transform data with Power Query 163
Build a data model 165
    Create relationships between the tables 165
    Create calculated columns 166
    Create measures 167
    Exercise 13: Data modeling 167
Conclusion 172
Questions 172

7. Integrate Analytics with Power BI 175
Introduction 175
Structure 175
Objectives 176
Power BI visualizations overview 176
    Bar and column charts 176
    Line and area charts 178
    Ribbon charts 180
    Waterfall charts 180
    Funnel charts 180
    Scatter charts 181
    Pie and donut charts 183

Maps, filled maps, and shape maps	183
Treemaps	185
Other chart types	185
Create a Power BI report	186
Exercise 14: Building a report	186
Publish a Power BI report	197
Exercise 15: Publishing a report	197
Create Power BI dashboards	199
Exercise 16: Creating a dashboard	200
Use Natural language query	202
Integrate analytics with apps and flows	203
Exercise 17: Integrating a dashboard	204
Conclusion	207
Questions	207

8. Chat with Power Virtual Agents 209

Introduction	209
Structure	209
Objectives	210
Use cases for Power Virtual Agents	210
Power Virtual Agents fundamentals	211
Create a bot	212
Create topics and conversation nodes	213
Integrate your bot with other IT systems	216
Exercise 18: Creating a chatbot	216
Test and publish your bot	226
Host your bot on a website and in Microsoft Teams	228
Exercise 19: Integrating a chatbot into a Power Apps portal	229
Conclusion	231
Questions	232

9. Bring Intelligence with AI Builder 233

Introduction	233

Structure	233
Objectives	234
Use cases for AI Builder	234
Document processing	234
Products recognition	235
Automated text analysis	235
AI Builder fundamentals	236
Overview of the AI Builder models	237
Text-processing models	238
Sentiment analysis	238
Category classification	239
Entity extraction	239
Key phrase extraction	239
Language detection	240
Text translation	240
Image-processing models	240
Invoice processing	240
Text recognition	240
Receipt processing	240
Identity document reader	241
Business card reader	241
Document processing	241
Object detection	241
Image classification	241
Data-processing models	242
Prediction	242
Configure and test a custom model	242
Example 3: Extract information from vendor invoices	242
Integrate your model with model-driven apps	253
Integrate your model with canvas apps	253
Integrate your model with Power Automate	254
Example 4: Test vendor invoice processing	254

Conclusion 259

Questions 260

10. Administer the Power Platform.. 261

Introduction 261

Structure 261

Objectives 262

Overview of the Power Platform administration 262

Users and groups administration 263

Administration of Power Platform environments 264

Configuration settings in Power Platform environments 265

Power BI administration 266

Power Platform environments overview 266

The Power Platform Admin Center 268

Power BI Admin Portal 269

Power Platform environment strategies 270

Simple project 270

Complex project with multiple teams 271

Complex project with multiple releases 271

Solution management fundamentals 272

Exercise 20: Exporting a Power Platform solution 275

Application lifecycle management (ALM) fundamentals 277

Automate Power Platform fundamentals 278

Conclusion 279

Questions 280

11. Secure and Govern the Power Platform 281

Introduction 281

Structure 281

Objectives 282

IT security fundamentals 282

Authentication in the Microsoft cloud 283

Advanced authentication concepts 284

Multi-factor authentication (MFA) 285
Integration between on-premises active directory and Azure Active Directory 285
Conditional access 285
Authorization in Microsoft Dataverse 285
The Microsoft Dataverse users 286
The ownership of records 288
The business units 289
The security roles 290
Basic authorization model explained 293
The Teams 296
The Hierarchy Security 298
The Column-Level Security 298
Authorization in Power Apps 300
Model-driven apps authorization 300
Canvas apps authorization 301
Portal apps authorization 302
Authorization in Power Automate 303
Authorization in Power BI 303
Build secure Power Platform solutions 304
Power Platform governance fundamentals 305
Data policies 305
Exercise 21: Creating a data policy 307
The Center of Excellence Starter Kit 310
Power BI CoE starter kit report 310
Power Platform admin view 312
Admin—Command Center 313
Other apps 314
Conclusion 315
Questions 316

Index 317-325

CHAPTER 1
Introducing Microsoft Power Platform

Introduction

In this introductory chapter, you will learn the low-code/no-code paradigm for creating business applications and what impact it does have on your business. Next, we will introduce the Microsoft Power Platform as a cloud service, providing you with exactly such a low-code solution. You will see what components contain the Power Platform and learn the licensing fundamentals. Finally, we will provide you with step-by-step guidance on how to provision your own Power Platform environment for learning the next topics covered in this book.

Structure

In this chapter, we will discuss the following topics:

- Business IT in the 21. century
- The low-code/no-code paradigm
- Power platform fundamentals
    - Components
    - Licensing overview
    - System requirements

- How to start with Power Platform

Objective

After reading this chapter, the reader will be able to have a basic understanding of the low-code/no-code paradigm in creating business applications and how Microsoft Power Platform can help you to adopt this approach. You will learn the foundation of Power Platform and set up your own working environment for the practical exercises which will accompany your Power Platform journey in this book.

Business IT in the 21st century

The world of business IT is constantly changing at a very high pace. The whole IT industry is barely older than an average length of a human life today, but in this relatively short period of time, we are facing tremendous development. Let us just remember how it was at the very beginning as information technology found its way into the business. IT was represented by huge data centers full of those mainframe computers processing programs and data prepared on punch cards and later magnetic tapes. The IT staff was a group of mysterious experts running around in white cloaks and providing not-so-well understandable operations to keep the whole infrastructure up and running. No single person without a deep understanding of IT technology was able to make any use of it.

And what do we have today? Almost everybody has a smartphone with a much higher computing capacity than all of those legacy mainframe systems ever had. A large majority of professionals are using IT systems on a daily basis. IT is everywhere, not just in PCs, tablets, and smartphones but also in smartwatches, TVs, and even refrigerators. The industry is full of IT as well. Companies from start-ups to corporations are using cloud computing, mobile devices, and machines of any kind equipped with internet-enabled sensors to leverage the benefits of the **Internet of Things (IoT)**. We are facing a super-fast evolution of **artificial intelligence (AI)**, augmented, and mixed reality. This leads to unprecedented growth of data produced by humans and machines. Companies of any size need to leverage this data to provide better products and services to their clients. And they need to do it fast.

On the other hand, we also see issues with adopting these fast-evolving trends. The business needs new modern solutions immediately, and yesterday was already too late. A major issue is represented by a lack of skilled and experienced IT experts. This leads to a clear conclusion that implementing IT solutions today and tomorrow must be done differently than how it was this done yesterday. The possible answer to this challenge is called low-code/no-code.

The low-code/no-code paradigm

So, what is that low-code/no-code actually? Simply put in one sentence, it is an approach where everybody can build business solutions. Really everybody? Well, yes, at least everybody who is interested to do so and has a certain affinity to information technology. A university degree in IT or any other deep understanding of the world of IT is not required because technology has removed all the road blockers for entering this world. For a more precise definition, let us have a look at Wikipedia.

> **Low-code development platform** (https://en.wikipedia.org/wiki/Low-code_development_platform)
>
> *"A low-code development platform (LCDP) provides a development environment used to create application software through a graphical user interface instead of traditional hand-coded computer programming. A low-coded platform may produce entirely operational applications or require additional coding for specific situations. Low-code development platforms reduce the amount of traditional hand coding, enabling accelerated delivery of business applications. A common benefit is that a wider range of people can contribute to the application's development—not only those with coding skills. LCDPs can also lower the initial cost of setup, training, deployment and maintenance."*
>
> **No-code development platform** (https://en.wikipedia.org/wiki/No-code_development_platform)
>
> *"No-code development platform (NCDPs) allow programmers and non-programmers to create application software through graphical user interfaces and configuration instead of traditional computer programming. No-code development platforms are closely related to low-code development platforms as both are designed to expedite the application development process. However, unlike low-code, no-code development platforms require no code writing at all, generally offering prebuilt templates that businesses can build apps with. These platforms have both increased in popularity as companies deal with the parallel trends of an increasingly mobile workforce and a limited supply of competent software developers."*

The preceding definitions are very well describing the approach; let us briefly analyze the benefits and possible drawbacks.

Lack of skilled IT professionals

Low-code/no-code is an ideal solution for filling the ever-growing gap between demand and availability of IT professionals. Anyone with a certain affinity for building business applications can become a *"citizen developer"* or *"maker"*.

Time to market

Modern IT solutions must be provided fast. In the traditional IT-driven approach, an IT project must be planned, prepared, and executed in a traditional way consisting of procurement, contracting of vendors, contracting of implementation partners, or planning own IT resources, and finally implementing the solution. This is not only a lengthy but also a very expensive approach. Low-code/no-code means the organization must adopt the respective platform once and then leverage this platform for repeatedly building solutions according to the current demand using its own business users as the implantation staff.

Price

There is no doubt that a do-it-yourself approach using a low-code/no-code platform is much cheaper than the classic approach with a standard project setup and an external consultancy.

Scope

Is a low-code/no-code approach suitable for implementing any business solution? The answer is clearly: no. It is important to have a clear understanding of where it is possible and where it is not. Companies and organizations have different types of information systems. If we are talking about business-critical IT systems, the low-code/no-code approach is most likely impossible. Just think about an extreme example of an IT system controlling the operations in a nuclear plant, usually a highly sophisticated system with the highest possible reliability and security standards. Or a less extreme example could be the main ERP system for a corporation—here, we will most likely see a standard solution from a vendor such as SAP, Oracle, or Microsoft implemented by highly skilled experts.

So, what is the right scope for a low-code/no-code approach? Let us try to identify a few examples:

- A company is running a legacy IT solution, which is not planned to be replaced in the near future, but a lack of flexibility makes it impossible to use this solution on the go, on a mobile device. This is a typical use case from the real world, where the low-code/no-code approach can bring quick benefits. You can use such a platform and build the mobile app for your users while at the same time continue using the proven legacy solution.
- A company would like to progress in the digital transformation by leveraging the long-hanging fruits and automating some obvious business processes, such as time-off requests, travel and expenses reports, or every kind of approval. Again, with low-code/no-code, you can build such small solutions quickly with little effort and achieve significant benefits.

- An organization would like to start replacing paper-based business processes with digital processes.
- A company would like to move away from Excel-based analytics, where every employee just creates his own analytics, to a more centralized self-service analytical solution, where the work of an individual can easily be shared with others.

These are just a few examples from many, illustrating the right scope of a low-code/no-code approach.

So, what is the take for you as a business user or manager interested in accelerating the digital transformation in your organization:

- Adopt a low-code/no-code platform.
- Ensure management support and establish an initial internal expert group—a center of excellence, to facilitate the broad adoption of the platform.
- Elaborate on strategy, goals, and success metrics to achieve the best outcomes using the platform.
- Establish an internal community, and ensure training and learning opportunities are available.
- Identify use cases, long-hanging fruits, or generally all areas where digitalization can bring the most benefits and start building real solutions.
- Foster the use of the platform for more and more scenarios to achieve a proper saturation so that the platform is used optimally to achieve the desired results.

To make your decision easier, let us together have a look at one of the market leaders, the well-known company Microsoft, and their low-code/no-code cloud offering called *Microsoft Power Platform*.

Power Platform fundamentals

So, what is actually the Microsoft Power Platform? Shortly said, it is a collection of multiple cloud services for building business applications with the low-code/no-code approach. The Power Platform is one of the market leaders, as you can see, for example, on the Gartner Magic Quadrant for enterprise low-code application platforms (**https://powerapps.microsoft.com/en-us/blog/microsoft-is-a-leader-in-the-2021-gartner-magic-quadrant-for-enterprise-low-code-application-platforms/**).

The Power Platform can be used for building the following types of business solutions:

- **Business applications** for any device—PCs, tablets, and smartphones, and for internal or external users.
- **Automation solutions**, automating processes across a wide range of different IT system types, such as modern cloud or on-premises systems with an API, legacy IT systems without any API, or even standard desktop applications.
- **Analytical solutions** for analyzing various possible data types coming from different data sources.
- **Chatbots**, extend the business applications with an AI-based chat service.

The various business solution types can be further extended with capabilities such as artificial intelligence, augmented reality, or the **Internet of Things (IoT)**.

Let us now have a closer look at the various components the Power Platform consists of.

Power Platform components

The Microsoft Power Platform at a high level consists of the following components, as illustrated in the diagram:

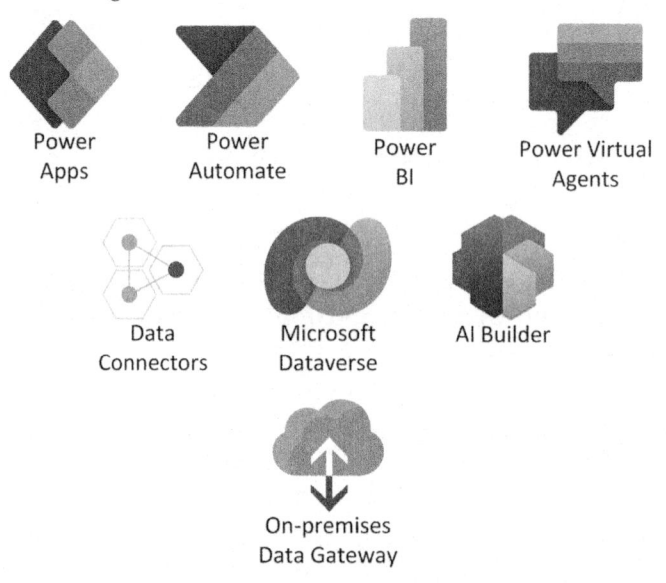

Figure 1.1: Structure of the Power Platform

Let us now have a closer look at the individual components of the Power Platform.

Microsoft Dataverse

Microsoft Dataverse is the hearth of the Power Platform, and even though it is not very visible to the end user, it is driving or supporting almost every other Power Platform component. Shortly said, Microsoft Dataverse is the Power Platform native relational database and, at the same time, a comprehensive application platform for building business applications. Microsoft Dataverse is hosting the following important features for your business solutions:

- The **data model** and the **business data** for certain types of Power Apps.
- The data model and data for other Power Platform components such as Power Automate approvals, AI Builder, or Power Virtual Agents.
- **Automation capabilities** such as Business Rules, Workflows, and more.
- A strong and flexible **security model** for implementing complex authentication requirements.

You will see many more details about the Microsoft Dataverse features later in this book.

Power Apps

Power Apps is a collection of three technologies that are used to build business applications for the end users. The result of our effort with Power Apps is a business application that can run either on a PC, a tablet, or a smartphone. Power Apps consist of the following three major types of technologies:

(1) **Model-driven apps**, which is used for building robust, enterprise-ready business application primarily used on PCs. These applications can be used only by internal users of your organization.

(2) **Canvas apps**, which is used for building smaller specific applications for mobile devices. These applications are also used by internal users of your organization.

(3) **Portal apps**, which is used to build business applications for your external parties such as customers, partners, vendors, citizens, or patients. Basically, you can build web-based applications directly integrated with Microsoft Dataverse, where selected business data can be easily shared with external parties.

We will dive deeper into these three application types in the subsequent *Chapter 2: Building Enterprise Solutions with Power Apps* and *Chapter 3: Enable Mobility and Integrate Partners with Power Apps* of this book.

Power Automate

Power Automate is again a collection of three different technologies used for building cross-applications and cross-technology automation solutions. Power Automate can be used for building independent automation or can be part of an overall business solution when combined with Power Apps. Power Automate consists of the following three major types of technologies:

- **Cloud flows**, which are used for building cross-application and cross-technology automation across IT systems having an API.

- **Desktop flows,** is a specific technology that falls into the **Robotic Process Automation (RPA)** category of software products. With the desktop flows, you can build automation across legacy and desktop applications having no API, where no technical interface can be built.

- **Business process flows**, which are used within model-driven Power Apps to change the working style of the users from data-centric to process-centric.

Further details about Power Automate will be discussed in *Chapter 4, Automate Processes with Power Automate* and *Chapter 5, Use Power Automate on Clients* of this book.

Power BI

Power BI is a collection of on-premises and cloud services dedicated to building visualizations and analytical solutions. Power BI is able to connect to a broad variety of different source databases and IT systems to get the right data for your required solutions. With the raw data from the sources, you can start consolidating your future data model using a powerful tool called **Power Query** to bring the data into the required structure. After that, you can build your visualizations and the required analytics and insights. The final solution can then be consumed either on the Power BI portal separately or the mobile application, or it can also be integrated into your Power Apps-based business solution.

You will learn more about Power BI in *Chapter 6, Start with Power BI* and *Chapter 7, Integrate analytics with Power BI* of this book.

Power Virtual Agents

Power Virtual Agents is a low-code/no-code graphical designer for building chatbots. The chatbots technology is growing constantly at a high pace, and more and more monotonous work is today replaced with chatbots. Using chatbots instead of humans in certain scenarios cannot just save labor costs but also provide a predictable functionality available 24 × 7. Power Virtual Agents let you build chatbots for external as well as internal audiences because your chatbots can be integrated into a variety of channels such as websites, mobile apps, and so on used by the public audiences, but also into Microsoft Teams, which, in turn, is a scenario for supporting internal users.

Power Virtual Agents will be discussed in more detail in *Chapter 8, Chat with Power Virtual Agents* of this book.

AI Builder

AI Builder is a typical example of a complex technology adopted successfully into the low-code/no-code world. Today's business applications require more and more artificial intelligence functionality, and implementing this in a traditional way requires deep AI and custom development expertise. AI Builder removes these road blockers by providing a no-code tool to establish AI models and integrate them into your business applications. AI Builder currently offers 17 different AI models, some of which are already pre-trained; others must be trained with your own data to achieve the desired functionality. After preparing an AI model in the AI Builder, this can be easily integrated into your Power Apps or Power Automate solutions.

We will go into the details of the AI Builder in *Chapter 9, Bring Intelligence with AI Builder* of this book.

Data connectors

Power Platform data connectors are a collection of more than 600 connectors, which make it easily possible to connect to a broad variety of different IT systems and technologies. The purpose of the data connectors is to hide the complexity of connecting to system interfaces while building Power Platform solutions. Instead of developing interface components with code, you just identify the right data connector for your desired technology and connect using just proper configuration. The data connectors are used specifically when building Power Apps/Canvas apps and Power Automate cloud flows. We mentioned already that there are—as of now—more than 600 data connectors available in the Power Platform, but this number is constantly growing, and you can expect around 10–15 new data connectors coming each and every month.

Data connectors are not specifically covered in any of the subsequent chapters, but you will learn more about the possibilities in chapters discussing Power Apps and Power Automate.

On-premises data gateway

The on-premises data gateway is a technology component used for establishing a secure communication channel between the Power Platform cloud solutions and your own on-premises data center. The purpose of this technology is to make it easily possible to include your own on-premises IT systems, such as databases, business applications, and more, into the Power Platform-based solutions.

The on-premises data gateway can be used in the following scenarios:

- A Power Apps/Canvas app needs to connect to on-premises IT systems.
- A Power Automate cloud solution needs to connect to on-premises IT systems.
- A Power BI analytical solution needs to leverage data from on-premises databases or business applications.
- You need to build hybrid automation consisting of Power Automate cloud flows and desktop flows.
- You need to import data from on-premises data sources into Microsoft Dataverse using the import tool called Dataflows.

You will find a handful of use cases and practical examples of using the on-premises data gateway in the subsequent chapters of this book.

The fusion development

Power Platform is a low-code/no-code cloud service, and Microsoft is investing heavily to make the platform more and more suitable for the "*makers*" or "*citizen developers*". However, when the complexity of the required business solution breaks a certain level, custom development might be necessary. There are multiple places where a Power Platform solution can be extended with custom development, such as building custom data connectors, custom automation code for Dataverse, or extending the functionality with integration with Microsoft Azure. Microsoft describes this approach as fusion development, where teams of business experts, citizen developers, and professional IT developers work together to build the required business solution's capabilities.

Power Platform licensing overview

The Power Platform is a **Software as a Service** (**SaaS**) type of cloud solution. It is usual to license this type of solution using a monthly per-user/per-product fee. For Power Platform, this is the base licensing model; however, Microsoft recently extended the licensing possibilities for Power Platform also with a consumption-based model.

There are basically the following licensing possibilities:

- Microsoft 365/Office 365 licensing

- Power Platform standalone licensing
- Dynamics 365 licensing
- Power BI licensing
- Power Platform trials
- Power Platform developer plan
- Power Platform pay-as-you-go (consumption-based) licensing

Let us have a closer look at the possibilities of the various licensing models.

> Note: Please note that the licensing is subject to frequent changes, so the most current version of the product licensing needs to be considered. More information can be found here: https://docs.microsoft.com/en-us/power-platform/admin/pricing-billing-skus

Microsoft 365/Office 365 licensing

Microsoft provides certain limited Power Platform capabilities also as part of the various Microsoft 365/Office 365 licenses.

The fundamental principles for this type of licensing are as follows:

- It is possible to build Power Apps/Canvas Apps and Power Automate/Cloud flows.

- It is possible to leverage all **standard data connectors**. The standard data connectors group contains all connectors to the Microsoft 365/Office 365 services along with a growing number of third-party connectors for various popular services. The use of premium connectors is not allowed with this license model.

- It is possible to use Microsoft Dataverse in limited functionality for certain Microsoft 365 subscription plans, especially to use a specific Microsoft Dataverse environment type called *"Default"*. You will find further details about Power Platform environments in *Chapter 2, Building Enterprise Solutions with Power Apps* of this book.

- It is further possible to use Microsoft Dataverse for Teams in limited functionality for certain Microsoft 365 subscription plans in order to build Power Apps/Canvas Apps, Power Automate/Cloud flows, and Power Virtual Agents chatbots. All of these solution components can be accessed only from within Microsoft Teams.

> **Note: For further details about using Microsoft Dataverse within the Microsoft 365/Office 365 subscriptions, please refer to the following resources:**
>
> https://docs.microsoft.com/en-us/power-platform/admin/pricing-billing-skus#dataverse-capabilities-with-microsoft-365-licenses
>
> https://docs.microsoft.com/en-us/power-platform/admin/about-teams-environment

Generally speaking, are the possibilities for building business applications rather limited with this license model; for leveraging the full Power Platform potential, a real Microsoft Power Platform is necessary.

Power Platform standalone licensing

The Power Platform standalone licensing options offer the most capabilities to leverage all Power Platform services. There are generally the following standalone licensing options:

- **Power Apps per app plan**, which allows the use of one single Power Apps app per user.
- **Power Apps per user plan**, which allows the use of unlimited Power Apps app per user.
- **Power Automate per user plan**, which allows the use of unlimited Power Automate cloud flows per user.
- **Power Automate per flow plan**, which allows for organization-wide use of a single Power Automate cloud flow.

In addition to these basic license types, multiple Power Platform components require additional licenses, specifically:

- Power Apps portals
- Power Automate for desktop (the RPA component in Power Automate)
- Power Virtual Agents
- AI Builder
- Power BI (see details about the Power BI licensing later in this chapter)

To make the things even more complex, multiple license plans allow certain use of other Power Platform services, such as a Power Apps license also allows the use of Power Automate, and so on.

Dynamics 365 licensing

Microsoft Dynamics 365 does not belong to the Power Platform, at least from the licensing point of view. However, the CRM apps, such as Marketing, Sales, Customer Service, Field Service, and Project Operations, are technologically running on Power Platform. That is why it is important to understand the licensing options also for these products. Dynamics 365 offers pure SaaS licensing per user and month, or per other KPI per month according to this overview:

- Dynamics 365 Sales, Dynamics 365 Customer Service, Dynamics 365 Field Service, and Dynamics 365 Project Operations are all licensed with the per user/per months license model

- Dynamics 365 Marketing provides a combined per app/per month and per marketing contact/per month license model

- There are multiple AddOns for the various Dynamics 365 apps, which are licensed separately with different license models

Note: For further details about using Microsoft Dynamics 365 licensing, please refer to the following resources:

https://dynamics.microsoft.com/en-us/pricing/

You will learn more details about the Microsoft Dynamics 365 apps and the typical use cases, where those apps can be considered in the upcoming chapter of this book.

Power BI licensing

Microsoft Power BI is an established technology, which used to be separate until it was brought under the Power Platform umbrella. There are, however, still significant technological differences between Power BI and the other parts of the Power Platform, as you will learn in the subsequent chapters of this book.

The licensing model of Power BI is influenced by the technology features and consists of the following licensing options:

- **Power BI Free**, which is free of charge and allows limited consumer-only access to content

- **Power BI Pro**, which allows the creation and publishing of content

- **Power BI Premium per user**, which allows the creation of advanced content, such as paginated reports, using advanced AI, dataflows, and some other advanced features

- **Power BI Premium per capacity**, which is the highest licensing level, offers all available Power BI features on a dedicated cloud infrastructure

> **Note: For further details about using Microsoft Power BI licensing, please refer to the following resources:**
>
> https://powerbi.microsoft.com/en-us/pricing/

For Power BI, there are also some cross-licensing options, where certain other Power Platform licenses allow limited use of Power BI.

Power Platform trials

Power Platform trials are an easy and free option to test the capabilities of Power Platform for a limited period of time. You can easily activate a trial license and create a Power Platform environment within a few minutes. Power Platform trials can be used for a duration of 30 days, after which they expire. It is further possible to one more time extend the lifetime of a trial environment for additional 30 days. Power Platform trials have no serious limitations, so you can use this option to make yourself familiar with everything of interest.

Power Platform developer plan

Another interesting free licensing option is the **Power Platform developer plan** license. This license type makes it possible to create one single permanent Power Platform environment free of charge. The only serious limitation is that the environment can be used only by one single user—the creator of the environment.

> **Note: Note: For further details about the Power Platform Developer Plan licensing, please refer to the following resources:**
>
> https://powerapps.microsoft.com/en-us/developerplan/

The purpose of this environment is to learn and test various Power Platform features, however, not to run production applications.

Power Platform pay-as-you-go (consumption-based) licensing

The latest Power Platform licensing model is the **pay-as-you-go license**. This license model is dedicated to Microsoft customers already having a Microsoft Azure subscription because the billing of the Power Platform usage is based on consumption and is part of the Microsoft Azure billing.

> **Note:** For further details about the Power Platform pay-as-you-go licensing, please refer to the following resources:
>
> https://docs.microsoft.com/en-us/power-platform/admin/pay-as-you-go-overview

This license type is suitable for customers with the large number of users, where the Power Platform apps and flows are expected to be used infrequently so that a standard SaaS licensing would be more costly.

Summary

Power Platform licensing is very complex, and for full implementation of the platform into an organization, especially a large organization, a thorough analysis of the licensing options and an ROI analysis of the selected licensing model would be appropriate.

Power Platform system requirements

Microsoft Power Platform is a cloud solution with few exceptions. So, the system requirements to use it are quite simple:

- For the use of any Power Platform component on a PC, you need an internet connection and one of the supported web browsers: Microsoft Edge, Google Chrome, or Mozilla Firefox.

- For the use of any Power Platform component on a Mac computer, you need an internet connection and one of the supported Web browsers: Apple Safari or any of the three Web browsers mentioned previously.

- To use apps on a mobile device (tablet or smartphone), you need a **Power Apps Mobile** application, available for free on all platforms (Android, iOS, and Microsoft). This application will host your Power Apps (model-driven and canvas). Power Apps Portals will run using the mobile browser

- To use flows on a mobile device, you need a **Power Automate Mobile** application, and other details are the same as for Power App Mobile.

- To use Power BI on a mobile device, you need a **Power BI Mobile** application, and other details are the same as for Power App Mobile.

- To use Microsoft Dynamics 365 apps on a mobile device, you need a **Dynamics 365 for phones** or **Dynamics 365 for tablets**.

- For certain capabilities of your model-driven apps, **Microsoft Office products** (Microsoft Word, Microsoft Excel, and Microsoft Outlook) could be required.

> **Note: For further details about the Power Platform system requirements, please refer to the following resources:**
>
> https://docs.microsoft.com/en-us/power-platform/admin/online-requirements

In order to support some of the specific Power Platform capabilities, the following on-premises components are required:

- You need the **Power Automate Desktop** tool for developing and running desktop flows (RPA). The tool can be downloaded directly from the Power Automate portal, which will be introduced in the next section of this chapter.

- You need the **On-Premises Data Gateway** tool to allow a secure and reliable connection between the Power Platform cloud components and your on-premises IT systems; if you need to integrate them into your Power Apps, Power Automate flows, or Power BI solutions. This tool can also be downloaded directly from the Power Automate portal.

- You need the **Power BI Desktop** tool to build Power BI solutions. You can download and install the tool either from the Microsoft Store (for Windows 10 or 11) or as a standalone installation file.

You will learn the details about using the mentioned tools along your journey into the Power Platform in the subsequent chapters of this book.

How to start with Power Platform

Now, after you have got a first impression of the Power Platform, it is the right time to start something practical. This book is packed with a lot of practical and proven examples, and we would like to encourage you to do all of the hands-on exercises because we strongly believe in the learning-by-doing method.

In this section, we will introduce you to the necessary tools for the first steps, together with a description of how you can get access to them.

Power Platform tools

For your practical experiments with the Power Platform, you will need the following tools:

- Power Platform Admin Center
- Maker Portal
- Power Automate Portal
- Power Automate Desktop

- On-Premises Data Gateway
- Power BI Desktop
- Microsoft SQL Server (advanced)
- MySQL (advanced)

Let us now describe in more detail what are the preceding tools for and how to get access:

Power Platform admin center

The **Power Platform admin center** is a portal for administrators, used for tasks such as creating or deleting Power Platform environments, configuring various settings of the environments, creating backups of environments, restoring environments from backups, and much more.

For the purpose of this book, we will use the Power Platform Admin Center only for creating some environments; we would need practical examples.

The Power Platform Admin Center has the following URL: **https://admin.powerplatform.microsoft.com/**

Maker Portal

The **Maker Portal** is the main tool used for building Power Platform solutions, and it is used to create and work with Power Platform solutions, extend the Dataverse, create apps, flows, and so on. We will spend a lot of time using this tool in the subsequent chapters of this book.

The Maker Portal has the following URL: **https://make.powerapps.com/**

Power Automate portal

The **Power Automate portal** is specifically dedicated to work with Power Automate. Although part of the Power Automate functionality is also available in the Maker Portal, some specific features are available only in this dedicated portal.

You can also download the following two desktop tools directly from the Power Automate portal:

- Power Automate desktop
- On-premises data gateway

The Power Automate portal has the following URL:

https://make.powerautomate.com

Please postpone the installation of the two mentioned desktop tools until you reach *Chapter 4, Automate Processes With Power Automate* of this book since after the installation, there is a follow-up configuration required.

Power BI Desktop

The **Power BI Desktop** is used to build Power BI solutions before they are deployed to the Power BI cloud. The tool can be downloaded and installed using one of the two possible ways:

- Installation from the **Microsoft Store** (for Windows 10 or 11). To get directly to the installation of the tool from the store, please use the following URL: **https://aka.ms/pbidesktopstore**

- A **standalone installation** using an installation file. To get directly to the download page of the standalone installation, please use the following URL: **https://aka.ms/pbiSingleInstaller**

You can install Power BI Desktop right away or postpone it until you reach *Chapter 6: Start with Power BI* of this book.

Microsoft SQL Server (advanced)

Some of the practical examples in this book are more advanced, requiring the use of more complex installations. We encourage you to try these examples as well if you want to. For those examples to work, you need to install **Microsoft SQL Server** and **MySQL** locally on your PC. Both products can be acquired free of charge. Following are the steps to install the Microsoft SQL Server on your local PC:

1. Navigate to the following webpage: **https://www.microsoft.com/en-us/sql-server/sql-server-downloads**

2. Locate the *"Developer"* product version and download the installation file onto your local PC. The developer version is free of charge.

3. Navigate to the following Web page, containing the installation documentation: **https://docs.microsoft.com/en-us/sql/database-engine/install-windows/install-sql-server?view=sql-server-ver15**

4. Start the installation using the downloaded installation file, and select *"Basic"* installation type. Follow the installation steps to install a local SQL Server instance on your PC. Refer to the installation documentation in case something is not clear. Do not forget to make a note of any settings and credentials you configure during the installation.

MySQL (advanced)

The second database system used in some of the advanced exercises later in this book is **MySQL**. Following are the steps to install the MySQL database on your local PC:

1. Navigate to the following Web page: **https://dev.MySQL.com/downloads/installer/**
2. Select your operating system and click on **Download** next to the installation file with the name "`MySQL-installer-web-community-8.0.28.0.msi`".
3. On the next page, confirm "`No thanks, just start my download`" to download the installation file.
4. Navigate to the following Web page containing the installation documentation: **https://dev.MySQL.com/doc/refman/8.0/en/MySQL-installer.html**
5. Start the installation using the downloaded installation file and follow the installation steps to install a local MySQL instance on your PC. Refer to the installation documentation in case something is not clear. Do not forget to make a note of any settings and credentials you use during the installation.

In the subsequent chapters of this book, you will use all of those cloud portals and local tools and databases in a series of exciting practical examples, so do not hesitate to invest some time to understand and perform all of the preceding installations.

Power Platform mobile

In order to try some of the exercises from this book on your mobile device, please locate and install the following mobile apps in your device store (Apple AppStore or Google Play store):

- Power Apps mobile
- Power Automate mobile
- Power BI mobile

The mobile applications are free of charge.

Prepare Power Platform environments

The last preparation step to be able to start with practical examples is the provisioning of your cloud environment. Following are the required steps we are going to perform:

- Provision of a Microsoft clout tenant
- Activate a Power Platform developer plan license

Since all Microsoft cloud services require a cloud tenant, we need to have one as a prerequisite for all other steps.

Provision of a Microsoft cloud tenant

There are multiple ways how a new Microsoft cloud tenant can be created. A popular way is to activate a Microsoft 365/Office 365 trial subscription, which creates at the same time a new cloud trial. Please use the following steps:

- Navigate in an incognito/in-private mode of your browser to the following webpage: **https://www.microsoft.com/en-us/microsoft-365/enterprise/office-365-e3** and click on the link **Free trial**:

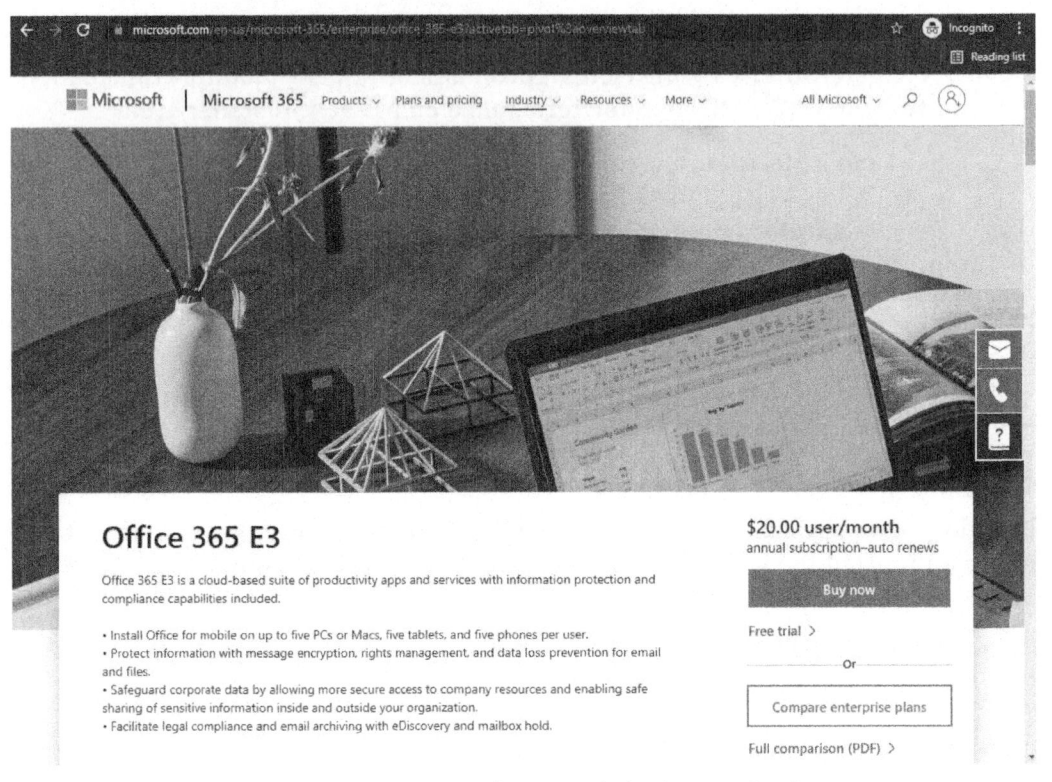

Figure 1.2: Provisioning of a Microsoft cloud tenant, Step I.

Introducing Microsoft Power Platform ■ 21

- Enter your private E-mail address and click "**Next**". It is important to enter a private e-mail to force the system to create a new tenant.

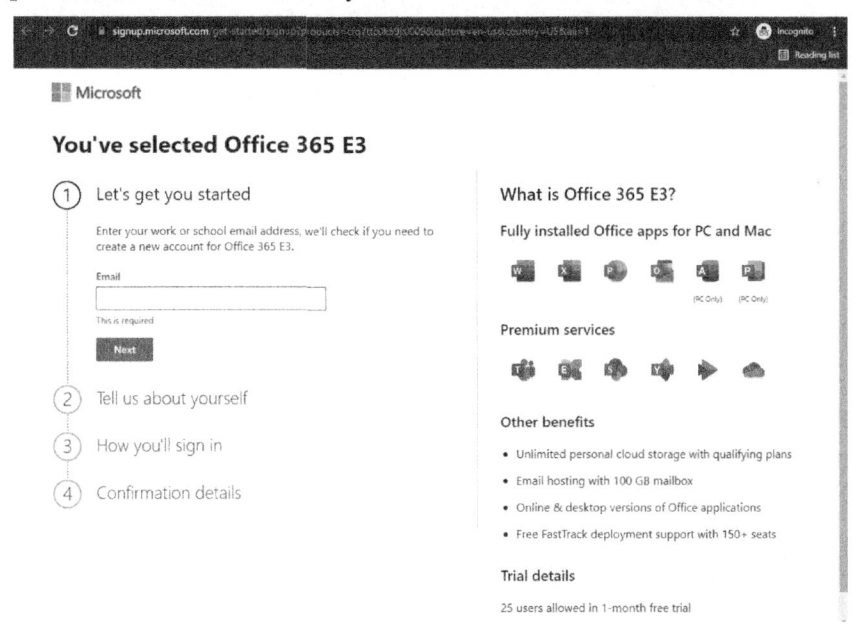

Figure 1.3: *Provisioning of a Microsoft cloud tenant, Step II.*

- Click on the **Set up account** button.

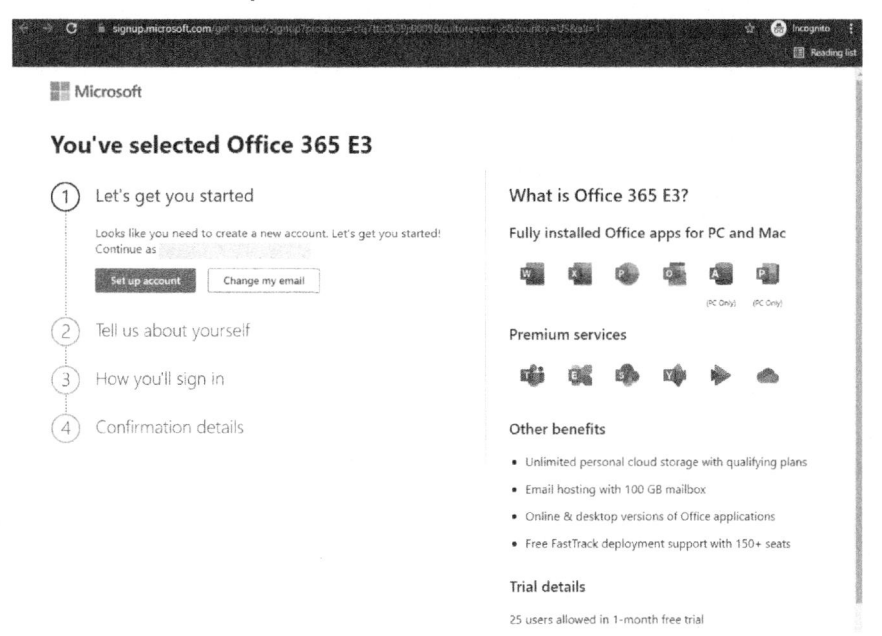

Figure 1.4: *Provisioning of a Microsoft cloud tenant, Step III.*

22 ■ *Microsoft Power Platform Up and Running*

- Fill in the information and click "**Next**".

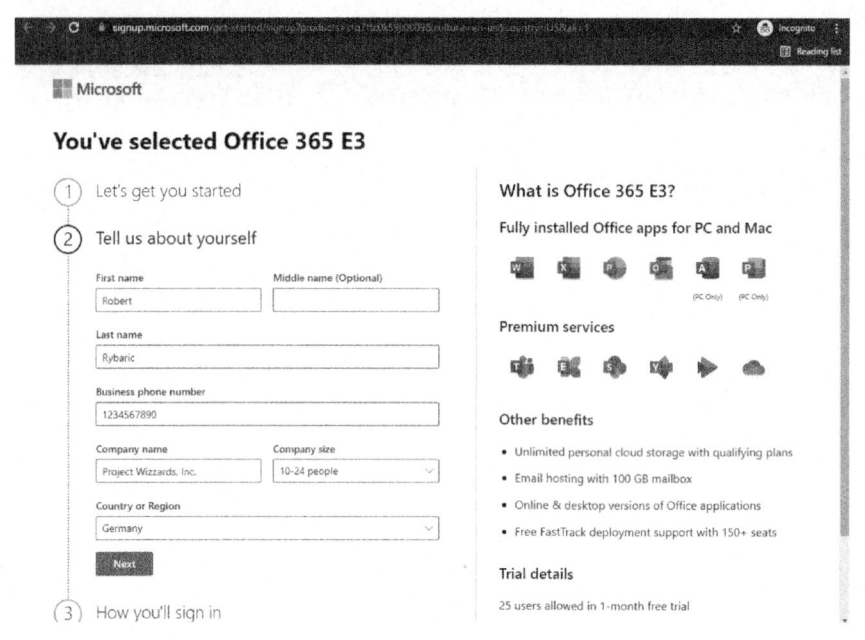

Figure 1.5: *Provisioning of a Microsoft cloud tenant, Step IV*

- In the next step, your identity will be verified, so select the option **Text me**, select a real phone number and click **Send verification code**.

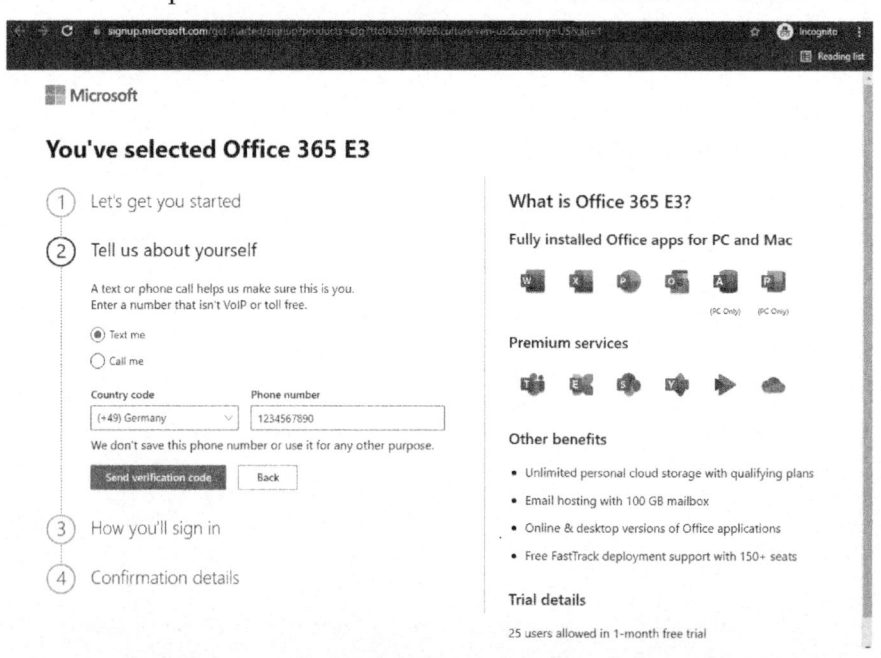

Figure 1.6: *Provisioning of a Microsoft cloud tenant, Step V*

Introducing Microsoft Power Platform ▪ 23

- After you obtain the SMS message, enter the six-digit verification code into the respective field, and click on **Verify**. Next, check the suggested username and tenant name and make any changes if you like. Define your password for the account which is going to be created and click on **Next**.

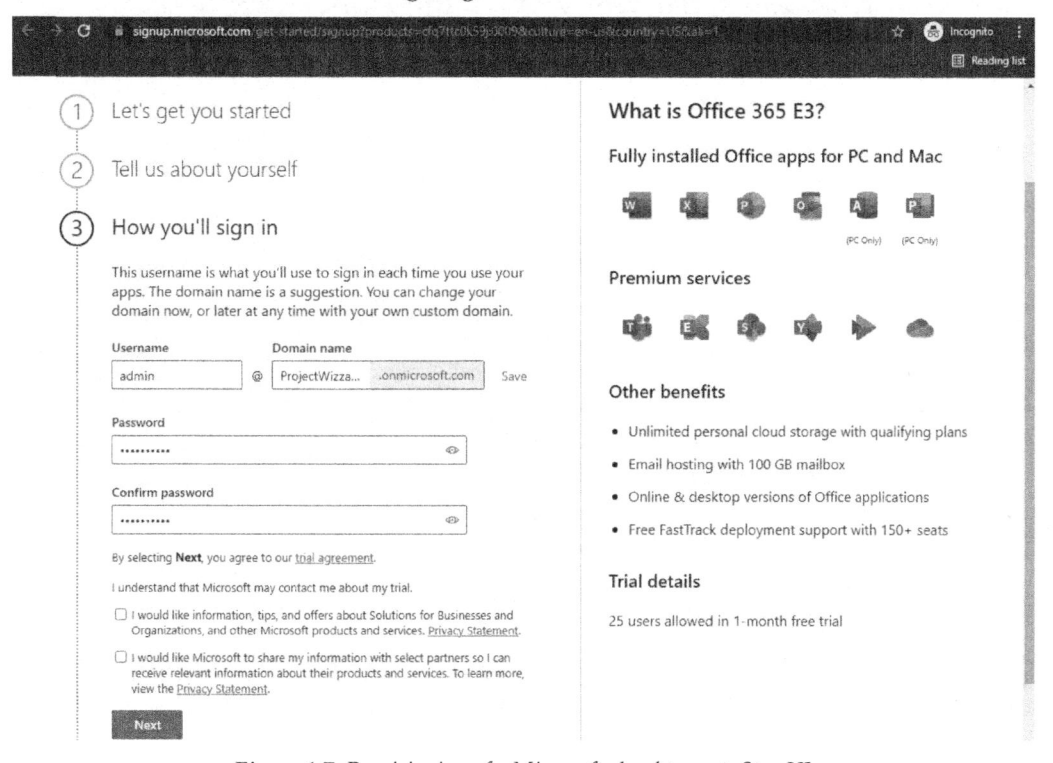

Figure 1.7: Provisioning of a Microsoft cloud tenant, Step VI.

That was the last step, and you will get a confirmation e-mail delivered to the private e-mail address you indicated at the beginning of the provisioning. Keep the browser session open for the next provisioning process.

> **Note: Save the username and password in a safe place, and you will need those credentials for all exercises in this book.**

After we have successfully created a Microsoft cloud tenant, the last step is to activate a Power Platform Developer plan license, which will at the same time provision a Power Platform environment of type "*Developer*".

Activating a Power Platform developer plan license

For the activation of the license, please perform the following steps:

- Open a new tab in your existing browser session from the previous section and enter the following webpage URL: **https://powerapps.microsoft.com/**

en-us/developerplan/ and click on the link **Existing user? Add a dev environment**.

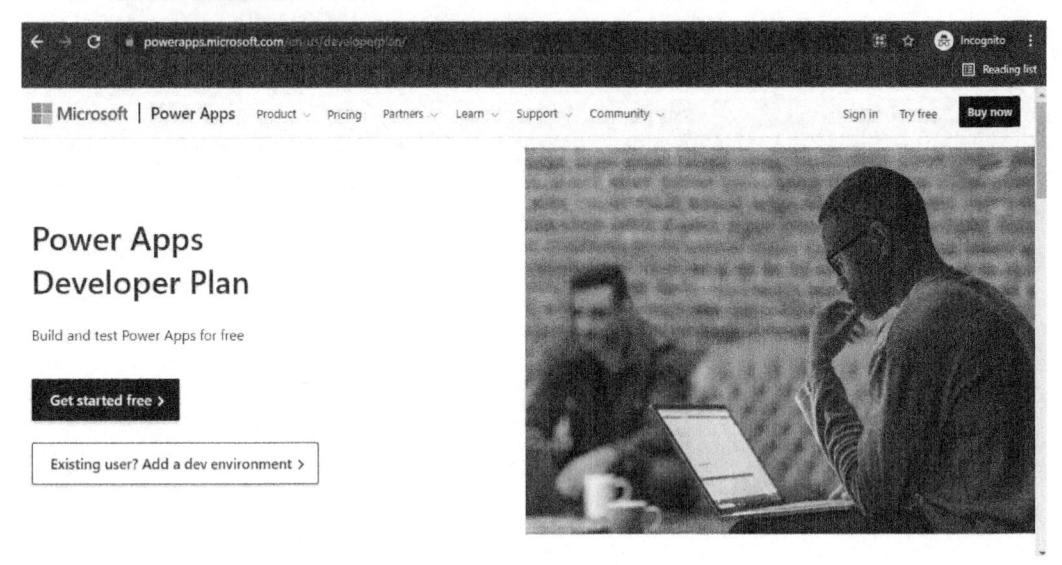

Figure 1.8: Activating of a Power Platform Developer plan license, Step I

- Confirm your preferred country in which the environment will be created and click **Accept**:

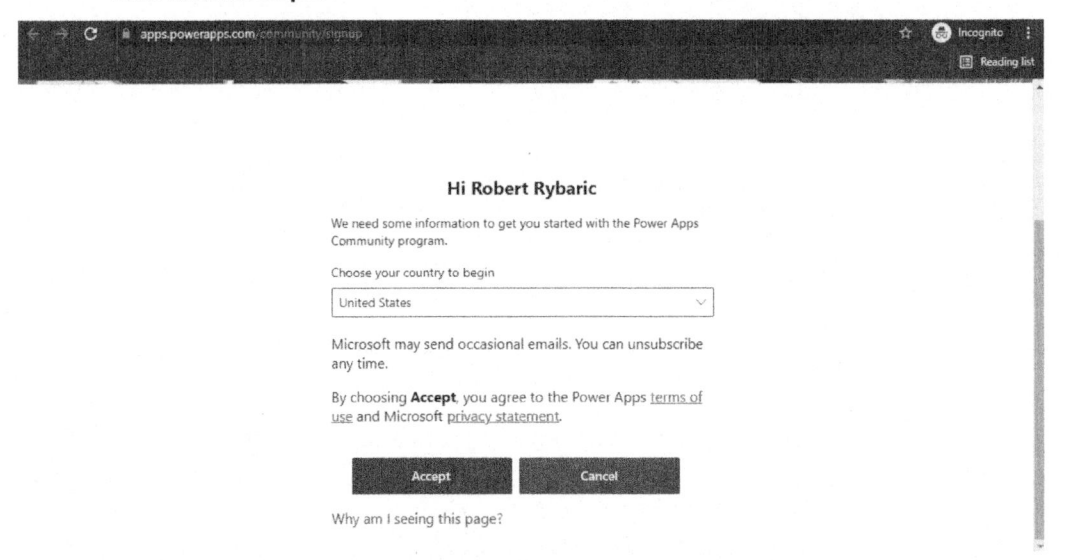

Figure 1.9: Activating of a Power Platform Developer plan license, Step II

- That was the last step, and you will be forwarded to the Maker Portal Web page where you can immediately start working in your fresh Power Platform environment.

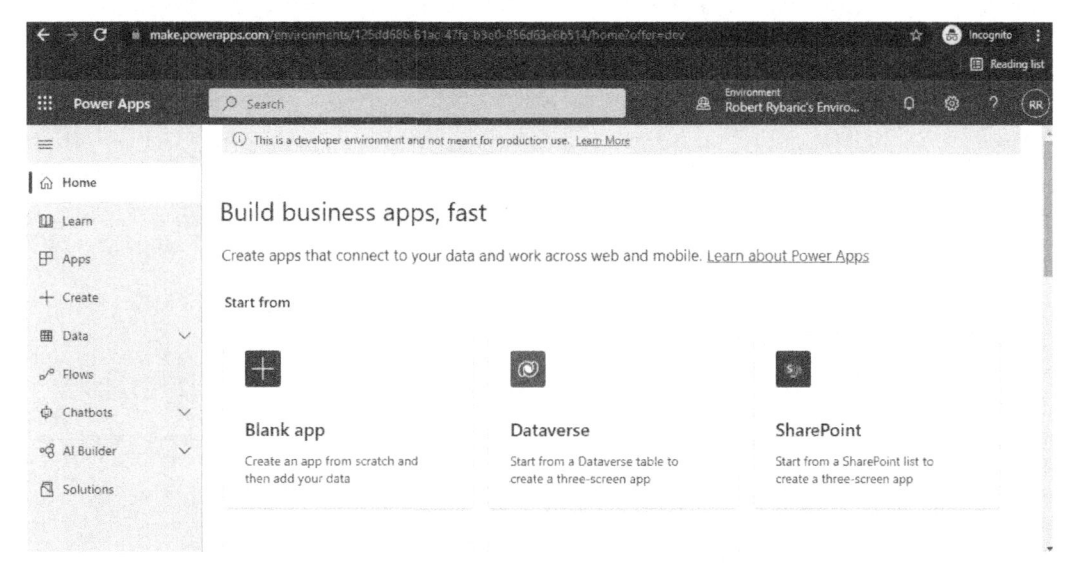

Figure 1.10: Activating of a Power Platform Developer plan license, Step III

Now, everything is ready for the interesting practical examples, which will follow in the next chapters of this book.

Conclusion

In this chapter, you have got a very basic overview of the Microsoft Power Platform, as one of the leading low-code/no-code cloud services on the market. You should now understand the purpose and benefits of using low-code/no-code in your business and should also have a first understanding of the structure and licensing of the Power Platform. You should also be prepared to start some first practical examples in your freshly provisioned Power Platform ecosystem.

In the upcoming chapter, we will start with the first Power Platform component, the Power Apps. You will learn the basics about Power Apps, the Microsoft Dataverse, and model-driven apps. You will implement the first practical exercises with the technology—create a data model and create a model-driven app.

Questions

1. What are the benefits of adopting a low-code/no-code approach for building business applications?

2. What is the Microsoft Power Platform, and which components does it contains?

3. Do you understand all the licensing portions for licensing Power Platform?

4. Do you understand the role of the most important Power Platform portals and tools?

CHAPTER 2
Building Enterprise Solutions with Power Apps

Introduction

In this chapter, we will have a deeper look inside the probably most important Power Platform component, i.e., the Power Apps. You will see how this technology can help you to build enterprise-ready business applications using the model-driven type of Power Apps. After that, we will provide a short overview of Microsoft's first-party model-driven apps—the Dynamics 365 apps, covering the typical business workloads such as marketing, sales, customer and field service, and project operations.

Structure

In this chapter, we will discuss the following topics:

- Use cases for Power Apps
- Types of Power Apps
- Microsoft Dataverse fundamentals
- Model-driven apps fundamentals
- Build enterprise-ready model-driven apps
- Dynamics 365 considerations

Objective

After reading this chapter, you will have an understanding of what is the Power Apps technology and how it can be used for building business applications. You will learn more about the three main types of Power Apps, model-driven apps, canvas apps, and portal apps. Next, we will fully focus on the key technologies of Microsoft Dataverse and model-driven apps. You will learn how to create a data model for your business application in Microsoft Dataverse and how you can build model-driven apps. In this chapter, you will start with practical examples, and you will create your own data model and a model-driven application.

Use cases for Power Apps

In the first chapter of this book, you learned that Power Apps is a technology for building business applications for the end users. Let us dive a bit deeper into the possible use cases for Power Apps. Because this chapter is dedicated to the model-driven app, let us focus on the typical use cases of this particular technology. Power Apps/model-driven apps technology can always be used when it comes to building robust, enterprise-ready business applications, which should be used across the whole organization, by many users, even geographically distributed across the whole planet. Those apps can handle very complex data structures and also large amounts of data—millions of business records in various tables are quite usual and easy to achieve. The technology support multi-language and multi-currency-equipped applications. Simply said—the typical use cases can be found in the enterprise area for every kind of major business workload.

Next, in preparation for our practical examples, let us have a look at a fictitious company Project Wizards, Inc., and the business challenge they decided to solve with the help of Microsoft Power Platform.

Introducing Project Wizards, Inc.

Let us have a look at the case study, which will be used in all the subsequent chapters for developing a simple end-to-end solution. The main role plays a fictitious company, *Project Wizards, Inc.,* focused on the installations and implementations of various machinery and equipment for their customers.

The company is still using Excel as their main tool for managing their projects, but they have already recognized that their growing business needs a more professional IT solution for managing the main part of their activities—the project execution. They have formulated the following set of requirements:

- The new solution must:
    - Be a cloud solution in order to eliminate any infrastructure costs.

- - Be able to track all customer and contact person data.
  - Provide the capability for creating and managing projects.
- For every project, it must be possible to specify project tasks with planned duration and assign them to the employees.
- The employees must be able to track the completion of their tasks on mobile devices.
- It must be possible to track products and materials used in the projects.
- The managers must be able to approve the completed tasks of the employees.
- The customer must be able to see and approve the products and materials used in the project using a customer portal solution.
- The solution must provide deep analytics of the collected project data.
- The customer portal must contain a chatbot for answering common customer questions.
- Project Wizards Inc. would also like to see and evaluate the possibility of fully automated vendor invoice processing. This capability is, however, not planned in the current project management solution.

After analyzing these requirements, Project Wizards, Inc. decided to adopt the Microsoft Power Platform and build their new project management solution using a low-code/no-code approach.

This case study will accompany you in this book; you will learn the theoretical background for every important part of the Power Platform and then implement the required functionality according to the preceding requirements set.

Types of Power Apps

In the first chapter of this book, we have already provided a brief overview of the Power Apps technology. Let us now have a close look into the details of the three types of Power Apps, their main features, and use cases. The overview will give you an indication in which situation is the use of which type of Power Apps technology most suitable.

Model-driven apps

Model-driven apps have the following main features:

- Model-driven apps can only be used by internal authenticated users of an organization.

- A model-driven app is bound to **Microsoft Dataverse**, which means you need to first have a data model for your business application created, and after that, you can create the model-driven app itself.
- All business data you plan to use in your model-driven app will reside in the Microsoft Dataverse.
- The model-driven app's technology is very well suitable for building *robust, enterprise-ready business applications*, handling complex data structures and large amounts of data.
- Due to the nature of Microsoft Dataverse, a model-driven app can include *complex internal automation* and *complex security configurations*.
- Model-driven apps can be best used on a PC. The use of mobile devices is possible; however, due to the small screens, the user interface must be designed appropriately.
- The user interface and look and feel of model-driven apps are very standardized; the technology offers you a framework to quickly configure the content but does not allow full flexibility in designing the user interface according to your specific preferences.
- With model-drive apps, you can configure an offline capability, supporting the use of the app on a mobile device in case there is no data connection available.

The following screenshot represents a typical model-driven app user interface:

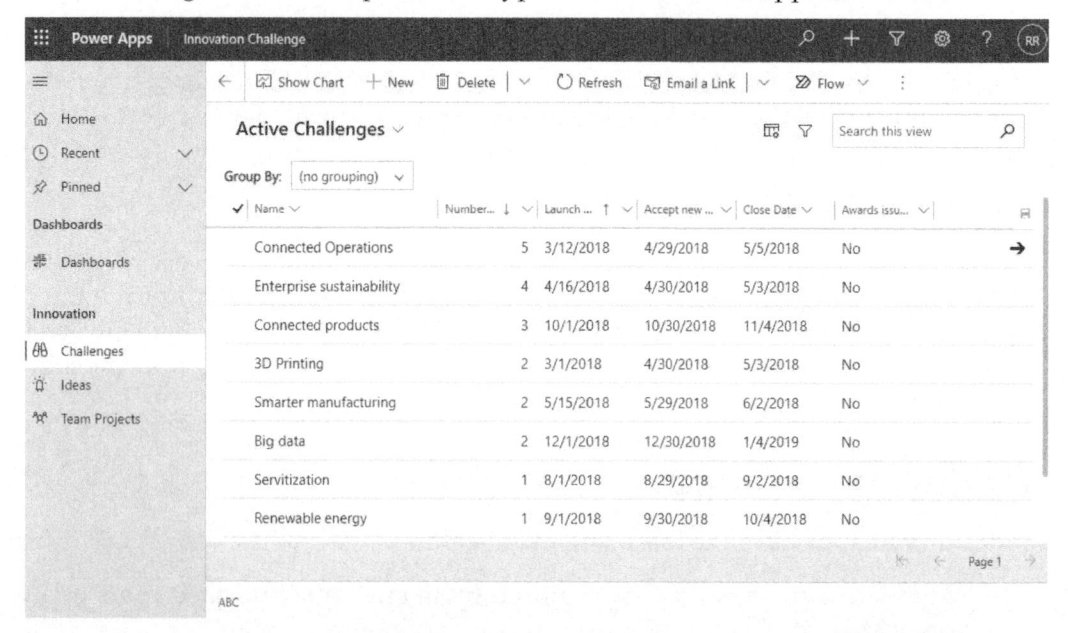

Figure 2.1: Example of a model-driven app

Next, let us have a deeper look at the canvas apps.

Canvas apps

Canvas apps have the following main features:

- Canvas apps can only be used by internal authenticated users of an organization.
- Canvas apps are *fully independent* of Microsoft Dataverse; canvas apps can but must not use Dataverse as the storage for your business data.
- Canvas apps use the *data connectors* to connect to any necessary IT system or solution, and you can create multiple connections to multiple different IT systems with multiple different data connectors within a single canvas app.
- The canvas apps technology is best suitable for building *smaller, single-purpose applications*, preferably for *mobile devices*—tablets and smartphones, even though it is possible to use them on PCs as well.
- There is *no standard user interface*, and you have full freedom and flexibility to design your canvas app UI according to given requirements and your preferences.
- When building canvas apps, it is necessary to use expressions and implement the logic of the application. The expressions are using their own, Excel-like formula language, called **Power Fx**.
- Canvas apps can support offline capability; however, the implementation requires more effort than in the case of model-driven apps.

On the following screenshot, you can see a possible look and feel of a canvas app:

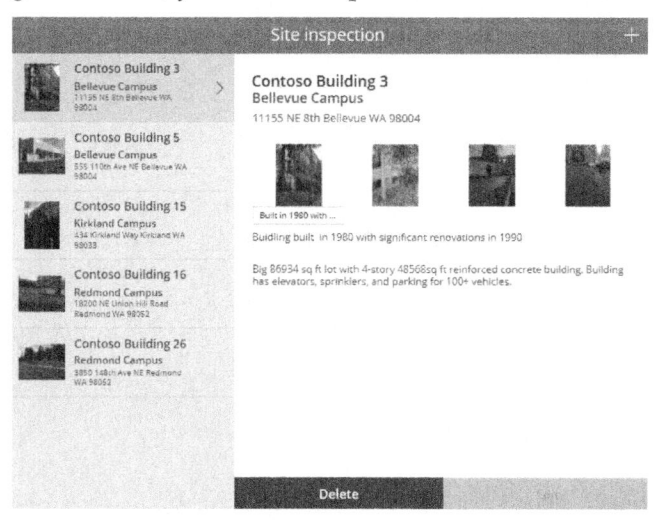

Figure 2.2: Example of a canvas app

The last Power Apps type we are going to present is the Power Apps portal apps technology.

Portal apps

Portal apps have the following main features:

- Portal apps is the only Power Apps technology that is used for building applications for *external audiences*—your customers, partners, vendors, and so on.
- Portal apps rely entirely on Microsoft Dataverse, which is used as a repository for the whole portal content management.
- Portal apps technology supports by default *responsive design* so that the portals can be used on any device: PC, tablet, or mobile.
- Portal apps are publicly available websites, but the technology supports the creation of portals with *public* and *private* content. The public content is by default available to every anonymous visitor, whereas the private content can be used only by authenticated users.
- Portal apps technology makes it easily possible to *integrate business data* stored in Microsoft Dataverse into the portal solutions.

On the following screenshot, you can see how a freshly created Power Apps portal looks:

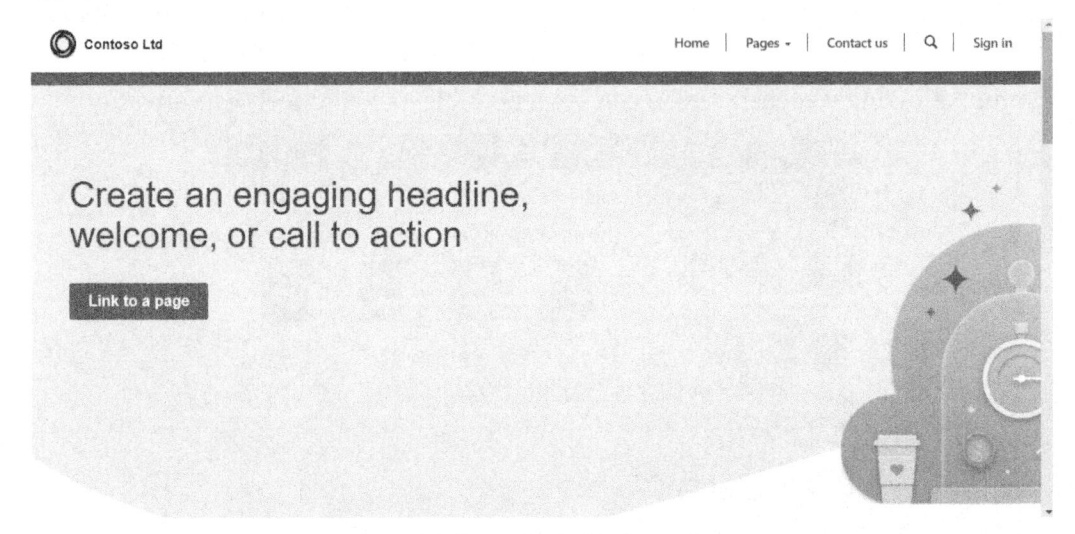

Figure 2.3: Example of a blank portal app

This overview should give you an understanding of the three types of Power Apps and their typical usage scenarios.

Power Apps for Project Wizards, Inc.

In this section, we have learned the main features of the three Power Apps types. With this knowledge, we can immediately identify the implementation approach for *Project Wizards, Inc.*:

- The main project management application will be implemented as a *model-driven app*. This app will be used for maintaining all data, such as customers, contact, and projects, with the necessary details.

- The mobile project tracking application for the project employees will be implemented using the *canvas apps* technology

- The customer portal solution will be implemented using the *Power Apps Portals*.

After we are able to specify the application types, we will first fully focus on the main project management application. In order to be able to build it, we need to know how to create a data model in Microsoft Dataverse and how to build the model-driven app with Power Apps.

Microsoft Dataverse fundamentals

In this section, we will fully focus on one single feature of the Microsoft Dataverse, and that is the database feature. You can use Microsoft Dataverse to configure a data model for your business application. Microsoft Dataverse contains a relational database, which means that you are provided with the capability to:

- Create and modify *database tables* for storing your business data.

- Connect those tables with *relationships* to make the data model consistent.

- Enhance the database tables with *columns* to store the individual data pieces of your business data.

For a better understanding of what the preceding structures mean, please refer to the following example of a simplified data model of a sales order:

Customer	
PK Customer ID	PK
Customer Name	String
Customer Address	String

Product Catalogue	
PK Product ID	PK
Product Name	String
Unit Price	Dec

Sales Order	
PK Sales Order ID	PK
Customer ID	FK
Sales Order Date	Date

Sales Order Line	
PK Sales Order Line ID	PK
Sales Order ID	FK
Product ID	FK
Quantity	Dec

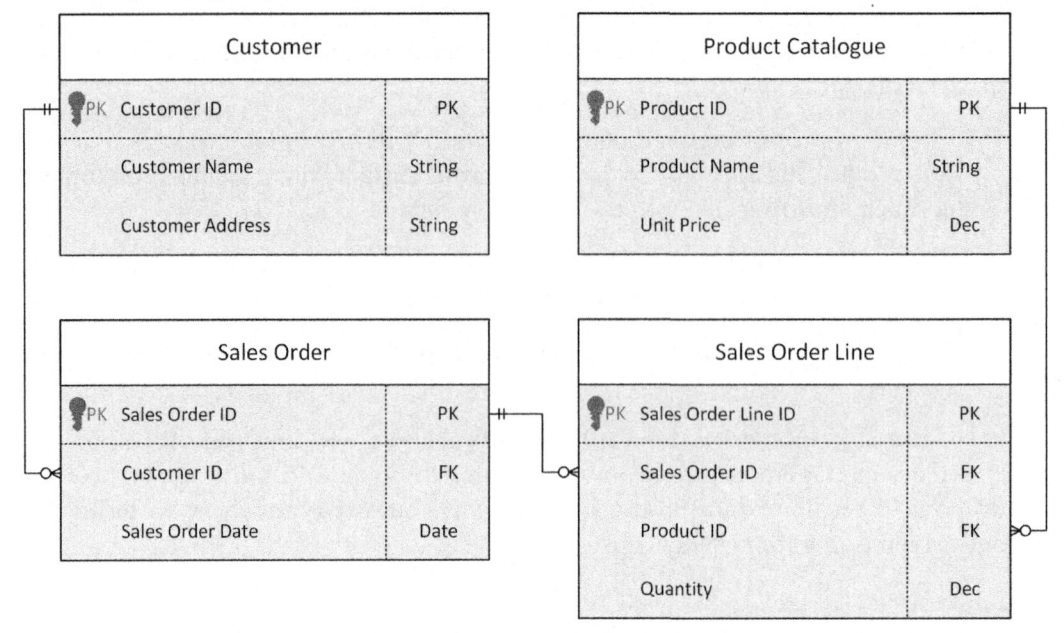

Figure 2.4: Simplified data model for a sales order

In *figure 2.4*, you can recognize the following structures:

- **Database tables**: **Customer** for storing customer data, **Product Catalogue** for storing data about products and services, **Sales Order** for storing the header data of sales orders, and the **Sales Order Line** table for storing the line items for every ordered product.

- *Relationships between the tables*, represented by the connection lines, are used to ensure that records in the four tables are always correctly connected with each other.

- **Columns**: For storing the individual pieces of information, such as **Customer Name**, **Sales Order Date**, or **Quantity**.

It is important to understand that Microsoft Dataverse comes with a predefined standard data model, which contains a lot of useful tables for general use, like the table **Account** for storing data about business customers or **Contact** for storing data about personal contacts.

There are many more specific details about the structures in Microsoft Dataverse, but for our introduction to the Power Platform, it is more important to quickly learn the basics along with practical exercises. Now is the right time to start with the first real exercise.

Exercise 1: Creating a data model

We will need to first analyze the requirements set of Project Wizards, Inc. and then go ahead with the practical implementation steps.

Analysis and preparations

After analyzing the requirements for the project management solution, we have identified the following data objects:

- **Customer object**, holding all the necessary details about the business customers.
- **Contact object**, holding all the details about the contact persons. The contacts will be usually assigned to a customer because the majority of the contacts are employees of the customers.
- **Employee object**, holding information about their own employees.
- **Project object** for maintaining all the details about the customer projects.
- **Project task object** for tracking the tasks which need to be performed in the project. Every project task needs to be assigned to a project and to an employee who will be responsible for performing that task.
- **Product catalogue object** for maintaining all the standard products and materials used in the organization within the projects.
- **Project product object** for tracking the products and materials needed for the project execution. Each project product will be assigned to a project and connected with a product from the product catalogue.

For a better visual understanding of the data model, please refer to the following simplified database diagram (for now, without columns):

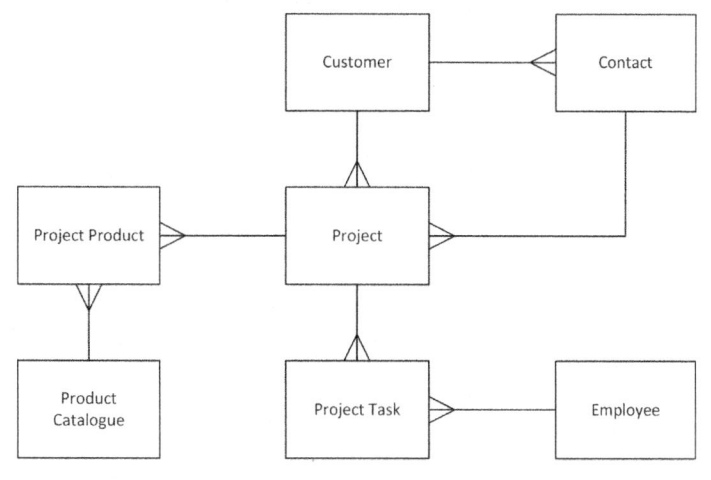

Figure 2.5: Data model

Next, we need to decide how to implement the data model in Microsoft Dataverse. As you have learned earlier in this section, Microsoft Dataverse comes with a default data model, which can be used as a foundation for individual data modeling efforts. In our data model, we have identified existing tables, which we will reuse:

- The **Account** table will be used to implement the Customer data object
- The **Contact** table will be used to implement the Contact data object
- The **User** table will be used to implement the Employee data object

The remaining data objects will be implemented by creating custom tables.

Practical implementation

In this exercise, we will implement the data model in Microsoft Dataverse. The implementation will consist of the following steps:

- Create a Power Platform solution and a publisher
- Add existing Microsoft Dataverse tables into the solution
- Create all remaining tables as custom tables
- Create all necessary relationships between the tables
- Create all necessary columns in the custom tables

Since we are starting the implementation process from the beginning, now, we need to create a solution that will contain everything we create in this and all subsequent chapters of this book. A solution is used in the Power Platform as a container supporting deployment processes from one environment to another.

> **Note:** Please note that the guidance for the practical examples will be very detailed at the beginning, but as you progress in your learning, the guidance will be less detailed and with less screenshots, reflecting your learning progress.

Creating a Power Platform solution and a publisher

This task consists of the following steps:

Navigate to the Maker Portal (**https://make.powerapps.com/**) and sign in with the cloud credentials you created in *Chapter 1, Introducing Microsoft Power Platform* of this book.

- In the Maker Portal, navigate to "`Solutions`".
- Click on "`+ New solution`".
- In the solution creation dialog, enter the **Display name** as "`Project Management`".

- In the solution creation dialog, click on the "**+ New publisher**".

- Enter the **Display name** for the publisher as "**Project Wizards Inc.**" and **Name** as "**ProjectWizardsInc**" (must not contain any spaces).

- Change the **Prefix** to "**pw**", representing the company name "*Project Wizards Inc*".

- The configuration of the publisher should correspond to the following screenshot:

Figure 2.6: Configuration of the solution publisher

- Click "**Save**" to save the publisher, which will return back to the solution

- In the solution configuration, select the newly created publisher

- The configuration of the solution should correspond to the following screenshot:

Figure 2.7: Configuration of the solution

- Click "**Create**" to create the solution

This was the last step of this task, and you should now see your solution as the first in the list of the solutions, corresponding to the following screenshot:

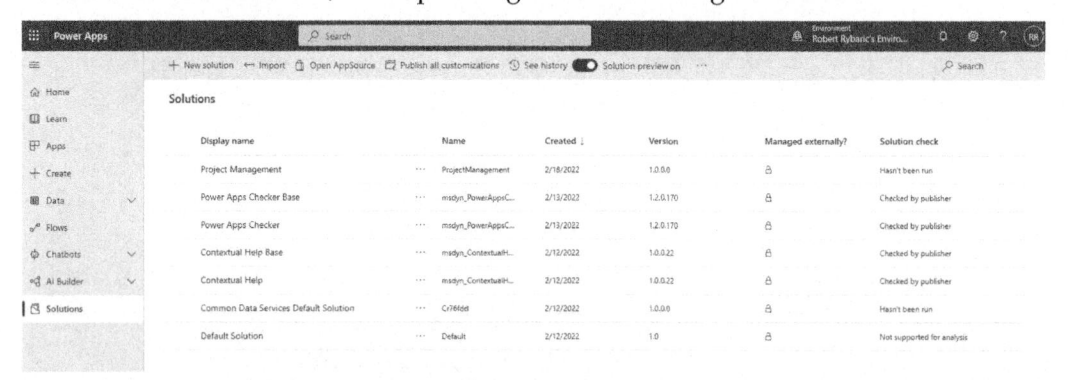

Figure 2.8: List of the Power Platform solutions

In the next task, we open the newly created solution and add the default tables "**Account**", "**Contact**", and "**User**" to the solution.

Adding existing Microsoft Dataverse tables to the solution

This task consists of the following steps:

- Click on the solution name "**Project Management**" to open it.
- Since this is a newly created solution, it is empty.
- Click on the "**Add existing**" selection control and select "**Table**" according to the following screenshot:

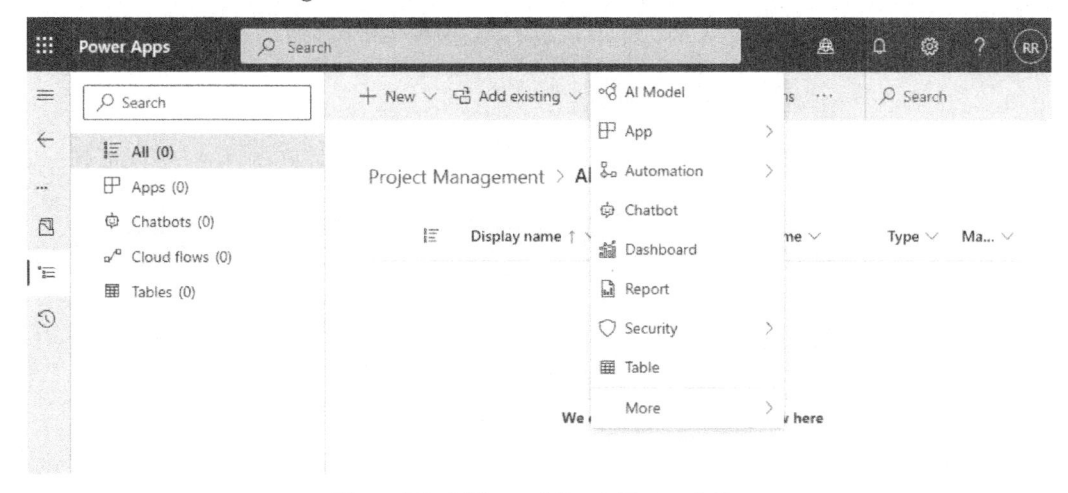

Figure 2.9: Adding existing table to solution

- In the list of tables, select the tables "**Account**", "**Contact**", and "**User**"—you need to scroll down in the list of the tables to identify and select all of them.
- After you have selected all three tables, click "**Next**" and then "**Add**" without making any changes to the default settings. As a result, you will find the three tables as new objects in the solution, according to the following screenshot:

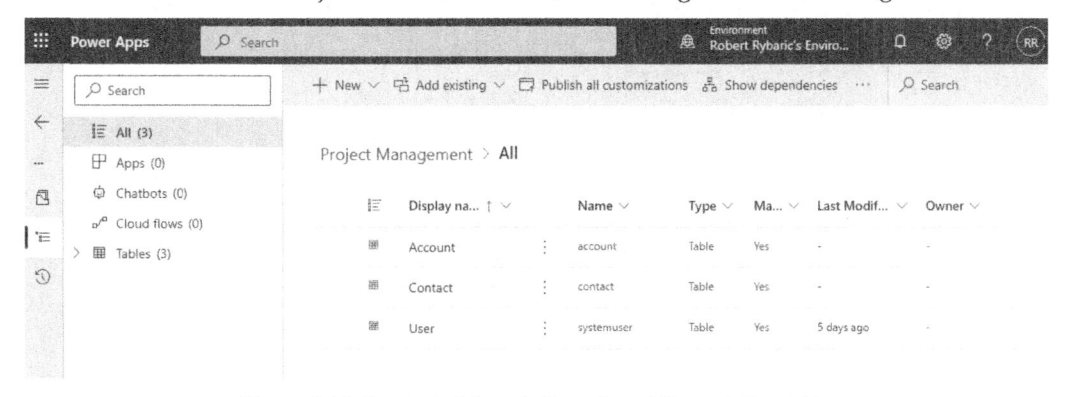

Figure 2.10: Content of the solution after adding existing tables

This was the last step of this task; in the next task, we will create the custom tables for our data model.

Creating all remaining tables as custom tables.

This task consists of the following steps:

- Click on the "**New**" selection and select "**Table**" according to the following screenshot:

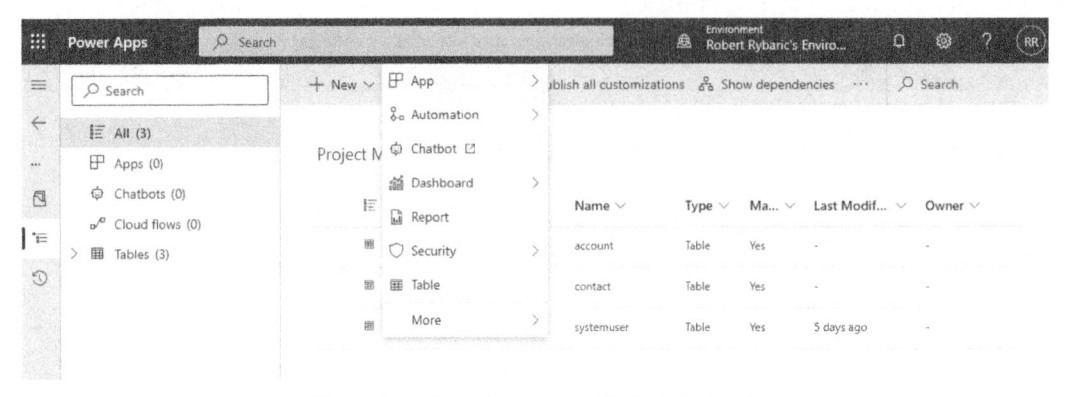

Figure 2.11: Creating a new table in Solution I.

- A table creation dialog will pop up; enter **Display name** as "**Project**", and the **Plural name** will be automatically filled in as "**Projects**" according to the following screenshot:

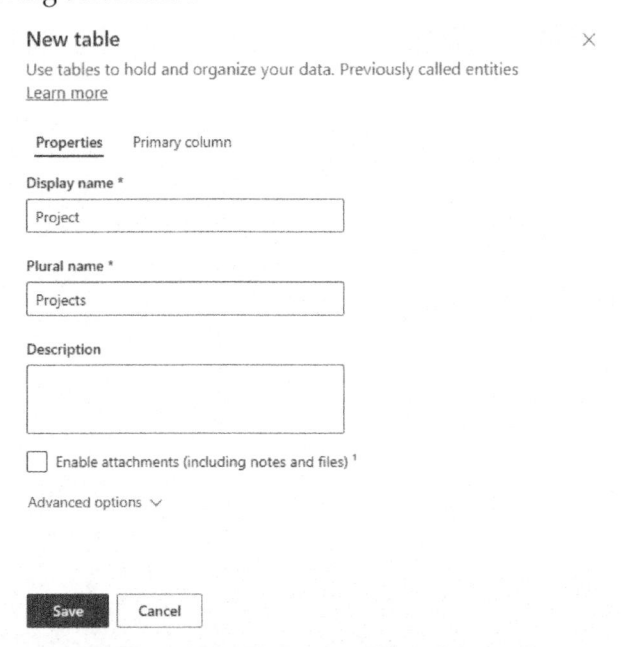

Figure 2.12: Creating a new table in Solution II.

- Click "**Save**", and the table will be created in the solution, and after a few seconds, you will see the newly created table in the list of the solution components. Please note that the content of the "**Name**" column has the prefix "**pw_**", according to the defined prefix in the solution publisher:

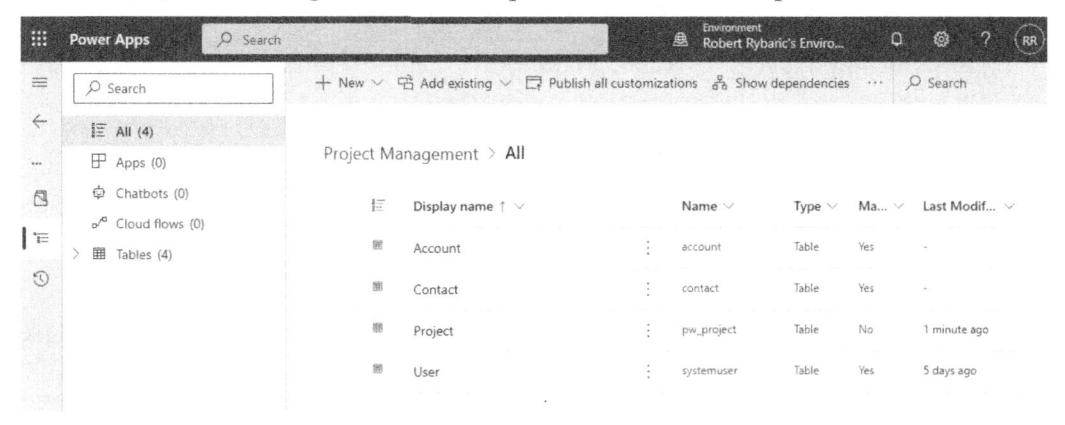

Figure 2.13: Newly created custom table with solution prefix

Repeat the described procedure to create the three remaining custom tables. Give the tables the following display names:

- **Product Catalogue**
- **Project Task**
- **Project Product**

Now, we have created the custom tables, and our data model in the solution has all seven required tables ready for the subsequent configuration steps. In the next task, we extend our data model with the required relationships.

Creating all necessary relationships between the tables

If you remember the main characteristics of a relational data model in Microsoft Dataverse, for all related tables, a **relationship** needs to be created. In this task, we create the relationships which are missing between the seven tables in our data model. Some of the relationships exist already in the default data model, such as the one-to-many relationship between the account and the contact table.

The task consists of the following steps:

- Navigate to the Maker Portal, open the solution "**Project Management**", open the table "**Project**", and switch to the tab "**Relationships**".
- Click "**+ Add relationship**" and select the type "**Many-to-one**". In the relationship definition dialogue, select the table "**Account**" in the selection control for "**Related (One)**".

- Rename the **Lookup column display name** from "`Account`" to "`Customer`" and click "**Done**" after that, always click the button "`Save Table`".

Repeat the procedure described previously to create the following additional relationships from within the table "`Project`":

Relationship type	Related table	Lookup column display name
Many-to-one	Contact	Customer primary contact
One-to-many	Project Product	Project
One-to-many	Project Task	Project

Table 2.1: Additional relationships for the table "Project"

Verify that the list of the custom relationships for the table "`Project`" corresponds to the following screenshot:

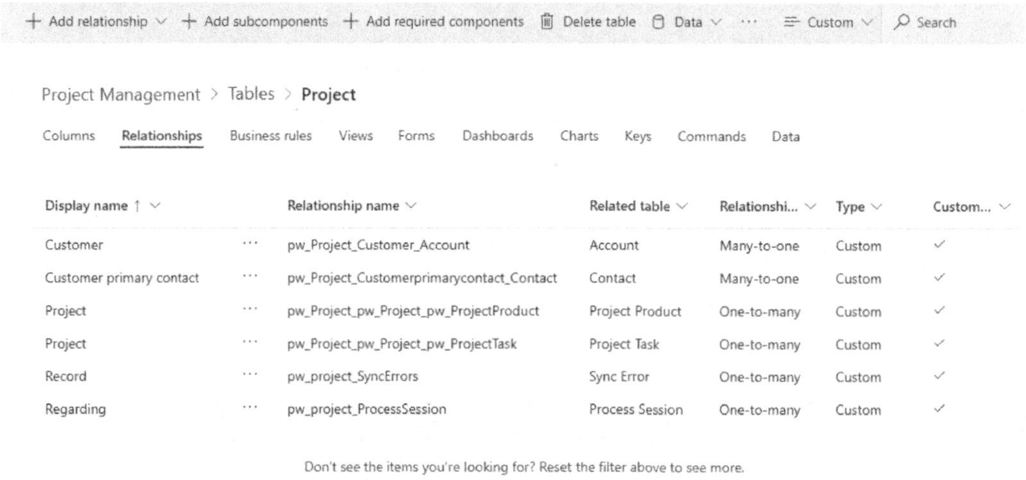

Figure 2.14: Custom relationships of the table "Project"

There is still one more relationship that needs to be created between the tables "`Project Catalogue`" and "`Project Product`". In order to create this last relationship, please perform the following steps:

- Navigate to the Maker Portal, open the solution "`Project Management`", open the table "`Project Catalogue`", and switch to the tab "**Relationships**".

- Click "`+ Add relationship`" and select the type "`One-to-many`". In the relationship definition dialogue, select the table "`Project Product`" in the selection control for "`Related (Many)`".

- Click "**Done**" and then click "`Save Table`".

Verify that the list of the custom relationships for the table "**Product Catalogue**" corresponds to the following screenshot:

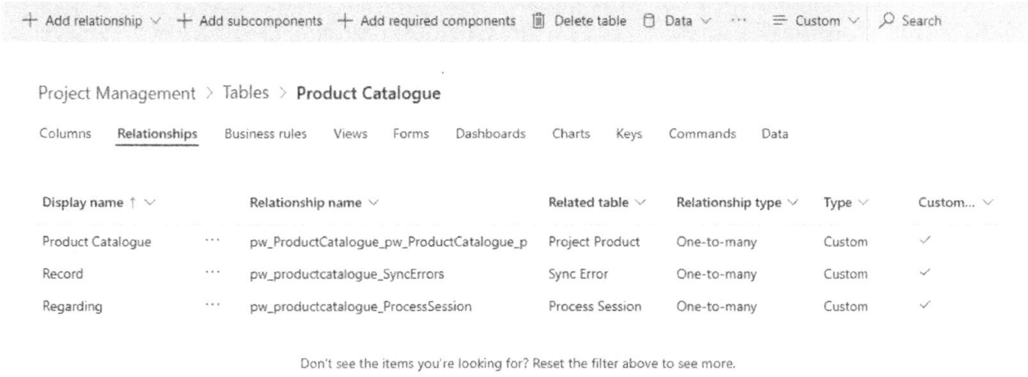

Display name ↑	Relationship name	Related table	Relationship type	Type	Custom...
Product Catalogue	pw_ProductCatalogue_pw_ProductCatalogue_p	Project Product	One-to-many	Custom	✓
Record	pw_productcatalogue_SyncErrors	Sync Error	One-to-many	Custom	✓
Regarding	pw_productcatalogue_ProcessSession	Process Session	One-to-many	Custom	✓

Figure 2.15: Custom relationships of the table "Product Catalogue"

In the last task, we extend all four custom tables with the necessary columns to store the required business data.

Creating all necessary columns in the custom tables

In this task, we need to extend the custom tables with additional columns, according to the following overview:

Columns for the "**Product Catalogue**" custom table:

Column	Data type	Description
Product ID	Text	Product ID
Name	Text	Column was created during table creation
Description	Multiline Text	Product description
Cost	Decimal Number	Unit cost value for the product
Price	Decimal Number	Unit price value for the product

Table 2.2: Structure of the table "Product Catalogue"

Columns for the **Project Task** custom table:

Column	Data type	Description
Name	Text	Column was created during table creation
Start Date	Date Only	Planned task start date
Duration	Whole Number	Estimated task duration in hours
Cost Rate	Decimal Number	Cost rate for this task
Bill Rate	Decimal Number	Bill rate for this task

Total Cost	Decimal Number	Calculated value = Duration x Cost Rate
Total Price	Decimal Number	Calculated value = Duration x Bill Rate
Task Status	Choice	Choice values: Planned, Completed, Approved

Table 2.3: Structure of the table "Project Task"

Columns for the **Project Product** custom table:

Column	Data Type	Description
Name	Text	Column was created during table creation
Quantity	Decimal Number	Quantity of the product used
Total Cost	Decimal Number	Calculated value = Quantity × Cost [form the Product Catalogue]
Total Price	Decimal Number	Calculated value = Quantity × Price [form the Product Catalogue]
Product Status	Choice	Choice values: Planned, Used, Approved

Table 2.4: Structure of the table "Project Product"

Columns for the **Project** custom table:

Column	Data Type	Description
Number	Autonumber	Automatically generated project number
Name	Text	Column was created during table creation
Total Work Cost	Decimal	Rollup value for the column "Total Cost" from the table "Project Task"
Total Work Price	Decimal	Rollup value for the column "Total Price" from the table "Project Task"

Table 2.5: Structure of the table "Project"

Please note that in every custom table, the column **Name** was created along with the table so that this column does not need to be created manually.

This task consists of the following steps for every table and every column—the following description will illustrate the steps for the table "**Product Catalogue**" and the column "**Product ID**":

- Navigate to the Maker Portal, open the solution "**Project Management**", open the table "**Product Catalogue**", and in the upper right corner, switch from the "**Default**" view of the columns to the "**Custom**" view. This will hide the system columns and so keeps a better overview of the result of our work.

- Click on "**Add column**", and in the column creation dialogue and enter the following information:
    - **Display name**: Product ID
    - **Name** will be automatically populated as "**pw_ ProductID**". Do not change this value.
    - **Data type** will be automatically selected as "**Text**". Keep this value. For all subsequent columns, you need to select the correct data type according to the definition described in *Table 2.2*.
    - Click "**Done**".
- Repeat the preceding steps for all additional columns required for the table "**Product Catalogue**" as specified in *Table 2.2*. For each column, select the display name and the correct data type.
- After you have entered all columns in the table "**Product Catalogue**", verify that the custom columns list looks like as shown in the following screenshot:

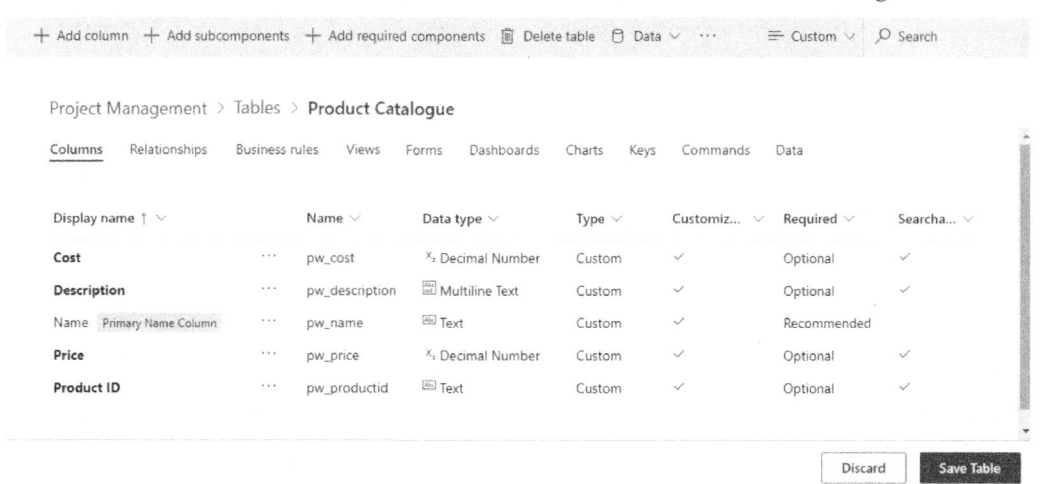

Figure 2.16: Custom columns in the table "Product Catalogue"

- Click on "**Save Table**".

Repeat the preceding task steps for all three remaining custom tables and create all required columns.

There are some specific settings for some of the columns. In the following section, you can see how to configure those specifics.

Configuration of calculated and rollup columns

46 ■ *Microsoft Power Platform Up and Running*

Some of the required columns are described as either "**Calculated**" or "**Rollup**". Microsoft Dataverse provides the capability to automatically calculate the content of these types of columns based on a defined formula. To configure a column as calculated or rollup, perform the following steps—this is a description for the column **Total Cost** in the table **Project Task**:

- Specify all the standard settings such as **Display name**, **Data type**, and so on and then click on "**+ Add**", right to the label "**Calculated or Rollup**".

- Select the proper calculation type (Calculated or Rollup) and confirm the saving of the column by clicking "**Save**" in the confirmation dialogue. The column will be saved, and a pop-up window with the formula designer will show up.

- Configure the formula as illustrated in the following screenshots. Click on the "**+ Action**" and select the field "**Cost Rate**" from the list of the fields. Then enter an asterisk character (*) representing multiplication, and then select the column "**Duration**". Confirm the formula by clicking on the checkbox on the lower right side, as illustrated in the following screenshot:

Figure 2.17: Configure the calculated column "Total Cost" in the table "Project Task" I.

- After confirming the formula, verify that the formula looks like as shown in the following screenshot:

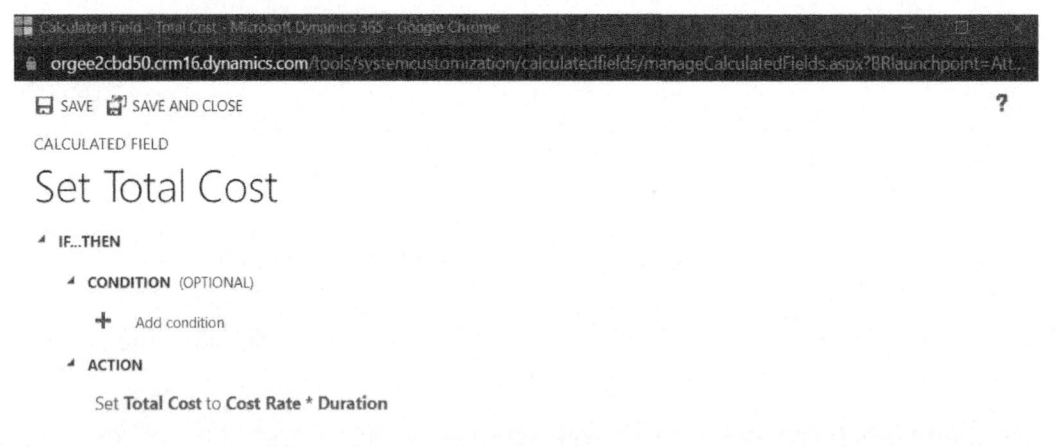

Figure 2.18: Configure the calculated column "Total Cost" in the table "Project Task" II.

The configuration of other calculated or rollup columns is described in the following sections.

Table **Project Task**—Column "Total Price"

Perform the same configuration as for the column **Total Cost** using the following formula:

$$Total\ Price = Bill\ Rate * Duration$$

Table **Project Product**—Column "Total Cost"

For this calculated column, a more complex setup is required because we are going to configure a formula containing columns from two different tables. To configure the formula, use the following steps:

- First, select the column "`Quantity`" from the table "`Project Product`".
- Enter the asterisk (*) representing multiplication
- Select the table "`Product Catalogue`" from the list of columns (yes, the list contains also references to related tables, not just columns from the same table)
- Enter a . (The dot character) representing the selection of columns from the related table
- Finally, after the dot character, select the column "`Cost`" from the related table "`Product catalogue`".

The whole formula, before confirming, should look like as shown in the following screenshot:

Set Total Cost (decimal number)

= pw_quantity * pw_productcatalogue.pw_cost

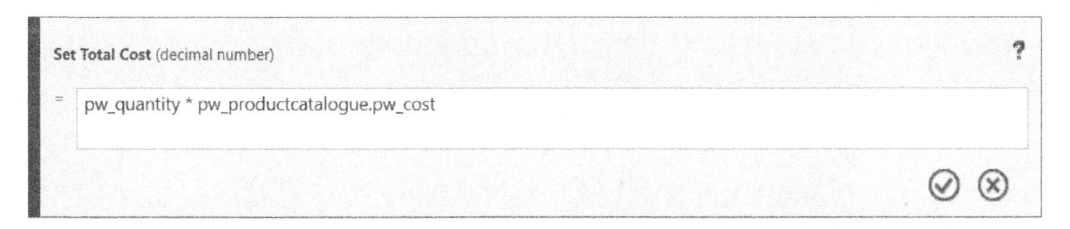

Figure 2.19: Configure the calculated column "Total Cost" in the table "Project Product" I.

Confirm the formula and save and close the formula designer window.

Table **Project Product**—Column "Total Price"

Perform the same configuration as for the column "`Total Cost`" using the following formula:

$$Total\ Price = Quantity * (Product\ Catalogue)\ Price$$

Table **Project**—columns "Total Work Cost" and "Total Work Price"

This is a column of type rollup, which needs a little more complex configuration. Please perform the following steps:

- Create the column, give it the **Display name** and **Data type**, click on the "**+ Add**" and select "**+ Rollup**".

- Confirm saving the column and wait until the pop-up window with the rollup formula configuration appears.

- Select the related entity by clicking on the "**+ Add related entity**", select "**Project Tasks (Project)**", and confirm.

- Specify a filter by clicking on "**+ Add condition**", Select the column "**Task Status**", operator "**Equals**", type "**Value**", and check the value "**Approved**", according to the following screenshot:

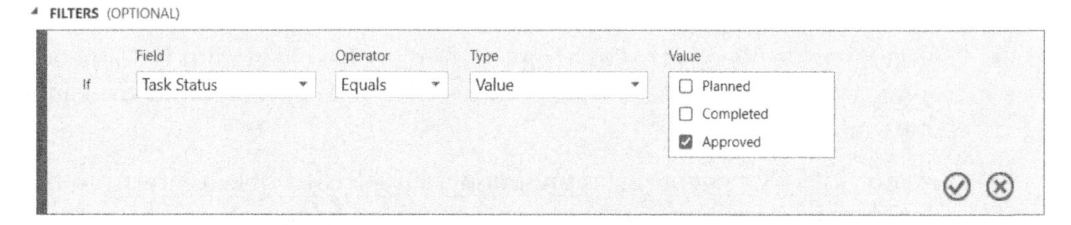

Figure 2.20: Configure filter for a rollup column

- Confirm the filter and create an aggregation by clicking on "**+ Add aggregation**", select the "**Aggregate function**" as SUM and the "**(Project Task) Total Cost**" column as the "**Aggregated Related Entity Field**", according to the following screenshot:

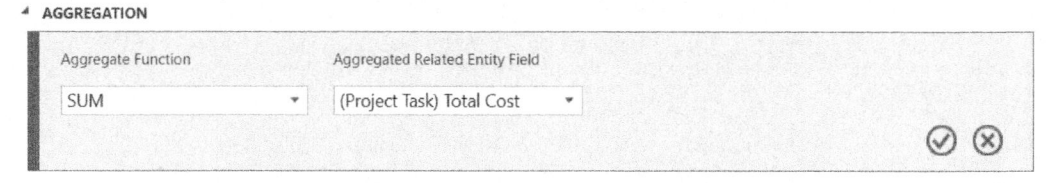

Figure 2.21: Configure aggregation for a rollup column

- Confirm the aggregation and click on "**Save and close**".

Configure the rollup field "**Total Work Price**" using the same procedure by selecting the expected configuration as described in the preceding *Table 2.5*.

> Note: Please note that for configuring the filters in the rollup columns, you first need to have the status columns created in the tables, so please create those columns according to the following description.

Configuration of columns with choice data type

In the tables "**Project Task**" and "**Project Product**", there is a column "**Task Status**" and "**Product Status**" of data type "**Choice**" required. Please configure the columns according to the following steps:

- Create the column, give it the **Display name,** and select the **Data type** "**Choice**" (not "**Choices**", which is a different data type) for the column.
- Open the list of available choices and click on the "**+ New choice**" at the top of the list.
- In the choice configuration dialogue, replace the first value, "**New option**", with our first status value for the respective column, which is "**Planned**".
- Click "**Add new item**" and enter the second value; click "**Add new item**" one more time and enter the third value. The configuration of choice should look like as shown in the following screenshot:

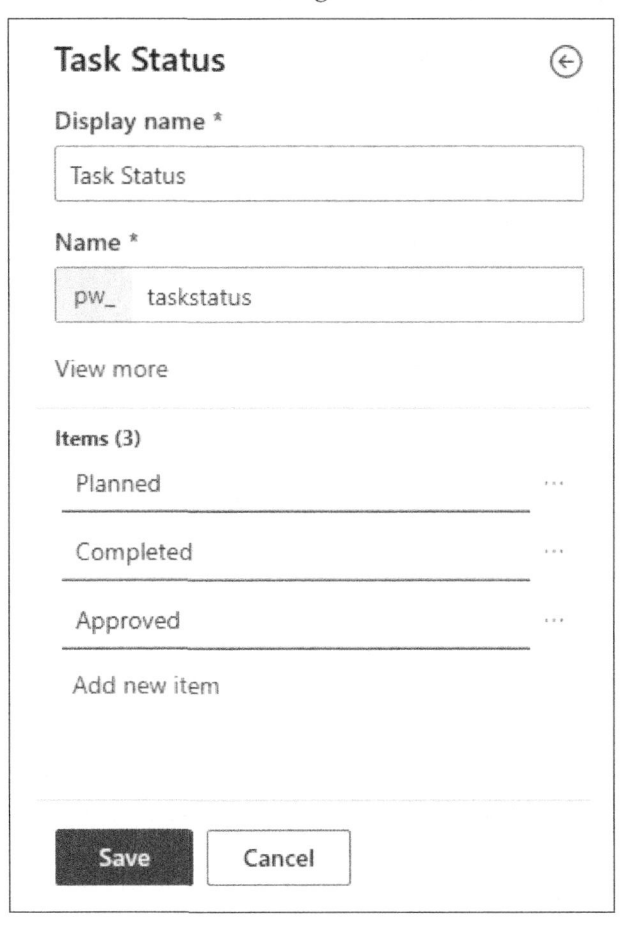

Figure 2.22: Configure a choice

- Click on "**Save**" to save the choice values; after that, you will return back into the column creation dialogue.

- Select the Default value as "**Planned**" and finish the creation of the column.

Repeat the same procedure for the "**Product Status**" in the table "**Project Product**". Add the three values as defined in *Table 2.4* and select the "**Planned**" value as default.

Configuration of a column data type Autonumber

The column "**Number**" in the table "**Project**" is of data type **Autonumber**. Please configure this column using following steps:

- Create the new column with the **Display name** "**Number**" and select the **Data type** "**Autonumber**".

- Keep the **Autonumber type** as "**String prefixed number**" and enter "**PROJ**" into **Prefix**.

- Keep other settings by default and finish the creation of the column.

Navigate to the top-level node "**All**" in your solution and click on the button "**Publish all customizations**". This procedure will move all your changes into operation so that they can be used by end users.

Congratulations! You have just finished your first practical exercise, and your data model in Microsoft Dataverse is ready to be used.

Model-driven apps fundamentals

You have learned the main characteristics of model-driven apps earlier in this chapter. Now let us have a close look at some details. The model-driven app consists of the following main components:

- The *user interface components* of the app, specifically the *forms*, *views*, *charts*, and *dashboards*. They are used to present the data from Microsoft Dataverse in the app but also to actively work with the data—enter new records, modify, or delete existing records and much more.

- The configuration of the *main navigation* of the model-driven app is called the **site map**. This main navigation is represented on the left side of the app and consists of a three-step hierarchy of areas, groups, and sub-areas.

- The configuration of the *model-driven* app itself gives us the possibility to decide which of the elements implemented in Microsoft Dataverse, such as table forms, views, charts, and so on, will be available in the app and which will not.

The configuration of the preceding elements of the model-driven app is performed from within the Maker Portal using respective graphical designer tools.

Now, after this short introduction, let us right away start with the practical implementation of our model-driven app for Project Wizards, Inc.

Exercise 2: Creating a model-driven app

We will need to first analyze the requirements set and then go ahead with the practical implementation steps:

Analysis and preparations

After analyzing the requirements for the project management solution, we have decided to build a simple model-driven app with the following structure:

- A simple site map navigation to the following tables: "**Account**", "**Contact**", "**Project**", and "**Product Catalogue**".
- The work with the "**Project Tasks**" and "**Project Products**" data will be embedded onto the Project's main form and will not have separate navigation.
- The model-driven forms and views will be configured to contain all relevant data from the custom tables.
- The user interface of the default tables "**Account**", "**Contact**", and "**User**" will not be modified.
- To make things simple, there will be no charts and dashboards in the app.

Now, let us start the practical implementation of the app.

Practical Implementation

In this exercise, we will implement the model-driven app with the name *Project Management* using the already created data model in Microsoft Dataverse. The implementation will consist of the following steps:

- Update the autogenerated main forms for the tables "**Project Catalogue**", "**Project Task**", "**Project Product**", and "**Project**".
- Update the autogenerated views for the same tables as preceding.
- Create the model-driven app "**Project Management**" using the app designer.

First, we will start with updating the main forms of the four custom tables. Microsoft Dataverse creates automatically for every custom table a main form with minimal content, so we need to just modify and extend the content.

Updating the autogenerated main forms

For updating the content of the main forms in our custom tables, we will be using the model-driven forms designer. For the configuration, perform the following steps:

- In the Maker Portal, open the Project Management solution, locate and open the table "**Project Catalogue**", go to the tab "**Forms**" and click on the form with the name "**Information**" and the form type "**Main**". The forms designer will be opened.

- In the left navigation pane, select the column list and, using drag-and-drop, move the columns on the form in the order as illustrated in the following screenshot:

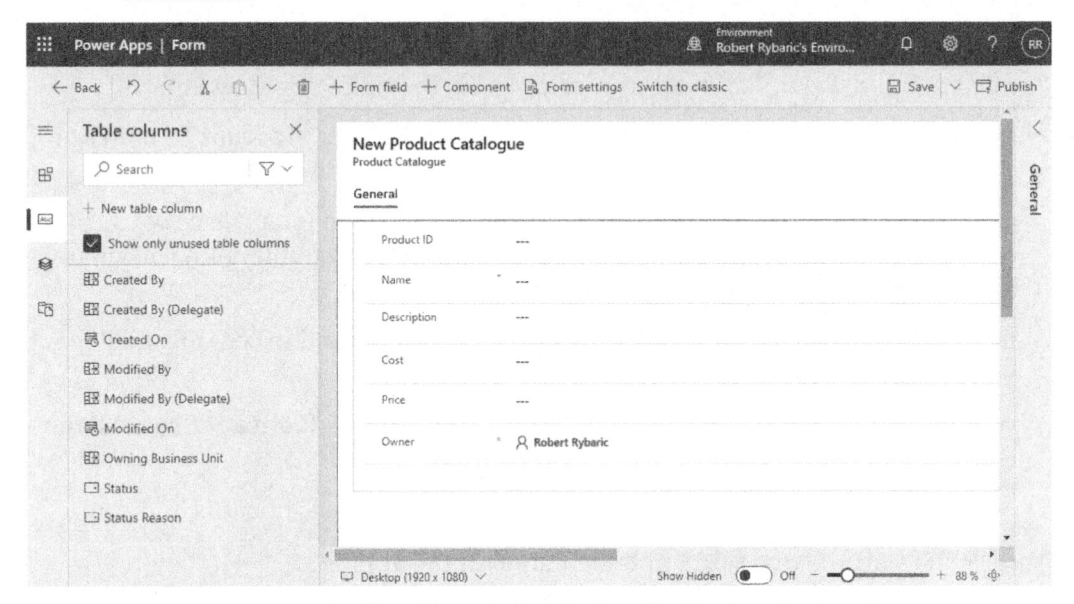

Figure 2.23: Configure the main form for the table "Product Catalogue"

- Click "**Save**" and then "**<- Back**" to return to the Maker Portal

Repeat the same steps for the tables "**Project Task**" and "**Project Product**":

- Add the following columns to the "**Project Task**" table in the specified order: "**Project, Name**", "**Start Date**", "**Duration**", "**Cost Rate**", "**Bill Rate**", "**Total Cost**", "**Total Price**", "**Task Status**", and "**Owner**".

- Add the following columns to the "**Project Product**" table in the specified order: "**Project**", "**Product Catalogue**", "**Name**", "**Quantity**", "**Total Cost**", "**Total Price**", "**Product Status**", and "**Owner**"

You may play with the design of the main forms and use capabilities like placing some of the columns into the header (such as "**Task Status**" and "**Product Status**"), changing the formatting of the tab to two-column, distributing the columns appropriately, and so on.

For the table "**Project**", we are going to use a different, more complex configuration to show not just the project column data but also all related project tasks and project products on the main form in two sub-grids. For this configuration, please perform the following steps:

- Add the following columns on the form in the specified order: "**Number**", "**Name**", "**Customer**", "**Customer primary contact**", "**Total Work Cost**", "**Total Work Price**", and "**Owner**"
- Select the tab "**General**" on the left navigation area, select "**Components**", and click on **Subgrid**
- Configure the following settings for the sub-grid:
    - Check "**Show related records**"
    - Select the table "**Project Tasks**"
    - Click "**Done**"
- A new sub-grid will be added to the form, change the autogenerated cryptic label of the sub-grid to "**Project Tasks**"
- Repeat the adding of another sub-grid, and configure the second sub-grid:
    - Check "**Show related records**"
    - Select the table "**Project Products**"
    - Click "**Done**"
- A second sub-grid will be added to the form, change the autogenerated cryptic label of the second sub-grid to "**Project Products**"

- Verify the main form look like as shown in the following screenshot:

Figure 2.24: Configure the main form for the table "Project"

You may play with the design of the main form like placing some of the columns into the header (like "**Owner**"), changing the formatting of the tab to two-column, distributing the columns or sub-grids appropriately, and so on.

Updating the autogenerated views

For updating the content of the views in our custom tables, we will be using the model-driven views designer. For the configuration, perform the following steps:

- In the Maker Portal, open the Project Management solution, locate and open the table "**Project Catalogue**", go to the tab "**Views**", and click on the view with the name "**Active Product Catalogues**". The views designer will be opened.

- By clicking on the column name in the list of columns on the left side, you can add a column to the view. Using this approach, insert the following columns into the view in the following order: "**Product ID**", "**Description**", "**Cost**", and "**Price**".

- Delete the column "**Created On**" by clicking on the column header and selecting "**Remove**".

- You can visually change the order of the columns, their width, order and filter of the records, and many more.

Repeat the same procedure with the other three custom tables to create the following view design:

- For the table "**Project**", modify the view "**Active Projects**" to include the following columns: "**Number**", "**Name**", "**Customer**", "**Customer primary contact**", "**Total Work Cost**", and "**Total Work Price**".

- For the table "**Project Task**", modify the view "**Active Project Tasks**" to include the following columns: "**Name**", "**Start Date**", "**Duration**", "**Cost Rate**", "**Bill Rate**", "**Total Cost**", "**Total Price**", and "**Task Status**".

- For the table "**Project Product**", modify the view "**Active Project Products**" to include the following columns: "**Product Catalogue**", "**Quantity**", "**Total Cost**", "**Total Price**", and "**Product Status**".

Note: Please note that we are not going to configure any other from the remaining five autogenerated table views in the custom tables.

Creating the model-driven app "Project Management"

The last task in this exercise is the creation of the model-driven app itself. Please perform the following steps:

- In the Maker Portal, open the "**Project Management**" solution, and select "**+ New**" → "**App**" → "**Model-driven app**".

- Select the "Modern app designer" and click "**Create**".

- Give the model-driven app the name "**Project Management**" and click "**Create**".

- On the left navigation side, select "**Navigation**".

- Select the pre-created group "**Group1**", and on the right side in the properties, change the **Title** to "**Projects**".

- Select the pre-created subarea with the name "**Subarea1**", and on the right side in the properties, change the **Title** to "**Projects**". Select **Content type** as "**Table**". Select the **Table** as "**Project**". In the main area of the app designer, you will see the result of the configuration.

- On the left side, click on "**+ Add**" and select "**Group**". Change the **Title** of the newly created group to "**Catalogues**".

- Stay on the group "**Catalogues**", click "**+ Add**", and select "**Subarea**". Select **Content type** as "**Table**". Select the **Table** as "**Product Catalogue**" and the **Title** will be automatically set to the name of the table. Click "**Add**".

- Click on the group "**Catalogues**", click "**+ Add**", and select "**Subarea**". Select **Content type** as "**Table**". Select the **Table** as "**Account**", and the **Title** will be automatically set to the name of the table. Click "**Add**".

- Click on the group "**Catalogues**", click "**+ Add**", and select "**Subarea**". Select **Content type** as "**Table**". Select the **Table** as "**Contact**", and the **Title** will be automatically set to the name of the table. Click "**Add**".

- Click on "**Save**" on the right side of the command bar.

- Click "**← Back**" on the left side of the command bar. This will return you back to the solution "**Project Management**".

- Click on "**Publish all customizations**" after the publishing finish, click on "**← Back to solutions**".

This was the last step in the creation of a model-driven app. Quite fast and simple, right?

Congratulations! You have just finished the second practical exercise, and you have now a simple yet fully functional model-driven app ready for Project Wizards Inc. For now, please refrain from testing the app because there is something interesting for you in the next section.

Building enterprise-ready model-driven apps

You have learned how to build modern and robust Power Apps app using the model-driven technology quickly and easily. What else is the technology offering in order to make the applications, even more, enterprise-ready? Let us first focus on the integration possibilities:

- You can integrate Microsoft Dataverse with Microsoft Exchange to get the possibility to work with e-mails, appointments, tasks and contacts directly from within model-driven applications.

- You can integrate Microsoft Dataverse with Microsoft SharePoint to get a seamless document management capability directly into your model-driven applications.

- You can integrate the model-driven applications into Microsoft Teams so that your employees can continue working within their known environment but enhanced with integrated business applications.

- There are multiple additional integration possibilities, making the life of the app user even more comfortable, for example, integration with OneDrive for private embedded document storage or with OneNote for an integrated note-taking extension.

- The open and well-documented interface of Microsoft Dataverse makes it easily possible to integrate with a broad variety of other business applications and IT systems.

Another important aspect of an enterprise business application is the possibility to import data from different sources to be prepared for a fast start and broad acceptance of your apps. Power Platform offers multiple easy-to-use data import options from data sources such as text files, Excel files, or various database systems.

In order to learn how to easily import data into Microsoft Dataverse using the native data import capability, we are going to import sample data into our Project Management solution.

Exercise 3: Importing sample data

To really enjoy your newly created model-driven app, *Project Management*, it is important to get some sample data in. There are prepared import files for importing such sample data. You can find the import files at the following location:

https://github.com/bpbpublications/Microsoft-Power-Platform-Up-and-Running

Note: Do not be concerned about the data itself, the data was extracted and prepared for this book from a sample Microsoft SQL Server database, provided free of charge. The data is fictitious and does not refer to any existing organization or individual.

Please download the files and proceed with importing while keeping the order according to the following list. There are dependencies between the data, and a wrong import order would prevent the data from being imported correctly:

1. Accounts (Import file: **Accounts.xlsx**)
2. Contacts (Import file: **Contacts.xlsx**)
3. Product Catalogue (Import file: **Product Catalogues.xlsx**)
4. Projects (Import file: **Projects.xlsx**)
5. Project Tasks (Import file: **Project Task.xlsx**)
6. Project Products (Import file: **Project Products.xlsx**)

Please follow the next steps for importing data from the files into Microsoft Dataverse:

- Navigate to the Power Platform Admin Center: **https://admin.powerplatform.microsoft.com/**

- From the list of the environments, select your developer environment.
- Click on "**Settings**" in the command bar.
- Open the settings group "**Data management**" and select "**Imports**". An empty list of import jobs will be populated.
- Click on "**Import Data**".
- Click on "**Choose File**", select the file "**Accounts.xlsx**", and click "**Next**".
- Set "**Allow Duplicates**" to Yes and click "**Submit**", then "**Finish**".
- The data import is an asynchronous process, and you can see the progress in the view "**My Imports**". Make refreshes of this view and wait until the "**Status Reason**" column shows the value "**Completed**". In the column "**Successes**", there should be the same number as in the column "**Total Processed**". In the columns "**Partial Failures**" and "**Error**", there should be 0. Do not start the next import until the current import is not finished.

Repeat the preceding procedure for the tables "**Contacts**", "**Product Catalogue**", "**Projects**", "**Project Tasks.xlsx**", and "**Project Products.xlsx**" in this order.

> **Note:** Please note that the import files expect exactly the same table and column names as described earlier in this chapter. Should your import fail, you might need to verify whether the naming you have used is correct.

Congratulations! Now you have not just the model-driven application "**Project Management**" but also a whole bunch of sample data imported into the tables. It is time to test your work. Go to the Maker Portal, navigate to Apps and open the "**Project Management**" app. Check all the navigation elements to see the data you have imported. Try to understand the usage patterns of a model-driven app to open a record from the view, modify some data in a form and save the modification, create new records, delete records, and so on.

Dynamics 365 considerations

There is not just the plain Power Platform, offering the possibility to build your own Power Apps and other components, but Microsoft is also offering its own Power Apps from the Microsoft Dynamics 365 product family. It is very important to understand what workloads these apps are covering to be able to take the right decision when planning for a new business solution. You have always the choice of *make* or *buy* and it is a question of comparing costs against the value and the return of investment in the decision-making process. To make the decision-making easier, let us have a quick look at the capabilities of the respective Dynamics 365 apps.

Dynamics 365 Marketing

Dynamics 365 Marketing covers the whole marketing execution workload consisting of building customer segments, creating marketing mails and marketing pages, creating customer journeys to execute complex, and multi-step marketing campaigns. The app also covers lead management and automated lead scoring. The second large capability is called event management and is used to plan, prepare, and execute complex events along with the necessary logistics. The last functional block is dedicated to real-time marketing, covering capabilities like responding to various customer events in real-time with SMS or push notifications.

Dynamics 365 Sales

Dynamics 365 Sales supports the whole sales lifecycle in an organization, starting with leads, qualifying leads to opportunities and then continuing with quoting, sales orders, and invoices. This main capability is accompanied by goal management, forecasting and a complex AI-driven add-on called Sales Insights. This add-on uses the Dynamics 365 data along with e-mails and other sources to provide AI capabilities helping the sales staff be much more effective and productive in their daily work.

Dynamics 365 Customer Service

Dynamics 365 Customer Service is an app for managing the customer service processes within an organization. You can create tickets and resolve them with the help of a rich knowledge base management capability. The ticketing is supported by SLA and entitlement capabilities. There are multiple add-ons and extensions providing multi-channel customer service, integration with IoT devices to convert reactive customer service into a proactive service, and much more.

Dynamics 365 Field Service

Dynamics 365 Field Service is specifically dedicated to organizations having a large and complex field service unit to automate the whole process from creating a work order, scheduling it to the best resources, performing the on-site work by the field service technicians up to closing and billing the work orders. Part of Dynamics 365 Field Service is also an inventory management capability to support the material flows as well as customer asset management, which can be extended with to the IoT capability, similar to the customer service app. There are also some very interesting add-ons available for automated scheduling of work orders or for supporting remote service using the HoloLens devices.

Dynamics 365 Project Operations

Dynamics 365 Project Operations can be used in organizations with complex project-oriented businesses. The app extends the standard sales capability of Dynamics 365 Sales with project-related sales processes in order to offer a seamless hand-over from sales to project for won project opportunities. The project management part of the app provides you with capabilities for project planning, WBS, resourcing and staffing, and time and expense management.

Make or buy?

The information in this section is intended to give you a first impression of what else is available from the Power Platform product family which can serve your needs. It is recommended to always compare the requirements for a new business application with the capabilities of the Dynamics 365 apps described previously. Direct feature comparison and an ROI analysis can give you a reasonable decision-making justification for either make a pure Power Platform solution from scratch, or rather look into some of the Dynamics 365 applications.

Conclusion

In this chapter, you have learned the basics of Power Apps and the typical use cases for building business applications using this technology. We were focusing on the Microsoft Dataverse and model-driven apps; you have seen how to easily build a data model for a business application. In the next part, you have learned more about model-driven apps, and you could build the Project Management model-driven app on your own. You have gained a good foundation understanding for the upcoming chapter of this book, where we will drive our attention to the other Power Apps types.

Questions

1. What are the three types of Power Apps, and what are their main features and use cases?
2. What is the Microsoft Dataverse, and how can it support building business applications?
3. What is the purpose of relationships between Microsoft Dataverse, and how can they be established?
4. What are calculated columns and rollup columns in Microsoft Dataverse, and what is the difference between them?
5. What are the main parts of a model-driven app?

CHAPTER 3
Enable Mobility and Integrate Partners with Power Apps

Introduction

In this chapter, we will continue presenting the Power Apps technology by looking into the two other Power Apps types. First, we will discuss the canvas apps technology, which can be used to quickly build business applications for your mobile workforce. After that, we will focus on the third Power Apps type—the portal apps. This technology can serve you for establishing portal solutions integrating your customers, partners, or any other external parties into your business processes.

Structure

In this chapter, we will discuss the following topics:

- Use cases for Power Apps
- Canvas apps fundamentals
- Connect to data with canvas apps
- Build user interface and functionality with canvas apps
- Enable employee mobility with canvas apps
- Portal apps fundamentals

- Configure simple portal apps
- Integrate your customers with portal apps

Objective

After reading this chapter, you will be able better understand the other two Power Apps types. You will know, what are the main features of canvas apps, and how they are built and deployed to users. Next, you will dive deeper into the portal apps and learn the basics of creating portals and publishing data from Microsoft Dataverse onto the portal surface. You will build your own canvas app and portal app in a series of practical exercises.

Use cases for Power Apps

As you know already from the previous chapter, what are the typical use cases for model-driven Power Apps. Let us now fully focus on the canvas apps and portal apps.

Canvas apps is primarily a technology for building internal applications for mobile devices. A typical use case is when you need to modernize existing legacy applications that are not yet intended to be replaced. Legacy applications are typically monolithic and robust but not very flexible. In today's modern working life, the mobility of the workforce is one of the key success factors. And a mobile workforce needs support in the form of mobile applications for the main enterprise workloads. Here comes the canvas apps technology in play. You can quickly and easily develop single-purpose mobile applications with canvas apps and leverage a large number of data connectors to connect to your legacy systems. When you intend to build a new modern enterprise IT system, then it is equally beneficial to consider using the canvas apps technology to build the mobile solution for that scenario.

The **portal apps** technology is typically used to build portal solutions for your external stakeholders, let it be customers, partners, vendors, citizens or even patients. The most appropriate use case is to extend either a Microsoft Dynamics 365 application or a custom Microsoft Dataverse-based solution with an external-facing portal component. There are multiple portal templates available for direct integration with Microsoft Dynamics 365 applications, which makes the deployment even easier and faster. You can deploy a customer self-service portal, a partner portal, or a portal for field service or project service purposes.

Canvas apps fundamentals

In *Chapter 2, Building enterprise solutions with Power Apps*, we have learned about the main characteristics and usage scenarios of canvas apps. Let us now dive deeper and learn how can the canvas apps be built. The basic structure of a canvas app consists of the following main parts:

- **Screens** represent the individual functional blocks and are displayed on the mobile device of an app user. The screens can be either in phone format or in tablet format.

- **Controls**, which are placed on screens where they provide the required functionality—user interface elements showing data, active controls for manipulating data or provide interactive functionality, and so on. There is a whole bunch of built-in control types available for use on the screens.

- **Data connections** provide an easy way to connect the canvas app to various data sources and IT systems and solutions.

- **App logic**, represented by the **Power Fx** expressions, is used to provide the required functionality of the canvas app, such as navigating from one screen to another, working with data, calculations and transformations of data, and many more.

When creating canvas apps, you need to work according to the following main steps:

- Create a new canvas app, and decide on the form factor: phone or tablet.
- Connect to all necessary data sources by using the Power Platform data connectors.
- Create the user interface: the screens and the controls.
- Configure the app logic using the Power Fx expressions.
- Test, publish and share the app.

Canvas apps can be created using one of the following three possible approaches:

- From a template: In the Maker Portal, you can find multiple templates that can be used to directly create a canvas app. This approach is best suitable for learning purposes because it is unlikely that your desired app can be found under those templates.

- From data: You can select a data source using some of the Power Platform data connectors to let the canvas apps designer generate a single-connection-based app. This approach can be used when you need to build a simple application very quickly.

- As blank app: This is the most common app creation approach. While it requires more effort compared with the previous approaches, it gives you full flexibility in designing your app exactly according to your requirements and preferences.

Canvas apps are created using a graphical designer tool called Power Apps Studio. This tool can be started directly from the Maker Portal. The structure of the Power Apps Studio tool is illustrated in the following screenshot.

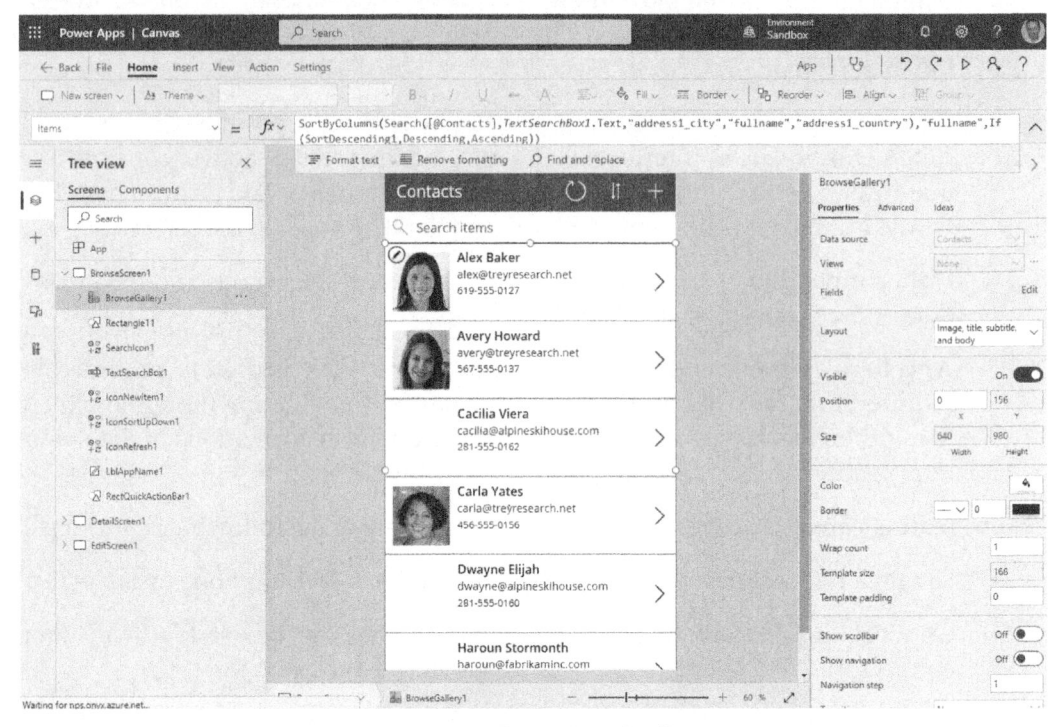

Figure 3.1: Power Apps Studio

On the left side, you will find the main navigation areas; in the middle, there is the working canvas to perform the visual design of the app; on the right side, there are properties of screens and controls, and above the main area, there is an editor for configuring the Power Fx formula expressions.

We will use this tool to build the Project Tracking app described as follows.

Design of the Project Tracking app

In *Chapter 2, Building enterprise solutions with Power Apps*, we have created the Project Management model-driven app, which will be primarily used by the administrators and project managers. In the second step, we need to create an app for the project members to execute the assigned project tasks and report on the status.

After we have analyzed the requirement set from Project Wizards, Inc., we have specified the following detailed required features for the app:

- The employees are all equipped with company mobile phones; therefore, it is required to build a phone format app.

- In order to make the use of the mobile app as simple as possible, the app will have just one single screen containing the whole functionality.

- On the screen, every employee needs to have a list of all project tasks assigned to them.

- The list should contain the following information: *"Project Name"*, *"Name of the project task"*, *"Estimated Duration"*, and *"Task Status"*.

- The employee must not see the commercial data assigned to the project task ("Cost Rate", "Bill Rate", "Total Cost", or "Total Price").

- When an employee selects a task from the list, it should be possible to change the status of the task from *"Planned"* to *"Completed"*, or vice versa, from *"Completed"* to *"Planned"*, in case the employee marks a task as completed by mistake.

- Project tasks with the status *"Approved"* should be locked so that the employee cannot modify the values anymore.

- The employee should have the possibility to switch the list of the task between *"All"*, showing all tasks assigned to them, or *"Open"*, showing only tasks with the status *"Planned"* and *"Completed"*, but not *"Approved"*.

In the subsequent sections of this chapter, we will go ahead and build the canvas app according to the specification.

Let us start first with creating a canvas app and connecting to data.

Connect to data with canvas apps

Canvas apps use the Power Platform Data Connectors to connect to data. There is a very large number of public connectors for every possible technology and business application. Most of the connectors provide a table feature, which makes it possible to directly connect data to canvas apps controls. Even connectors without the table property can be used to connect to data using some of the most suitable actions.

Connecting an app to data means identifying proper data connectors for our required IT technology, selecting the connector, and configuring a connection. The configuration usually requires specifying the exact data source, such as database name, SharePoint site URL and list name, or Dataverse table, along with some additional information such as authentication and so on.

Connecting to a particular data source, such as a Dataverse table or SharePoint list, creates a *connection*. You can have multiple connections in a canvas app, and each can be configured using any available data connector.

> Note: For further details about the data connectors, please refer to the following product documentation: https://docs.microsoft.com/en-us/connectors/

After this short introduction to connecting to data, we are ready for the next practical exercise.

Exercise 4—Create app and connect it to data

In this exercise, we start building the Project Tracking app for Project Wizards, Inc. by creating the app and connecting it to data. We already know the most important facts about the app: the form factor selected at the time of creation will be *"Phone"*, and the app will connect only to the Microsoft Dataverse tables *"Project Task"* and *"Project"*.

Create new table views

There is one additional requirement we need to implement upfront. The app should show every user the list of project tasks assigned to them only, and not any tasks assigned to some other employee. Further, there should be the capability to switch between all assigned tasks or assigned open tasks.

The easiest way to implement this requirement is to create specific table views in the table *"Project Task"* in Microsoft Dataverse, which will filter the records appropriately. These views will then be used as the data source in the canvas app. Please follow the following steps to create such a view:

- In the Maker Portal, open the Project Management solution, locate and open the table "**Project Task**", go to the tab "**Views**", and click "**+ Add view**".
- Give the new view the name "**My Project Tasks**" and click "**Create**".
- Keep the existing column "**Name**" and add the following columns: "**Duration**" and "**Task Status**".
- On the left pane "**Table columns**", switch the column list from "**Project Task**" to "**Related**".
- Expand the node "**Project (Project)**", and from the column list add the column "**Name**", representing the project name to the view.
- On the right side, click on "**Edit filters** …". In the filter editor, click on "**+ Add**" and select "**+ Add row**".

- In the filter query row, select "**Owner**" for the column and "**Equals current user**" for the condition. Select "**Ok**" to confirm the filter.

- Back in the main view designer select "**Save**".

- Click on the small down arrow right from the **Save** button and select "**Save As**". In the view naming dialog, give the new view the name "**My Open Project Tasks**" and confirm with "**Save**". A copy of the previously created view will be created.

- The structure of the view does not need any change, and only the filter condition needs to be updated. Click on "**Edit filters** …" to open the filter designer.

- Click "**+ Add**" and then "**Add row**". This will add a second condition to the filter. Select the column "**Task Status**", confirm the operator "**Equals**", and select both the values "**Planned**" and "**Completed**". You must select the first value and then the second value separately. Confirm the new filter with "**Ok**".

- Click "**Save**" and then "**<- Back**".

- Note that the new views with the names "**My Project Tasks**" and "**My Open Project Tasks**" are added to the view list.

- Click on the upper node "**All**" in the structure of the solution, click on "**Publish all customizations**", and wait until the publishing procedure finish.

The next steps will be the creation of the canvas app and setting up the data source.

Create a new canvas app

Please follow the following steps to create a new canvas app:

- In the Maker Portal, open the Project Management solution, click "**+ New**", select "**App**", and "**Canvas app**".

- Give the app the name "**Project Tracking**", select the format "**Phone**", and click "**Create**". This will open the Power Apps Studio. Skip the suggested steps.

- The created canvas app is empty, having just one single screen with the name "**Screen1**". Select the screen in the left navigation tree, click on the three dots, and select "**Rename**". Give the screen the name "**Main Screen**".

- In the left navigation area, move from "**Tree view**" to "**Data**".

- Click "**Add data**", and in the data selection dialogue, search for the table "**Project Tasks**". When found, click on the table name—this will create a connection to the table.

- Click again "**Add data**", and in the data selection dialogue, search for the table "**Project**". When found, click on the table name—this will create another connection to the table.

- Click in the main menu on "**File**". You will be offered an app directly saving dialogue. Verify that the name of the app is "**Project Tracking**" and that the "**Save as**" selection remains as "**The cloud**". In the lower right corner, click on "**Save**".

- In the upper left corner, click the left arrow (<-) button to navigate back to the designer view.

- Click on the "**<- Back**" button to navigate back to the solution.

- Verify that the canvas app was added to the solution.

- This is the last task in the exercise. You have successfully created the basic structure of the Project Tracking app. In the subsequent exercises, we will together build the app user interface and functionality.

Build user interface and functionality with canvas apps

After a canvas app is connected to all necessary data sources, the next steps are to configure the user interface and the required functionality. Although the user interface is created in a graphical design, the functionality needs to be implemented using the Power Fx expression language. Microsoft has made significant efforts to make this expression language user-friendly so that everybody regularly using Excel expressions will find Power Fx pretty similar.

Let us first focus on the user interface creation capabilities.

Canvas apps user interface

The canvas apps technology is dedicated to creating apps for mobile devices. That is why the UI is optimized for use on such devices. The apps consist of screens and controls placed on the screens.

The canvas app technology supports currently the creation of apps in two form factors: phone and tablet. You need to choose the form factor when creating the app.

> Note: The form factor of a canvas app cannot be changed once the app is created, so be careful when deciding which is the right form factor for your app.

A canvas app can have *one* or *multiple* screens. It is important to understand that mobile apps need to be simple to ensure user acceptance. That is why you should always consider just a limited number of screens for your app.

Screens can be created in Power Apps Studio as either *blank* screens or screens inherited from one of the multiple available *templates*.

After all the required screens are created, it is time to start placing *controls* on the screens. There are multiple different control types available to cover many different application purposes, such as:

- Displaying *text blocks*, using controls such as "`Label`" or "`HTML text`".
- *Displaying data* from the connections, using controls such as "`Image`", "`Gallery`", "`Data table`", "`Form`", "`Column chart`", "`Line chart`", or "`Pie chart`".
- Providing *data input* for the user, with controls such as "`Text input`", "`Rich text editor`", "`Pen input`", "`Drop down`", "`Combo box`", "`Date picker`", "`List box`", "`Check box`", "`Radio`", "`Toggle`", "`Slider`", or "`Rating`".
- *Triggering actions*, using controls such as "`Button`" or "`Icon`".
- There are many other special controls like the media controls, communicating with the mobile device hardware components (camera, microphone, and speaker) or the mixed reality controls for developing mixed reality apps.

Working with controls means *selecting* the right controls for the required purpose, *placing* the controls on the screen, and *configuring* the control *properties*. Every control has many properties to configure the control look and feel, functionality, behavior and more; for example:

- The exact *position* and size of the control.
- The *color scheme* of the control (foreground color, background color, disabled color, and hover color).
- The *formatting* of the text is displayed on the control (font type, size, style, weight, and alignment).
- Configuration of the *connection* to some data elements.
- Configuration of the *actions* to happen when the user interacts with the control.

In the next exercise, we will create the user interface for our *Project Tracking* application.

Exercise 5—Create and design an app screen

Our application will have a single screen with a simple user interface consisting of the following controls:

- A *label* control to display the header of the app.
- A *toggle* control to switch the list of project tasks between all tasks and open tasks.
- A *gallery* control to display the list of the project tasks assigned to the signed-in user.
- A *button* control to set the project task status as "**Completed**".
- Another *button* control to revert the project task status back to "**Planned**".

In the following parts of this exercise, we will subsequently configure the main controls on the screen.

Configure the application header

Please follow the following steps to configure the application header:

- In the Maker Portal, open the "**Project Management**" solution, locate the "**Project Tracking**" canvas app, select the app, and in the command bar, click "**Edit**". This will open the **Power Apps Studio** with our app containing the single empty screen as we have configured it in the previous exercise.
- In the upper command bar, select "**Insert**" and then "**Label**".
- On the left side of the tree view, rename the label from "**Label1**" to "**Header**".
- On the right side, on the properties pane, change the "**Text**" property of the label from "**Text**" to "**Project Tracking Application**".
- On the properties pane, change the following values of the label in the first group of the properties:
    - Font size: 32
    - Font weight: Semibold
    - Text alignment: center

- Next, change the following values in the second group of the label properties:
    - Position—X: 0
    - Position—Y: 0
    - Position—Width: 640
    - Position—Height: 80
- Finally, in the third group of the label properties, change the following values:
    - Color: White
    - Color—Fill: Dark blue

Next, we will add the toggle control to switch the list of the assigned project tasks between a full list and a list of only open tasks.

Configure the toggle control

Please follow the following steps to configure the toggle control:

- In the upper command bar, select "**Insert**", then "**Input**", and finally "**Toggle**". A toggle control will be placed in the upper part of the screen.
- Rename the toggle control to "**Project Task Filter**".
- On the properties pane on the right side, change the following property values of the control:
    - Default: On
    - Label position: Left
    - Position—X: 330
    - Position—Y: 90
    - Position—Width: 300
    - Position—Height: 50
- In the property selector on the upper left side, select the respective property and set the values according to the following:
    - FalseText: "**Open Tasks**"
    - TrueText: "**All Tasks**"

Next, we need to add a gallery control to the screen to display the list of the assigned project tasks.

Configure the gallery

Please follow the following steps to configure the gallery:

- In the upper command bar, select "**Insert**" and then "**Gallery**". From the gallery templates, select "**Vertical**". This will add gallery control to the screen.
- In the dialog "**Select a data source**", click on the connection "**Project Tasks**". This will connect the gallery with the "**Project Task**" table, and the gallery will be populated with the data from the table.
- On the left side, rename the gallery from "**Gallery1**" to "**Project Task List**".
- On the right side, on the properties pane, change the "**Layout**" of the gallery from "**Image, title and subtitle**" to "**Title, subtitle and body**".
- Next, change the sizing properties of the gallery as follows:
    - Position—X: 0
    - Position—Y: 150
    - Position—Width: 640
    - Position—Height: 890
- On the left side in the tree view of the application, expand the gallery "**Project Task List**" to see the controls inside the gallery control. The structure of the app should look like as shown in the following screenshot:

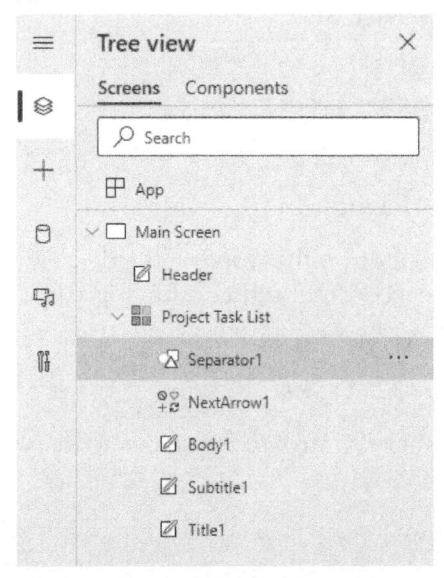

Figure 3.2: Structure of the App I.

Enable Mobility and Integrate Partners with Power Apps ■ 73

- We need to add a new control inside the gallery because we need to display four column values from the "**Project Task**" table. In order to achieve this, click on the three dots right from the "**Title1**" and select "**Copy**". Then select the three dots right from the "**Title1**" again and select "**Paste**". This will create a duplicate of the label control "**Title1**" with the name "**Title1_1**" according to the following screenshot:

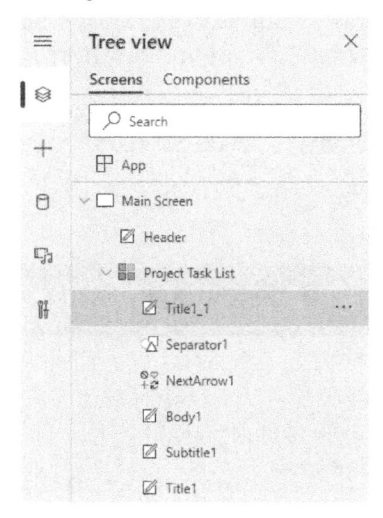

Figure 3.3: Structure of the App II

- Next, we need to change the positions and connection to data of the four labels inside the gallery to represent the data properly graphically from the table "**Project Task**". On the footer of the Power Apps Studio, use the zoom control to make the design area bigger and move the four labels inside the gallery into the following positions, where the order of the controls should be: **Title1_1**, **Title1**, **Subtitle1**, and **Body1** according to the following screenshot:

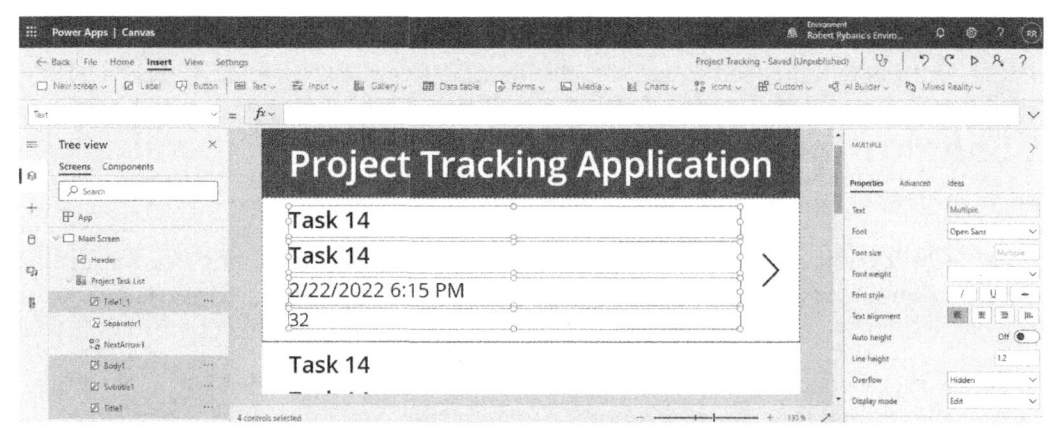

Figure 3.4: Structure of the gallery control

- If the label **Body1** is too high by default, change the height of the control to 24.

- Next, select the label **control Title1_1** in the property selector on the left side of the command bar, make sure the selected property is "**Text**", and change the value to **ThisItem.Project.Name**.

- Select the label control **Subtitle1** and change the **Text** property to "**Estimated duration:**", ThisItem.Duration, and "hours".

- Select the label control **Body1** and change the **Text** property to "**Task status:**" and **ThisItem.' Task Status'**.

- The final design of the gallery should look like as shown in the following screenshot:

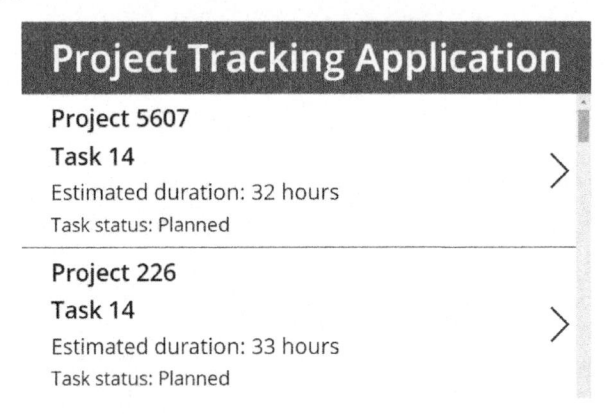

Figure 3.5: Final design of the gallery control

- Feel free to try to change some other properties of the four labels inside the gallery to achieve some interesting visual effects, but do not change any properties of the gallery itself.

In the last task of this exercise, we will add and configure two buttons to the screen. These controls will be used to modify the Task Status of the selected task.

Configure the buttons

Please follow the following steps to configure the buttons:

- On the left side of the designer, click on the "**Main Screen**" in the upper command bar, click "**Insert**", and select the "**Button**" control. The control will be placed in the upper part of the screen.

- First, we need to rename the button to "**Set Complete Button**". After that, we change the "**Text**" property of the button control to "**Set Complete**".

- Next, we need to place the button control properly at the bottom of the screen. Select the button control and change the sizing properties to the following values:
    - Position—X: 30
    - Position—Y: 1060
    - Position—Width: 280
    - Position—Height: 60
- After that, we create the second button and configure it the same way as described previously with the following properties:
    - Name: "**Revert Button**"
    - Text: "**Revert**"
    - Position—X: 340
    - Position—Y: 1060
    - Position—Width: 280
    - Position—Height: 60
- The final design of the application should look like as shown in the following screenshot:

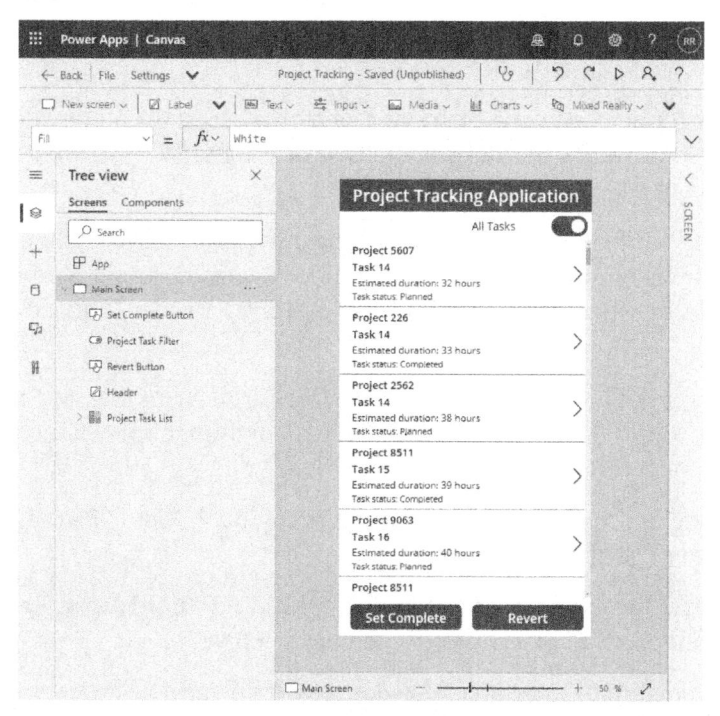

Figure 3.6: Final design of the application

- In the main navigation of the Power Apps Studio, click on "**File**" and then click on "**Save**". After that, click on the left arrow "<-" in the upper left corner.
- Click on the "**<- Back**" button to leave the Power Apps Studio and return back to the solution.

This was the last task in this exercise. Now, your application is almost ready, and it just does not do anything apart from showing the list of tasks because the app functionality is still missing.

In the next part, we will focus on the functionality of a canvas app implemented using the expression language Power Fx.

Fundamentals of Power Fx

As mentioned earlier in this chapter, the **Power Fx** is the Excel-like expression language, which acts as a glue to bring all the screens and controls together to provide the required functionality. The Power Fx expressions (or formulas) need to be properly attached to the screen or control properties.

The following examples can illustrate the typical scenarios of using Power Fx:
- A label control should be connected to a column from a data connection to display the content of the column. The Power Fx formula is assigned to the **Text** property of the control. Sounds familiar? Sure, because we have done exactly this in the previous exercise, without even knowing that we are already working with Power Fx.
- A button (or icon) control should perform a certain action upon click. The Power Fx formula defining the action is assigned to the **OnSelect** property of the control.
- A gallery or Data table control should provide a search, filter, sort, or other capabilities on top of the pure display of records from a table. The Power Fx formula defining the capabilities is assigned to the **Items** property of the control.

There is quite a large number of Power Fx expressions available, but the purpose of this book is not to provide a detailed reference of all those expressions. Let us instead illustrate them on a few simple examples:
- To navigate from the current screen to the screen "**Details Screen**": **Navigate('Detail Screen')**.
- To submit the entered data from the Edit Form "**Contacts Form**" control to the connection: **SubmitForm('Contacts Form')**.
- To define a global variable "**NewPersonName**" and assign a value "**John**" to it: **Set(NewPersonName, "John")**.

Do you think that having to learn Power Fx is too complicated and can stop you from using the canvas apps technology? That is for sure not the case. The recommended way is to learn the formulas gradually, just in case you need to solve a particular business problem while building an app. There is no need to spend days or weeks to first learn all the existing formulas because many of them will be most likely never used.

> Note: For further details about the Power Fx formulas, refer to the product documentation: https://docs.microsoft.com/en-us/powerapps/maker/canvas-apps/formula-reference

In order to learn some of the Power Fx formulas in a very practical way, let us bring our canvas app Project Tracking to life.

Exercise 6—Configure app functionality

First, let us summarize what the expected functionality of the app is:

- The app should show every user only the project tasks assigned to them.
- When a project task is selected, it should be possible to change the "**Task Status**".
- When the "**Task Status**" = "**Approved**", the status should not be open for change.

How can we achieve these three required capabilities? Let us have a look into it:

- In the Maker Portal, open the "**Project Management**" solution, locate the "**Project Tracking**" canvas app, select the app, and in the command bar, click "**Edit**". This will open the **Power Apps Studio** with our app.

- At the beginning of Exercise 4, we created custom views in the table "**Project Task**" to filter out only tasks assigned to the signed-in user. In order to bring that filtering into the gallery control "**Project Task List**" select the gallery, in the property selector on the upper left side, select the property "**Items**", and assign the following Power Fx expression: `Filter('Project Tasks', If('Project Task Filter'.Value, 'Project Tasks (Views)'.'My Project Tasks', 'Project Tasks (Views)'.'My Open Project Tasks'))`. This is a little bit more complex formula, that is why the following explanation:

    o The **Items** property of the gallery defines the content to be displayed in the gallery.

    o The **Filter** expression filters data from a data connection based on a condition.

- o The **If** expression is a logical branching expression, evaluating a condition and selecting values based on the result of the expression, which needs to be either True or False.
  - o The whole expression retrieves the value of the toggle control "**Project Task Filter**". When the value is true ("**All Tasks**"), then the Items property of the gallery is filtered by the view "**My Project Tasks**" when the value is false ("**Open Tasks**"), then the Items property of the gallery is filtered by the view "**My Open Project Tasks**".
- We also need to ensure that the selected item in the gallery will be highlighted so that the app user can see which line was selected. To achieve this, select the property "**TemplateFill**" of the gallery and assign the following Power Fx expression: **If(ThisItem.IsSelected, Color.Azure, Color.White)**. The selected item will have a light blue color background, called "*Azure*", whereas the other items will have a white background. You can replace the color "*Azure*" with some other light color if you like so.
- Select the button "**Set Complete Button**", in the property selector on the upper left side select the property **OnSelect** and assign the following Power Fx expression: **Patch('Project Tasks', LookUp('Project Tasks', 'Project Task' = 'Project Task List'.Selected.'Project Task'), {'Task Status': 'Task Status'.Completed})**. This expression will locate the selected row and physically change the Task Status to "**Completed**" upon clicking on the button.
- Stay on the button and select the property **DisplayMode**. Assign the following Power Fx expression: **If('Project Task List'.Selected.'Task Status' = 'Task Status'.Approved, DisplayMode.Disabled, DisplayMode.Edit)**. This expression will ensure that the button will be disabled for any project task which is already approved.
- Repeat the previous two steps with the button "**Revert Button**". Set the property **OnSelect** to the following Power Fx expression: **Patch('Project Tasks', LookUp('Project Tasks', 'Project Task' = 'Project Task List'.Selected.'Project Task'), {'Task Status': 'Task Status'.Planned})**. Set the **DisplayMode** property to exact the same expression as for the button **Set Complete Button**.
- In the main menu, select **File** and then **Save**. Return back to the Power Apps Studio and click on **<- Back**.

This was the last step in this exercise. Now, your application is ready to be used. In the next section, we will prepare the app for real use on a mobile device.

Enable employee mobility with canvas apps

In the previous sections, you have learned how to develop simple canvas apps. But how to bring a developed app into production? Well, there are some last steps which need to be performed:

- After every modification, a canvas app needs to be *saved*. When the app is saved, a *new app version* is automatically created.

- In order to be able to use a canvas app on a mobile device, the app needs to be *published*. After every modification of an existing app, you need to save the app and then publish it.

- Even the published app is not yet ready for the target audience. A published app needs to be *shared* with the target user population.

Let us now practice these steps in our next exercise.

Exercise 7—Publish, share, and test the app

In *Exercise 6*, we have developed and saved the final version of the app. In order to test the app on our mobile device, please follow the following steps:

- In the Maker Portal, open the "**Project Management**" solution, locate the "**Project Tracking**" canvas app, select the app, and in the command bar, click "**Edit**". This will open our app in the Power Apps Studio.

- Select "**File**", and in the menu item "**Save**", you will find a button "**Publish**". Click on the button and confirm the publishing by clicking on "**Publish this version**".

- There is no need to share the app because we are the only user in the Power Platform environment.

- Click "**<- Back**" to return to the solution.

- Take your mobile phone, go to the Apps Store (iPhone) or Google Play Store (Android phone) and locate the *Power Apps* application from Microsoft. Install the application on your mobile device.

- After the installation open the Power Apps app and sign-in with your cloud credentials (username and password).

- You should find your application, *Project Tracking*, in the Power Apps app. Start the application and try out the implemented capabilities. The capability of switching between all tasks and open tasks cannot be tested now because there are no approved tasks yet.

This was the last step in this exercise.

Congratulations! You have achieved the next milestone in having a fully functional mobile application for the project employees of Project Wizards Inc.

In the next section, we are going to investigate the third and last Power Apps type—the portal apps, and how they can be used in the business.

Portal apps fundamentals

A Power Apps portal solution is a publicly available website with content configured by you. The final portal solution consists usually of a public part, available to every anonymous visitor and a private part, available only to authenticated portal users. The biggest benefit of this technology is the easy way how can be business data, stored in Microsoft Dataverse, surfaced on the portal.

Portal apps consist of two main technological components:

- The content management part is implemented in Microsoft Dataverse. You have full control over the content of the portal and can design the portal structure according to the requirements and your own preferences.
- The website hosting environment, where the portals are hosted. This is a Microsoft internal Azure environment where a customer does not have access.

When you plan to use s portal app, you need to perform the following main steps:

- Create a portal app in your Power Platform environment. This step requires a basic configuration consisting of specifying the name of the portal, the URL and the portal language. Then you can trigger the creation of the portal, which takes usually some 1–2 hours to complete.
- Configure the portal app structure and content. This step requires using the configuration tools to specify the Web pages with the content and any other required portal functionality. Part of the configuration is also to specify which data from Microsoft Dataverse should be surfaced on the portal and what is the required security setup to control access to that data for your portal users.

Portal apps are created using two different tools:

- **Power Apps Portals Studio**: This is a graphical designer tool similar to Power Apps Studio. You use this tool to design the basic structure of the portal—the Web pages with their content.

- **Portal Management app**: This is a model-driven app used to perform the detailed design of every single aspect of a portal solution. You can use this app to specify the Web page templates, the forms and lists used to render Microsoft Dataverse data on the portal, the security of the portal and much more.

Now, let us analyze the requirements of Project Wizards, Inc. to be able to configure the portal app structure.

Design of the Project Wizards customer portal

The portal solution should make it possible for Project Wizards, Inc. customers to see and approve the products used in the projects.

After we have analyzed the requirement set from Project Wizards, Inc., we have specified the following detailed required features for the app:

- Project Wizards, Inc. customers should be able to navigate to the portal solution on any device (PC, tablet, phone) and easily find a list of the products used in the projects.
- The list should contain the following information: "`Project Name`", "`Name of the product`", "`Quantity`", "`Total Price`", and "`Product Status`".
- The list should only show project products with the "`Product Status`" values "`Used`" or "`Approved`", but not "`Planned`".
- The portal user should be able to change only the value of "`Product Status`". The other values need to be read-only.

In the subsequent sections in this chapter, we will create a portal app and perform the necessary configuration according to the requirements.

Configure simple portal apps

In this section, you will learn the basics of the portal configuration using the Power Apps Portals Studio.

After you create a Power Apps Portals app in your Power Platform environment, you can use the **Power Apps Portals Studio** to perform the basic portal configuration. With this tool, you can:

- Add *new Web pages* to the portal. After adding a new Web page, you can configure the content.

- Add *layout components* to a Web page. Currently, there are one-column, two-columns, and three-columns sections available to be added.
- Add *controls* into the columns of the sections. Currently, there are the following controls available:
  - **Text**: This is used to include blocks of formatted texts.
  - **Image**: This is used to include images.
  - **IFrame**: This is used to include external content referenced by an URL.
  - **Form**: This is used to provide the Microsoft Dataverse data processing capability.
  - **List**: This is used to provide a list of Microsoft Dataverse records.
  - **Breadcrumb**: This is used to include an additional navigation control.
  - **Power BI**: This is used to include a Power BI visualization.
  - **Chatbot**: This is used to include a Power Virtual Agents chatbot.
- Specify configuration *properties* of the controls.
- Use *theming*; either select any of the standard themes or upload your own theme. Creating and uploading your own themes requires Web development expertise.
- Configure *table permissions* to control access to Microsoft Dataverse data rendered on the portal.

For every additional, deeper configuration of the portal app, it is necessary to use the **Portal Management** model-driven application.

In the following exercise, we are going to build a portal solution for Project Wizards, Inc. For this to accomplish, some additional user interface elements must be created first in Microsoft Dataverse. In the second part, the whole configuration of the portal solution will be performed using the **Portal Management** model-driven app as well as **Power Apps Portals Studio**.

Exercise 8: Create a customer portal

In this exercise, we are going to build a simple Power Apps Portals application for the customers of Project Wizards, Inc. The application will make it possible for the customer employees to find and approve the project-related products.

Note: Due to the complexity of the Power Apps Portals technology, we will implement just a simplified version of a real portal solution.

Create the portal application

First, we need to provide the portal application. Since the creation takes a considerable amount of time, please create it according to the next steps and allow for 1–2 hours until the application is ready:

- In the Maker Portal, navigate to "**Create**" and select "**Blank app**". From the selection of the three app types, select "**Blank website**", and click "**Create**".
- In the subsequent dialog, give the portal app the name "**Project Wizards Customer Portal**" and select a unique Address (the address consists of your individual first part, followed by "**.powerappsportals.com**"). The first individual part must be unique. After you enter your individual value, the tool verifies whether the address already exists; if yes, you will be forced to change the address before proceeding.
- Select the English language and do not check "**Use data from existing website record**".
- Click "**Create**". The portal app provisioning starts, and you will be notified when the app is ready.

After the provisioning of the portal application is finished, we can continue with the configuration of the app.

Prepare a model-driven view and model-driven form

The Microsoft Dataverse data is rendered on the portal using pre-configured model-driven views and forms. In order to have the required functionality on the portal, we need to first configure a specific view and form.

Note: The Power Apps Portals technology installs multiple Power Platform solutions into the environment. Do not be surprised that your solution "Project Management" is no more the first one on the list of solutions.

Please follow the next steps:

- In the Maker Portal, open the "**Project Management**" solution, locate and open the "**Project Product**" table, navigate to **Views**, and click "**+ Add view**".

- Give the new view the name: "**Portal Project Products**" and click "**Create**".
- Add the following columns in this order: "**Project**", "**Product Catalogue**", "**Quantity**", "**Total Price**", and "**Product Status**".
- Remove the "**Name**" column.
- Click on the "**Edit filters …**", add a new query row and configure the query as "**Product Status**", "**Equals**" and the values "**Used**" and "**Approved**". This will ensure that no products with the status "**Planned**" will be listed in the view. Confirm with "**Ok**"
- Click "**Save**" and then "**<- Back**" to return to the solution.
- Stay in the "**Project Products**" table, navigate to Forms and click "**Add form**" and select "**Main Form**". A form designer opens, and the new form is a copy of the standard main form, which we have configured in the previous chapter.
- Make the following changes to the form:
    - On the right side, in the properties pane, set the "**Display Name**" of the form to "**Portal Project Product**".
    - Select the "**Project**" column, and on the right side, on the properties pane select "**Read-only**". Set the columns "**Product Catalogue**" and "**Quantity**" also to "**Read-only**".
    - Select the "**Name**" column and on the right side, on the properties pane select "**Hide**". Set the "**Total Cost**" and "**Owner**" columns also to "**Hide**".
    - After the changes, there should be five columns visible on the form, "**Project**", "**Product Catalogue**", "**Quantity**", and "**Total Price**" as read-only columns and "**Product Status**" as a read-write column.
- Click "**Save**" and then "**<- Back**" to return to the solution. In the solution, navigate to "**All**" and click on "**Publish all customizations**".

In the next task, we will go ahead and configure the portal solution in the Power Apps Portals Studio.

Configure the portals solution I

First, you need to verify whether the portal app was already created. In the Maker Portal, in the upper violet navigation bar, click on the "*Bell*" icon. You should see a notification "**Your site is ready**". If that notification is present, you can continue with the first part of the portal app configuration. This part will be performed in the Power Apps Portals configuration app called *"Portal Management"*:

- In the Maker Portal, navigate to "**Apps**" and open the model-driven app "**Portal Management**". In this app, we need to configure a portal form used to update the status of the project product.

- In the "**Portal Management**" app navigate to "**Content**" -> "**Basic Forms**". Click on "**+ New**" to create a new portal form configuration and configure the following settings:
    - **Name:** *"Project Product Form"*.
    - On the right side from the "**Table Name**", select the table "**Project Product (pw_projectproduct)**".
    - On the right side from the "**Form Name**", select the form "**Portal Project Product**". This is the form we created in the previous part of this exercise.
    - On the right side from the "**Tab Name**", select "**General**".
    - **Mode:** "**Edit**".
    - **Record Source Type:** *"***Query String***"*.
    - **Website:** select the "**Project Wizards Customer Portal**".

- Verify that the configuration corresponds to the following screenshot:

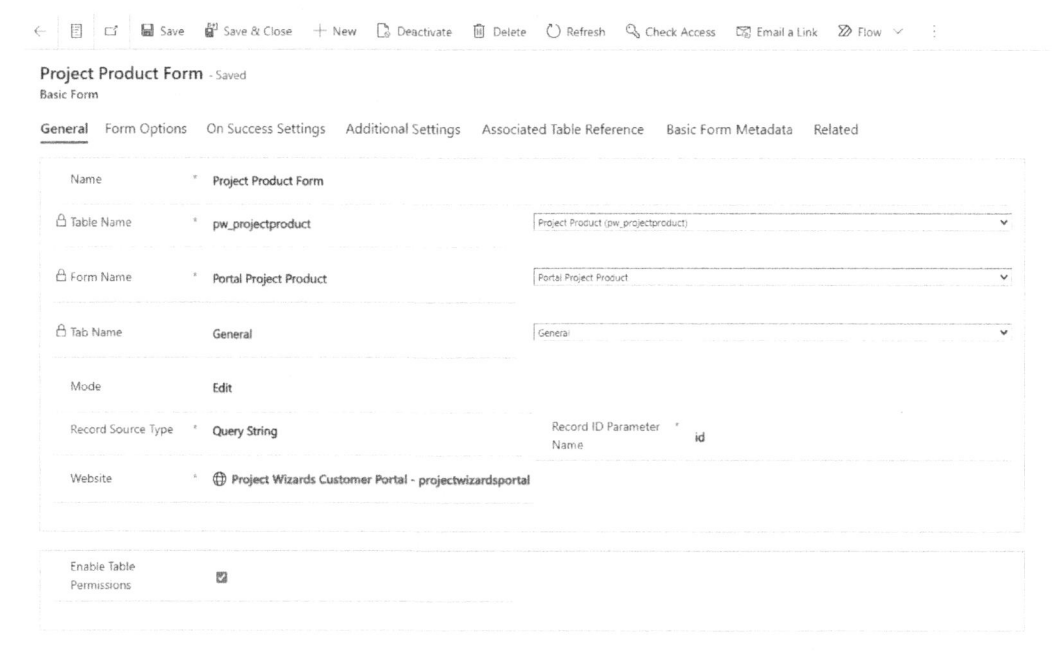

Figure 3.7: Configuration of the portal form

- Click "**Save & Close**".

Now, we have a configured portal form and can proceed with the second part of the configuration, which will be performed in the **Power Apps Portals Studio**.

Configure the portals solution II

Please follow the next steps to finally configure the portal app:

- In the Maker Portal, navigate to "**Apps**", mark the portal app "**Project Wizards Customer Portal**", and click on "**Edit**" in the upper command bar. This will open the **Power Apps Portals Studio**.

- In the upper left corner, select "**+ New Page**" and then the layout "Blank". A new blank page will be added to the portal app.

- On the right side of the properties, set the "**Name**" to "**Project Products**" and the "**Partial URL**" to "**project-products**". Note that the designer tool automatically saves the changes you make, and the new page is automatically included in the upper navigation bar of the portal app.

- The newly created page is empty; there is just one single one-column section at the top, below the common portal app navigation. Click on the single column in this section, and on the left side of the toolbox select "+" and then "Text". A text box is added to the column.

- Enter "*Project Products List*" into the text box. Format the text as you like (you can select the font size, bold, italic, or underline style of the text).

- In the toolbox, select "+" again and then "One column section". A new section will be added below the first section. Click on the single column in the section, and on the left side of the toolbox, select "+" and then "List". A list control is added to the column. The list control will render the project product records on the page.

- On the right side in the properties, configure the following settings for the list control:
    - **Name**: "*Project Products List*"
    - **Table:** "Project Product (pw_projectproduct)"
    - **Views:** from the available views, select the view "**Portal Project Products**" only. This is the view that we have created in the previous part of this exercise.
    - Set the toggle "**Edit record**" to "**On**", and keep all other toggles to "**Off**". Additional settings for the record editing will show up.

- Set "`Target type`" to "`Form`" and select the "`Project Product Form`" this is the portal form we configured in the previous part of this exercise.
- Verify that the configuration corresponds to the following screenshot:

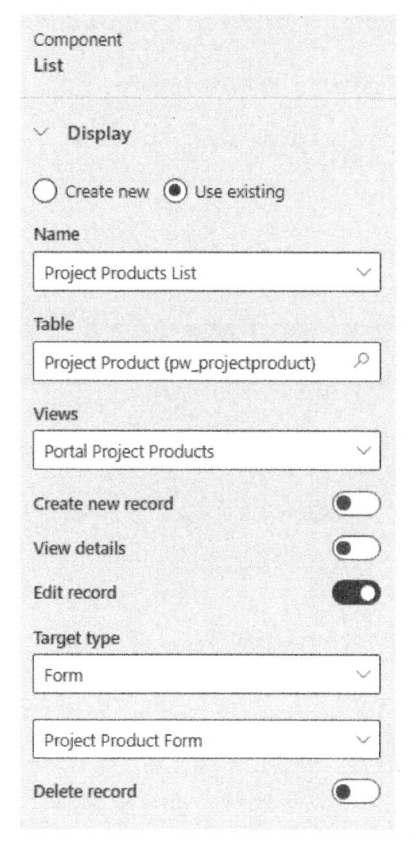

Figure 3.8: Configuration of the list control

- Under "`Permissions`", click on the link "`Manage table permissions`". This will navigate to the table permission settings.
- In the upper left corner, click on "`New permission`". In the quick create form on the right side, configure the following settings:
    - **Name**: "Project Products Permissions".
    - **Table:** "Project Product (pw_projectproduct)".
    - **Access type:** "`Global access`".
    - **Permission to:** check the options "`Read`" and "`Write`".

- Click on "**+ Add roles**" and select all three roles: "**Administrators**", "**Anonymous Users**", and "**Authenticated Users**".
- Verify that the configuration corresponds to the following screenshot:

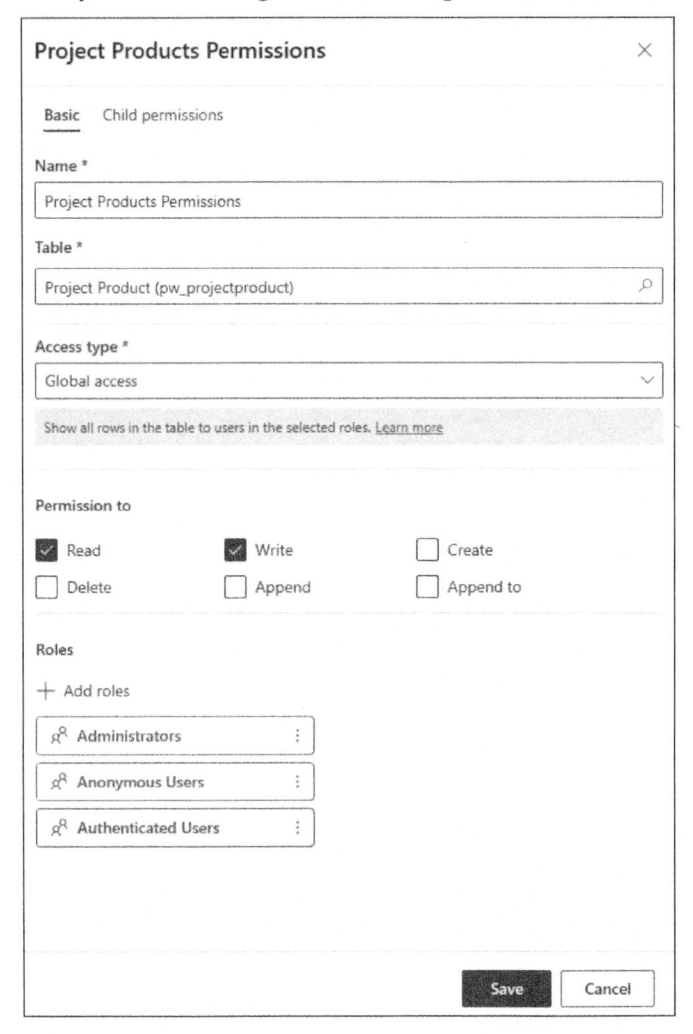

Figure 3.9: Configuration of the table permissions

- Click "**Save**" to save the table permission.
- In the left navigation, go to "**Pages and navigation**", navigate back to our page "**Project Products**" and click on "**Sync configuration**" on the upper command bar.
- Click on "**Browse website**" to verify the final configuration of the page. You will not see any records in the Project Product List because the view is

filtered to show only "**Used**" or "**Approved**" products, while in our database, all project products are still in the "**Planned**" state.

This was the last step in this exercise.

Congratulations! You have now created fully functional yet simple Power Apps Portals solutions for Project Wizards, Inc. The portal will be used by their customers to approve the products used in the projects. In order to test the functionality, navigate to our "**Project Management**" model-driven app, open some project records, open some assigned project products and change the "**Product Status**" to "**Used**". Those project products will show up on the portal, and you will be able to test the change in the "**Product Status**".

> Note: The security configuration we have implemented in this exercise does not correspond to the security best practices because it gives full access to the Project Products to everybody, even anonymous visitors of the portal. In real-life scenarios, there is a deep security setup, defining various permission levels to access any parts of the Power Apps portal. Data like our project products will be normally made available only to authenticated users and also strictly filtered by the customer so that employees of a customer will get access only to records belonging to that specific customer.

In the following section, we will dive deeper into the practical aspects of providing portal solutions with Power Apps to customers.

Integrate your customers with portal apps

The most important last step in a Power Apps Portals configuration is to setup the **security**. The purpose of a portal solution is to share some Microsoft Dataverse data with external parties, which needs to be done in a controlled way. As we have learned already, a portal solution contains a public part, which is available to every portal visitor, and even an anonymous and private part, which is only available to an authenticated portal user.

The **portal users** are managed in Microsoft Dataverse in the **contact** table. After a Power Apps Portals solution is provisioned, the **contact** table is extended to accommodate the additional information required for portal user management. In order to setup an enterprise-level portal security, the following two aspects need to be configured:

- **Portal user's authentication:** The authentication is used to verify the portal user's identity. The Power Apps Portals technology offers the possibility for internal authentication, where the username and password of every portal user are stored directly in the contact table in Microsoft Dataverse, or an external authentication, where you can decide to configure integration with *Facebook*, *Twitter*, *Google*, *LinkedIn*, or *Microsoft* identity. You can configure multiple authentication providers for s single portal solution to give your portal users the flexibility to choose their preferred identity.

- **Portal user's authorization:** The authorization is used to specify to which portal Web pages and to which surfaced Microsoft Dataverse data can a particular portal user get access. There is a very detailed concept of defining the permissions so that you can configure your security exactly corresponding to the overall security requirements of the organization.

There are multiple other aspects to be considered when designing an enterprise-level portal solution, like the following:

- Replacing the default URL of a Power Apps Portals website **https://<your name>.powerappsportals.com** with your own DNS name.
- Enable integration with **Microsoft SharePoint** and **Microsoft Power BI**.
- Setup **IP ranging** to restrict access to your portal solution to certain geography only.

All of those settings are available and can be performed in the portal administration.

Conclusion

In this chapter, you have learned some deeper details about canvas apps and portal apps. You should now be able to identify the typical use cases where any of the three types of Power Apps can be used. We went through the details of the canvas apps technology, and you have created a canvas app for our scenario. In the second part of the chapter, we focused on the portal apps and how they can be provisioned and configured. In addition, we have also created a portal app for our customer, Project Wizards, Inc.

In the upcoming chapter, we will drive our attention to the Power Automate technology and specifically on the cloud and desktop flows and how they can be used together to build enterprise-ready automation solutions.

Questions

1. How are canvas apps connected with various data sources?
2. What are the main building blocks of a canvas app user interface?
3. Which are the typical situations where Power Fx needs to be used?
4. How are canvas apps deployed to the end users?
5. What are the main building blocks of a portal app?
6. What are the tools used to configure a portal app?
7. What are the main building blocks of the portal apps security?

CHAPTER 4
Automate Processes with Power Automate

Introduction

In this chapter, we will drive our attention to the **Power Automate** cloud service. You will learn the various possibilities for building cross-application hyper-automated solutions and automating cloud, legacy, and desktop systems. We will explain the role of the Power Automate cloud flows and desktop flows in building this type of automation scenarios. You will learn how this technology can help you on your digital transformation journey.

Structure

In this chapter, we will discuss the following topics:

- Use cases for Power Automate
- Types of Power Automate automations
- Cloud flows fundamentals
- Automated cloud flows
- Scheduled cloud flows
- Desktop flows fundamentals

- Build hyper-automated solutions

Objective

After reading this chapter, you will be able to understand the value of Power Automate in building automated solutions within your organization. You will specifically learn the two major Power Automate components, the cloud flows and the desktop flows. In this chapter, you will continue building solution components for our fictitious organization Project Wizards, Inc., by building an approval solution for approving the project tasks of the project employees. Finally, you will see a possible solution design for the automated vendor invoice processing.

Use cases for Power Automate

After you have learned the basics of Power Apps and built apps for Project Wizards, Inc., we are going to drive our attention to the next big Power Platform component, the **Power Automate**.

Power Automate is a group of technologies dedicated for building cross-application and cross-technology automation in an enterprise. Part of a digital transformation of an organization is also the desire to automate as much as possible in existing business processes. Business processes are often very complex, crossing various borders, borders of different technologies, and borders of different organizational structures. The complexity evolved with time, and the processes are many times very conservative, historical, and not easy to modernize and digitize. It is not uncommon to still see a lot of paper-based processes requiring a lot of human work—fill in forms, transport forms from one place to another, collect approvals and signatures, and finally, enter the result into a legacy IT system. So how can a product like Power Automate help to drive digital transformation here? Let us discuss a few examples:

Approvals are a natural part of every organization. Organizations are structured hierarchically, and things required by employees, teams, and organizational units must be first approved by the respective authority within the organization. It can be as simple as a travel expense approval from a direct manager of an employee but also as complex as a sequential approval procedure for approving a large multi-million deal. And the processes are almost always managed either on paper or using some not-so-state-of-the-art tools such as e-mails or Excel sheets. Power Automate is an ideal solution for building unified, fully electronic approval processes, as you will learn later in this chapter.

Cross-application automations were always a pain point due to the challenges imposed by various, not really compatible IT systems, which should suddenly talk to each other. Traditionally these challenges were solved mostly by complex custom development solutions using or even not using traditional middleware software products. By no means was building these automations possible for a non-IT professional. With Power Automate, there is a solution available that can easily, with the help of the numerous data connectors, connect to every possible IT system and, in a graphical designer, configure an automation process.

Process-oriented business solution is another example of a discrepancy between IT and human users. Traditionally, business solutions such as ERP or CRM systems are based on data maintenance. It is expected that the user navigates across the business solution and enters new data or modifies existing data. This is, however, not the typical working style of a business professional. A businessperson usually follows a business process to achieve the desired goal. The process has stages, and in every stage, there are some tasks to accomplish. Power Automate offers a solution for this scenario as well. The solution is called Business Process Flows and will be explained in more detail in *Chapter 5, Use Power Automate on Clients*.

Let us now enter the stage and learn the basics about Power Automate.

Types of Power Automate automations

Power Automate, like Power Apps, is actually a group of multiple services with the same common goal—to provide low-code/no-code components for building cross-application and cross-technology automation solutions. Because the landscape of possible IT systems can be thoroughly complex, we need to have something for every type of situation. For that reason, Power Automate is offering the following three types of services:

(1) **Cloud Flows**: The primary purpose of cloud flows is to build automations across IT systems and solutions, having an API to which a connection using one of the many data connectors can be made. It is not relevant whether the IT system or solution is deployed in the cloud or in our own data center; it just needs to have an API interface. For on-premises systems, we have an excellent connectivity option using the on-premises data gateway.

(2) **Desktop Flows**: There are still many IT systems and solutions which simply do not have any API interface, and building one is not possible or reasonable. To have the possibility to automate also across such systems, Power Automate is offering desktop flows, which are able to automate using a front-end approach, basically automatically replicating the steps of human use of the system. This kind of solution is also known as **Robotic Process Automation (RPA)**.

(3) **Business Process Flows**: The primary scenario of business process flows is to provide a guided end-user experience in model-driven apps. As the flows can be integrated with cloud flows, the overall solution can provide the same

level of cross-application and cross-technology automations, specifically for the benefit of model-driven app users.

In this chapter, we will focus on the background automations, so in the next sections, you will learn about cloud flows and desktop flows and how can they be used to build enterprise-level hyper-automated solutions.

Cloud flows fundamentals

Let us first dive deeper into the first Power Automate component—the cloud flows. As mentioned in the previous section, cloud flows are used in scenarios where the automation solution can connect to the IT systems and solutions are automated via a data connector.

A general structure of every cloud flow consists of the following three parts:

(1) **The trigger**: The trigger is used to start the execution of the cloud flow. There are multiple possibilities of how a cloud flow can start; that is why we have three main trigger types described later in this chapter. Every cloud flow must have one single trigger.

(2) **The actions**: The actions are implementing the required automation of the cloud flow. There are many possible types of actions, and most of the actions are implemented using the data connectors.

(3) **The logic**: A cloud flow can optionally also contain business logic, implemented by components like branching or looping.

In *figure 4.1*, there is a structure of a simple cloud flow illustrating all the mentioned parts. The flow implements a Twitter posting automation, including an approval:

Figure 4.1: Power Automate cloud flow example

Figure 4.1 shows you:

- A **trigger** was implemented using the SharePoint data connector. The trigger starts the execution of the flow whenever a new item in a specified SharePoint list is created by a human user or automatically.

- An approval **action**, approving the content coming from the SharePoint list item.

- A **condition**, evaluating the decision made in the approval. If the decision is positive (the *If yes* path), there is another action, posting the content of the SharePoint list item on Twitter; for the negative decision (the *If no* path), there is no further action.

Power Automate cloud flows can be created either in the Maker Portal or in a specific Power Automate portal. The graphical designer used for building cloud flows is identical in both portals.

Next, we will have a deeper focus on the typical action types used in most of the cloud flows.

Cloud flows action types

As already mentioned, most of the cloud flow actions are implemented by using some of the data connectors, which means that the types of actions depend on the type of technology, the data connector is connecting to. For illustration, just a few examples of typical actions:

- Data connectors connecting to database systems, such as Microsoft Dataverse, SQL Server, Azure SQL, MySQL, Oracle, or IBM DB2 are typically implementing database actions such as **inserting** a new record, **updating** an existing record, **deleting** an existing record, or **retrieving** one or multiple records from a database table.

- The SharePoint data connector offers a large number of different actions to *download*, *upload* or *copy files*, manipulate *folders*, manipulate the *item* in SharePoint lists, and many more.

- The Teams data connector provides you with the capabilities to manipulate *teams* and their *members*, work with *chat*, work with *messages*, or send an *adaptive card* to a channel.

- The Office 365 Outlook data connector can manipulate *e-mails*, *contacts*, *events*, work with *calendars*, and many more.

Generally, it is expected that every data connector supports at least the most important capabilities provided by the underlying technology.

Not all cloud flow actions are, however, implemented using data connectors. The best example is the very popular *approval action*. This action type is used to implement approval processes within an organization. Since approval processes exist literally in every organization, big or small, it is one of the most used actions when building Power Automate solutions. The approval action can be used to implement all the typical approvals as follows:

- **Single approval:** the approval needs to be granted by one single approver, and their decision is final.

- **Sequential approval:** the approval process consists of a cascade of approvers; the final positive decision is only taken when every single approver in the chain approves. The flow action manages the whole process by sending the approval request to the first approver and waiting for their decision. In case the decision is positive, the action sends the request to the second, and so on. Whenever any single approver in the chain rejects, the whole approval ends with the outcome as rejected.

- **Parallel approval:** the approval action sends the approval request to a group of approvers at the same time and waits until the first approver decides to approve, in which case the whole approval process ends as approved. In case every single approver decides to reject, the whole approval ends up with the final decision as rejected.

Next, let us examine the cloud flow logic components.

Cloud flows logic

The use of logic components in cloud flows is optional; however, there is barely a real Power Automate flow not using any logic. The logic components are used to better structure the automation and support things like branching, looping, or error handling. The most important logic components are the following:

- **Condition:** The flow of the logic is branching, based on a condition, into two directions. If the condition evaluates to *"Yes"*, the flow continues to the first direction for *"No"* into a second direction.

- **Switch:** The flow of the logic branches into multiple directions based on the evaluation of a specified item. For the known and desired values of the item, a separate branch is configured. This type of branching is suitable for situations where the possible values of the item are well known, and a good example could be a Microsoft Dataverse column of the data type **"Choice"**.

- **Apply for each loop:** The loop is used to iteratively process a collection of items, for example, collection or records, which were retrieved in a previous action. The purpose of the loop is to perform certain additional actions for every item in the collection. For example, if we need to send a birthday greeting to a subset of contacts from the Microsoft Dataverse table "**Contact**" having a birthday on that given day, we can first retrieve all contacts having a birthday and then, in a loop, send them the personalized e-mail greetings.

- **Do until loop:** This loop is like the "*Apply for each*" loop, but in addition to the plain looping capability, there is an embedded condition, which is evaluated on every subsequent iteration. If the condition evaluates to "Yes", the loop terminates, and the flow of the logic continues with the next step after the loop.

- **Error handling:** Error handling is an important concept in cloud flows, making it more robust. Basically, we can evaluate the outcome of a given action, whether the action was finished successfully or with an error. For all possible outcomes, there can be a separate flow of logic; for the failed outcome, we can configure a compensation for the failure.

There are multiple other logic components and options in Power Automate cloud flows, such as scope, terminate, and more.

Now, let us familiarize ourselves with a bit more complex topic in the world of cloud flows with the expressions.

Cloud flows expressions

Cloud flows provide an excellent way to use any values touched in the flow of the logic in the subsequent steps of the logic. This approach is called **dynamic content**. Before we dive into expressions, we need to understand this concept first. It is a matter of fact that the trigger, as well as most of the actions, touch some data. For example, the trigger can be fired based on a new item created in a SharePoint list. This means that the content of the SharePoint list item is available for the whole subsequent actions in the flow. Some of the subsequent actions can, for example, retrieve a record from a Microsoft Dataverse table. The values of each column from that record are as well available in all subsequent actions after that specific action. This capability makes the life of a Power Automate maker significantly easier

98 ■ *Microsoft Power Platform Up and Running*

because all those pieces of data can be directly used in a graphical way, as illustrated in the following screenshot:

Figure 4.2: Power Automate dynamics content example

In *Figure 4.2*, you can see an example of the dynamic content. The flow begins with the SharePoint trigger, which starts the flow when a new item is created in a specified SharePoint list. After that, the next action inserts a record into a Microsoft Database table. Using the dynamic content, we can select any of the elements of the SharePoint list entry along with a whole bunch of metadata coming from the SharePoint list. In the example, the content of the SharePoint list column "**Name**" is used to be stored in the column "**Name**" in the Microsoft Dataverse table.

You can now ask yourself: But wait, what should I do when I need to modify the respective value from the dynamic content before I use it the way as illustrated? And that is exactly when the expressions come to place. Expressions are first and foremost used to transform the dynamic content or any other content we need to use in the logic of our flow. There is a large list of expressions available in Power Automate. Instead of going to the detail, let us illustrate the capability by modifying the previous example. What if we need to put the following into the Microsoft Dataverse record created in action: "`Project name:`" and after that, the content of the column "`Name`" from the SharePoint list? In this case, we simply replace the direct use of the dynamic content with a formula, as illustrated in the following screenshot:

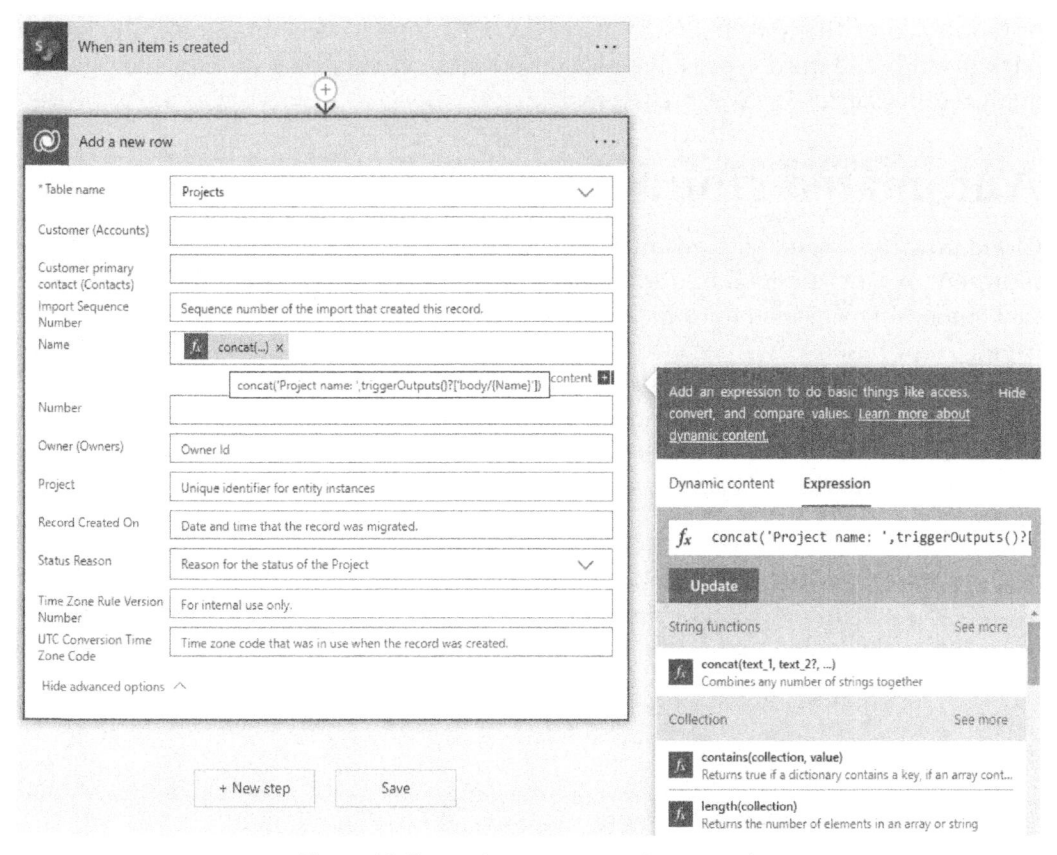

Figure 4.3: Power Automate expressions example

In *Figure 4.3*, you can see the implementation of the preceding example, where the dynamic content was replaced with the expression: `concat('Project name: ',triggerOutputs()?['body/{Name}'])`. The expression was, however, created interactively by configuring the content of the expression in the right pane, so there is no need to bother with the cryptic second part of the expression. The expression `concat()` contains two arguments; the first is the plain string **'Project name: '**, and the second was selected directly from the dynamics content list as the value "**Name**". The cryptic second part is the *real* technical representation of the dynamic content value "**Name**" coming from the flow trigger.

> **Note:** For further details about the expressions in cloud flows, please refer to the following product documentation: https://docs.microsoft.com/en-us/azure/logic-apps/workflow-definition-language-functions-reference

With this, we have finished the basic overview of the capabilities of the Power Automate cloud flows. What is still missing is a deeper overview of the already mentioned three different types of triggers. In this chapter, we will, however, focus only on two of them, which start the Power Automate flow automatically in the background. The third type, which is started interactively by a human user, will be analyzed in *Chapter 5: Use Power Automate on Clients*.

Automated cloud flows

Cloud flows equipped with an automated trigger is the most used flows because they represent exactly the idea of automation: something happens in an IT system, and that something starts an automated background process. Automated flows are also called event-based flows because they are triggered by an event in the respective IT system. The trigger in event-based flows is always implemented by one of the many data connectors so that the particular events to be triggered may be very different. Let us try to name a few examples of possible events, depending on the type of the data connector:

- Data connectors connecting to database systems, such as Microsoft Dataverse, SQL Server, Azure SQL, MySQL, Oracle, or IBM DB2, are typically implementing triggers like: a new record was created, an existing record was modified, and an existing record was deleted.

- The SharePoint data connector offers triggers like: an item in a list being created, a file is uploaded to a folder, and many more.

- The Office 365 Outlook data connector provides triggers like: a new e-mail arrived in the inbox or a new event created in the calendar.

Since in the event-based flows, the trigger is implemented using a data connector, there is no common configuration of the trigger but rather a data connector-specific configuration, which is very different from one data connector to another. In order to illustrate the configuration possibilities of an event-based trigger, we take the Microsoft Dataverse trigger as an example, used for the typical database transaction types to create, update, or delete a record. The configuration possibilities are documented in the following screenshot:

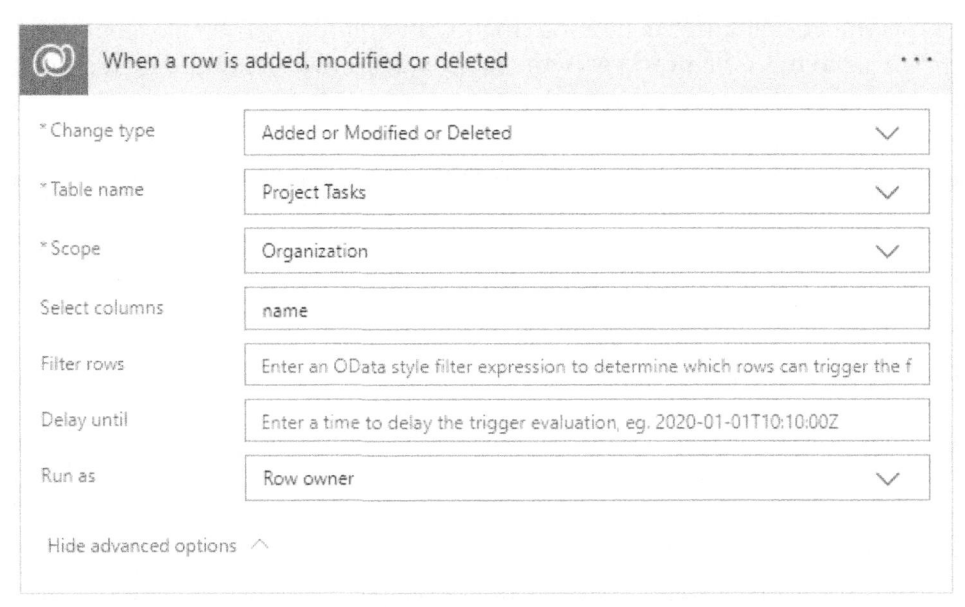

When a row is added, modified or deleted	
*Change type	Added or Modified or Deleted
*Table name	Project Tasks
*Scope	Organization
Select columns	name
Filter rows	Enter an OData style filter expression to determine which rows can trigger the f
Delay until	Enter a time to delay the trigger evaluation, eg. 2020-01-01T10:10:00Z
Run as	Row owner

Hide advanced options ∧

Figure 4.4: *Microsoft Dataverse trigger example configuration*

In *Figure 4.4*, we can see the following configuration options:

- **Change type:** This setting represents the transaction type to trigger the flow: the record was created (Added), the record was updated (Modified), or the record was deleted. In the Microsoft Dataverse trigger, those three basic transactions can be combined so that one single Power Automate flow can handle not just one of them but eventually all three, or any combination of two of them.

- **Table name:** You must select the respective Microsoft Dataverse table, which transactions will trigger the flow.

- **Scope:** The scope is a security setting specifying the subset of records for which the flow will be triggered. If you want the flow to start for every record, regardless of the owner of the record, select "**Organization**".

- **Select columns:** This setting can limit the execution of the flow to just those records where one or more from the specified columns is created or modified.

- **Filter rows:** This setting can also limit the number of records by filtering the records using a query condition.

- **Delay until:** This setting can delay the execution of the flow until a given date and time.

- **Run as:** This setting defines the security context in which the flow for subsequent Microsoft Dataverse actions will run.

After this theoretical introduction into the world of Power Automate cloud flows, it is time to again do some practice. In the next exercise, we will implement another of the Project Wizards, Inc. requirements.

Exercise 9: Create an approval flow

One of the requirements of Project Wizards, Inc. is that the managers must be able to approve completed project tasks. Before we go ahead with the implementation, let us first analyze the requirement and prepare a detailed solution design.

Analysis and preparations

After analyzing the requirements for the project management solution, we have decided to build a cloud flow to implement the management approval of the completed project tasks:

- The automation should be event-based; when a project employee changes the project task status to "**Completed**", the automation should be triggered automatically in the background.

- As the event happens in a Microsoft Dataverse table, the flow trigger will be implemented using the Microsoft Dataverse data connector.

- The only event interesting for the automation is the update event when the value of the "**Task Status**" is modified. The configuration of the trigger will be based on the "**Modified**" event only.

- The only change, which should trigger the automation, is the change of the column "**Task Status**" in the "**Project Task**" table. We will filter the trigger by this single column.

- Other settings of the trigger will be configured according to the common best practices.

- The business logic of the flow will perform the following steps:
  - Test whether the value of the "**Task Status**" is "**Completed**" the subsequent steps will be performed only for this specific value.
  - Start an approval process. This action will be simplified compared with a real-life solution because we cannot send the approval request to a manager. Instead, we will send the request to ourselves.
  - Verify the decision of the approval. For approved requests, the value of the column "**Task Status**" will be modified to "**Approved**", for rejected requests, there will be no change.

o   For both decisions, the employee will be notified by e-mail about the decision.

Now, having a solution design, we can start with the practical implementation.

Practical implementation

In the flow, we need to use a numerical representation for the value "**Completed**" of the column "**Task Status**". This is because the column "**Task Status**" is of data type "**Choice**", and this data type has not just the visible text value, like "**Completed**", but also a corresponding numerical value, which is invisible to the end user, but very important for our flow. Please perform the following steps to figure out the value first:

- In the Maker Portal, open the Project Management solution, navigate to "**Choices**", and click on the choice "**Task Status**". This will open on the right side a side pane with the three values of choice. Click the three dots right to the value "**Completed**" and select "**View more**". This will show the numerical value for "**Completed**", according to the following screenshot:

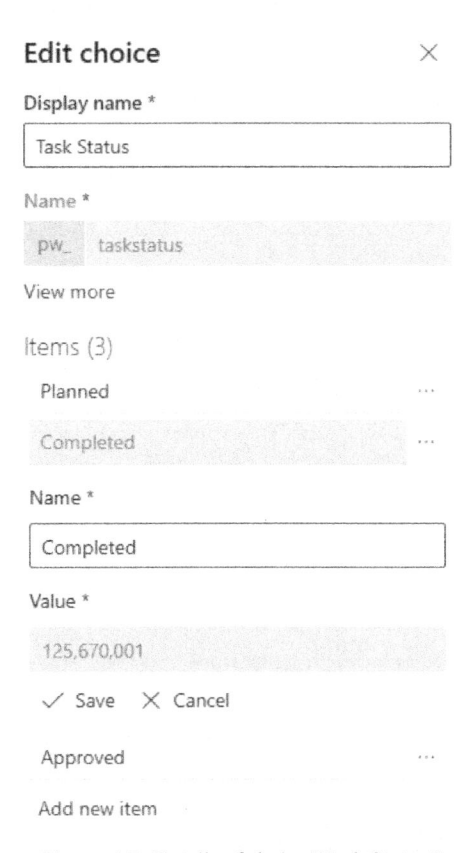

Figure 4.5: Details of choice "Task Status"

- Make a note of the numerical value; in our example, it is the value of 125 670 001; however, it can be a different value in your environment. Close the choice "**Task Status**" without making any changes.

Now, we are ready to start creating a Power Automate cloud flow:

- Navigate back to "**All**" and click on "**+ New**", then "**Automation**", "**Cloud flow**", and finally "**Automated**".

- In the flow creation dialogue, give the flow the name "**Project Task Approval**". In the field "**Choose your flow's trigger**" search for "**Dataverse**" and from the list of possible trigger types, select the green trigger with the name "**When a row is added, modified or deleted**". You will see two types of triggers, the green ones are implemented with the current "**Microsoft Dataverse**" data connector, and the grey ones are implemented with the "**Microsoft Dataverse (legacy)**" data connector, which should not be used for new implementations anymore.

- Click on "**Create**", which will open the Power Automate designer directly within the Maker Portal.

- Configure the trigger according to the following screenshot:

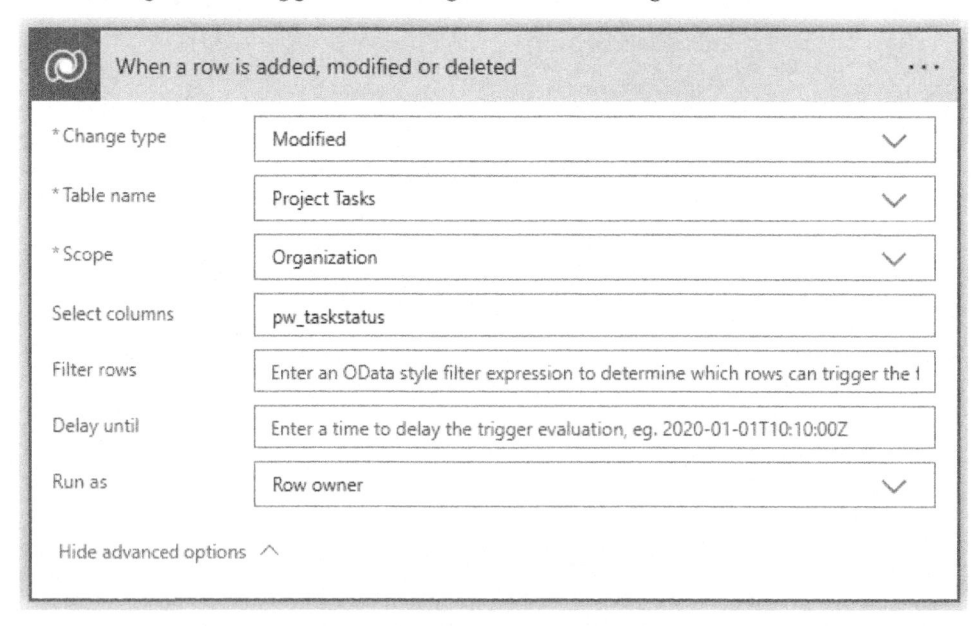

Figure 4.6: Configuration of the trigger

- The configuration contains the following elements:
    - **Change type:** Modified—we only need the update transaction to trigger the execution of the flow.

- o **Table name:** Project Tasks—we need to trigger updates of records in this table.
- o **Scope:** Organization—we want the flow to trigger for every record in the table, regardless of the owner of the record.
- o **Select columns:** pw_taskstatus—we only want to trigger if there is a change in the column "**Task Status**". The value "**pw_taskstatus**" is the technical name of that column.
- o **Run as:** Row owner—we want that if there is any change in the task status, that change should be performed in the security context of the owner of the Project Task record.

- It is a best practice to rename the trigger and the actions in a flow to reflect the details configured in the trigger or actions. Click on the tree dots to the right of the trigger name and select "**Rename**". Change the name of the trigger to "**When the task status of a project task change**". Confirm by pressing ENTER.

- The next step is to verify the value in the column "**Task status**" the approval logic should be only triggered for records with the value of "**Completed**". Below the trigger, click on "**+ New step**". This will open the selection dialog for actions. In the search box, search for "**Control**" and from the search result select "**Control**" with the dark grey background color. After clicking on the "**Control**", there will be a short list of possible controls offered; select the "**Condition**" with the dark grey background color. This will add the condition after the trigger. The condition is presented with a condition configuration tile and two possible outcomes, one for "**If yes**" with a green background and one for "**If no**" with a red background.

- Configure the condition by first clicking on the field with the shadow text "**Choose a value**". Clicking on that field will open the list of dynamic content values. These values are coming from the Microsoft Dataverse record from the table "**Project Task**". Scroll in the list to find the column with the name "**Task Status**" and click on the column, and this will transfer the column into the condition field.

- Keep the operation as "**is equal to**".

- Put the numerical representation of the task status "**Completed**" into the last field with the shadow text "**Choose a value**". The configured condition should look like this as shown in the following screenshot:

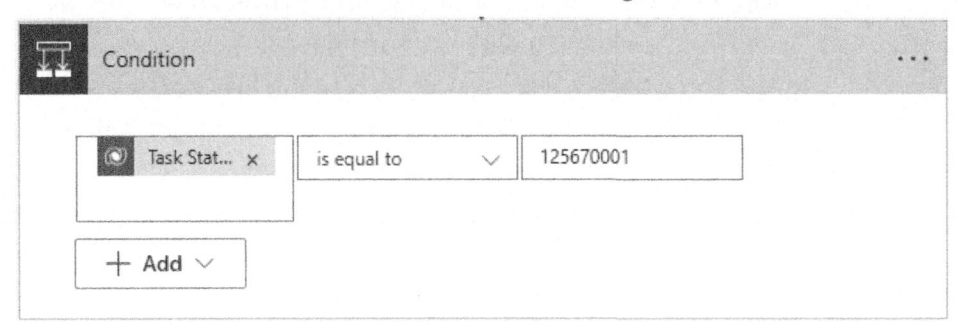

Figure 4.7: Configuration of the condition

- The remaining part of the flow will be implemented in the left box with the green label "**If yes**". Click on "**Add an action**" inside this box. In the search box, enter "**Dataverse**". Click on the green "**Dataverse**" connector, and from the list of actions, select "**Get a row by ID**".

- Select the table "**Projects**" from the list of tables. Click on the field "**Row ID**", and the dynamic contents pane opens. Scroll in the pane, find the column "**Project (Value)**", and click on the column to copy the value into "**Row ID**". Rename the action to "**Get the project**".

- Click on "**Add an action**" inside the box below the previous action. In the search box, enter "**approval**". From the list of the results, select the action "**Approvals**" with the violet background. From the list of possible approval types, select "**Start and wait for an approval**".

- Configure the approval according to the following screenshot:

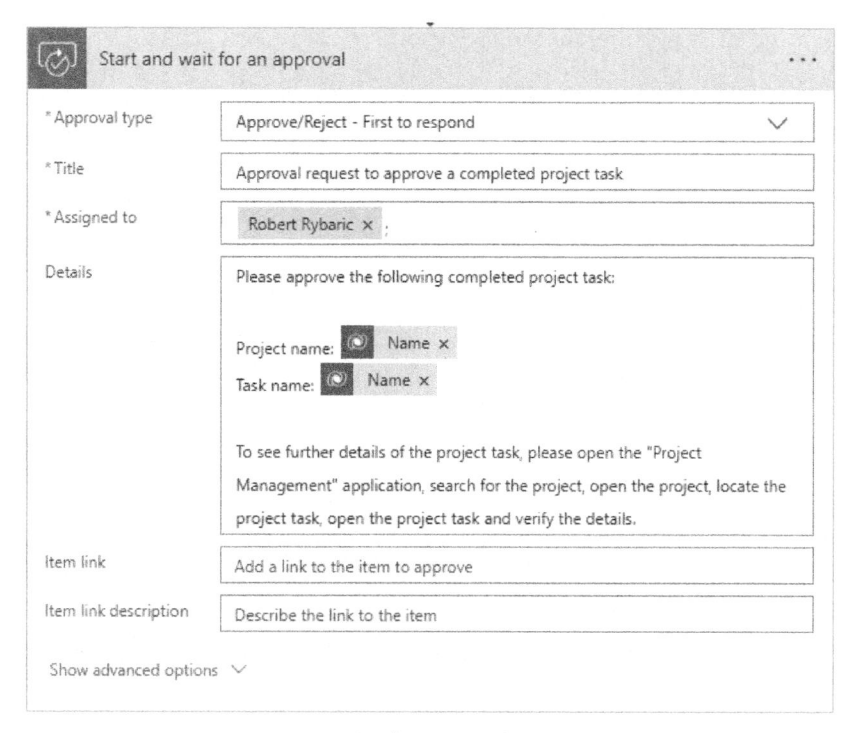

Figure 4.8: Configuration of the approval

- The configuration settings explained:

    o **Approval type:** select the value "**Approve/Reject - First to respond**".

    o **Title:** enter the text from the screenshot; you can modify the text if you like.

    o **Assigned to:** you need to assign your own cloud account because we are going to send the approval request to ourselves. To do so, start typing "**admin**" in the field "**Assigned to**", you should be offered your full cloud account, select and confirm. In case the cloud account you created in *Chapter 1, Introducing Microsoft Power Platform* does not start with "**admin**", type the real start of your account to get the account.

    o **Details**: This part is a combination of text and dynamic content. Put the text parts first. For the **project name**, you need to place the cursor after the text "**Project name:**" and select the dynamic value "**Name**" from the group "**Get the project**". For the **task name**, you need to select the dynamic value "**Name**" from the group "**When a task status of a project task change**".

- Rename the approval action to "**Approve project task**".
- Click again on "**Add an action**" inside the box below the approval action. Search for "**Control**" again and select the "**Condition**" exactly as we have done in the previous steps.
- Rename the inserted condition to "**Check decision**". Configure the condition according to the following screenshot:

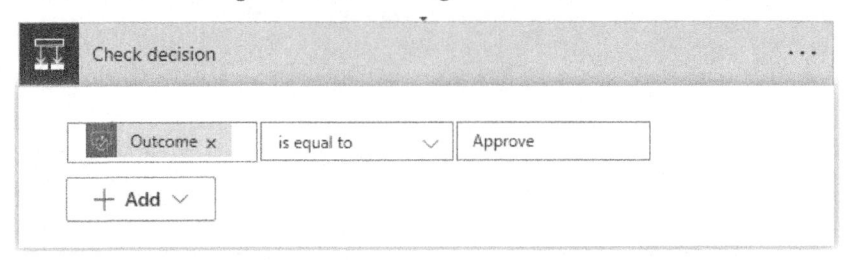

Figure 4.9: Configuration of the second condition

- Click on the "**Add an action**" in the left column "**If yes**" below the second condition. Select the Microsoft Dataverse data connector and select the action "**Update a row**".
- Configure the new action according to the following screenshot:

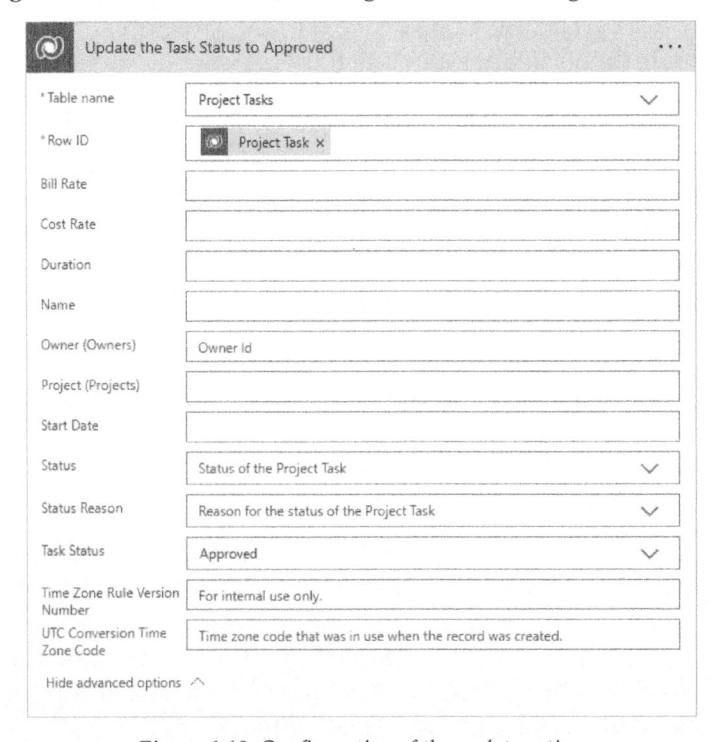

Figure 4.10: Configuration of the update action

- For the configuration, you need to select the table "**Project Tasks**", for the "**Row ID**" the dynamic content value "**Project Task**" from the trigger and for the "**Task Status**" the value "**Approved**". Rename the update action.

- The last task in the flow will notify the employee about the approval decision. This action needs to be placed into the flow two times for both approved and rejected decisions.

- Click "**Add an action**" below the update action and search for "**Office 365 Outlook**". Select the action "**Send an e-mail (V2)**". Configure the action. Repeat the same with the "**If no**" outcome and configure the action. The whole last part of the flow should look like as shown in the following screenshot:

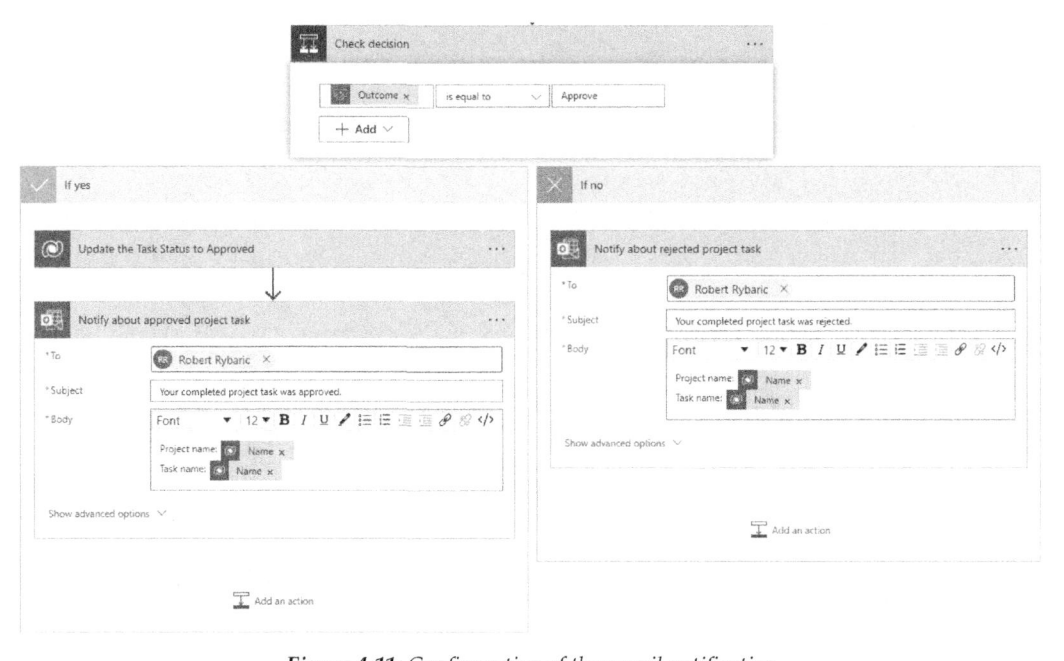

Figure 4.11: Configuration of the e-mail notification

- Configure the "**To**" field to send the e-mail to yourself. Enter a text into the "**Subject**" field.

- Configure the "**Body**" with the project name and the task name exactly the same way, as is the Details field of the approval action configured.

110 ■ *Microsoft Power Platform Up and Running*

- Your finished cloud flow should have the final structure according to the following screenshot (the actions are collapsed for space reasons):

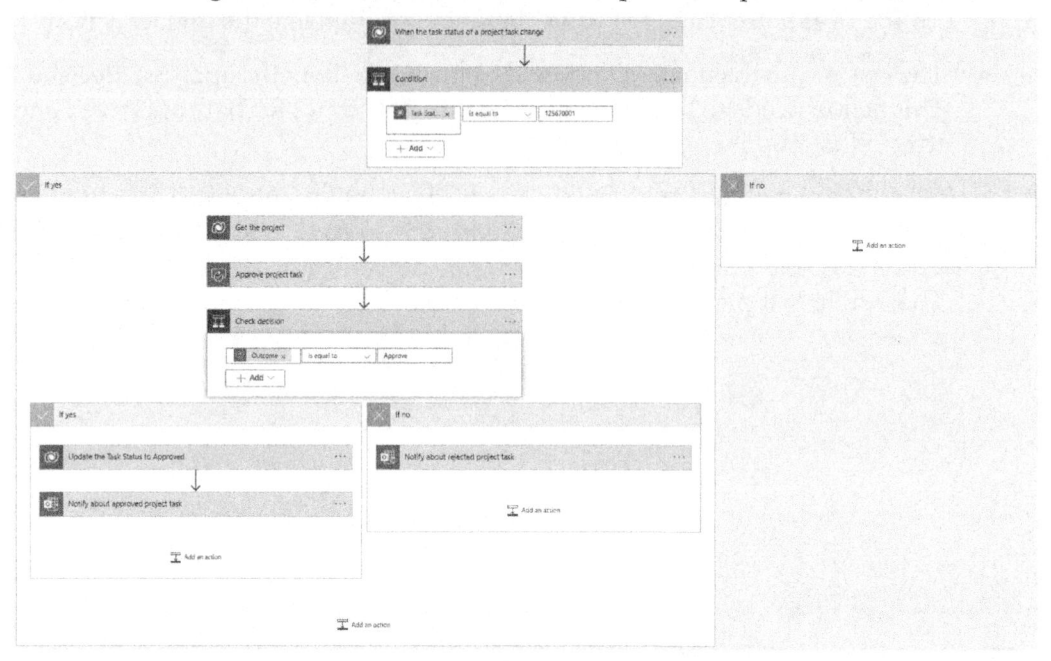

Figure 4.12: Final structure of the cloud flow

- On the upper right side of the flow designer, click on the "**Save**" button. An error message will be presented that the approvals were not yet installed on the environment. You can ignore the message; it is just an information. The approval action requires the installation of additional solutions, which will be automatically performed during the first run of the flow. That is also the reason why the very first run of an approval flow takes up to 20 minutes to complete. After the first run, all subsequent runs will work normally.

- Navigate back from the Power Automate designer to the solution by clicking on the left arrow in the upper left corner of the designer.

- For testing purposes, it is important to install a mobile application, *"Power Automate"*, on your mobile phone. Take your mobile phone, go to the Apps Store (iPhone) or Google Play Store (Android phone) and locate the *"Power Automate"* application from Microsoft. Install the application on your mobile device.

- After installation, open the Power Automate app and sign-in with your cloud credentials (username and password).

Congratulations! You have successfully created your first Power Automate cloud flow. Now, it is time to make the test. Please proceed with the following steps:

- Open the "*Power Apps*" app on your mobile phone, and the "*Power Automate*" mobile app must stay opened as well.

- Open the "**Project Tracking Application**" in the "*Power Apps*" app and change the task status to "**Completed**" on one of the tasks marked as "**Planned**". This will trigger the execution of the flow, and an approval request should be delivered to you. Keep in mind that the first execution of the approval will take around 20 minutes to install the prerequisites.

- Approval requests are delivered to the approver using multiple channels: e-mail, Microsoft Teams notification, on the Power Automate portal, but also on the "*Power Automate*" mobile app.

- Switch on your mobile phone to the "*Power Automate*" mobile app, navigate to "**Account**", and verify whether the app is connected with the correct environment—it should be the same environment you are working within the Maker Portal. If necessary, change to the correct environment before proceeding.

- Next, navigate to "**Activity**" and select "**Approvals**". You should find an approval request according to the following screenshot:

Figure 4.13: *Approval request for Power Automate mobile app*

- Click on the request to see further details—you should find the whole approval request details, as you have configured those in the flow.

- Select "**Approve**" and confirm with the upper right button "**CONFIRM**".

- Switch back to the "**Project Tracking Application**" in the *Power Apps* mobile app and verify that the approved tasks have the status changed correctly to the value "**Approved**". Verify that for the approved tasks, and there is no more possible to change the status. Also, verify the functionality of the toggle button "**Open Tasks / All Tasks**", which should show or hide the approved tasks.

This is the end of the exercise. You have learned how to create a simple Power Automate flow equipped with an event-based trigger. Next, we will have a look at the scheduled flows.

Scheduled cloud flows

Scheduled cloud flows represent the second category of cloud flows, and they are triggered based on a configured schedule rather than on an event in an IT system. The main purpose of the scheduled flows is to perform any kind of batch jobs.

Let us just imagine the following scenario: we have in our Microsoft Dataverse 100.000 contacts, and for most of them, we have a correct date of birth. We would like to automatically send a greeting e-mail every day to all our contacts having a birthday on that day. Here comes a scheduled flow very handy because we can configure the scheduler trigger to run every day at say, 8:00 a.m., select all contacts from the contact table and send a personalized e-mail to those contacts.

The only difference between an automated event-based flow and a scheduled flow is the trigger, and the flow logic can be the same. The specific scheduler trigger has a very simple configuration, according to the following screenshot:

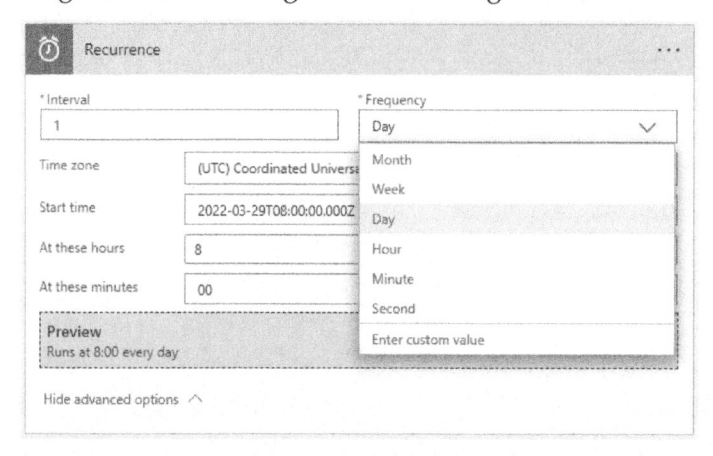

Figure 4.14: Power Automate schedule trigger

As we can see in *figure 4.14*, the schedule trigger can be configured for a broad time interval range from seconds up to months. For each configuration, you can add some details, for example, at what time the flow should start and when the trigger is configured for daily execution.

There is a third trigger type for Power Automate cloud flows, but that will be discussed in *Chapter 5, Use Power Automate on Clients*. Now, we focus on another type of Power Automate, on the desktop flows.

Desktop flows fundamentals

Cloud flows are excellent for building automations across IT systems and solutions having an API interface. But often, enterprise automation requires automating legacy or desktop applications where no interface exists. There are many examples out there where organizations are using legacy systems for decades without the need to replace and modernize them simply because they are robust, stable, and fit for purpose. But when it comes to enterprise automations, these legacy systems, without any API interfaces, just cannot be included in a Power Automate cloud flow automation because there is no data connector which can be used for connecting to them.

To automate such solutions, there is a new approach available called **Robotic Process Automation (RPA)**. The essence of an RPA solution is to replicate the human interaction with the legacy system instead of trying to connect via an interface. Power Automate Desktop is an RPA type of solution, and that is why we can use Power Automate to build automations covering both IT systems and solutions with an API interface and those not having it.

Let us shortly describe the basic capabilities of the Power Automate Desktop. First, the product is not a cloud tool but rather a desktop application, which must be installed locally on your computer. Power Automate Desktops offers the following capabilities:

- Configure a *business process* as a series of *manual steps* with a legacy application, consisting of steps such as start the application, open an application screen, enter data to the fields on the screen, click on a button or a keyboard key to save the data, search for some data, retrieve the content of the fields, and so on.

- The configuration of the steps can be done either *manually* or using a *recording capability* of Power Automate Desktop. For the latter case, the user of the legacy application just starts the recorder and performs the business process on the legacy application from start to end. The recording can then be used for automation.

- The created desktop flow can be in either case configured, polished, and equipped with variables used for communicating with other components of the final automation solution.

The following screen illustrates the Power Automate Desktop tool:

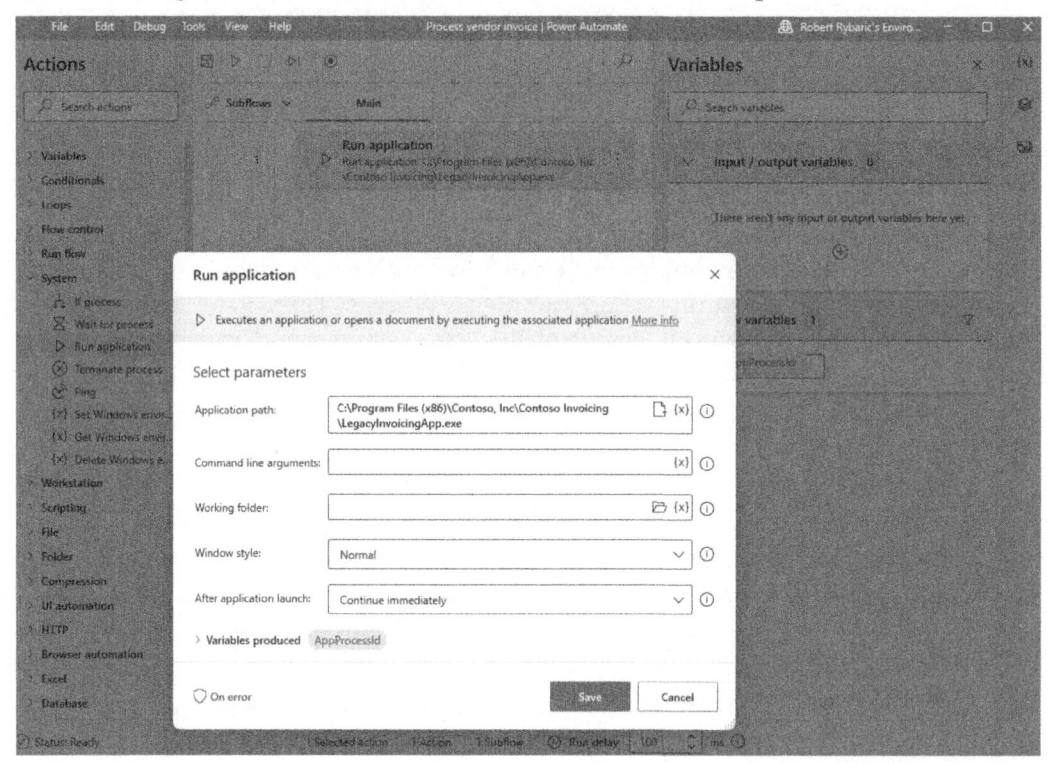

Figure 4.15: Power Automate Desktop

As we can see in *figure 4.15*, the tool offers a broad variety of different actions for managing every possible aspect of the local computer, the operating system, the different applications and desktop or cloud services. In *Figure 4.15*, you can also see an example configuration of a step to start a desktop application, *"Contoso Invoicing"*. On the right side of the tool, there is the area for configuring input and output variables to communicate with the other parts of the automation solution, specifically with a Power Automate cloud flow.

In the next section, you will learn how to build an overall automation solution consisting of Power Automate cloud flow and desktop flow.

Build hyper-automated solutions

The ultimate goal when building automation solutions in an organization is to build an end-to-end solution across all required existing IT systems and solutions, regardless of technology, type, or age of the solution. In such scenarios, there can be multiple IT systems having an API interface as well as multiple without such an interface. What can Power Automate offer to cover such scenarios? A combination of Power Automate cloud flows equipped with public or custom data connectors, and Power Automate Desktop flows to handle IT systems without any interface. In addition, such a solution can include another component of Microsoft Power Platform, the AI Builder, to include artificial intelligence in the whole automation process. In the following example, you will see a possible solution for Project Wizards, Inc. to cover their requirement for automated processing of vendor invoices. In the example, we are not going to actually implement the solution since the complexity of such a solution breaks the scope of this book, but it will give you an idea of what is possible using the right Power Platform technologies.

Example 1—Create a sample vendor invoice processing solution

Project Wizards, Inc. has a lot of vendors for the products and materials they are using within their customer projects. Currently, they are using a legacy ERP solution for processing vendor invoices. The solution is aged and does not have any meaningful API interface, and there is no way to build one. They are satisfied with the ERP system, but not with the huge amount of manual work the invoice processing requires. Their vendor invoice processing consists today of the following steps:

- The vendors are sending their invoices electronically to a dedicated e-mail address **vendors@projectwizards.com**

- The vendors are sending their invoices in different formats, mainly as PDF files, but some are sending scans of paper invoices as image files such as JPG, PNG, and other similar formats.

- The accounts payable department staff needs to open every single received e-mail message and analyze the content. If there is any attachment, then it is one or more invoices.

- The staff needs to open the invoice and enter the invoice data such as vendor name and address, invoice number and date, the products delivered with quantity, unit price, total price, and so on manually into the legacy ERP system.

- The manual entry sometimes leads to errors, so the data entered needs to be double-checked by another staff member.

Project Wizards, Inc. would like to understand what could be the options to automate the manual processing to the maximum possible extent. After analyzing the situation at the company, we have prepared a following high-level design of a possible solution implemented using the Power Platform:

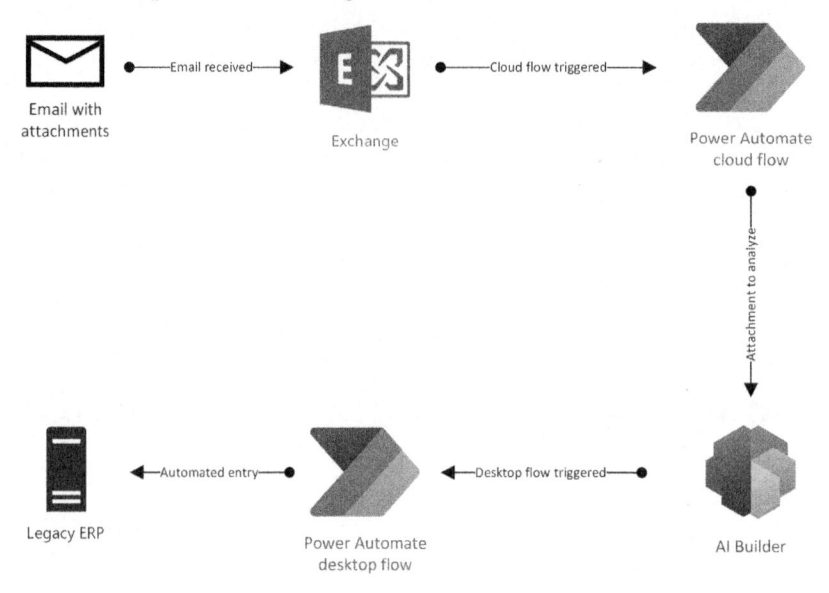

Figure 4.16: Vendor invoice processing automated

The solution design depicted in *figure 4.16* can fully automate the whole vendor invoicing processing. Building the solution would require the following steps:

- Collect at least five different vendor invoices (invoice files, received via e-mail) from every vendor. Use these files to prepare and train an AI model of the type "**Form processing**" in the tool AI Builder. This AI model will be able to automatically recognize the required pieces of information from the invoice files, such as invoice number, invoice date, vendor name, vendor address, product name, unit price, total price, and so on. You will learn a lot more about the AI Builder in *Chapter 9, Bring Intelligence with AI Builder* of this book.

- Use Power Automate Desktop to record the exact steps required to enter all required data of a new vendor invoice into the legacy ERP solution. The result of this recording will be a desktop flow to automate vendor invoice entry.

- Build a Power Automate cloud flow to implement the master automation. This flow will be triggered by incoming e-mail messages in the inbox **vendors@projectwizards.com**. The flow will implement the following main actions:

    o Verify whether there are attachments in the e-mail message. If yes, perform a loop across all attachments.

- o In the loop, send the attachment to the AI Builder model to analyze the content and return the required data as text elements.
- o Next, in the loop, call the Power Automate Desktop flow to automatically perform the entry of the vendor invoice into the legacy ERP system. You will need to provide the data from the AI Builder model as parameters to the desktop flow.
- o Optionally send an automated e-mail notification to the vendor with a confirmation that their invoices were processed.

It is needless to say that this solution design impressed Project Wizards, Inc. heavily, and they decided to have a deeper look into the possible real implementation just after their current project management solution was completely built.

Conclusion

In this chapter, you have learned the fundamentals of Power Automate. You have seen that Power Automate consists of three different types of services. We have focused primarily on those parts of Power Automate, which are used for background enterprise automation. Next, we discussed the cloud flows and, specifically, the automated cloud flows. In this part of the chapter, you could use your new knowledge to build a Power Automate flow for automated approvals of project tasks for our fictitious company Project Wizards, Inc. In the last part of the chapter, we have described some details about the scheduled cloud flows and the desktop flows. Finally, we have elaborated a solution design for Project Wizards, Inc. for a possible future solution to automate their vendor invoice processing.

In the upcoming chapter, we are going to focus on the other parts of Power Automate, which are more visible to the end user, like the on-demand cloud flows or Business Process Flows. We will also see how can flows be integrated into Power Apps.

Questions

1. What is Power Automate?
2. What are the three main building blocks of Power Automate?
3. What are the specifics of Power Automate cloud flows, and for which automation can they be used?
4. What tools are used to build Power Automate cloud flows?
5. What three types of triggers do Power Automate cloud flows support?
6. When is it required to use Power Automate Desktop?
7. What tools are used to build desktop flows?
8. What is the benefit of combining cloud flows and desktop flows?

CHAPTER 5
Use Power Automate on Clients

Introduction

In this chapter, we will continue the journey into the Power Automate cloud service by looking into specific scenarios of personal automation and automating Power Apps. First, you will see what the possibilities are to build one-click personal automations, easily triggered from a mobile device. After that, we will present you with the possible options and how an automated solution can be integrated with Power Apps. You will learn how to call automation from model-driven and canvas apps and how you can streamline business processes by implementing business process flows.

Structure

In this chapter, we will discuss the following topics:

- Use cases for Power Automate
- Button cloud flows fundamentals
- Use button flows for personal automation
- Business process flows fundamentals
- Dataverse automations fundamentals

- Use cloud flows in Power Apps
- Use Dataverse automations in Power Apps

Objectives

After reading this chapter, you will be able to understand all the possibilities to automate business applications using Power Automate but also using different automation types within Microsoft Dataverse. In the first part, we will focus on the third type of Power Automate flows, and the button flows are triggered manually by the end user. In the next part, we will discuss the last component of the Power Automate family, the business process flows, what they are, and how they can be used to change the way of working within model-driven apps. Then, we will drive our attention to the automation, which is available directly within Microsoft Dataverse, specifically to the Business Rules, classic workflows, and classic custom actions. In the last part of this chapter, you will see multiple examples and scenarios where the various Power Platform automation types are most suitable. Part of this chapter is also two practical exercises for our fictitious customer Project Wizards, Inc., as well as an example of how to build on-demand automations.

Use cases for Power Automate

In *Chapter 4, Automate Processes with Power Automate*, we have introduced the most typical use cases where automation is required to accompany a business solution. In that chapter, we have focused our interest on background automation, automation that is not visible to the end user, and the end user neither triggers nor influences those automations. But there are also many scenarios where automation needs to be *visible* and *available for the end user to start them*. And that is exactly what we are going to cover in this chapter.

We will cover scenarios where an end user needs to directly trigger automation from Power Apps, regardless of model-driven apps or canvas apps. Specifically, in model-driven apps, there are multiple places where automation should be available for an end user. Of course, there are scenarios where automation does not need to be part of a Power Apps application but can be triggered directly with the capabilities of Power Automate. All of those scenarios will be covered in the next sections of this chapter.

Button cloud flows fundamentals

First, it is time to look into the third type of Power Automate cloud flows, the *button flows*. There are multiple differences between the background flows (automated and scheduled) and the button flows:

- The button flow is the only flow not running in the background but rather *manually started by a human user*.

- The button flows are equipped with a trigger called *"Button trigger"*. This trigger has some specific settings and capabilities described as follows.

- As the button flow is expected to be used by human users, it must be *deployed* to the intended user population by *sharing*, exactly as this is done for Power Apps.

Saying that button flows are started by human users needs a bit of explanation. Actually, it is simple, and we have indirectly used this approach in the previous chapter. Button flows are typically started by end users on mobile devices using the **Power Automate mobile app** from Microsoft. Every button flow shared with a user will be available within this app.

The next interesting topic is what additional possibilities are provided by the button trigger. A button trigger delivers automatically a certain number of implicit parameters to the cloud flow, and these parameters are called trigger tokens. The following is the overview of the tokens:

- *Name* and *e-mail address* of the user who triggered the flow. This is an important information, giving personalization possibilities to the flow. The information is easily available since the end user starts a button that flows from their mobile application, where they need to be signed in.

- *Date and timestamp*, including the *time zone* of the moment when the user started the flow. This information is also easy to obtain since, in every modern mobile device, there is a running clock and an automated time zone identification.

- *GPS coordinates* and eventually the *full address* of the device from the moment of starting the flow. Power Automate mobile is able to use the location service of the mobile device, and by leveraging the Bing Maps mapping service, this information can be collected.

All of the preceding information is available as *dynamic content* for the subsequent actions and logic of the flow, according to the following screenshot:

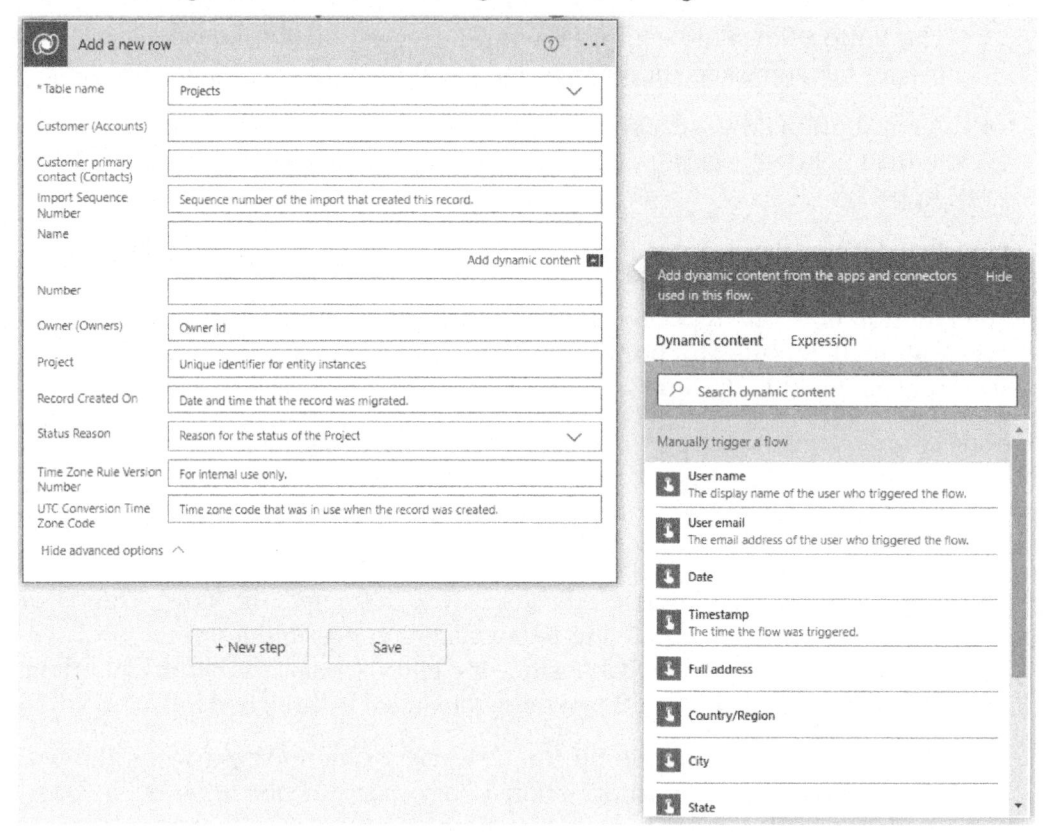

Figure 5.1: Button flow trigger tokens as dynamic content

> **Note:** It is not always allowed to use all of the trigger tokens, especially the GPS coordinates and the current address since it can be seen as employee position tracking. In some countries, this kind of tracking might be prohibited by law.

The second important capability of the button trigger is the possibility to create custom input parameters. If you need any input from the user for your button flow before the flow actually starts the execution, the input parameters are an excellent way to do this. Button flows equipped with input parameters can be considered as very simple apps, so in some specific cases, building a button flow can be even a very easy alternative to building Power Apps.

The input parameters can be of six different data types, as illustrated in the following screenshot:

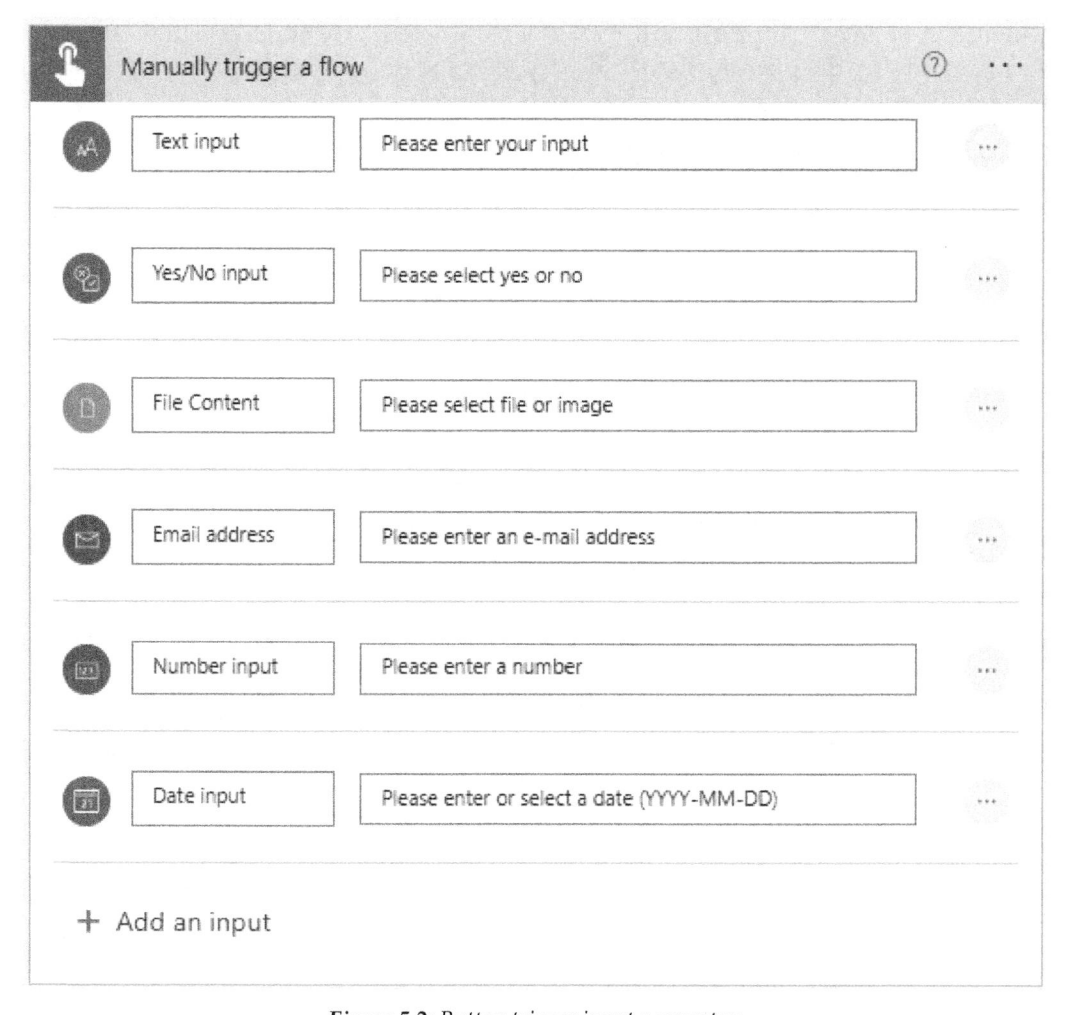

Manually trigger a flow		
Text input	Please enter your input	
Yes/No input	Please select yes or no	
File Content	Please select file or image	
Email address	Please enter an e-mail address	
Number input	Please enter a number	
Date input	Please enter or select a date (YYYY-MM-DD)	

+ Add an input

Figure 5.2: Button trigger input parameters

As you can see in *figure 5.2*, you can define any number of input parameters of the following possible data types:

- **Text**: input any text string
- **Yes/No**: select Yes or No, using a toggle control
- **File**: upload a file using a file selection dialogue
- **E-mail**: enter an e-mail address
- **Number**: enter any numerical value
- **Date**: select a date using a calendar control

When a user invokes a button flow with parameters, a data entry dialogue will show up, giving the user the possibility to enter the data. After that, the flow can be manually triggered with a button, as illustrated in the following screenshot:

Figure 5.3: Entering values into a button flow

As for the trigger tokens, the custom input parameters you eventually configure will provide the values entered by the end user as part of the *dynamic content* to the actions and logic of the flow.

What comes after the button trigger can be exactly the same as for the other two types of cloud flows, so the usual actions and logic, as described in *Chapter 4, Automate Processes with Power Automate*.

Use button flows for personal automation

As mentioned in the previous section, button flows are like simple Power Apps, so they can be used in every situation where a very simple mobile application is required. Let us examine some examples.

Vacation request

A vacation request is a typical business process known by every organization. Let us have a look at how this can be implemented with a button flow (simplified). Please refer to the following figure:

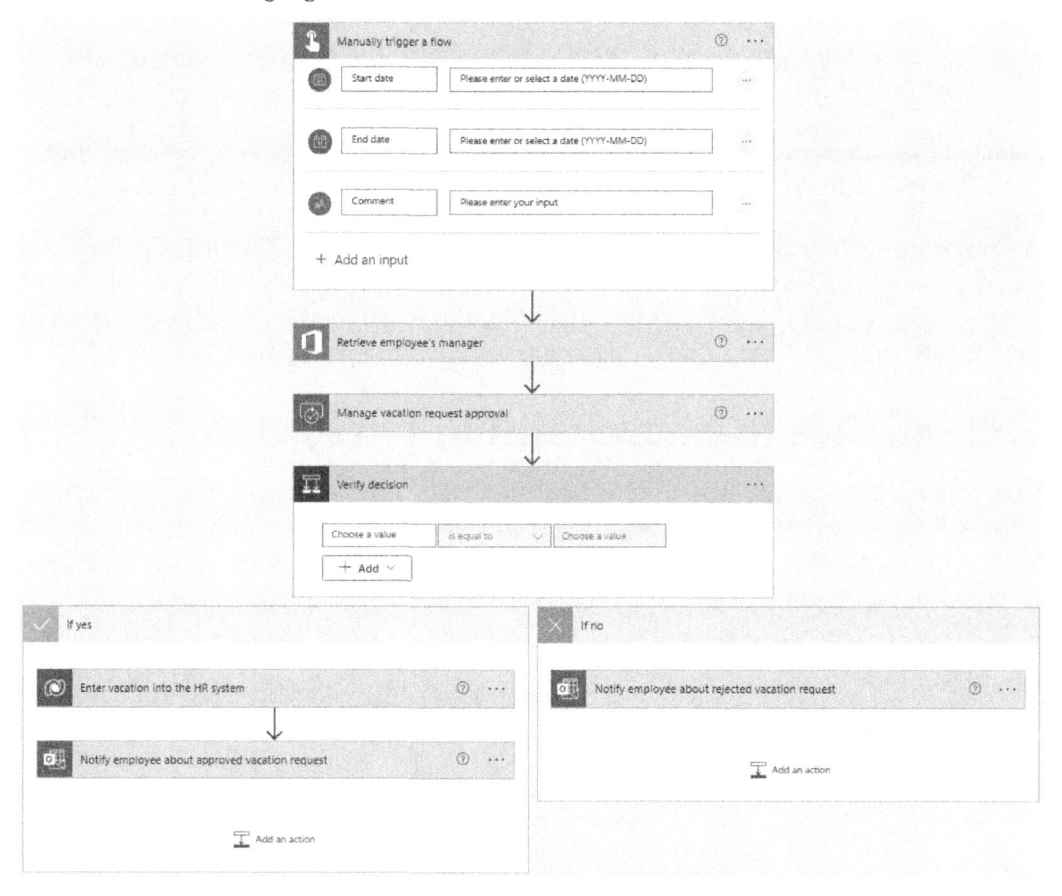

Figure 5.4: Vacation request flow example

On the screenshot *figure 5.4*, you can see the following business process:

- The flow starts with a *button trigger* containing *three custom input parameters*: "**Start date**", "**End date**", and "**Comment**". An employee would enter the start and end date for their vacation and an optional comment for their manager.

- The next step is to *retrieve the direct manager* of the employee.
- After that, an *approval action* comes, where the details would be sent to the manager for approval. The name of the employee is part of the trigger tokens so that this information does not need to be entered manually by the employee.
- After the approval, the *decision is evaluated*. For a positive decision (vacation approved), the flow is sending the request data into an HR system, and the employee is notified with an e-mail.
- For the negative decision (vacation rejected), the employee is notified with an e-mail.

Note: These examples are not part of the solution for Project Wizards, Inc., but you can try yourself and build the flows just to practice the technology.

A similar but certainly more complex would be another typical business process—a travel expenses reimbursement request. Part of such flow would be to take photos of the documents (flight/train tickets, hotel bills, and so on) and submit those as part of the button trigger by using the *file data type* for custom input variables.

Upload files to SharePoint or OneDrive

Many times, we need to easily upload files created on our mobile device (for example, photos, screenshots and even documents, and so on) into a document management system. This process can also be easily accomplished using a button flow. Please refer to the following figure:

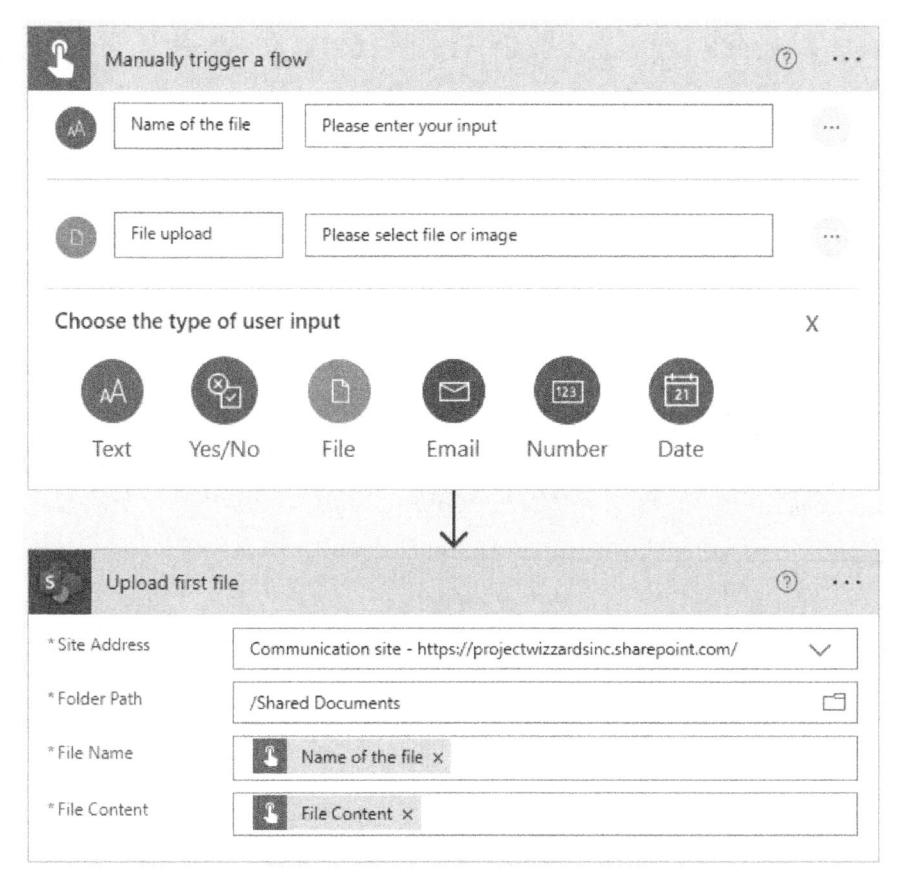

Figure 5.5: File upload flow example

On the screenshot *figure 5.5*, you can see the following business process:

- The flow starts with a *button trigger* containing *two custom input parameters*: "**Name of the file**" and "**File upload**". A user would enter a name for the file, under which the file should be uploaded to a SharePoint folder and then upload the file from their mobile device.
- In the next and last step, the file would be created in a defined SharePoint site, within a defined folder, with the specified file name.

Create an Azure Active Directory user

This flow would be a nice help for a Microsoft cloud administrator who needs to create new user accounts in Azure Active Directory very quickly while being offsite. Please refer to the following figure:

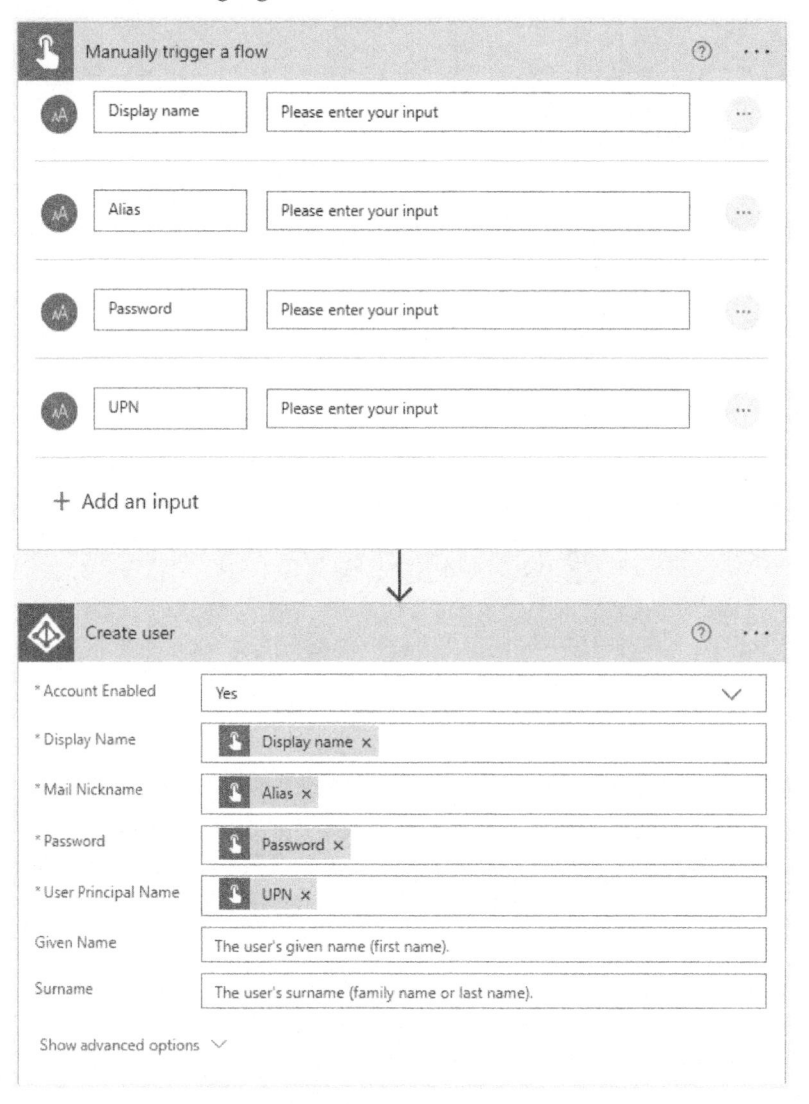

Figure 5.6: User creation flow example

On the screenshot *figure 5.6*, you can see the following business process:

- The flow starts with a *button trigger* containing *four custom input parameters*: "`Display name`", "`Alias`", "`Password`", and "`UPN`", which are required when creating a new user account.

- In the next and last step, an *Azure Active Directory action* is used to create the user, using the four mandatory parameters from the button trigger input.

Now, after we have concluded the overview of the cloud flows technology, we drive our attention to the last part of the Power Automate family, the business process flows.

Business process flows fundamentals

Even though **Business Process Flows (BPF)** belong to Power Automate, the technology as such, as well as the usage scenarios, are rather different. Simply said, the BPF is used within model-driven Power Apps to guide the user of the apps throughout a business process.

The main idea behind the BPF is to align the typical thinking of a business user with the use of an IT application. A typical business user usually works by following business processes. That means a particular business process has certain phases, and, in every phase, it is required to perform certain steps. A traditional business application is rather data-centric, which means that the user should create, modify, or delete records or perform similar steps with a focus on data. These two approaches are not compatible, which is one of the reasons for the low acceptance of traditional business applications.

BPF offers a solution for this issue by enhancing a model-driven app with the capability to follow a business process. On the following screenshot, there is an example of a BPF in one of the sample apps coming from Microsoft:

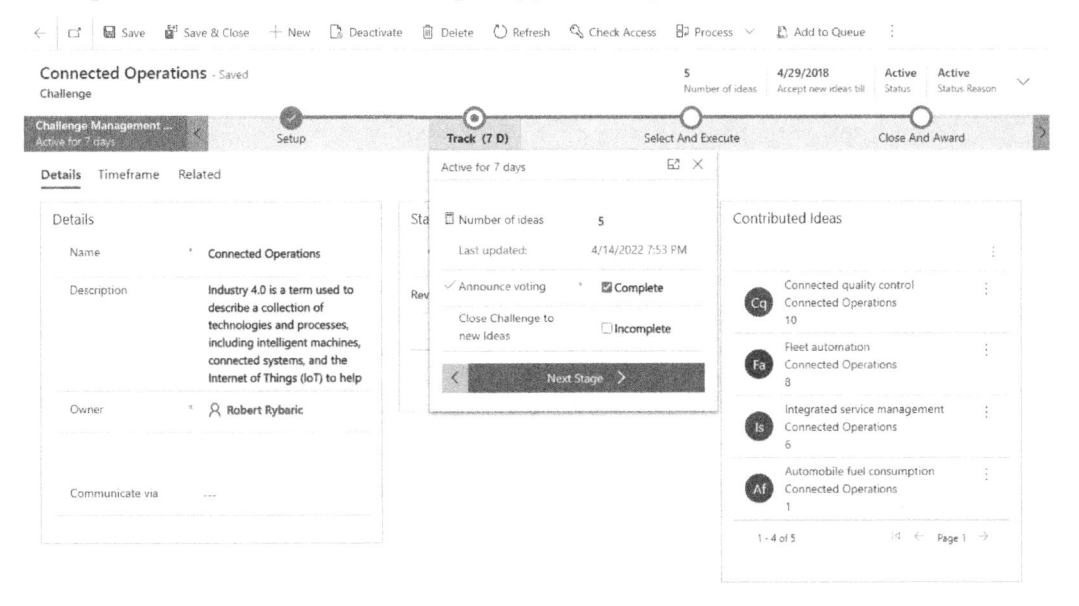

Figure 5.7: *Business process flow example*

The main capabilities of the BPF are the following:

- You can create a BPF consisting of *stages* representing the phases of a business process, and in each stage, you can have multiple *steps*. The stages are represented by the red circles in *figure 5.7*. The steps are visible for the current stage "`Track`" in the box with the blue button "`Next Stage ->`".
- There can be up to *30* stages and up to *30* steps in every stage in a BPF.
- The steps can be either *data steps* equivalent to the usual columns on a model-driven form, or they can also be *automations*, such as *classic workflows*, *custom actions*, or *Power Automate cloud flows*.
- The BPFs are connected with a Dataverse table so that they are always sitting on top of a model-driven main form, as illustrated in *figure 5.7*. It is possible to skip from one record in one table to another record in another table.
- The stages can be *dynamic*, and the logic can be equipped with conditions and based on the evaluation of the conditions, certain stages can be *skipped* or *replaced* with other stages.

The BPFs are used by the end-user of a model-driven app by starting a process with the creation of a record and then following the logic of the stages and steps from the beginning until the end. The user is required to perform all the tasks configured within a stage (enter data, start automations) and then move to the next stage. Using this approach, the user will, at some point of time, finish the BPF and confirm that by clicking on the button on the last stage.

The BPF technology is giving us, besides the main capability of guiding end users along business processes also, the possibility to *track* and *analyze* the usage of the processes, the duration each stage requires on average, and many more useful features.

To practice this amazing technology, let us dive into the next practical exercise and implement a business process flow for Project Wizards, Inc.

Exercise 10: Create a business process flow

In this exercise, we are going to streamline the preparation and execution of the projects for Project Wizards, Inc. As usual, let us first analyze the situation and prepare a solution design.

Analysis and preparations

There were no specific requirements implying the use of BPF, but it is always useful to think about this capability because it is known for increasing the acceptance of business applications. For Project Wizards, Inc., we can identify the following (simplified) phases of their main business process:

- Create a project and identify the customer
- Create project tasks
- Create project products
- Execute the project
- Close the project

To make it more straightforward to follow these phases, we are going to create a BPF with four stages with the following content (steps):

- **Stage 1**: Create a project and identify the customer—data steps for "`Customer`" and "`Customer primary contact`".
- **Stage 2**: Create project tasks—data step, confirming the creation of the project tasks.
- **Stage 3**: Create project products—data step, confirming the creation of the project products.
- **Stage 4**: Close the project—data step, confirming the project closure.

There will be no stage for the phase "`Execute the project`" because there is no meaningful content for steps in this phase.

As we do not have any structures yet for the three confirmations as described previously, we will create for that purpose *three Yes/No columns* in the table "**Project**". This is a popular approach since the data for such "**Confirmations**" can be stored in the business application, and at the same time, it looks like a confirmation business logic.

Practical implementation

The first step in the practical implementation will be the extension of the data model in the table "**Project**" in Microsoft Dataverse. Since this is already well-known, we are not going to provide a detailed description; just perform the following steps:

- In the Maker Portal, open the Project Management solution and open the table "`Project`".
- Go to "`Columns`" and create the following three columns:
    - "`Project tasks created`", the data type "`Yes / No`".
    - "`Project products created`", the data type "`Yes / No`".

        o "**Project closed**", the data type "**Yes / No**".

- Click "**Save Table**", navigate to the main node "**All**", and click on "**Publish all customizations**"

We are not going to place these three columns on the model-driven forms or views because they are only intended to support the business process flow.

The next step is to create that BPF; please perform the following steps:

- In the Maker Portal, open the Project Management solution, click "**+ New**", then "**Automation**", "**Process**", and finally "**Business process flow**".

- In the BPF creation dialogue, enter the following values and then click "**Create**":

    o **Display name**: "**Project Process**"

    o **Name** will be set-up automatically to "**pw_projectprocess**"

    o **Table**: select "**Project**"

- The business process flow designer will open in a new browser tab. As we are going to create a new BPF, the designer contains the first unconfigured stage with one unconfigured step, according to the following screenshot:

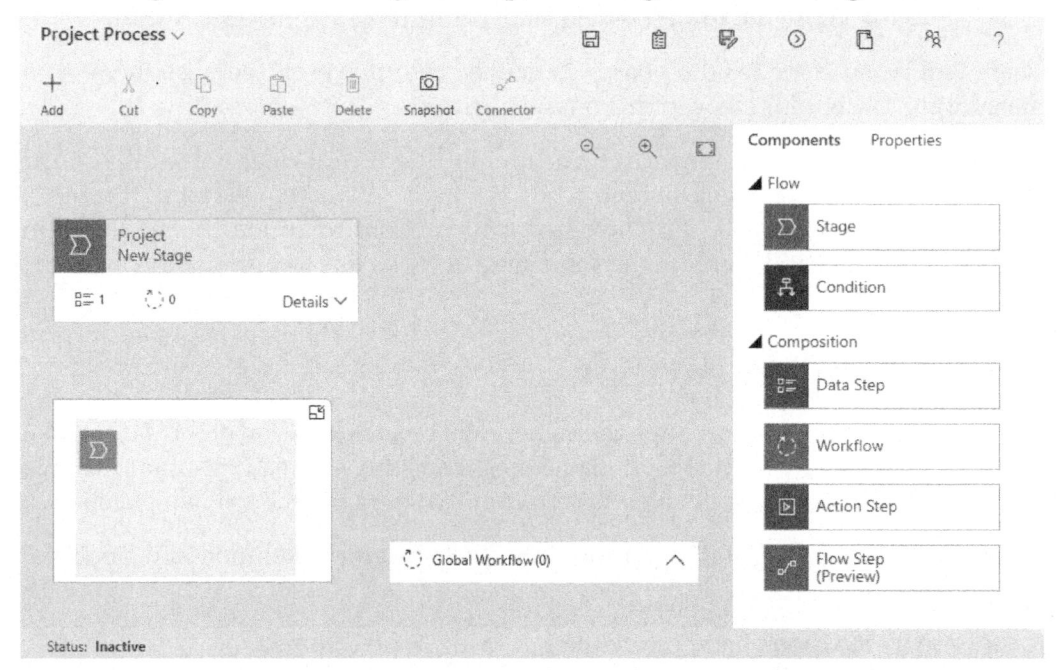

Figure 5.8: Business process flow designer for new BPF

- Click on the first stage, and on the right side in the properties pane, set Display Name to "**Identify the customer**". Click on "**Apply**".

- Click on the "**Details**" on the stage to open the content of the stage. The first step, which is a data step, will be displayed.

- Click on the first step, and on the right side in the properties pane, select the column "**Customer**". Select the checkbox "**Required**"; this will make this data step mandatory. Click on "**Apply**". The Step Name will be automatically set to the name of the selected column.

- On the right side in the properties pane, switch to "**Components**". Drag a data step and drop it on the stage *below the first data step*. You need to drop the step on the "**+**" sign shown *below the first data step*.

- Click on the new step, and on the right side in the properties pane, select the column "**Customer primary contact**". Click on "**Apply**". This data step will not be set to "**Required**".

- On the right side in the properties pane, switch to "**Components**" again, drag a new stage and drop it to the right of the first stage, on the "**+**" sign.

- Click on the new stage, and on the right side in the properties pane, set Display Name to "**Create project tasks**". Click on "**Apply**".

- Click on the "**Details**" on the stage to open the content of the stage. The first step, which is a data step, will be displayed.

- Click on the first step, and on the right side in the properties pane, select the column "**Project tasks created**". Select the checkbox "**Required**"; this will make this data step mandatory. Click on "**Apply**". The Step Name will be automatically set to the name of the selected column.

- On the right side in the properties pane, switch to "**Components**" again, drag a new stage and drop it to the right of the first stage, on the "**+**" sign.

- Click on the new stage, and on the right side in the properties pane, set **Display Name** to "**Create project products**". Click on "**Apply**".

- Click on the "**Details**" on the stage to open the content of the stage. The first step, which is a data step, will be displayed.

- Click on the first step, and on the right side in the properties pane, select the column "**Project products created**". Select the checkbox "**Required**"; this will make this data step mandatory. Click on "**Apply**". The Step Name will be automatically set to the name of the selected column.

- On the right side in the properties pane, switch to "**Components**" again, drag a new stage and drop it to the right of the first stage, on the "**+**" sign.

- Click on the new stage, and on the right side in the properties pane, set **Display Name** to "`Close the project`". Click on "`Apply`".

- Click on the "`Details`" on the stage to open the content of the stage. The first step, which is a data step, will be displayed.

- Click on the first step, and on the right side in the properties pane, select the column "`Project closed`". Select the checkbox "`Required`"; this will make this data step mandatory. Click on "`Apply`". The Step Name will be automatically set to the name of the selected column.

The final BPF should have a structure as illustrated in the following screenshot:

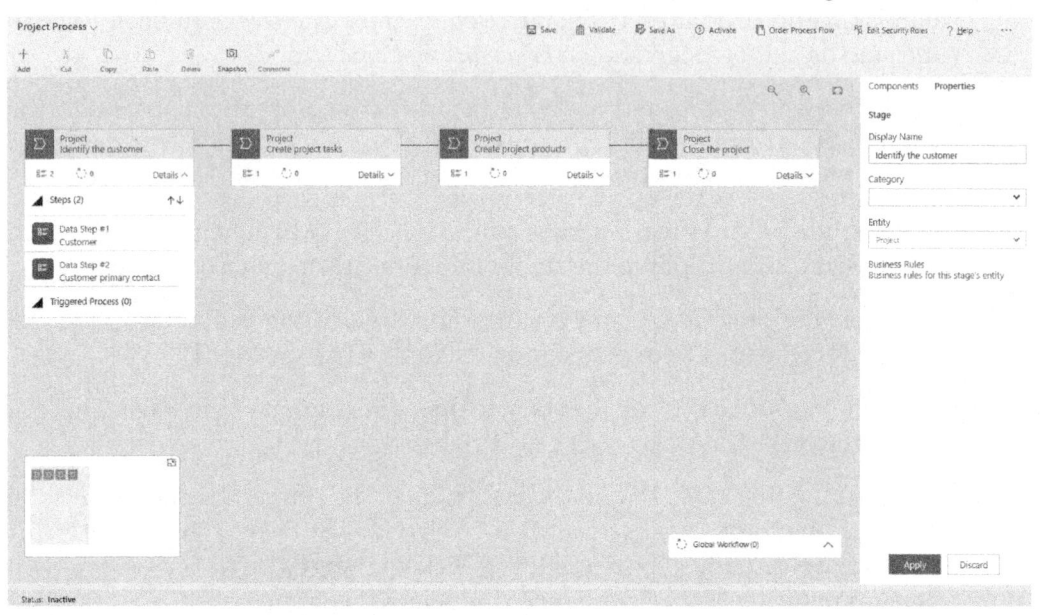

Figure 5.9: Business process flow "Project Process"

In order to start using the BPF, it must be *saved* and *activated*. Please perform the following steps:

- Click on "`Save`" this will save the BPF and, at the same time, perform an **error check**.

- In case there is no error reported in the designer, click on "`Activate`" and confirm the activation. Only activated BPFs can be used in model-driven apps.

- After successful activation, you can close the browser tab with the BPF designer.

- Back in the Maker Portal, with the solution "**Project Management**", click on "`Publish all customizations`".

- Click on the button "`<- Back to solutions`".

The last step in this exercise is to test the newly created BPF.

> **Note: When a business process flow is created in Microsoft Dataverse, and there are already some records in the respective tables, the BPF will not be automatically applied to existing records, only to new records created after the BPF is activated.**

To test the BPF, perform the following steps:

- In the Maker Portal, navigate to "**Apps**" and start the "**Project Management**" model-driven app.

- Navigate to "**Projects**" and open an existing project record. You will notice that there is *no BPF on the model-driven form*. This is because the records were created *before* we created the BPF.

- In the upper command bar, click on "**Process**" and then "**Switch Process**". In the pop-up window, you will find the process "**Project Process**".

- Select the process and click "**OK**". The Project form will reload, and the BPF will be displayed on the form according to the following screenshot:

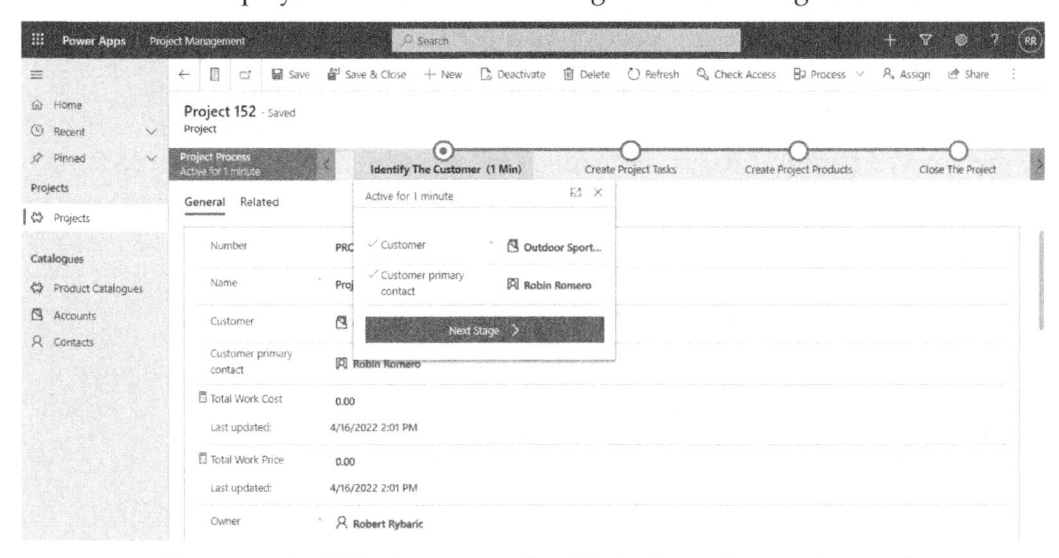

Figure 5.10: Applied business process flow "Project Process" on a project record

You can try the functionality by selecting the first stage, verifying the content, and then moving with the button "`Next Stage >`" throughout the whole BPF until the end. You will notice the functionality of the "Required" data steps so that some data entries will be *mandatory*.

The second test you can perform is to create a *new project record*. In this case, you will notice that the BPF is applied *automatically*.

Congratulations! You have created and tested a business process flow and enhanced the functionality of the Project Management model-driven app for Project Wizards, Inc.

In the next section, we will investigate another automation capability, the automations available within Microsoft Dataverse.

Dataverse automations fundamentals

You have already learned a lot about Power Automate, as *the* automation technology within the Power Platform. But guess what? There is also some automation available directly within Microsoft Dataverse. Building a Power Platform solution requires, among other things, knowing which type of automation is best suitable for the specific requirements.

Microsoft Dataverse contains the following types of automations:

- Business Rules
- Classic workflows
- Classic custom actions

In fact, business process flows are also technically part of Microsoft Dataverse, but in the Power Platform product structure, they are placed in the Power Automate family. Let us now have a look at the three mentioned Dataverse automations.

Business Rules

Business Rules is the simplest automation type within Microsoft Dataverse. With this technology, you can configure simple automations, being able to do the following:

- Show or hide a column on a model-driven form.
- Make a column on a model-driven form editable or read-only.
- Make a column on a model-driven form mandatory or optional.
- Set or clear a value of a column.
- Set a default value for a column.
- Show an error message within a column on a model-driven form.

- **Perform a recommendation action**: This is more complex automation, offering the capability to recommend something to the user of a model-driven app, and in case the user confirms the recommendation, the action will be performed. As an example, for this automation, you can imagine a recommendation to offer a discount of 2% to a customer in case the estimated opportunity close date is less than two weeks.

Business rules are configured using a simple graphical designer. In order to try this automation right away, we are going to perform the next practical exercise.

Exercise 11: Create a business rule

In this exercise, we are going to make sure that in case a user creates a project product record, the selection of a product from a product catalogue is never forgotten.

Analysis and preparations

There were no specific requirements for this verification, but every business application should be robust and potential error situations should be eliminated. When creating a project product, one of the important values is the selection of a product from the product catalogue. Without a product, the project product record will behave incorrectly, and the cost and price information would not be calculated.

> Note: A possible solution for this type of verification would be to make the "Product Catalogue" column in the "Project Product" table mandatory. Using Business Rules, we have, however, the possibility to define a specific error message text, which will be displayed to the user when trying to save a record without a selected product.

The implementation of this verification will be a simple business rule, checking whether there is a value in the column "**Product Catalogue**". In case the column is empty, there will be an error displayed within that column, and it will not be possible to save the record unless a product is selected.

Practical implementation

For the implementation, please perform the following steps:

- In the Maker Portal, open the Project Management solution and open the table "**Project Product**".
- Navigate to "**Business Rules**" and click "**Add business rule**". The business rule designer will open in a separate browser tab. You will notice that the designer is very similar to the BPF designer.

- The designer for a new business rule will always open with an unconfigured condition. A condition as a starting point of the business rule is mandatory.
- Before we continue with the configuration, click on the small down-arrow right from the name of the business rule: "**Project Product: New business rule**", as documented on the following screenshot. This will open the upper area and give you the possibility to set a name for the business rule:

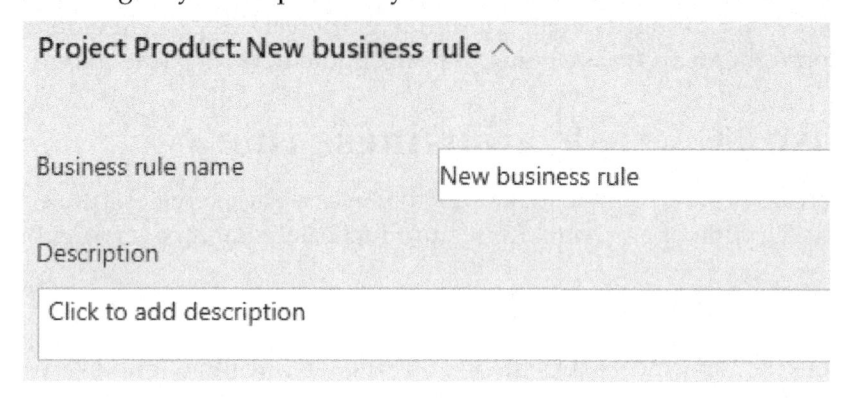

Figure 5.11: Giving a business rule a name

- Give the business rule the name "**Verify product catalogue**". After that, you can minimize the upper area again using the up-arrow to have more space for the designer.
- Click on the condition, and on the right side in the properties pane, give the condition the name "**Product not selected**".
- Next, we need to configure the condition. Please go to "**Rule 1**" and select the following values:
    - Source: **Entity**
    - Field: **Product Catalogue**
    - Operator: **Does not contain data**
- Click "**Apply**" to confirm the configuration.
- On the right side in the properties pane, switch from "**Properties**" to "**Components**".
- Drag the action "**Show Error Message**" and drop it to the right of the condition on the "**+**" sign.
- Click on the new action, and on the right side in the properties pane, give the action the name "**Display error message**".

- Next, we need to configure the action. Please go to the "Error Massage" and select the following values:
    - **Field**: `Product Catalogue`
    - **Message**: `"You need to select a product from the product catalogue!"`
- Click "**Apply**" to confirm the configuration.
- Verify that the business rule looks like as shown in the following screenshot:

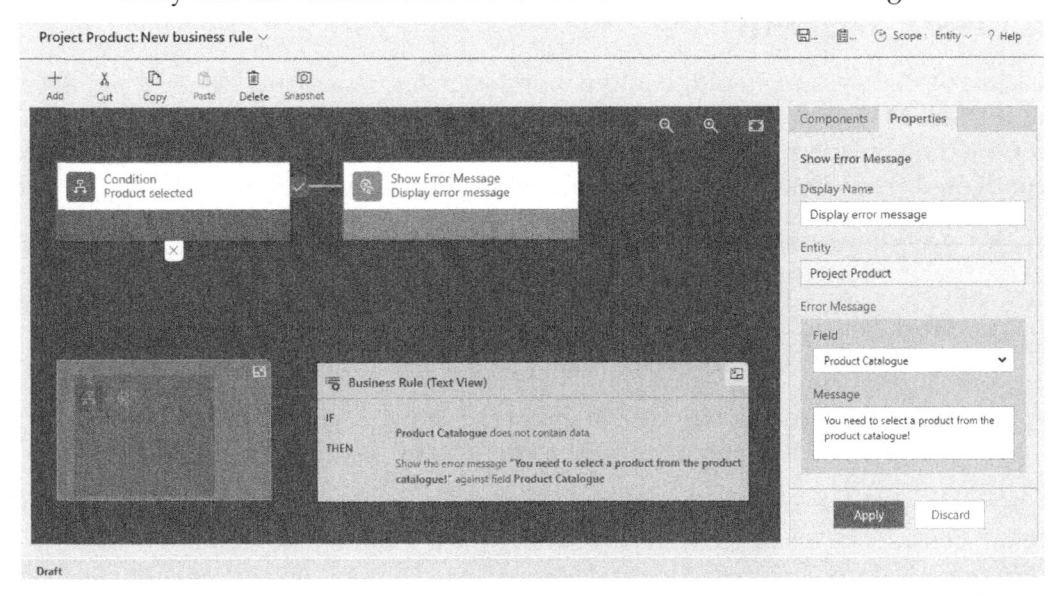

Figure 5.12: Business rule "Verify product catalogue"

As for BPF, a business rule must be saved and activated. Please perform the following steps:

- Click on "**Save**" this will save the business rule and, at the same time, perform an error check.
- In case there is no error reported in the designer, click on "**Activate**" and confirm the activation. Only activated Business rules will work within apps.
- After successful activation, you can close the browser tab with the business rule designer.
- Back in the Maker Portal, with the solution "**Project Management**", navigate to "**All**", and click on "**Publish all customizations**".
- Click on the button "`<- Back to solutions`".

The last step in this exercise is to test the newly created business rule. The test is very simple, in the Maker Portal, navigate to the apps, open the *"Project Management"* model-driven app, navigate to projects, open an existing project, and try to add a new project product. You will see an error message within the "**Product Catalogue**" column, which will stay there until you select a product from the catalogue.

Congratulations! You have successfully created a business rule and further enhanced the *"Project Management"* app for Project Wizards, Inc.

Classic workflows

Classic workflows are an older automation technology, available from the old days of the first Microsoft Dynamics CRM versions. The workflows are used preferably for building *event-based automations*; however, an on-demand execution can also be configured. The workflows have the following main features:

- Workflows can respond to typical events in Microsoft Dataverse, like when a record was created, modified, or deleted.
- Workflows can perform a limited set of actions, mainly around creating or updating records in various Microsoft Dataverse tables.
- When configuring for on-demand execution, the workflow will be available within model-driven apps for the end user for manual triggering.

Classic workflows are configured using a legacy workflow designer. They are today considered obsolete in most of the typical automation scenarios, and it is recommended to use Power Automate cloud flows instead, whenever possible.

Classic custom actions

Classic custom actions are similar automations like classic workflows, and they are also configured in the same legacy workflow designer. Custom actions, however, do not have any trigger; they must be started from a workflow, business process flow, or by code. Similar to classic workflows, they are considered as obsolete technology.

Use cloud flows in Power Apps

We have learned a lot about Power Automate cloud flows in *Chapter 4, Automate Processes with Power Automate*, and in this chapter, but one thing was not yet explained in detail, and that is the direct integration between Power Apps and Power Automate. There are many scenarios of how these two amazing technologies can work together; let us investigate some of the most typical.

Event-based automations

In this scenario, it is required that when something happens in Microsoft Dataverse, for example, a user creates, modifies, or deletes a record, automation should start and perform some specified actions. In this case, the cloud flow will use the Microsoft Dataverse trigger to catch the event and start the flow execution. In the further logic, we can use Microsoft Dataverse actions to perform some automations directly inside of Microsoft Dataverse, or we can use any other data connector to perform actions using other technologies. The best example for this scenario is *Exercise 9* from *Chapter 4, Automate Processes with Power Automate*, where we created an approval flow to approve the completion of the project tasks.

Scheduled automations

When building business applications, there are many times requirements for certain batch processing automations. It can be anything from mass deactivation or deletion of old records and mass data transfers between various IT systems to typical business requirements, like the one we already mentioned: to send a birthday greeting e-mail to contacts from the Microsoft Dataverse. A common pattern for these automations is the use of the Scheduler trigger, configured to start in the required time intervals. The logic after the trigger can be implemented by using any number of data connectors.

On-demand automations

On-demand automations we have not described yet. For this type of automation, it is expected that the user will be able to start the automation from a Power App manually. Let us have a look at how this can work.

For model-driven applications, there are two ways to provide a cloud flow for on-demand execution.

There is a specific Microsoft Dataverse trigger called "**When a record is selected**". This trigger is offered to build on-demand automations, which can be started from within a model-driven app. Let us take an example of how this approach could be used in our "**Project Management**" application. Let us assume we need a simple way to create an annotation record for the project's customer while working with the project record. This can be, of course, achieved manually, but it would need a whole bunch of clicks, and we would need to leave the project record we are just working on. So, a simpler way to do this is always more desirable.

Example 2: Create an on-demand automation

To implement this requirement, it is needed to build a cloud flow using the legacy Microsoft Dataverse data connector and to select the trigger called "**When a record**

142 ■ *Microsoft Power Platform Up and Running*

is selected". To give the user the possibility to specify the title and body text of the annotation, we can create custom input parameters, just like for a button trigger. Next, we would need to use the Microsoft Dataverse data connector and select the action "**Add a new row**". The whole flow is illustrated in the following screenshot:

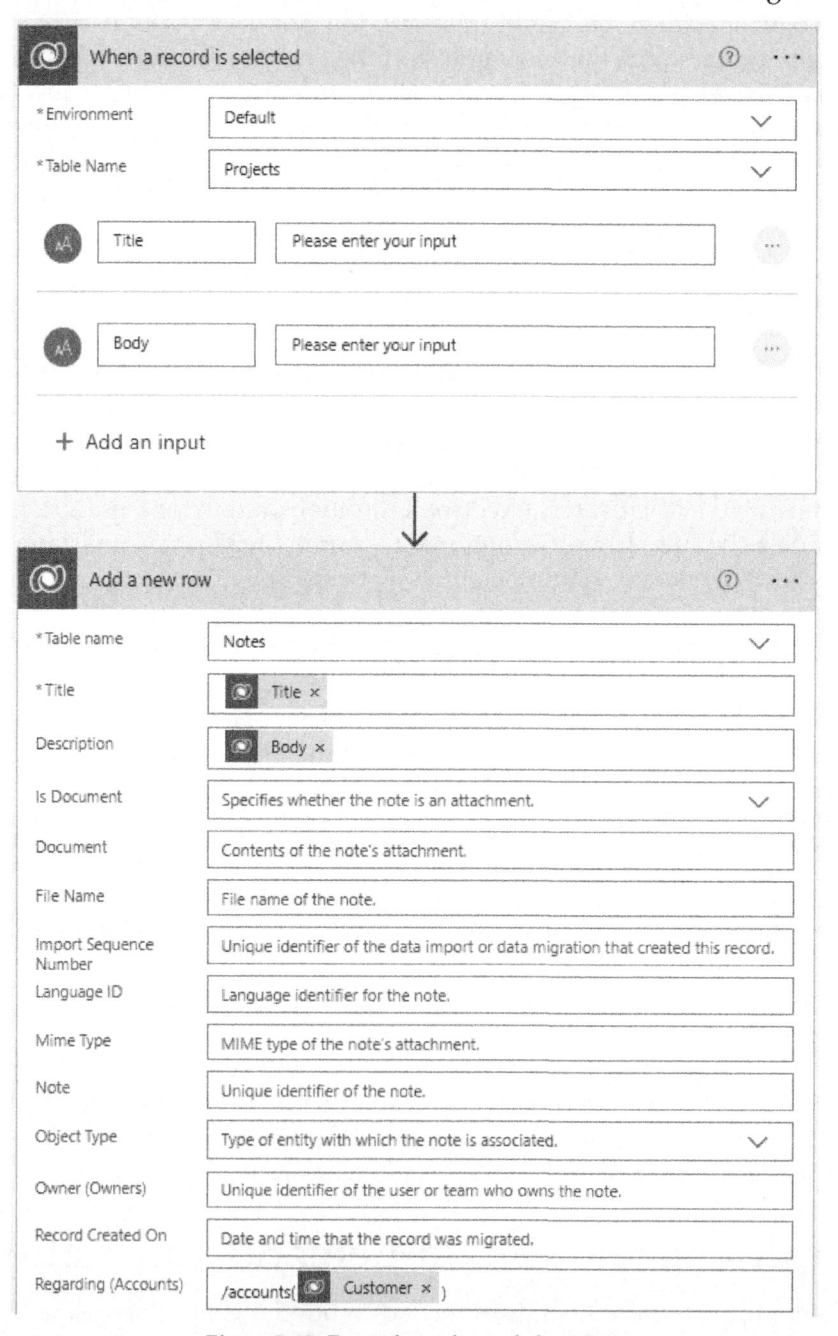

Figure 5.13: Example on-demand cloud flow

As you can see in *Figure 5.13*, there is the "**When a record is selected**" trigger configured with two custom input parameters "**Title**" and "**Body**". In the lower part, there is an action "**Add a new row**", configured to create a new record in the "Notes" table (Notes is the synonym for Annotations). The title and the description of the annotation will be provided by the custom input parameters. Please note the slightly more complex way to configure the connection of the annotation record to the account record (the project's customer).

After we create such a cloud flow, we will see a new entry in the command bar of the Project table, as illustrated in the following screenshot:

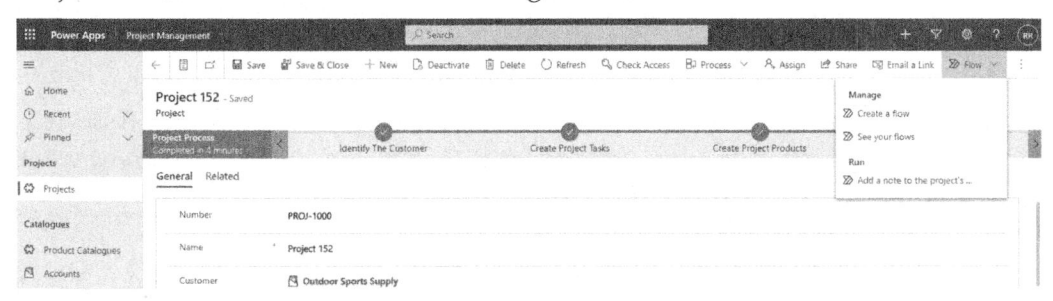

Figure 5.14: *On-demand cloud flow in a model-driven app*

As you can see in *figure 5.14*, there is a new entry in the command bar button "**Flow**". The new entry represents the on-demand flow. When you click on the flow name, there will be a dialogue presented for entering the desired title and body text for the annotation. After that, the flow can be started by a button. As a result of the flow execution, an annotation record will be attached to the project's customer record (account record).

Similar functionality can be provided for canvas apps. There is again a specific trigger for calling a Power Automate cloud flow from a canvas app with the name "*PowerApps*". This trigger can also be configured with custom input parameters to get values from the app.

Use Dataverse automations in Power Apps

In the previous sections, you have learned the basics of the Microsoft Dataverse automations. Let us now have a deeper look into scenarios where those automations can be used.

Frontend automations

Many times, when building business applications, specifically by using the model-driven apps technology, there might be requirements to perform certain simple manipulations on the frontend, on the model-driven forms. It can be anything from the following:

- Depending on a condition, show or hide a column, a section, or a whole tab.
- Depending on a condition, make a column read-only or read-write.
- Depending on a condition, make a column mandatory or optional.
- Set values or default values to columns.
- Depending on a condition, show an error message, warning, or information on a column or on a form level.
- Implement a recommendation process.

Although most of the scenarios can be implemented by using the Business Rules we discussed earlier in this chapter, some of them cannot, and you need to know what are the options. There are some scenarios which would need to be implemented using the JavaScript programming language:

- Show or hide a section or a whole tab (Business Rules support this only for columns, not for sections or tabs).
- Show a warning or information on a column or on a form level (Business Rules support only error messages on a column, no warning or information message and also not on a form level).

On-demand automations

Part of a business solution implemented using the model-driven apps technology could be on-demand automation, a feature giving the end-user the possibility to start automation manually. There are again multiple scenarios:

- A user should be able to start automation from the model-driven app's command bar.
- A user should be able to start automation from the business process flow stage or step.
- A user should be able to start automation outside a model-driven app.

Similarly, as in the previous part, most of the scenarios can be implemented using some of the low-code/no-code approaches we learned already in *Chapter 4, Automate Processes with Power Automate* or in this chapter. Let us make a summary:

- Starting automation from the model-driven app's command bar is possible from the command bar button **"Flow"**. Using this button, you can start either classic workflows that are configured as on-demand or Power Automate flows configured with the trigger "**When a record is selected**".

- Creating own buttons on the command bar and starting automations by clicking those buttons, however, requires advanced customization and JavaScript programming.

- Starting automation from a business process flow can be implemented using the knowledge we have already. From a business process flow, you can start either a workflow in the background (unattended) or a classic custom action or a Power Automate cloud flow using a specific button populated as part of the business process flow.

- Starting automation outside a model-driven app is also possible, using the Power Automate flows with the button trigger. In this case, the automation can be started from the Power Automate mobile app, installed on the user's mobile device.

Backend automations

There are multiple types of backend automations fitting into the most typical scenarios:

- An automation should start as a result of an event in Microsoft Dataverse. The end user needs to see the result of the automation immediately, for example, as a change of some data on the model-driven form.

- An automation should start as a result of an event in Microsoft Dataverse. The end user does not need to see the results immediately.

- An automation should perform a batch job, for example a nightly clean-up of some data in Microsoft Dataverse.

Microsoft Dataverse automations, as well as Power Automate, offer a solution for most of the scenarios with a low-code/no-code approach:

- The first scenario, also known as synchronous execution of automation, can be implemented either by using classic workflows (configured for synchronous execution) or using a custom development approach by developing the so-called Plugins. Interestingly, Power Automate flows cannot be used because they do not support synchronous execution.

- The second scenario, also known as the asynchronous execution of automation, has even more possibilities for implementation. We can use the classic workflows (configured for asynchronous execution), or Power Automate flows using the Microsoft Dataverse trigger. For very complex automations, again, a custom development approach can be used by developing the already mentioned Plugins.

- For the implementation of batch jobs, we have again multiple options. The easiest way is to use the Power Automate flows, equipped with the scheduler trigger. In case the automation is too complex to be implemented in a low-code/no-code way, we can use custom development and build solutions based, for example, on the Microsoft Azure Functions technology.

Conclusion

In this chapter, you have learned everything else about Power Automate automations, which was not covered in *Chapter 4, Automate Processes with Power Automate*. We have also covered automations, which are not part of Power Automate, but rather belong directly to Microsoft Dataverse. Specifically, you have learned about the button flows, automations, which are not running in the background but are triggered by the end users. We have also covered another end-user capability, the business process flows, used within model-driven apps to support the process-driven use of the apps. This knowledge was then used to build a business process flow for the application for Project Wizards, Inc. In the area of Microsoft Dataverse automations, we have covered Business Rules, classic workflows, and classic custom actions. In this section, we have built another automation for the *"Project Management"* model-driven app for Project Wizards, Inc. At the end of the chapter, we have explained multiple possible automation scenarios and the possibilities the Power Platform offers to implement them.

In the upcoming chapter, you will start learning the fundamentals of Power BI. This technology is used to build analytical solutions, which can be used either standalone or as part of a business solution created with the various components of the Power Platform.

Questions

1. What is the purpose of the button flows, are in which scenarios can they be used?
2. What are the specific configuration possibilities of the button trigger?
3. How can the button flows be used by the end users? What are the steps to deploy them?
4. What is business process flows, and in which scenarios can they be used?
5. What can be part of a business process flow?
6. What automation possibilities are part of Microsoft Dataverse?
7. Which capabilities are most suitable for model-driven apps frontend automations?
8. Which capabilities are most suitable for on-demand automations?

CHAPTER 6
Start with Power BI

Introduction

This chapter is fully dedicated to analytics. You will learn how analytics can enhance business applications. We will start by explaining the ways Power BI can connect various data sources and perform complex transformations to bring the data into the required form. Next, you will see the possibilities to create a consistent data model from disparate data sources. Having a clean and compact data model is the prerequisite for the subsequent step—building complex analytical visualizations.

Structure

In this chapter, we will discuss the following topics:

- Use cases for Power BI
- Power BI fundamentals
- The difference between Import and DirectQuery
- Power BI Desktop overview
- Connect to data with Power BI Desktop
- Transform data with Power Query

- Build a data model

Objective

After reading this chapter, you will be able to understand the basics of analytics with Power BI. In this chapter, we are focusing on the fundamentals and the data management with Power BI. You will learn the major difference between the two types of handling data in Power BI with either Import or DirectQuery. You will make yourself familiar with the primary tool used by every Power BI developer, the Power BI Desktop. You will see what types of data and from which different data sources can be used for building analytics. At the end of this chapter, you will learn the fundamentals of data transformation with Power Query and data modeling within Power BI Desktop.

Use cases for Power BI

Microsoft Power Platform has a clear scope, and that is, building business applications. So far, we have learned how to build Power Apps for the end user and how to automate business applications with Power Automate. Business applications also require an analytical and reporting part, which can present the data processed in the applications in a graphical form and provide deeper insight into the data as a foundation for decision-making within the organization. Exactly these requirements can be covered with the next Power Platform component we are going to investigate, the Power BI analytical service.

The typical analytical and reporting requirements for a business application can be structured into the following categories:

- **Self-service reporting and analytics**: This is typically required in every modern business application. The end users should be able to use the built-in tools and capabilities to configure their own ad-hoc analytics and reporting. In Power Apps, specifically in the model-driven apps, there are certain possibilities for self-service analytics and reporting, for example, the reporting wizard, the possibility to export data to Excel and analyze the data there, or create Excel templates with pre-created analytics. Which role plays the Power BI component here? Power BI is also considered as a low-code/no-code service so that skilled end users with access to Power BI can build their own ad-hoc reporting and analytics with this service and even integrate it with Power Apps or Power Automate.

- **Application-wide central analytics**: Usually, every modern business solution comes with certain pre-configured analytics and reporting. Typical examples in Power Apps are model-driven views, model-driven charts, or model-driven dashboards. Other examples are pre-built reports, delivered as part of the Microsoft Dynamics 365 applications. Power BI can, of course, be used as well to create more complex and sophisticated reports and analytics for requirements where the built-in capabilities of Power Apps are not sufficient anymore. Power BI dashboards or visualizations can be easily integrated into a business application created with the Power Apps technology.

- **Enterprise-wide central analytics**: This type of analytics is usually part of the centralized organization's IT strategy and can but must not be implemented using Microsoft tools. The main feature is that the data for these analytic solutions comes usually from various data sources, from multiple different business applications, databases, data warehouses, and so on. The data is consolidated, combined, and eventually enriched with the capabilities of an artificial intelligence component. In the world of Microsoft products and services, enterprise-wide analytics and reporting can be implemented with components like Power BI combined with services from Microsoft Azure such as Azure SQL, Azure Cosmos DB, Azure Data Factory, Azure Synapse Analytics, and many more.

In this and the upcoming chapter, we are going to focus mainly on leveraging the data stored in Microsoft Dataverse and make the best of it by analyzing it with the capabilities of Power BI.

Power BI fundamentals

Power BI is a collection of cloud services and tools with one common goal—build, deploy, and consume advanced analytical solutions. The main structure of Power BI is documented in the following diagram:

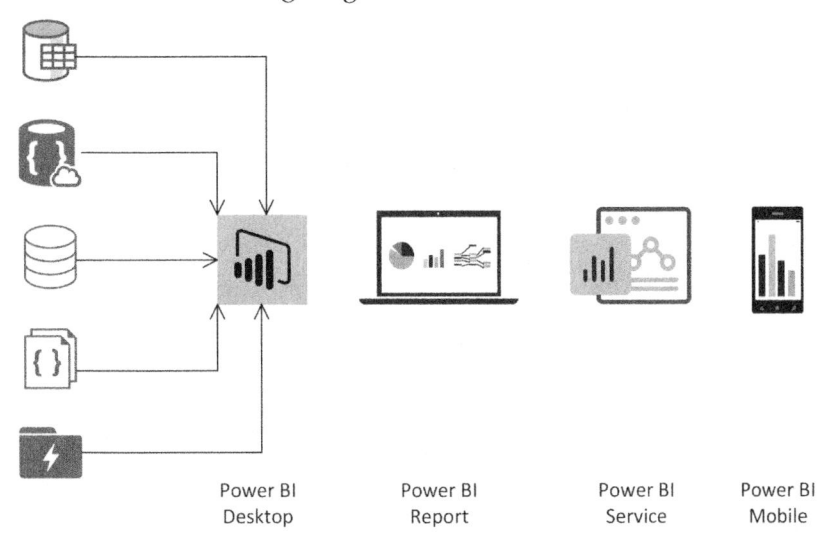

Figure 6.1: Power BI main structure

As you can see in *figure 6.1*, there are multiple components having the following functionality:

- Power BI Desktop: This is the main tool used by the Power BI developers. In contrast to most tools we have seen so far is the Power BI Desktop, a real desktop tool that needs to be installed, as described shortly in *Chapter 1, Introducing Microsoft Power Platform*. A Power BI developer is using this tool to build the Power BI solution.

- Power BI Report: This is the final product of the development of the Power BI Desktop. A report is a local file containing the visualizations and, in certain scenarios, also the data used in the visualizations.

- Power BI Service: This is the cloud service where the final analytical solution lands. The cloud service accommodates the visualizations and, in certain scenarios, also the data. In this service, it is necessary to perform some last configuration steps to prepare the solution for the end users. The solutions can be consumed by the end users directly from the Power BI Service using a browser.

- Power BI Mobile: This is a mobile application for smartphones and tablets, which can be used to consume the Power BI content by the end users. It uses the same concept as the Power Apps mobile or Power Automate mobile. The end user needs to install the app from the AppStore or Google Play Store and sign in with their cloud credentials. The end user will find everything made available to them in the app.

The creation of a final analytical solution, which can be consumed by the end users, requires certain steps to be perfumed by the Power BI developer:

- The Power BI developer needs to *install the Power BI Desktop* tool. As you have learned in *Chapter 1, Introducing Microsoft Power Platform*, there are two possible sources from which the installation can be performed.

- The Power BI developer needs to understand which data sources are necessary to build the required analytical solution. Deep knowledge of the database management systems and a good overview of the IT landscape within the own or customer's organization is required.

- The Power BI developer *connects* to each required data source and decides whether to use the Import or the DirectQuery approach. Details about those two approaches are explained in the next section of this chapter.

- The Power BI developer can *perform transformations* of the data from the data sources using a very powerful tool, *Power Query*, built-in into the Power BI Desktop. The transformations can change the structures of the raw data from the data sources into a form suitable for building the analytical solution.

- The Power BI developer performs a *consolidation* of the data with the goal to build a consistent and compact *data model* exactly corresponding to the requirements of the future analytical solution.

- The Power BI developer builds the *Power BI report*, which is a collection of various *visualizations* and data.

- The Power BI report is the final product created in the Power BI Desktop. When the report is finished, it needs to be *deployed* to the Power BI cloud service. This is done directly from Power BI Desktop.

- The subsequent steps are all performed already in the cloud, in the Power BI Service. The next optional step is to create a *Power BI dashboard*. A dashboard is a collection of the most important or popular visualizations from the report, a kind of start screen for the whole analytical solution.

- The Power BI developer needs to also ensure that the users *get access* to the Power BI solution. This can be achieved by setting up the access rights to the Power BI *workspaces, sharing* the Power BI artifacts, or creating and distributing a Power BI *app*.

This was a very brief overview of the fundamentals of Power BI. Next, we will dive deeper into one of the very important concepts in Power BI, and that is the way how Power BI handles data required for the visualizations.

The difference between Import and DirectQuery

Power BI service contains, besides other internal components, also storage optimized for storing data used within the visualizations. It is, however, not always necessary to physically transfer the data from the data sources to the Power BI cloud platform. That is why Power BI offers two fundamentally different approaches to how the data can be handled:

- **Import**: This approach means that the Power BI analytical solution contains the visualizations stored in the report but also the data stored in a structure called a *dataset*. When we publish a Power BI solution using the Import approach, both the report and the dataset are uploaded to the Power BI platform.

- **DirectQuery**: This approach means that the Power BI solution consists only of the report. The data remains at the data sources and will not be uploaded to the Power BI platform. The Power BI solution contains only the metadata—the description of the structure of the data and connection information to the original data sources.

There are many differences between these two approaches (also called modes) in how the data is handled, and it is important to understand those differences and the key implications.

Power BI supports a large number of various data source technologies, but not every data source technology offers both the Import and the DirectQuery access mode. You need to always refer to the documentation to understand what are the available options.

The **Import** mode is the default mode and is used for most of the standard analytical solutions. The benefit of this mode is specifically *performance* since the internal Power BI storage is optimized for the highest processing speed. The Import mode offers the *widest selection of analytical features*, for example, the Q&A feature, which will be explained in *Chapter 7, Integrate analytics with Power BI*. This mode has, however, also some *disadvantages*. The most important is the fact that the data used in the visualizations is a *copy* of the original data and, as such, *does not reflect the current state* of the data at the data sources. That is why a *refresh capability* needs to be used to either manually or automatically pull fresh data in certain intervals from the data sources. Another serious implication is that since the visualizations are working with a local copy of the data, any possible *authorization system* working at the original data source is *lost*. Due to that fact, a *separate authorization* needs to be implemented within Power BI to restrict access to certain data, depending on the user's role in the organization. Finally, the Import mode can be an issue when we need to process huge amounts of data.

The **DirectQuery** mode is a specific mode that is not used by default in the analytical solutions but can be configured during the data import phase. The biggest *benefit* is exactly what is the disadvantage of the Import mode—the Power BI visualizations are directly connected to the source data, which is always current and accurate, and no refresh is necessary. The same applies to the *authorization*—whenever are the source systems equipped with an authorization feature, this is automatically respected within the Power BI solution because the data is pulled on-demand via an API of the source systems. A *disadvantage* of the DirectQuery mode can be a *possible poor performance*, in case the underlying data source is not scalable enough to support the on-demand data queries fast enough. There is another possible performance problem with DirectQuery. Imagine you have a solution using DirectQuery, and that solution is heavily used by a very large number of users. This heavy usage can also negatively impact the business solutions using the data source, for example, a CRM or ERP application.

In order to gain a better understanding of these two modes, let us imagine an example where we use Microsoft Dataverse as a single data source for a Power BI solution. Microsoft Dataverse supports both the Import as well as the DirectQuery modes. We decide to implement a complex analytical solution using first the Import and then the DirectQuery mode. What is the result?

Import Mode

When using the import mode, the following will be the significant features:

- The solution will offer more analytical features.

- Even high-volume usage of the solution will have no negative impact on the performance of the Power Apps and other solution components using the Microsoft Dataverse data since Power BI is working with a copy of that data.

- The end users will not see the most current data. The Power BI developer would need to configure an automatic refresh of the datasets to make the data at least near real-time. However, automated refresh scheduling is limited to just a few refreshes per day.

- The end users will see unfiltered data from Microsoft Dataverse, even data they would normally have no access to within Power Apps. The Power BI developer would need to configure a separate Power BI authorization using a concept called **Row-level security** (**RLS**). Even using this approach will never map 100% to the complex authorization model of Microsoft Dataverse.

DirectQuery Mode

When using the DirectQuery mode, you will, in contracts, see the following capabilities:

- The solution will offer less analytical features.

- High-volume usage of the solution might have a negative impact on the performance of the Power Apps and other solution components using the Microsoft Dataverse data as the Power BI solution is using the Microsoft Dataverse data directly, through on-demand queries.

- The end users will always see the most current data due to the direct connection to Microsoft Dataverse—no refresh is needed.

- The end users will see exactly the same subset of the data from Microsoft Dataverse, which they can see in the Power Apps or any other Power Platform solution components. This is because Power BI is retrieving the data on-demand from the Dataverse API, and that interface respects the authorization settings of the users.

So, what is the take on this? You need to know your priorities and, based on those, decide which of the two modes is better for your planned solution. The good news is that you can combine both modes and use a *hybrid mode*, where part of your data will use the Import mode and another part the DirectQuery mode.

Power BI Desktop overview

As we have already learned, Power BI solutions are developed using a desktop tool called **Power BI Desktop**. The tool is very complex, and in order to start, you need to learn just the basics. When you start Power BI Desktop, you will see the following structure of the tool:

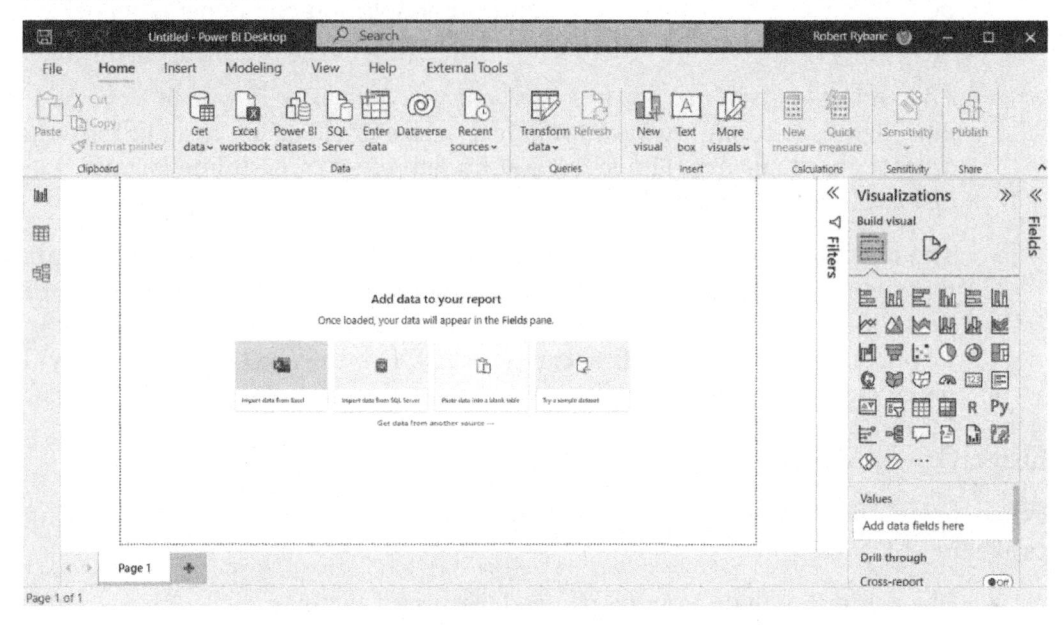

Figure 6.2: Power BI Desktop

As you can see in *figure 6.2*, Power BI Desktop contains the following main parts:

- In the upper right corner, you can see the *name of the signed-in user*. This is important when you need to publish your finished Power BI Report so that the tool knows into which tenant the report should be published.
- In the whole upper part, you can see the *complex ribbon* of the tool, consisting of multiple tabs and, on each tab, a lot of controls.
- On the left side, you can see the *three main views* of the solution you are developing, represented by the three small horizontally aligned buttons. The views are the following:
    - The *Report* view shows the working canvas on which you develop the report content, consisting of visualizations.
    - The *Data* view shows the preview of the dataset data you are using in your solution.

- o The *Model* view represents the relational data model of the dataset tables.
- In the Report view, you can see at the bottom of the tool the *pages* you create when developing the report. A Power BI Report can contain multiple pages.
- In the Report view on the right side, you will find the selection of the available *visualizations* as well as *configuration* and *property* settings for the visualizations.

The tool ribbon contains really a lot of controls, and it is certainly not required to learn the capability behind every single one of the controls. To start developing simple Power BI solutions, it is more than enough to know that you can *connect* to various data sources and start the **Power Query** data transformation tool from the ribbon.

Connect to data with Power BI Desktop

Connecting to one or multiple data sources is, in any case, the first step in developing a Power BI solution. Power BI offers a lot of data connectors to connect to every established database system (Microsoft SQL Server, Oracle, IBM DB2, MySql, PostgreSQL, Sybase, and so on) as well as to a lot of other data sources, such as different business solutions (Dynamics 365, SAP, Salesforce, Marketo, Zendesk, and so on), cloud technologies, and many more.

Note: Please note that the Power BI data connectors and the Power Platform data connectors are not the same, but they are completely different technologies.

You can get a full overview of the available data sources when you click on "**Get data**" and then "**More...**". You will see a selection of the connectors according to the following screenshot:

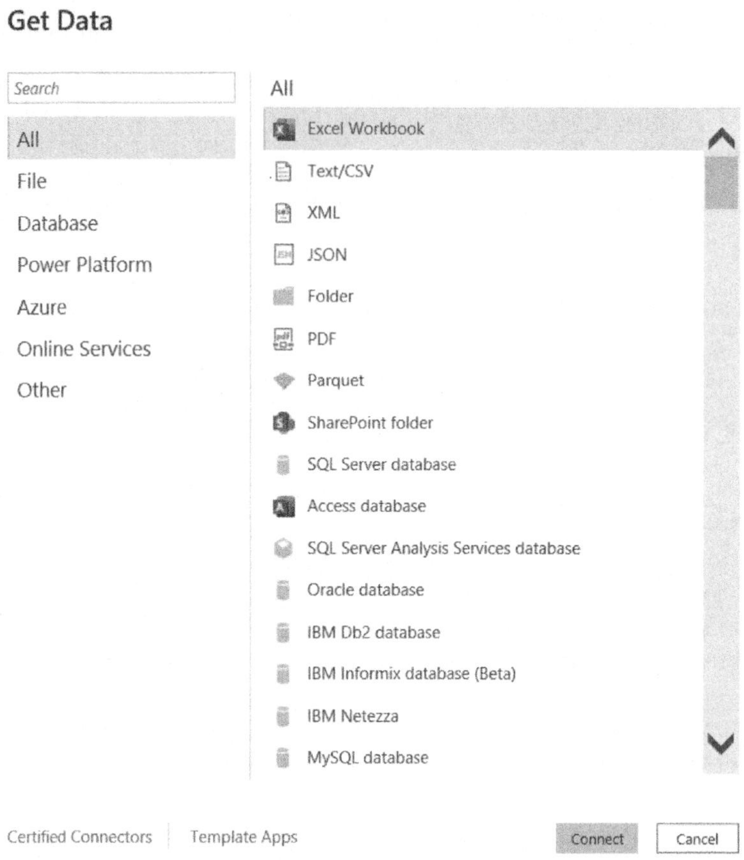

Figure 6.3: Power BI Desktop data sources selection

As you can see in *figure 6.3*, the data sources selection dialog offers a categorization to find the required data source quickly within the respective category.

After you select your preferred data source, you will need to configure the details of the connection. The details are individual and specific for each data connector.

Let us focus on Microsoft Dataverse as the data source for Power BI. When you select the category "**Power Platform**", you will find two data connectors related to Microsoft Dataverse, the "**Common Data Service (Legacy)**", which is the old connector with the old name of Dataverse, and the current "**Dataverse**" connector. Although the old connector supports only the Import mode, the current connector supports both the Import as well as the DirectQuery mode and should be used for all new Power BI solutions.

With this, we are ready to start our next exercise, which will connect to Microsoft Dataverse and load the data, we will use for our analytical solution.

Exercise 12: Connect to Microsoft Dataverse

In this exercise, we are going to perform the first step in the development of the analytical solution for Project Wizards, Inc. We use Power BI Desktop to connect to Microsoft Dataverse and select and load the data from the tables used in the Project Management solution.

For the implementation, please perform the following steps:

- If not yet installed, install the Power BI Desktop on your PC. Follow the guidance from *Chapter 1, Introducing Microsoft Power Platform* to perform the installation.
- Start the Power BI Desktop and close the initial pop-up window.
- Click on the upper right side on the "**Sign in**" button and sign-in with the cloud credentials you use for the exercises. Since there is not yet any Power BI license activated in the tenant you use for the exercises, a browser window with activation of the Power BI license will pop up. Make sure the cloud account you use for the exercises is selected, and if yes, confirm the trial license activation.
- On the ribbon, select the "**Get data**" button, and then "**More…**". Switch to the "**Power Platform**" category and select the data connector "**Dataverse**" with the green icon. Click "**Connect**".
- Next, the "**Navigator**" selection dialog will be displayed. You will see at least two nodes representing the two Power Platform environments in your tenant. Expand the node with the environment you use for the exercises (it is the one without the "(default)" in the name). When you expand the node, you will see the list of all Dataverse tables; however, not the Display names, but rather the schema names (technical names) of the tables.
- You can identify the custom tables from our data model by the prefix "pw_". Select the following tables from the list:
    - account
    - contact
    - pw_productcatalogue
    - pw_project
    - pw_projectproduct
    - pw_projecttask

- The selection will look like as shown in the following screenshot:

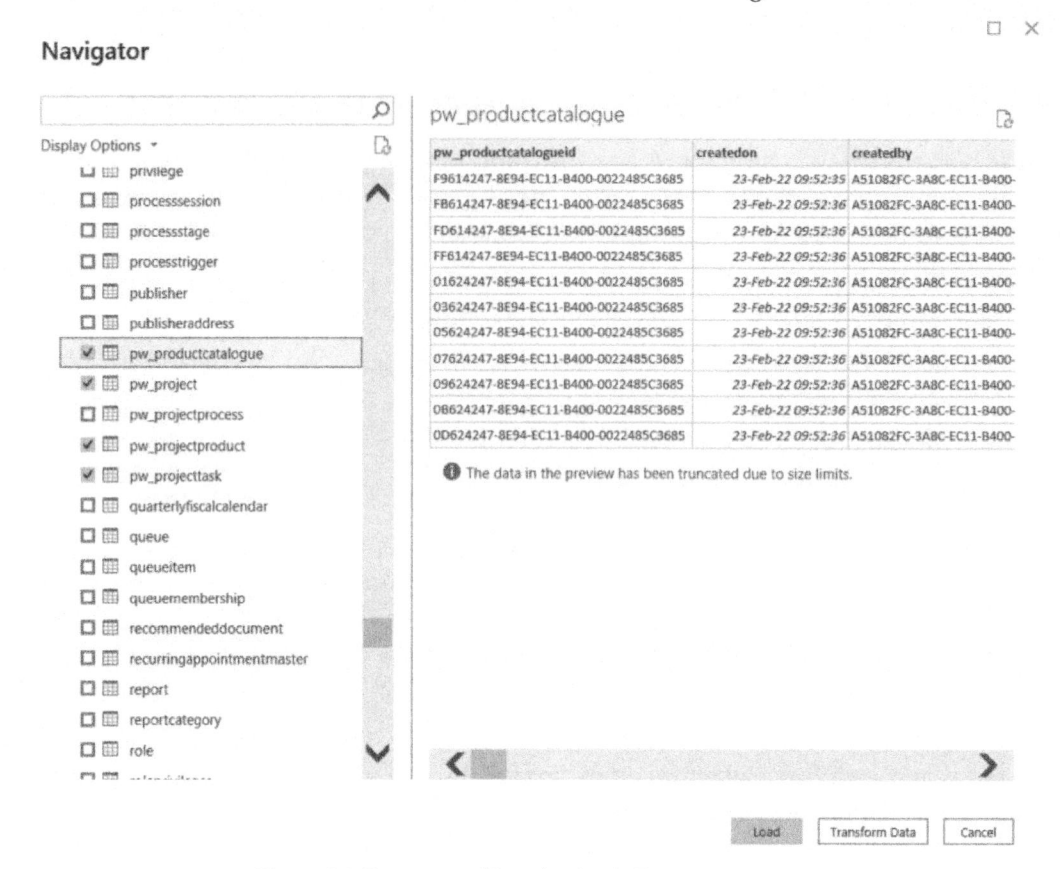

Figure 6.4: Dataverse tables selection in Power BI Desktop

- After you have selected all the six tables, click "**Load**".

Note: If there is a need to perform a transformation of the source data before loading it into the Power BI Desktop, clicking on the button "Transform Data" starts the Power Query transformation tool. For our exercise, we are not going to perform a transformation.

- After clicking the "**Load**" button, Power BI Desktop will offer a selection of whether you prefer an Import mode or DirectQuery mode. Since we need to practice some additional features in Power BI, we select the Import mode, even though the DirectQuery mode might have some benefits. Select the "**Import**" mode and confirm with "**OK**".

- The data from the six tables are now physically downloaded into the Power BI Desktop tool, where it will become part of the Power BI Report.

- Click on the "**Save**" icon in the upper left corner of the Power BI Desktop to save the report. Select a preferred folder to save the file and give the file the name: "`Project Wizards Analytics`".

- Verify the correct result of the data loading steps by switching from the "**Report**" to the "**Model**" view. You should see a data model consisting of the six imported tables with established relationships between them, according to the following screenshot:

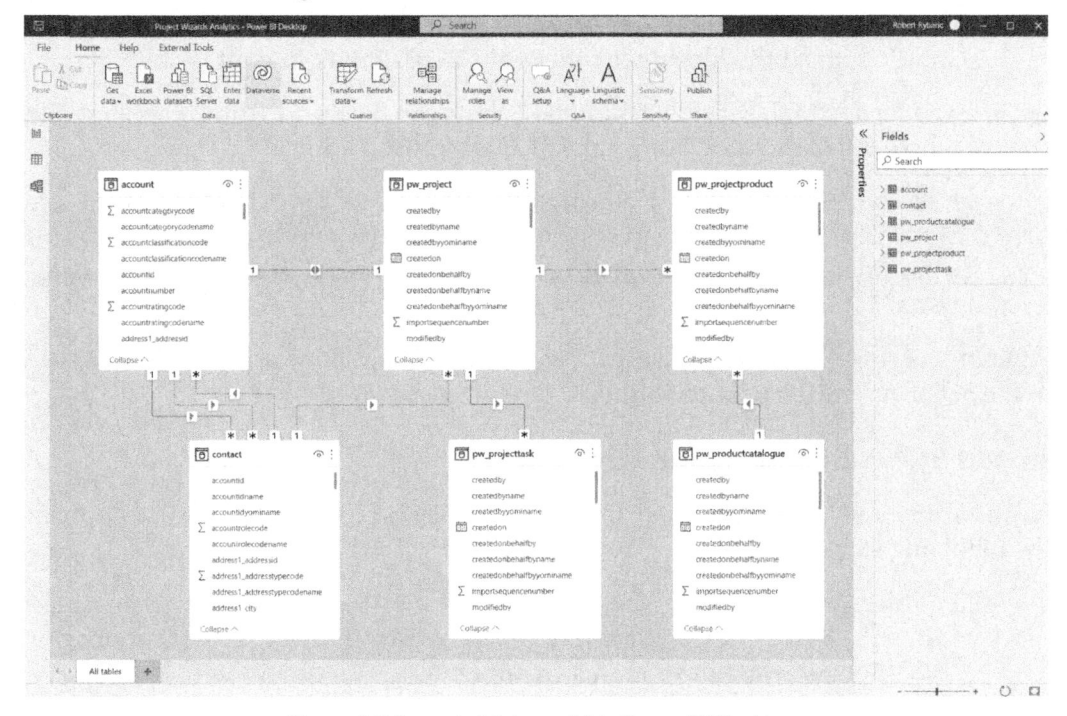

Figure 6.5: Imported data model in Power BI Desktop

This is the last step in the standard part of this exercise. Next, you can challenge yourself by implementing the advanced part.

Advanced part

You are invited to perform the advanced part of this exercise. However, the final analytical solution will also work without this part. In order to implement this part of the exercise, you need to have Microsoft SQL Server and MySql installed as described in *Chapter 1, Introducing Microsoft Power Platform*. You will also need the credentials you configured during the installation of both database systems.

Import sample database into SQL server

The first task is to import a sample database into your local Microsoft SQL Server installation. Please perform the following steps:

- Navigate to GitHub to the repository containing sample Microsoft SQL Server databases: **https://github.com/Microsoft/sql-server-samples/releases/tag/adventureworks**

- Locate the section "*AdventureWorksDW (Data Warehouse) full database backups*" and download the file **AdventureWorksDW2019.bak** to your local PC.

- The file is a SQL Server backup file, which can be used to directly restore the whole database into your local SQL Server installation.

- Use the SQL Server documentation to restore the database using the SQL Server Management Studio: **https://docs.microsoft.com/en-us/sql/relational-databases/backup-restore/restore-a-database-backup-using-ssms**

After the successful restore, you should find the database "**AdventureWorksDW2019**" in the SQL Server Management Studio.

Import SQL Server data into Power BI

Now, we are ready to import some data from SQL Server to Power BI. Please perform the following steps:

- In Power BI Desktop, on the ribbon, select the "**Get data**" button and then "**More...**". Switch to the "**Database**" category and select the data connector "**SQL Server database**". Click "**Connect**".

- Fill in the following values:
  - Server: localhost
  - Database (optional): AdventureWorksDW2019
  - Data Connectivity mode: Import
- Click "**OK**", according to the following screenshot:

Start with Power BI ■ 161

SQL Server database

Server ⓘ
localhost

Database (optional)
AdventureWorksDW2019

Data Connectivity mode ⓘ
● Import
○ DirectQuery

> Advanced options

OK   Cancel

Figure 6.6: Import data from SQL Server — configuration

- A dialog for selecting tables or views from the database **AdventureWorksDW2019** will be offered. Select the tables: "**DimGeography**", "**DimProduct**", and "**DimReseller**" as illustrated on the following screenshot:

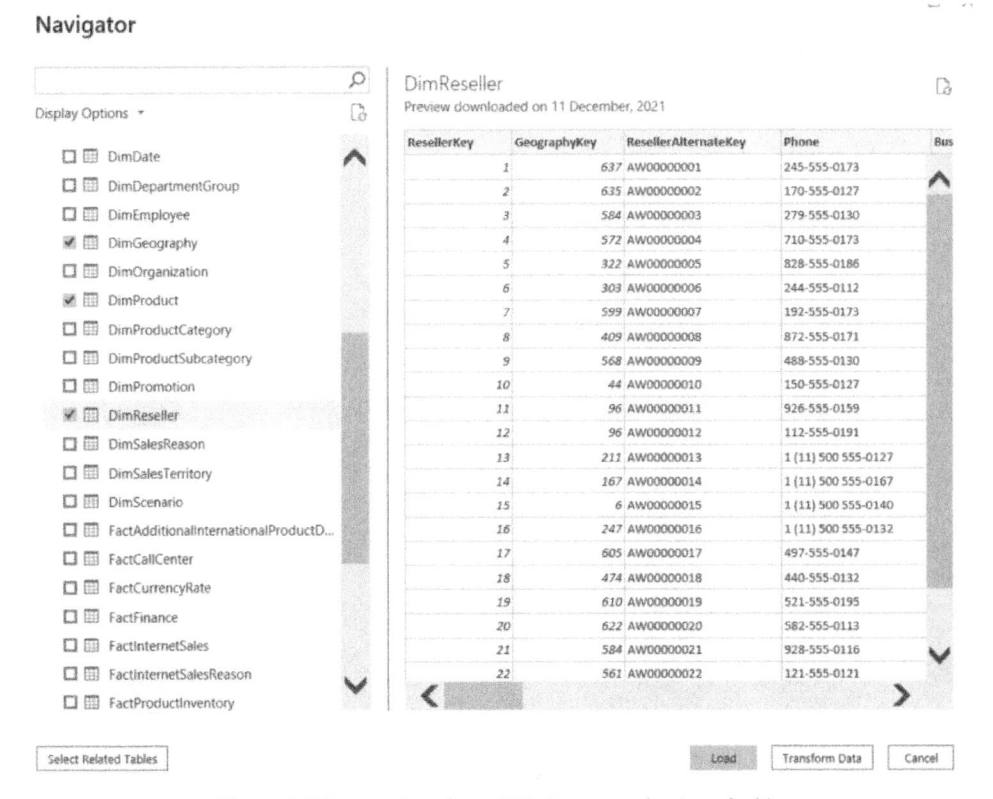

Figure 6.7: Import data from SQL Server — selection of tables

- Click "**Load**" to load the data from the three selected tables into the Power BI dataset.

Import MySQL data into Power BI

The next step will be to import some data from MySQL. MySQL comes with preinstalled sample data suitable for our scenario, so there is no need to first import any specific database. Please perform the following steps:

- In Power BI Desktop, on the ribbon, select the "**Get data**" button and then "**More...**". Switch to the "**Database**" category and select the data connector "**MySQL database**". Click "**Connect**".

- Fill in the following values:
    - **Server**: localhost
    - **Database (optional)**: world

- Please note that there is no selection for the data connectivity mode because the MySQL connector supports only the Import mode.

- Click "**OK**," according to the following screenshot:

MySQL database

Server
localhost

Database
world

> Advanced options

OK   Cancel

Figure 6.8: Import data from MySQL—configuration

- A dialog for selecting tables or views from the database `localhost.world` will be offered. Select the table: "`world.country`", as illustrated in the following screenshot:

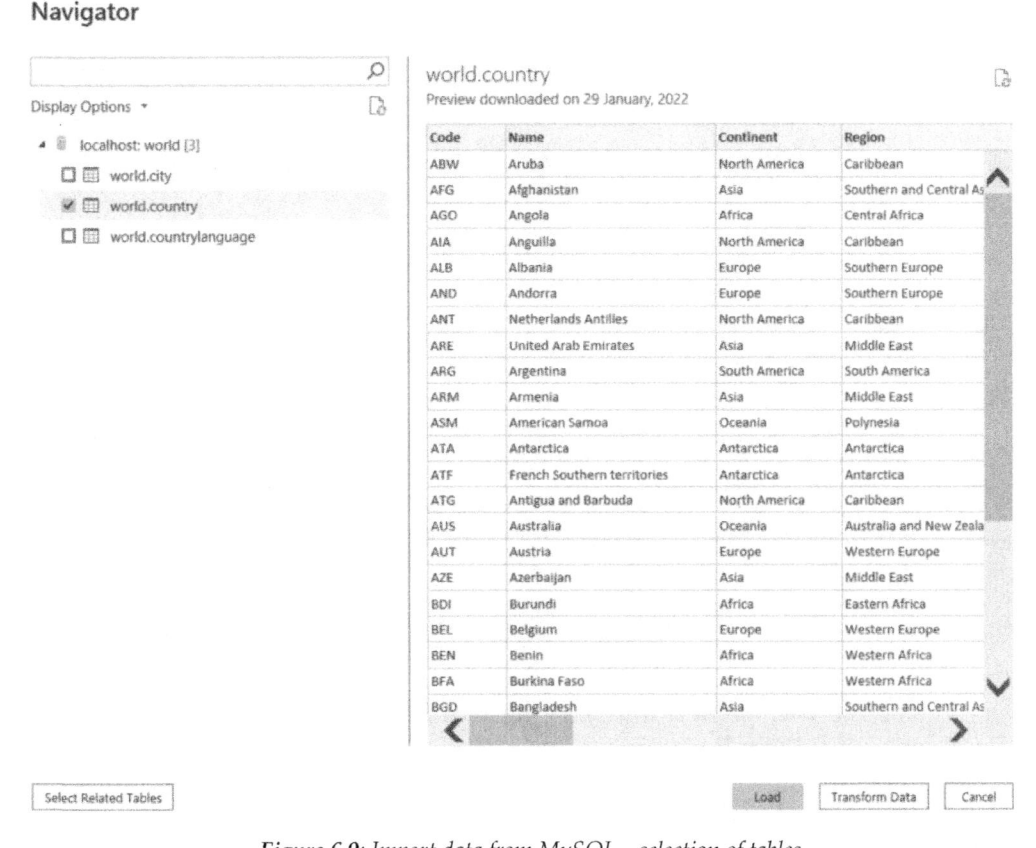

Figure 6.9: *Import data from MySQL—selection of tables*

- Click "**Load**" to load the data from the selected table into the Power BI dataset.
- Click the "**Save**" icon in the upper left corner of the Power BI Desktop to save your work. Now, you can close Power BI Desktop.

This is the last step in the exercise. We have imported all required data into Power BI and are prepared to build a consolidated data model.

Transform data with Power Query

Many times, when you import data from external data sources for your Power BI solution, the raw data is not in the required structure and need to be transformed. The best way to do it is to transform the data before it is actually loaded into Power BI Desktop so that any unnecessary or wrong data is eliminated and corrected upfront. Power BI Desktop offers a handy tool called Power Query, which can do the transformation. The tool can be started by clicking on the button "**Transform Data**" in the initial data import dialog or later directly from Power BI Desktop. When you open the tool, you will see the structure as illustrated in the following screenshot:

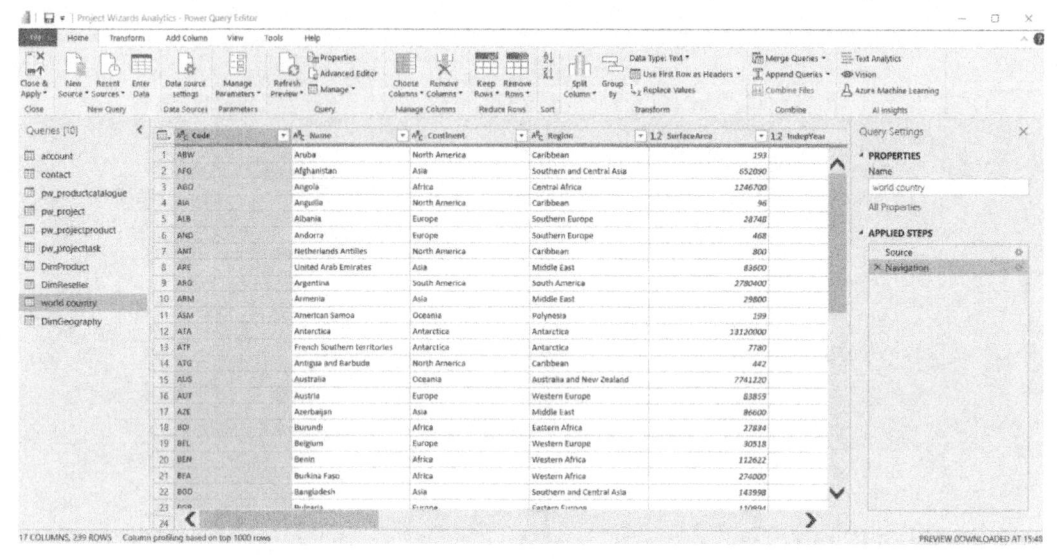

Figure 6.10: Power Query

Power Query is a very powerful tool, being able to perform a broad range of data manipulations, like the following:

- **Promote column headers:** You can transform the first row of the imported data into headers. This is very useful if you import text files, where the first row represents the column names.

- **Remove or rename columns:** You can eliminate columns for which you know that they will not be required for the solution and so save some storage space. You can also rename the columns to more meaningful names.

- **Add custom columns:** You can add custom columns with required values.

- **Split and merge columns:** You can perform a transformation by first splitting a column, then changing some values, and then merging the parts back.

- **Fill or replace column values:** You can fill columns with empty values or replace existing values with other values.

- **Group and summarize:** You can perform grouping and summarizations on table values.

- **Filter data:** You can filter data to eliminate data not needed for the solution.

- **Pivot/unpivot data:** You can pivot tables or unpivot tables to achieve the required structures of the data.

- **Transpose tables:** You can transpose tables to achieve the required structures of the data.

- **Combine data from multiple tables:** you can combine tables together to consolidate the data upfront before importing.

A nice feature of Power Query is the history of applied steps, which makes it possible to cancel some of the steps and return back to some previous steps in case we do something wrong.

Build a data model

The next step, after all the necessary data is imported into Power BI Desktop, is to build a consistent and compact data model from that raw data. This step is important to prepare the data into a final form, which can be directly used for building the visualizations. During this step, the following are the typical tasks:

- Create relationships between the tables
- Create calculated columns
- Create measures

Let us have a closer look at those most important tasks.

Create relationships between the tables

Depending on the types of data and the number of different data sources, it can happen that after we have imported the data, some of the tables are not connected. Having disconnected tables in a Power BI data model is quite unusual and does not bring value to the analytical solution, so we should always try to connect all tables with relationships.

Tables can be connected into relationships using key columns. For example, if we have a "`Customer`" table with key columns called "`Customer ID`" imported from one data source and an "Invoice" table with a key column called "`Customer Number`", and we know that the values in those two key columns are identical for the same customers, we can easily create a relationship between those tables, using the mentioned key columns.

> Note: Should those two tables be imported from the same data source, then most likely, the relationship would be automatically recognized by Power BI Desktop, and we would not need to create it manually.

Relationships between tables have certain properties, among which the most important is *cardinality*. The cardinality is something we have briefly learned in

Microsoft Dataverse, and it defines the connection type between the tables. In Power BI, there are four cardinality types:

(1) **One-to-many (1:*):** This is the most typical cardinality type, where on one side of the relationship, there is one record, and on the other side of the relation, there are multiple records. A typical example is our previous example with the customers and invoices. A customer can have multiple invoices, but an invoice can never have multiple customers.

(2) **Many-to-one (*:1):** This is just the opposite type as One-to-many, from the point of view of the table on the "*Many*" side of the relationship.

(3) **One-to-one (1:1):** This cardinality type represents a connection between single records from two tables. We can use this cardinality when we need to connect two tables from two different data sources containing similar types of information. For example, when we import two tables containing information about the customers just from two different databases, we would need to have these two connected together.

(4) **Many-to-many (*:*):** This is a rather unusual type of cardinality, where on both sides of the relationship, there can be multiple records. It is generally not recommended to use this cardinality and rather try to find a different way to connect tables together.

The next task type in the data modeling phase could be to create calculated columns.

Create calculated columns

Many times, it is required to analyze values that are not directly available in any of the tables used in the data model. But we know that those values can be calculated by using some existing values in the various other columns. For example, we have a table with sales data. In that table, there is a column representing the unit price and another column representing the quantity, but there is no column representing the total amount for that sale record. For our analytical solution, we need the total amount. For that reason, we can use the concept of calculated columns and create one. Power BI uses a specific formula language called Data Analysis Expressions (DAX) to define the calculations. With DAX, you can achieve the following:

- Create new, calculated columns in the existing tables, using many different transformations the DAX is supporting. For the previous example, we would create a calculated column with a simple multiplication formula.

- The calculations can contain columns from the main table but also columns from related tables.

- The calculations can contain logical expressions, for example, an IF expression for conditional calculations.

This concept is something very similar to the calculated columns available in Microsoft Dataverse.

The DAX language is, however, quite complex, and it is not in the scope of this book to learn it.

> Note: To learn more about DAX, please refer to the documentation: https://docs.microsoft.com/en-us/dax/

There is one more typical task in the modeling phase, the creation of measures.

Create measures

Another common requirement when building analytical solutions is to create aggregations of values in the columns, mostly in the columns containing numerical values. We know this approach from Microsoft Dataverse as well, where it is called rollup columns. But Power BI is a smart analytical tool, and the measures are many times created automatically. This happens always when we use some data from our data model in the visualizations. The visualization recognizes the data a creates a measure to represent the aggregation automatically. For example, when we have the sales table mentioned in the previous section with the unit price, quantity, and the calculated column for the total amount, we place the total amount column as the value on a bar chart. The bar chart will automatically aggregate the values and show a total amount from all sales records.

In case we need to create explicit measures, we can create them using the same DAX language as for the calculated columns.

Now, it is time for the next exercise. In the previous exercise, we imported all required data into our Power BI solution for *Project Wizards, Inc*. Now, we will continue and create a consistent data model from the imported raw data.

Exercise 13: Data modeling

In this exercise, we continue building the analytical solution by creating a proper data model from the data we imported from Microsoft Dataverse, SQL Server, and MySQL.

To start the exercise, please perform the following steps:

- Start the Power BI Desktop and close the initial pop-up window.
- Click on the upper right side on the "**Sign in**" button and sign-in with the cloud credentials you use for the exercises.

168 ■ *Microsoft Power Platform Up and Running*

- Click "**File**" and "**Open report**", and select the file "Project Wizards Analytics.pbix" you created in the previous exercise.

- On the left navigation pane, switch to the "Model" view. If you have not implemented the advanced part of *Exercise 12*, then you will see the same structure as in *figure 6.5*.

- If you have implemented the advanced part, rearrange the tables in the view in a structure as documented in the following screenshot:

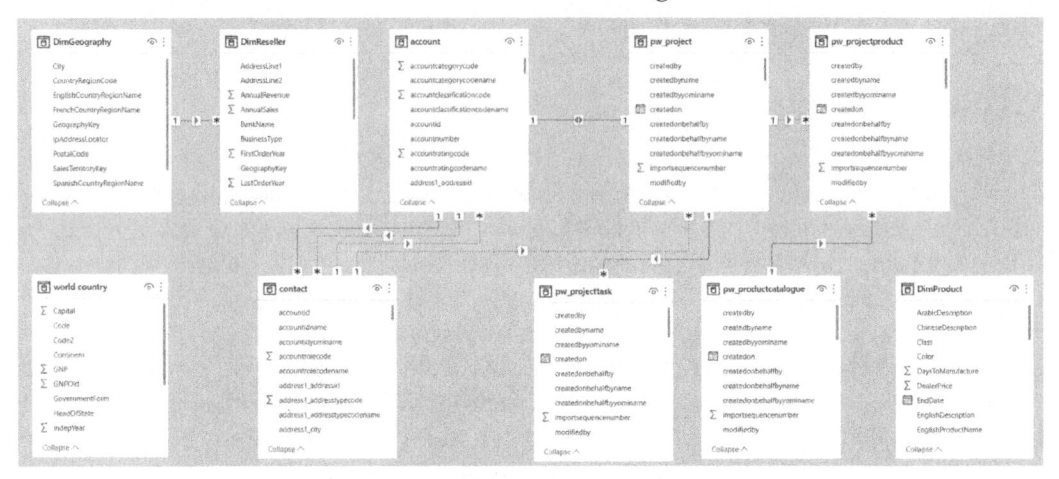

Figure 6.11: Full data model, including the advanced part

As you can see in *figure 6.11*, not all tables are already connected with the proper relationships. The tables from Microsoft Dataverse are connected since the Microsoft Dataverse connector has recognized and recreated the relationships. The same applies to the two SQL Server tables, "**DimGeography**" and "**DimReseller**". But the relationships between tables coming from different data sources are not connected. The next task will be to create those missing relationships.

We will need to create the following three additional relationships:

- A relationship between the table "**DimReseller**" from SQL Server and the table "account" from Microsoft Dataverse. The data we have imported at the beginning of *Chapter 2, Building Enterprise Solutions with Power Apps*, into the "**account**" table in Microsoft Dataverse are originally coming from the table "**DimReseller**" from SQL Server, so we can now easily create a relationship using the corresponding key columns. Those columns are as follows:

    o **DimReseller**: ResellerAlternateKey

    o **account**: accountnumber

- A relationship between the table "**DimGeography**" from SQL Server and the table "**world country**" from MySQL. There are no direct key columns we can use for creating the relationship, so we need to use the columns containing the name of the country in both tables:
    - **DimGeography**: EnglishCountryRegionName
    - **world country**: Name
- A relationship between the table "**DimProduct**" from SQL Server and the table "**pw_productcatalogue**" from Microsoft Dataverse. The data we have imported at the beginning into the "**pw_productcatalogue**" table in Microsoft Dataverse is originally coming from the table "**DimProduct**" from SQL Server, so we can now easily create a relationship using the corresponding key columns. Those columns are as follows:
    - **DimProduct**: ProductAlternateKey
    - **pw_productcatalogue**: pw_productid

For creating the relationships, please perform the following steps:

- Drag the column "**ResellerAlternateKey**" from the table "**DimReseller**" and drop it onto the column "**accountnumber**" in the table "**account**". Power BI Desktop will correctly recognize that this relationship needs to have the cardinality "On-to-one (1:1)". This is because in both tables, there are records about customers, and in each of both tables, there is always only one record with the same customer number.

- Drag the column "**Name**" from the table "**world country**" and drop it onto the column "**EnglishCountryRegionName**" in the table "**DimGeography**". Power BI Desktop will correctly recognize that this relationship needs to have the cardinality *"One-to-many (1:*)"*, where the table "**world country**" is on the "One" side and the table "**DimGeography**" on the "many" side. This is because in the table "**world country**", there is just one record for every country, whereas in the table "**DimGeography**", there are multiple customer records with the same country.

- Drag the column "**ProductAlternateKey**" from the table "**DimProduct**" and drop it onto the column "**pw_productid**" in the table "**pw_productcatalogue**". Power BI Desktop will recognize that this relationship needs to have the cardinality *"One-to-many (1:*)"*, where the table "**pw_productcatalogue**" is on the "One" side and the table "**DimProduct**" on the "many" side. This is because in the table "**pw_productcatalogue**", there is just one record with the same product ID, whereas in the table "**DimProduct**", there are multiple records with the same product ID. This could be an issue for our analytical solution, so we would need to consider this when building the visualizations in the upcoming chapter.

- The final data model should look like as shown in the following screenshot:

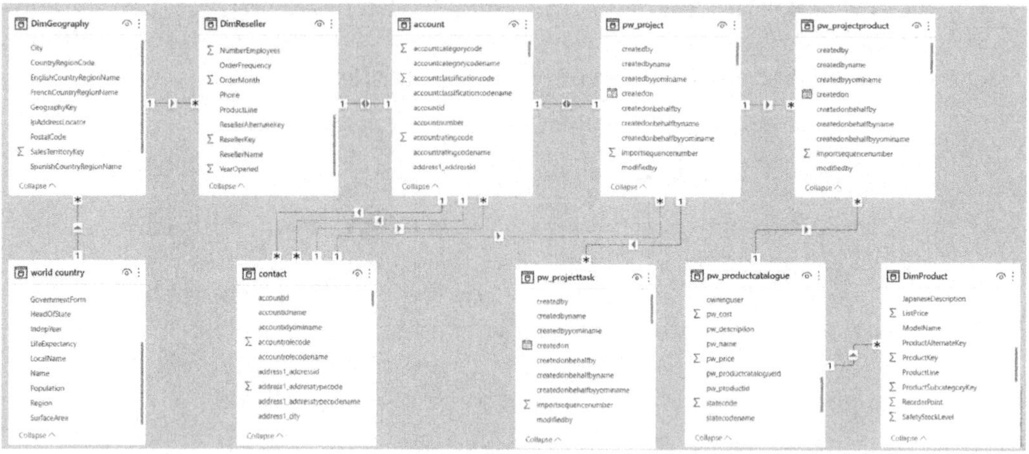

Figure 6.12: Full data model with all required relationships

In the next part of this exercise, we are going to examine the whole data model and verify whether all relationship settings are correct.

Everything seems to be correct, with one exception. Power BI Desktop has created an "*On-to-one (1:1)*" relationship between the tables "**account**" and "**pw_project**". This happened because, by coincidence, in the sample data we have imported into the tables, every project is related to a different customer, and Power BI thought there should be this type of cardinality. This is, however, wrong, and the analytical solution would not work when we create multiple projects for the same customer. To correct this, please perform the following steps:

- Select the relationship with the mouse, click on the right mouse button, and select "**Properties**".

- Since the table "**pw_project**" is the first in the relationship settings, change the cardinality to "*Many to one (*:1)*", as illustrated in the following screenshot:

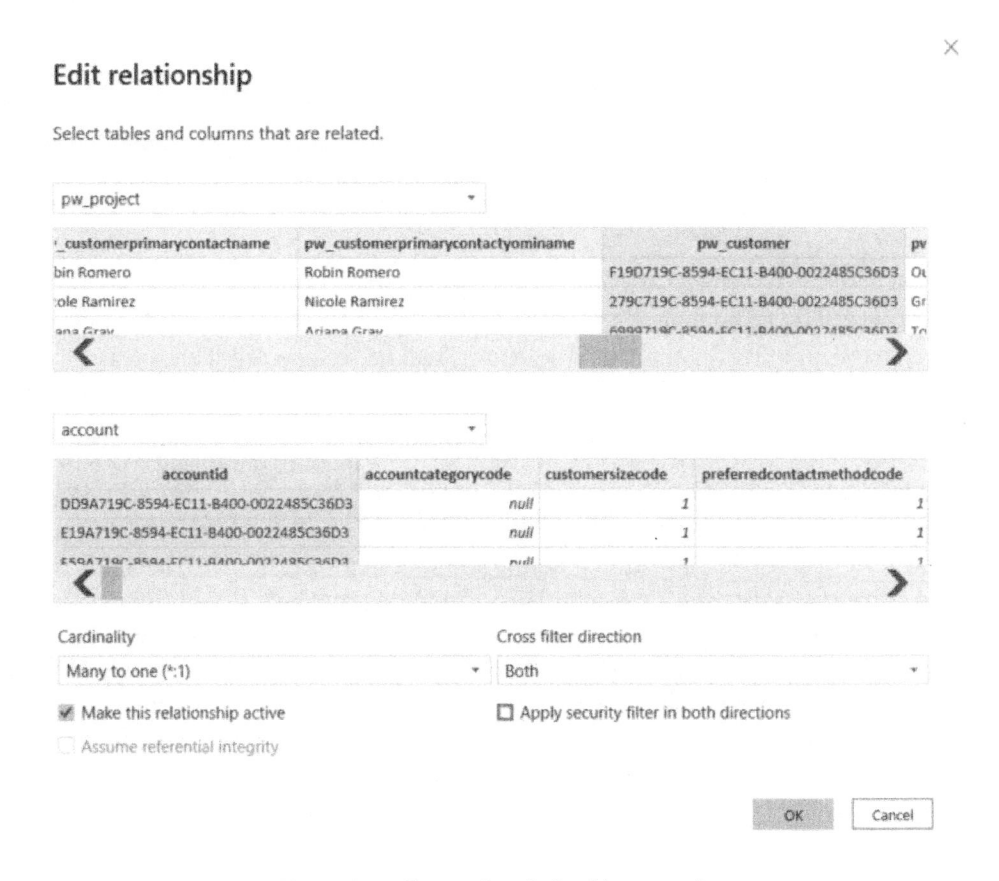

Figure 6.13: Change the relationship properties

- Click "**OK**". The change will be performed, and the final and correct data model should look like as shown in the following screenshot:

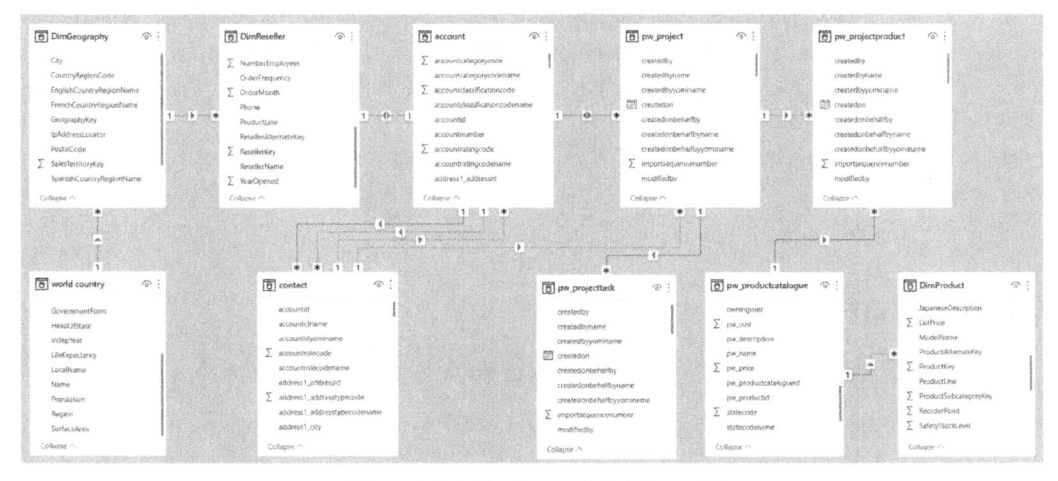

Figure 6.14: Final corrected data model

This is the last task in this exercise.

Congratulations! You have successfully imported data from different data sources and created a consistent data model, which can be used in the upcoming chapter for building the final analytical solution.

Conclusion

In this chapter, you have learned the basics of Power BI and some more details about the first part of creating an analytical solution. You have seen what are the typical use cases for Power BI and how Power BI can enhance a Power Platform-based business solution. You have made yourself familiar with the basic concepts of Power BI, its components, what Power BI consists of, and the tools used to create and consume the analytical solutions. In the next part, we presented the two fundamental methods, how data can be handled in Power BI, what are the benefits of those two and how to choose the right one for a solution. Next, you have learned the main tool a Power BI developer needs to use, the Power BI Desktop. After that, we dived deeper into the first step required for building the analytics—the connection to data and the Import of data required for the solution. In this section, you could prove yourself in the practical exercise by connecting to Microsoft Dataverse and importing the project management data into Power BI Desktop. This exercise has also an advanced part, in which we have imported some more data from additional two data sources. The next topic we have analyzed is the possibility of performing data transformations using the tool Power Query. In the last section of this chapter, we have seen what comes next; after the raw data for the analytical solution is imported—we have examined the possibilities to build a data model. In this section, we have, for the second time, performed a practical exercise by finalizing our data model with new relationships and correcting an existing one.

In the upcoming chapter, we will continue working through Power BI. We will make ourselves familiar with the Power BI visualizations and how they are used to build a Power BI report. Next, you will learn how to publish a finished report into the Power BI cloud and what can happen next. You will see how to create a dashboard and use some of the advanced capabilities of Power BI, like the natural language queries. Finally, you will learn how to integrate Power BI with Power Apps and Power Automate.

Questions

1. What types of analytic and reporting solutions do you know?
2. What are the main components and building blocks of Power BI?

3. What are the main end-to-end steps a Power BI developer needs to take when building an analytical solution?
4. What are the main differences, benefits, and disadvantages between an Import mode and a DirectQuery mode in Power BI?
5. What is the main structure of the Power BI Desktop tool?
6. How is Power BI Desktop connecting to the different data sources?
7. What are the possibilities to transform data with the Power Query tool?
8. What needs to be done after the raw data is imported to create a consistent data model?
9. What types of cardinalities does Power BI support?
10. What is the difference between calculated columns and measures, and what are they used for?

CHAPTER 7
Integrate Analytics with Power BI

Introduction

In this chapter, we will continue by diving deeper into the Power BI cloud service to help you understand how to create a final analytical solution. We will provide an overview of possible visualizations used for various analytical scenarios. In the next part, you will learn how Power BI analytics can be integrated with model-driven apps, canvas apps, portal apps, and Power Automate.

Structure

In this chapter, we will discuss the following topics:

- Power BI visualizations overview
- Create a Power BI report
- Publish a Power BI report
- Create Power BI dashboards
- Use natural language query
- Integrate analytics with apps and flows

Objectives

After reading this chapter, you will be able to understand which visualization types are available when building Power BI reports. You will learn the details about creating reports, placing visualizations, and configuring the visualizations properties. Here, you will have the possibility to work on the next practical exercise by building a report for Project Wizards, Inc. In the next part, you will see how to publish a final Power BI Report into the Power BI service, which will also be practically implemented with your report. Then, you will dive deeper into the various capabilities of the Power BI service, specifically the possibility to create dashboards or to use the natural language query capability. At this point, you will create a dashboard for your analytical solution. At the end of this chapter, you will learn what are the various possibilities to integrate Power BI with other Power Platform components, and you will then embed your dashboard into the Project Management model-driven app.

Power BI visualizations overview

The real power of the Power BI service is the visualization capabilities. Power BI can present the business data in a very broad variety of ways, from the simplest line charts, bar charts, or pie charts up to complex visualizations such as key influencers diagrams or decomposition tree diagrams. A huge benefit of the product is a large library of additional visualizations from Microsoft but also from third-party developers, which can be found in the AppSource repository.

> Note: Microsoft AppSource is a repository of various add-ons for all products from the Microsoft Power Platform family. You can find AppSource under the following URL: https://appsource.microsoft.com/

Let us now have a look at the typical visualizations and their main purpose and parameters.

> Note: Feel free to try it yourself and verify whether you would be able to implement the examples without a previous theoretical introduction on how to do that. A practical guided example for using visualizations will follow in the next section.

Bar and column charts

Bar and column charts present the data in an easy understandable way since the size of the bars or the columns represents the value of the respective numerical data column, and the number and labeling of the bars or columns represent the categories into which we divide the whole dataset.

Following are three examples of bar and column charts, based on the tables "`Project Product (pw_projectproduct)`" and "`Project Catalogue (pw_projectcatalogue)`" from our data model, using the columns "`Product Name`", "`Total Cost`", and "`Total Price`". Please refer to the following figure:

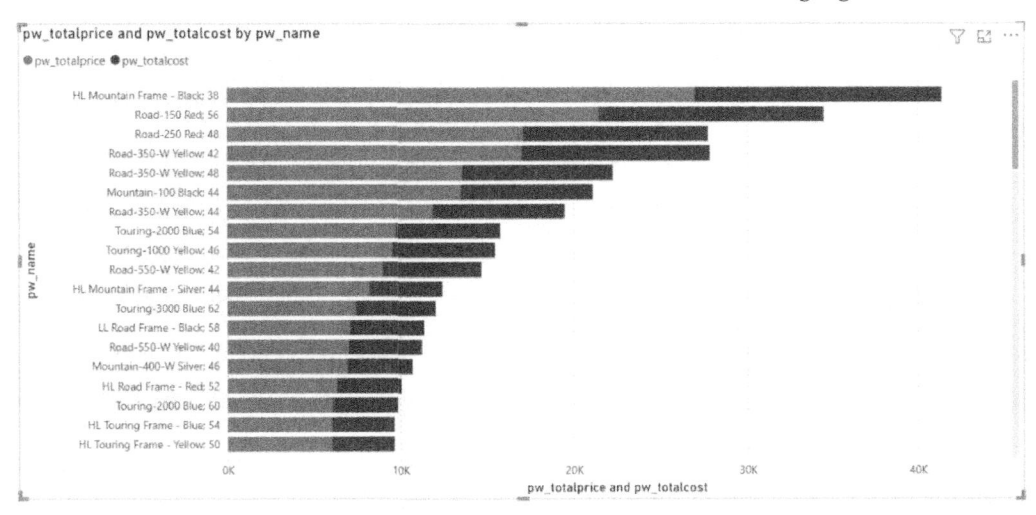

Figure 7.1: Stacked bar chart example

As you can see in *figure 7.1*, it is an example of a typical stacked bar chart, where the values, in this case, the Total Cost and Total Price, are stacked into a single bar. Please refer to the following figure:

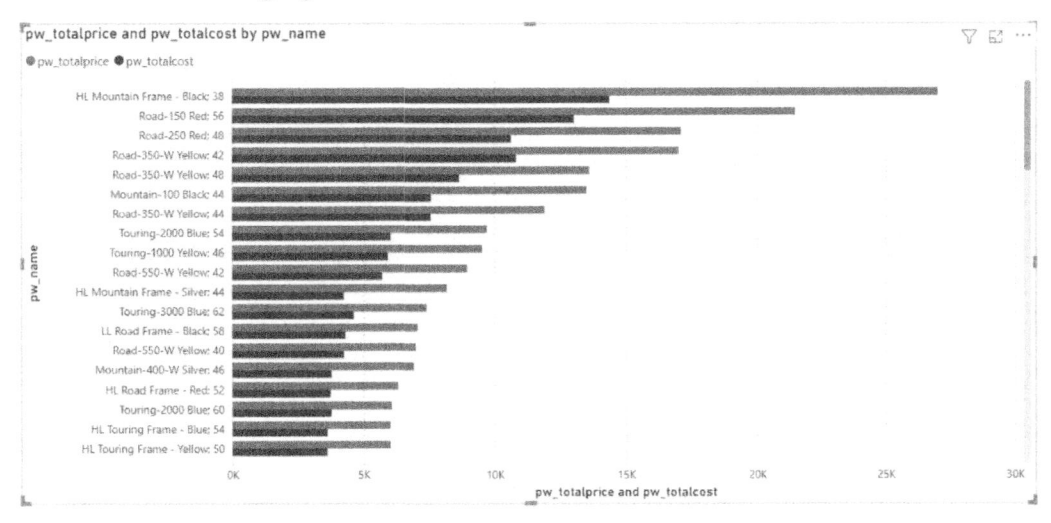

Figure 7.2: Clustered bar chart example

As you can see in *figure 7.2*, the clustered chart is different. With the same two facts, the bars are placed below each other, which gives a good opportunity to compare the values. Please refer to the following figure:

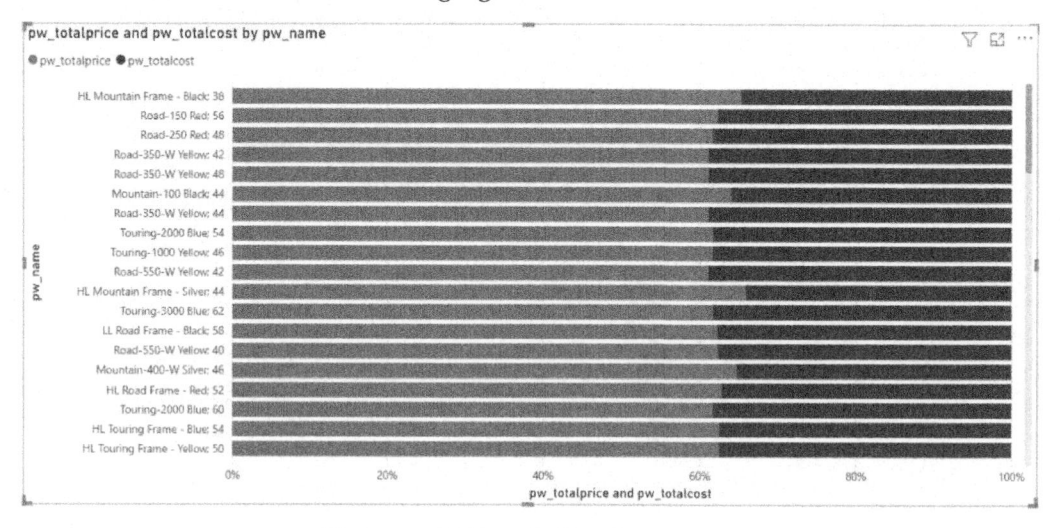

Figure 7.3: 100% stacked bar chart example

As you can see in the last example, in *Figure 7.3*, there could be even a 100% stacked bar chart, where again, the same two facts are visualized always with the same total length. For this type of chart, you can compare the relative distribution of the two fact values for every dimension value.

Line and area charts

Although bar and column charts are typically used to present data distributed across general categories, line and area charts are more suitable to present data based on a timeline, usually configured on the X-axis.

Following are two examples of line and area charts, based on the table "**DimReseller**" from our data model, using the columns "**YearOpened**", "**AnnualSales**", and "**AnnualRevenue**". Please refer to the following figure:

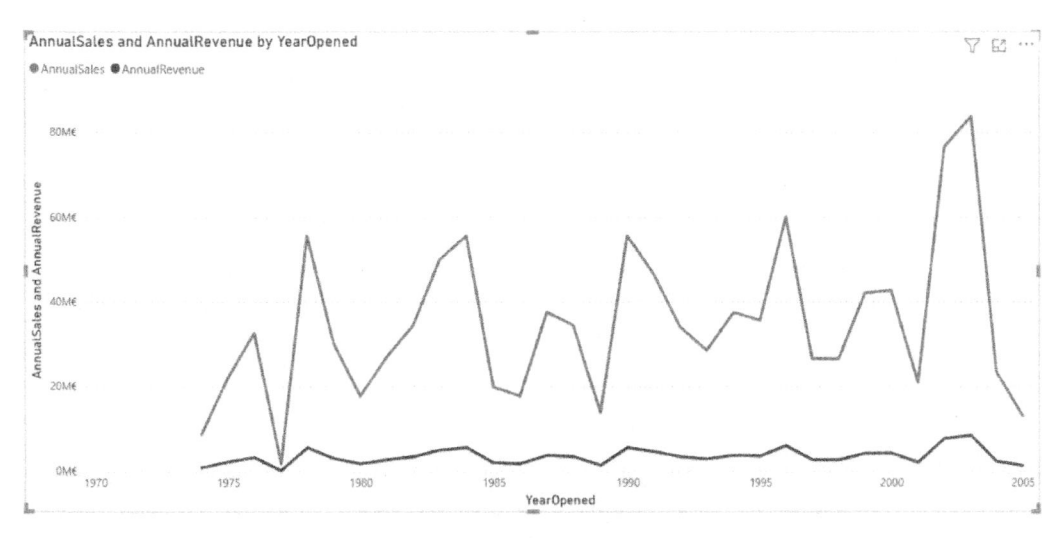

Figure 7.4: Line chart example

As you can see in *figure 7.4*, you can use multiple fact values to be visualized on one chart. This gives you the possibility to compare the values. Please refer to the following figure:

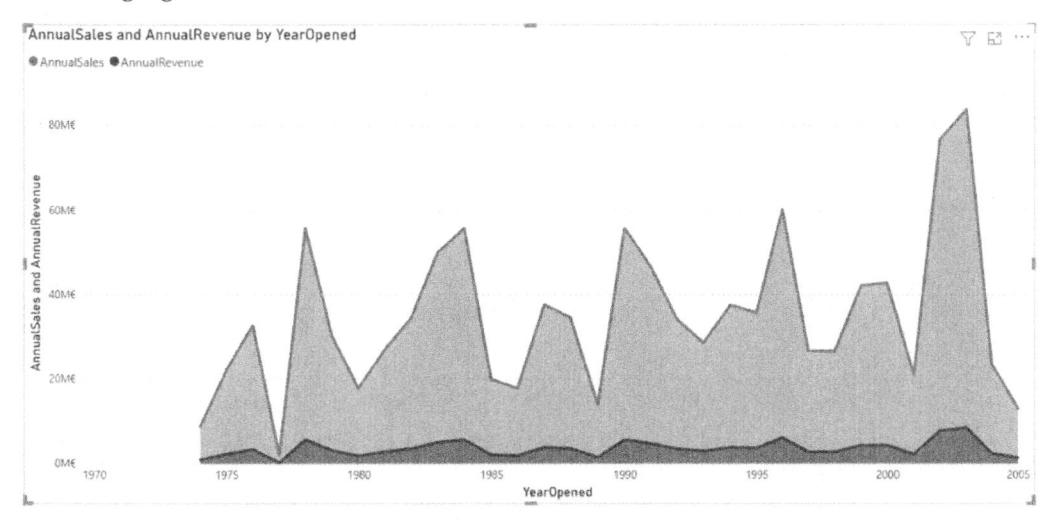

Figure 7.5: Area chart example

In *figure 7.4*, you can see the same example, however, using the area chart. This chart type is specifically presenting the *"volume"* of the facts data over the values of the dimension.

Ribbon charts

Ribbon charts are used to visualize data with the goal of discovering which data category has the highest value over different values on the X-axis. As with the line and area charts, the ribbon chart is also in many cases uses timeline data on the X-axis.

Waterfall charts

A **waterfall chart** is typically used to demonstrate increments or decrements of values from the first initial value until the last value, with timeline data on the X-axis. This type of chart is often used to document financial data, for example, the development the yearly or monthly revenue.

The following is an example of a waterfall chart, based on the table "`DimReseller`" from our data model, using the columns "`YearOpened`" and "`AnnualRevenue`":

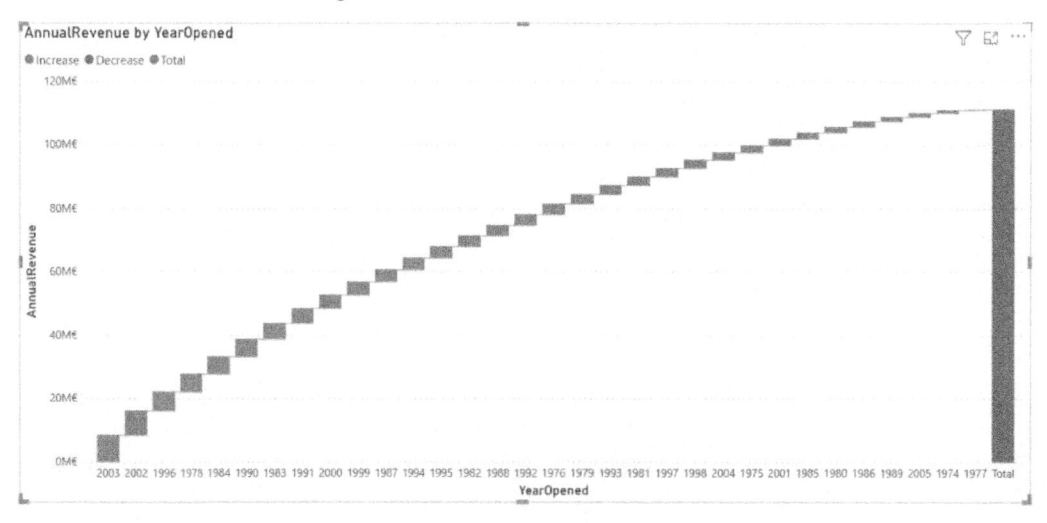

Figure 7.6: Waterfall chart example

Funnel charts

Funnel charts are used to visualize processes and demonstrate values per process stage. That is why they are very popular in sales-related business applications, where they provide the *"sales funnel"* showing the sales staff the estimated revenue in the sales pipeline per sales stage.

The following is an example of a funnel chart, based on the table "**DimReseller**" from our data model, using the columns "**YearOpened**" and "**AnnualRevenue**". This is not the typical use of the funnel chart but can still demonstrate the capabilities of this chart type:

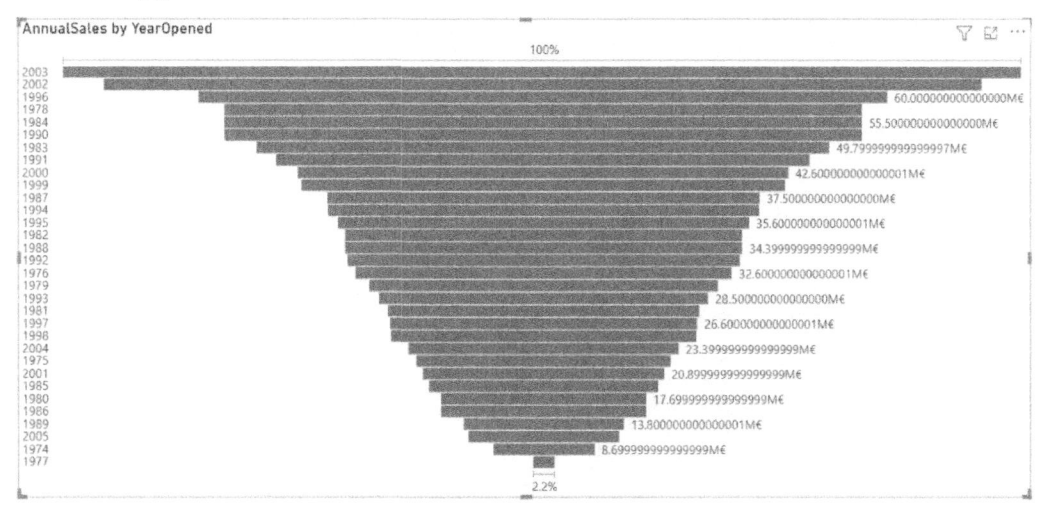

Figure 7.7: Funnel chart example

Scatter charts

Scatter charts are typically showing certain data representations depending on two values (represented by the X-axis and Y-axis). A variation of the scatter chart is called a bubble chart, which can bring a third dimension of the data, represented by the size of the bubble on the chart.

For better understanding, the following is an example of an analysis configured with the values of the tables "**DimReseller**" and "**DimGeography**" from our data model. The first example is demonstrating a scatter chart showing the "**AnnualRevenue**" of companies based on the "**StateProvinceName**" column. For better graphical representation, the chart is extended with a color-based legend, showing the data from distinct "**EnglishCountryRegionName**" values represented with different colors. The second example is a bubble chart, where the same data is enriched with the "**NumberEmployees**" values represented as sizes of the bubbles instead of just dots:

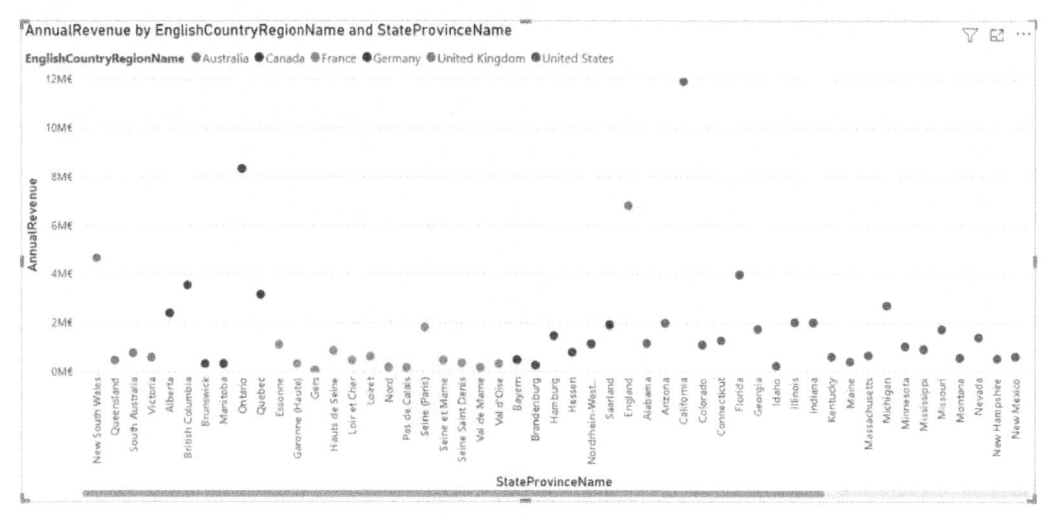

Figure 7.8: Scatter chart example

As you can see in *figure 7.8*, the scatter chart shows the revenue values only but distributed across states or provinces of the analyzed countries. Please refer to the following figure:

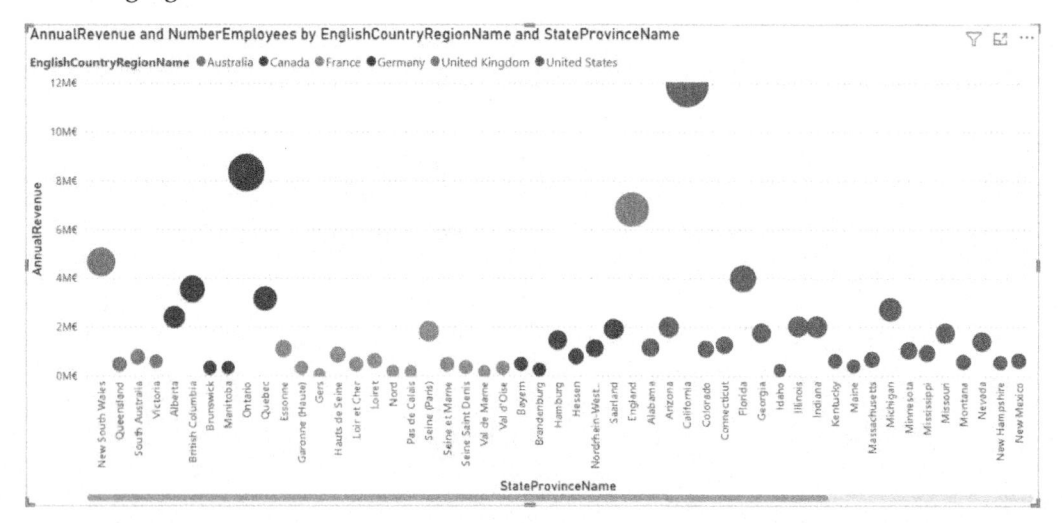

Figure 7.9: Bubble chart example

The bubble chart, presented in *figure 7.9*, adds a new fact to the visualization, which is the number of employees. This is shown by the size of the bubbles.

Pie and donut charts

Pie and donut charts are almost identical, and the main purpose is to present the relationship or relative portion of multiple parts of a whole value.

The following is an example of a donut chart, based on the tables "**DimReseller**" and "**DimGeography**" from our data model, using the columns "**EnglishCountryRegionName**" and "**AnnualRevenue**". Please refer to the following figure:

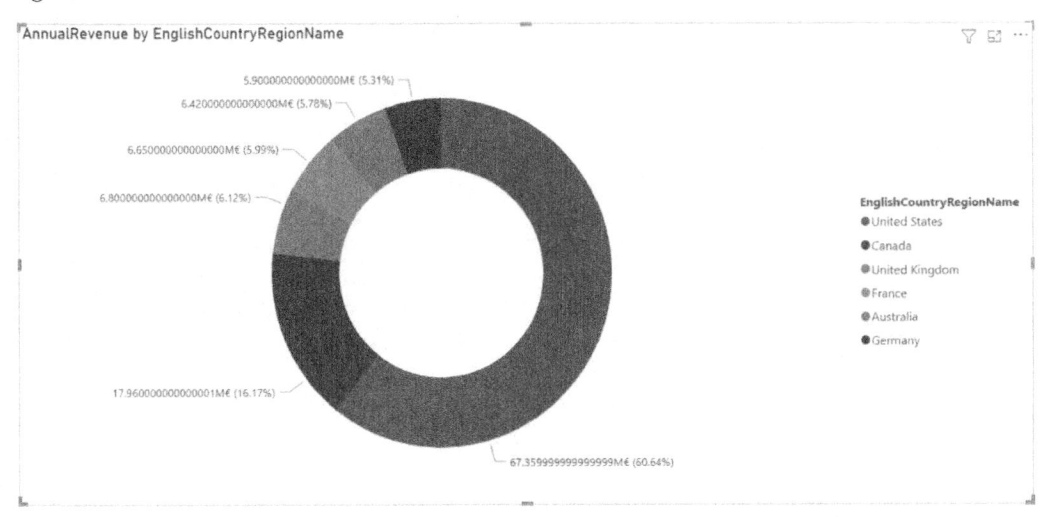

Figure 7.10: Donut chart example

Maps, filled maps, and shape maps

Power BI contains multiple mapping visualizations, which are typically used to present data based on geographical distribution. This is used for sales-related or other analysis, where we want to understand the values achieved in countries or geographical regions.

184 ■ *Microsoft Power Platform Up and Running*

Following are two examples of a bubble map and filled map, both based on the tables "**DimReseller**" and "**DimGeography**" from our data model, using the columns "**EnglishCountryRegionName**", "**StateProvinceName**", and "**AnnualRevenue**":

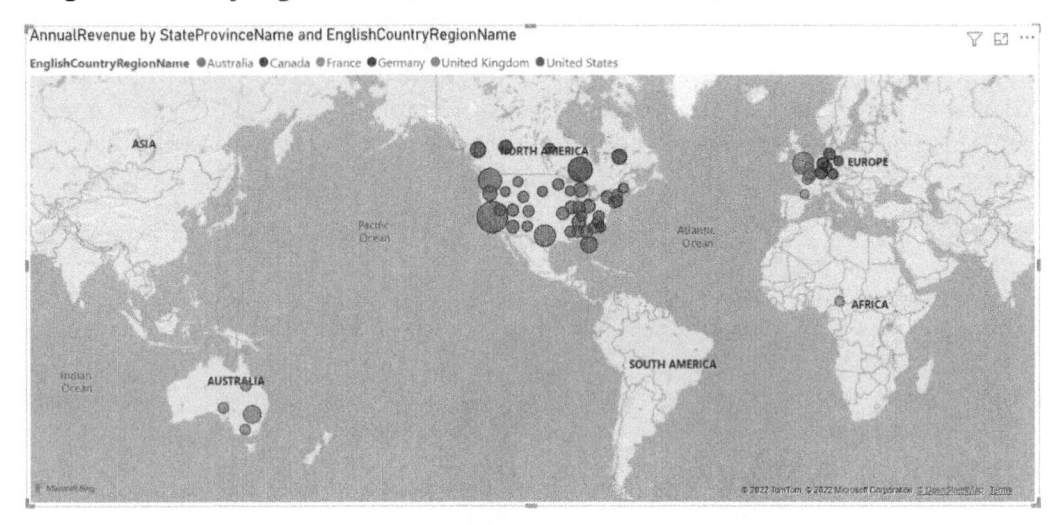

Figure 7.11: Bubble map example

As you can see in *figure 7.11*, the bubble map shows the revenue values as bubbles of different sizes. Please refer to the following figure:

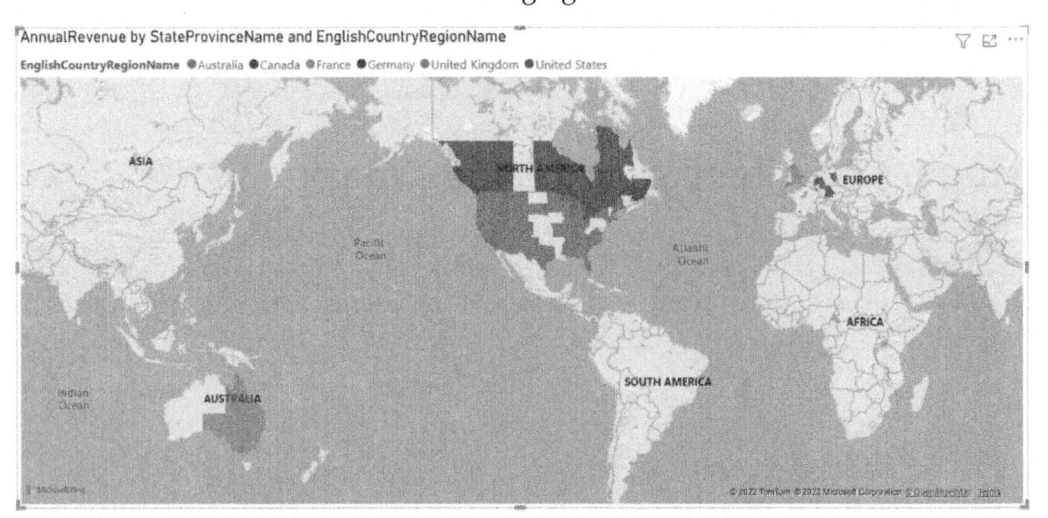

Figure 7.12: Shape map example

The shape map, presented in *figure 7.12*, shows the same data, but the revenue value is now implemented using the darkness of the shape of the map.

Treemaps

Treemaps show data on a rectangle consisting of smaller rectangles. The size of the smaller rectangles inside a treemap represents the analyzed values.

Following is an example of a treemap, based on the tables "`DimReseller`" and "`DimGeography`" from our data model, using the columns "**StateProvinceName**" and "**AnnualRevenue**":

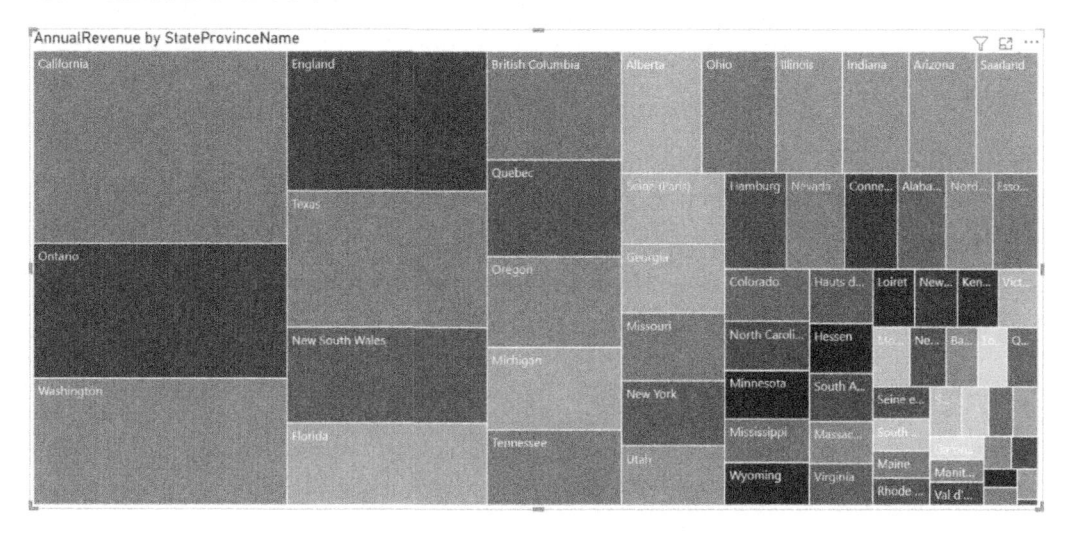

Figure 7.13: Treemap example

Other chart types

Besides the mentioned charts, there is much more Power BI can offer to support the right analytics to represent the business data. Here are a few more examples:

- **Slicers:** Slicers are used to provide an advanced filtering component to the report. Slicers are connected with some values from the dataset, which should be used to offer filtering to the end users.

- **Gauges:** Gauges are used to visualize a single value on a scale between minimum and maximum. The visualization is mainly used to demonstrate the current progress towards a goal value.

- **Tables and matrixes:** Tables and matrices are not charts but rather usual numerical representations of data from the dataset. Tables are able to show data from a dataset enhanced with headers, total values, and colored components, such as bubbles, foreground, or background colors. Matrices are enhanced tables, supporting more than just two dimensions as in usual tables.

- **KPIs**: KPIs are used to display one single numerical value, optionally accompanied by a goal value toward which the KPI value is heading.
- **Key influencers charts**: Key influencer chart is a complex chart showing which factors in the underlying data influenced most of the selected key metrics. For example, which factors influence the decision of our customers to place a second order or to provide positive feedback in a survey we offer them.
- **Decomposition tree charts**: A decomposition tree is another example of a complex chart, enabling multiple steps drilling down into data to gain additional insight into data not visible in a usual way.

Now, after we have seen how many possible types of visualizations can be found in Power BI, we will drive our attention to more practical aspects of creating the Power BI reports.

Create a Power BI report

Creating a Power BI report is the next step after we have successfully imported and transformed the data and created a consistent data model. This step is completely implemented using Power BI Desktop and consists of adding and configuring visualizations on the reporting canvas.

A Power BI report can consist of multiple pages. Depending on the number of planned visualizations, it is necessary to create the corresponding number of pages and give those pages meaningful names because they will be displayed to the end user in the Power BI service. Depending on the size of the visualizations, it is possible to place one or multiple visualizations on one page. Some visualizations are always small, like the KPIs or gauges; others need to be large because they present a large amount of data.

Every visualization needs to be configured to display exactly the right analytical view of the data. The configuration is performed on the configuration pane. Besides the basic configuration, which is typically very simple, there are always also many additional advanced configurations.

Now is again the best time to start something practical. In the next exercise, you will build and configure a Power BI report with the data from our data model.

Exercise 14: Building a report

In this exercise, we are going to build the Power BI report. Since we have imported data in the standard part of *Exercise 12* in *Chapter 6, Start with Power BI* from Microsoft Dataverse, and in the advanced part also from Microsoft SQL Server and MySQL, we will create two groups of visualizations. The first group will contain only data from Microsoft Dataverse, and the second will contain data from the additional data sources as well.

For the implementation, please perform the following steps:

1. Start the Power BI Desktop and close the initial pop-up window.
2. If not signed-in, click on the upper right side on the "**Sign in**" button and sign-in with the cloud credentials you use for the exercises.
3. Click "**File**" and "**Open report**" and select the file "**Project Wizards Analytics.pbix**".
4. You should be already in the "**Report**" area in Power BI Desktop; if not, navigate to that area using the left-side navigation buttons.
5. In the lower part of the report canvas, you will see the first page of the report with the name "**Page 1**". Double-click on the name and rename the page to "**Standard**".
6. The available visualizations are on the right side of the pane with the name "**Visualizations**". Right from the "**Visualizations**" pane, there is another pane with the name "**Fields**", which contains all the dataset tables in our report. You can expand every table to see the columns contained in the table. The columns are, however, presented with the schema (technical) names and not the display names. The technical column names are also automatically used in every visualization we place on the report page and configure. In order to equip the visualizations with more user-friendly names, we can rename the columns we plan to use. We will rename all required columns as a first step before we select and configure every visualization.
7. Expand the table "**pw_projectproduct**" to see all the columns. Rename the following columns by locating the column, double-clicking on the column, and renaming. Confirm the rename with the ENTER key and wait a few seconds after the rename is finished:
    - Rename "**pw_totalcost**" to "**Total cost**"
    - Rename "**pw_totalprice**" to "**Total price**"
8. Expand the table "**pw_productcatalogue**" to see all the columns. Rename the following columns by locating the column, double-clicking on the column, and renaming:
    - Rename "**pw_name**" to "**Product**"
9. Click on the visualization "**Clustered bar chart**" in the "**Visualization**" pane. This will place the visualization in the upper left corner of the canvas. In

188 ■ *Microsoft Power Platform Up and Running*

the lower part of the "**Visualization**" pane, you will find the configuration fields. Drag and drop the dataset columns to the configuration fields:

- Y-axis: "**Product**" from the table "**pw_productcatalogue**"
- X-axis: "**Total cost**" and then "**Total price**" from the table "**pw_projectproduct**"

10. Verify that the configuration corresponds to the following screenshot:

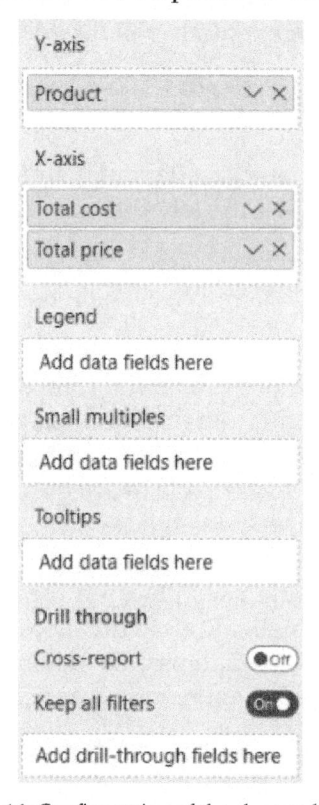

Figure 7.14: Configuration of the clustered bar chart

11. The size of the visualization is, by default, very small. Make the visualization larger by dragging the right and bottom edges to make it occupy the full upper left quadrant of the canvas, according to the following screenshot:

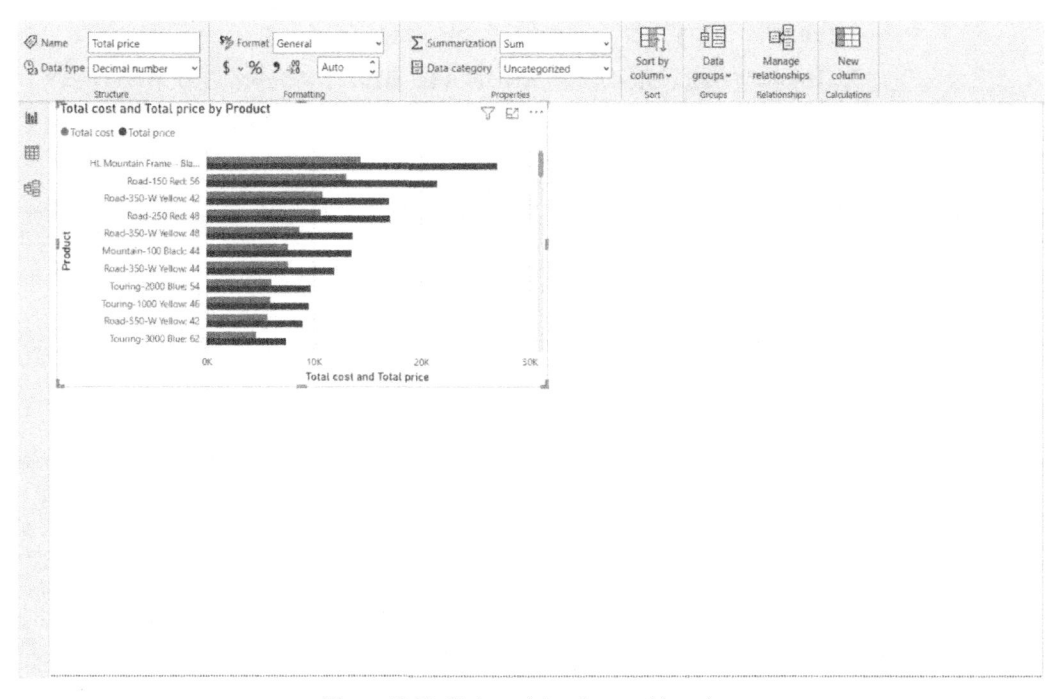

Figure 7.15: Sizing of the clustered bar chart

12. So, what is the first visualization representing? It is an analytical view of the products used in the projects of Project Wizards, Inc. showing which products are contributing the most revenue and at the same time generating the highest cost.

13. Next, click with the mouse away from the visualization so that it is no more selected.

14. Expand the table "**pw_project**" to see all the columns. Rename the following columns by locating the column, double-clicking on the column, and renaming:
    o Rename "**pw_name**" to "**Project**"
    o Rename "**pw_totalworkcost**" to "**Total Cost of Work**"
    o Rename "**pw_totalworkprice**" to "**Total Revenue of Work**"

15. Click on the visualization "**Donut chart**" in the "**Visualization**" pane. This will place the visualization below the first visualization on the canvas. In the lower part of the "**Visualization**" pane, you will find the configuration fields. Drag and drop the dataset columns to the configuration fields:

- Legend: "**Project**" from the table "**pw_project**"
- Values: "**Total Revenue of Work**" from the table "**pw_project**"

16. Verify that the report corresponds to the following screenshot:

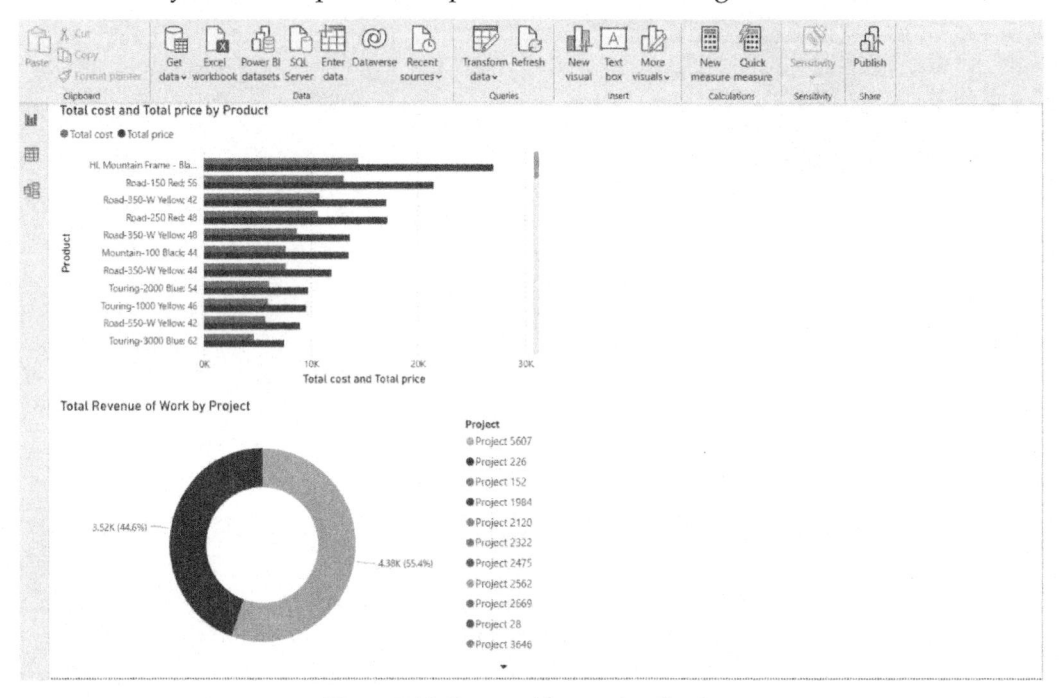

Figure 7.16: Report with two visualizations

17. So, what is the visualization representing? It is an analytical view of the projects of Project Wizards, Inc. showing the labor revenue split of the respective projects. You may be wondering why there are not all projects in the analysis and why are the revenue values so low? Remember the logic of the Project Management application—the revenue for labor is calculated only for project tasks that are completed and approved. The more tasks you flag as completed and approved, the more and higher values will be visible in this visualization.

18. Next, click with the mouse away from the visualization so that it is no more selected.

19. Expand the table "**pw_project**" to see all the columns. Rename the following columns by locating the column, double-clicking on the column, and renaming:
    - Rename "**pw_customername**" to "**Customer**"
    - Rename "**pw_number**" to "**Project Number**"

20. Click on the visualization "**Table**" in the "**Visualization**" pane. This will place the visualization right to the first visualization on the canvas. In the lower part of the "**Visualization**" pane, you will find the configuration fields. Drag and drop the following dataset columns from the table "**pw_project**" to the "**Columns**" field:
    - Customer
    - Project Number
    - Project
    - Total Cost of Work
    - Total Revenue of Work

21. So, what is the visualization representing? It is a table view on the "**Project**" table containing the selected columns. The table visualization places the column names in the first row and also a summary of every numerical column in the last row.

22. Next, click with the mouse away from the visualization so that it is no more selected.

23. Expand the table "**pw_projecttask**" to see all the columns. Rename the following columns by locating the column, double-clicking on the column, and renaming:
    - Rename "**pw_name**" to "**Task**"
    - Rename "**pw_totalprice**" to "**Revenue**"

24. Click on the visualization "**Treemap**" in the "**Visualization**" pane. This will place the visualization below the third visualization on the canvas. In the lower part of the "**Visualization**" pane, you will find the configuration fields. Drag and drop the dataset columns to the configuration fields:
    - **Category**: "**Task**" from the table "**pw_projecttask**"
    - **Values**: "**Revenue**" from the table "**pw_projecttask**"

192 ■ *Microsoft Power Platform Up and Running*

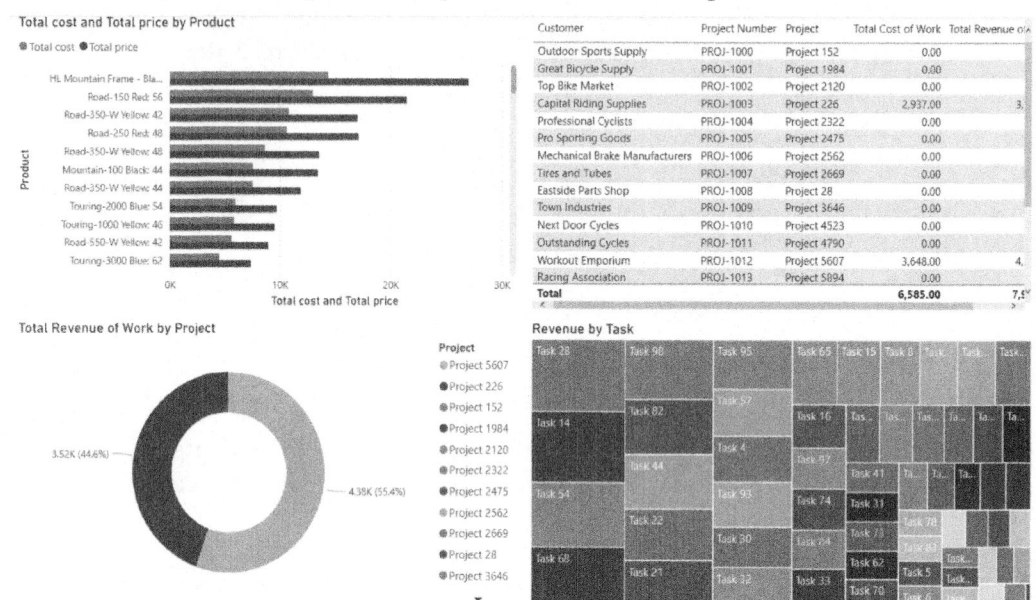

25. Verify that the report corresponds to the following screenshot:

Figure 7.17: Final report structure on the "Standard" page

26. So, what is the visualization representing? It is an analytical view of the project tasks of Project Wizards, Inc. showing the labor revenue on a treemap, where the revenue values of the respective tasks are visually represented by the size of the blocks.

27. Click on the "**Save**" icon in the upper left corner of Power BI Desktop to save the final solution.

With this last step, the standard part of the report is finished. In the next steps, we are going to enhance the report with some more visualizations, requiring data from the two additional data sources, which were imported in the advanced part of *Exercise 12* in *Chapter 6, Start with Power BI*.

Please perform the following steps:

1. In the "**Report**" area in Power BI Desktop, click on the "**+**" sign right from the first report page, "**Standard**". This will create a second page. Double-click on the name of the second page and rename it to "**Advanced**".

2. Select the "**Advanced**" page.

3. Click on the visualization "**Clustered bar chart**" in the "**Visualization**" pane. This will place the visualization in the upper left part of the canvas. In the lower part of the "**Visualization**" pane, you will find the configuration fields. Drag and drop the dataset columns to the configuration fields:

- Y-axis: "**Product Line**" from the table "**DimProduct**"
- X-axis: "**Total price**" and "**Total cost**" from the table "**pw_projectproduct**"

4. Resize the visualization so that it occupies the whole upper left quadrant of the page.

5. So, what is the visualization representing? It is an analytical view of the products used in the projects of Project Wizards, Inc. showing which product lines are contributing the most revenue and at the same time generating the highest cost. The product line is an information not available in Microsoft Dataverse but available in the table "**DimProduct**" imported from Microsoft SQL Server. But wait, the chart is showing the same data for all product lines, as shown in the following screenshot:

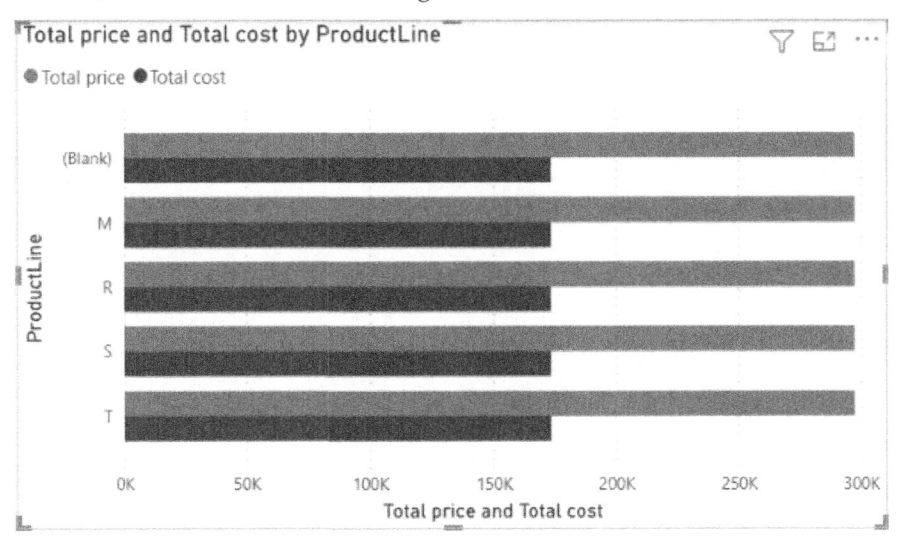

Figure 7.18: Clustered bar chart showing incorrect values

In order to understand the reason for this wrong behavior, we need to remember that the relationship created between the tables "**DimProduct**" and "**pw_productcatalogue**" is of type "**Many to one (*:1)**" because there are multiple products in "**DimProduct**" with the same "**ProductAlternateKey**", whereas there is always just one product with the same key in the "**pw_productcatalogue**" table. This is the root cause of the error—the data is not filtered correctly from the "**DimProduct**" table to the "**pw_productcatalogue**" table. But fortunately, there is a way to correct it.

Please perform the following steps:

1. Switch from the "**Report**" view to the "**Model**" view.

2. Click on the relationship between the tables "**DimProduct**" and "**pw_productcatalogue**" and with the right mouse button, select "**Properties**".

3. Change the "**Cross filter direction**" from "**Single**" to "**Both**" and confirm with "**OK**" according to the following screenshot:

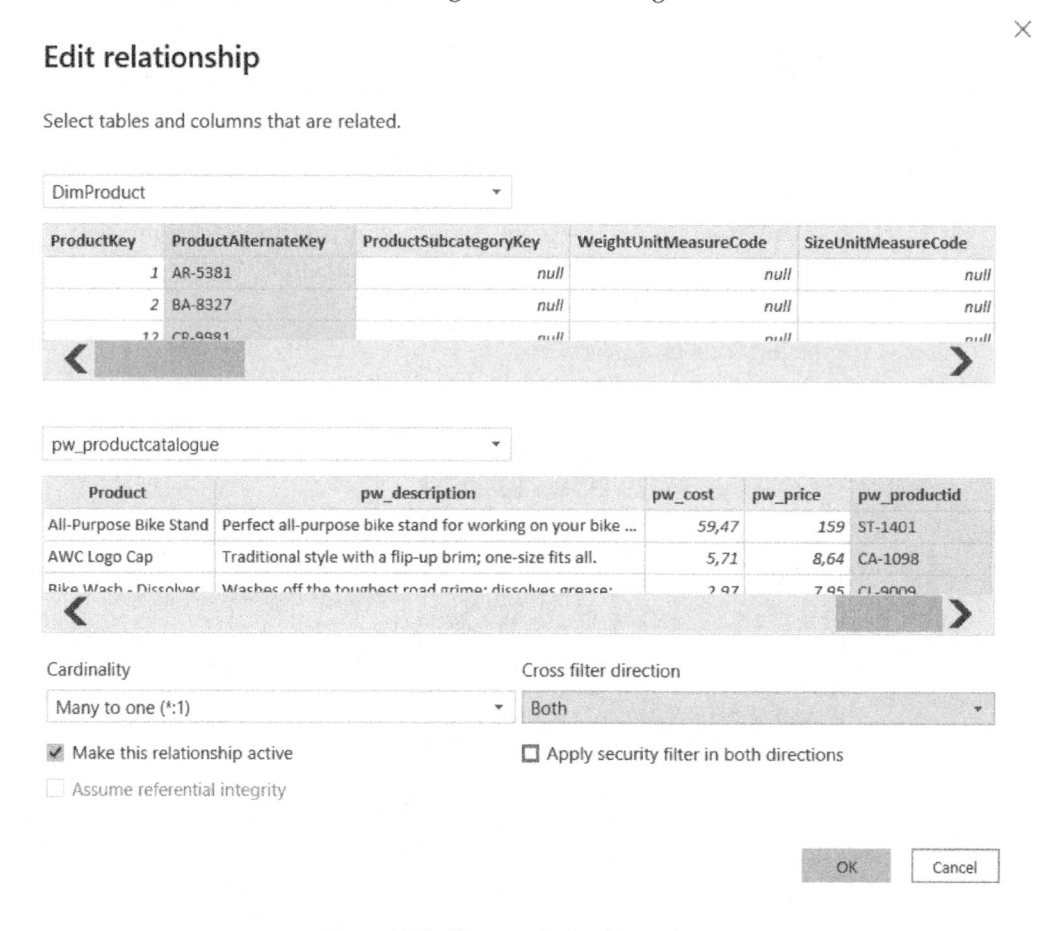

Figure 7.19: Change relationship settings

4. This change will ensure that the data will be correctly filtered in both directions of the relationship, and our chart will show the correct data.

5. Switch back to the "**Report**" view, where you will see the chart is showing the data correctly now.

6. Next, click with the mouse away from the visualization so that it is no more selected.

7. Click on the visualization "**Pie chart**" in the "**Visualization**" pane. This will place the visualization below the first one on the canvas. In the lower

part of the "**Visualization**" pane, you will find the configuration fields. Drag and drop the dataset columns to the configuration fields:

- **Legend**: "**Continent**" from the table "**world country**"
- Values: "**Population**" from the table "**world country**"

8. When you now click on the small down-arrow icon on the content of the field "**Values**", it will show you the possible aggregation types. Select the value "**Sum**" as illustrated on the following screenshot:

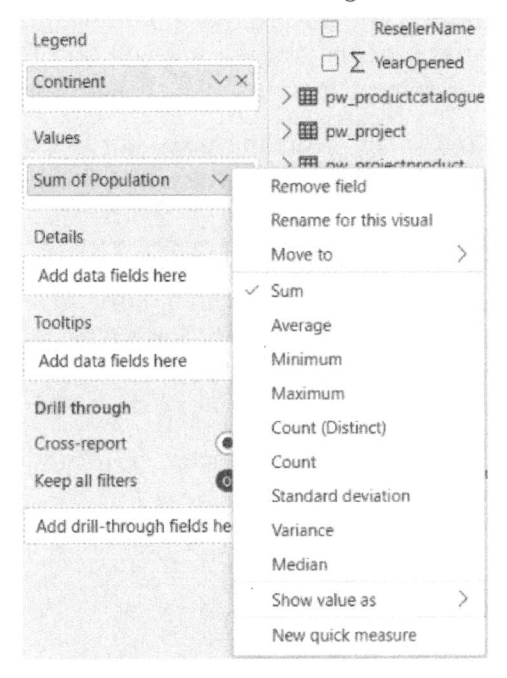

Figure 7.20: Change aggregation type

9. We need to perform the change since we want to see the sum of the population of each continent of the earth on the visualization.

10. Next, click with the mouse away from the visualization so that it is no more selected.

11. Click on the visualization "**Treemap**" in the "**Visualization**" pane. This will place the visualization right on the first one on the canvas. In the lower part of the "**Visualization**" pane, you will find the configuration fields. Drag and drop the dataset columns to the configuration fields:

- **Category**: "**EnglishCountryRegionName**" from the table "**DimGeography**"
- **Details**: "**StateProvinceName**" from the table "**DimGeography**"

o **Values**: "`AnnualRevenue`" from the table "`DimReseller`"

12. So, what is the visualization representing? It is an analytical view of the annual revenue clustered by regions and detailed by state or province names from the tables imported from the SQL Server database.

13. Next, click with the mouse away from the visualization so that it is no more selected.

14. Click on the visualization "`Slicer`" in the "`Visualization`" pane. This will place the visualization into the last free quadrant on the canvas. In the lower part of the "`Visualization`" pane, you will find the configuration fields. Drag and drop the dataset columns to the configuration field:

    o **Field**: "`Continent`" from the table "`world country`", then "`Region`" from the table "`world country`", and finally, "`Name`" from the table "`world country`"

15. So, what is the visualization representing? It is a slicer—a filtering control, which gives the user the possibility to filter the data on the other visualizations on the page, where this is applicable. For our page "**Advanced**", the slicer will filter the data in the treemap and in the pie chart, but not in the clustered bar chart because this visualization has no dependency on geography.

16. Please verify that the page "**Advanced**" is configured according to the following screenshot:

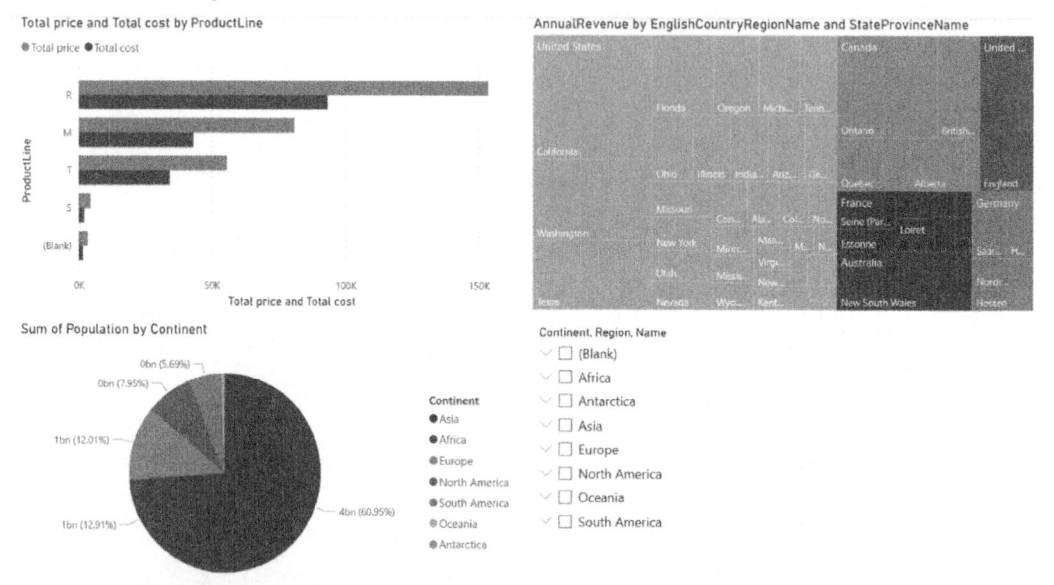

Figure 7.21: Final report structure on the "Advanced" page

17. Click on the "**Save**" icon in the upper left corner of Power BI Desktop to save the final solution.

This was the last step in the exercise.

Congratulations! You have just successfully created a two-page Power BI report and are ready for the next challenges with Power BI. The next task for a Power BI developer is to publish the finished report into the Power BI cloud service.

Publish a Power BI report

Publishing a Power BI report is the last step; a Power BI developer usually performs in Power BI Desktop. Publishing is nothing else, just uploading the report into the Power BI service. Important information to know before publishing are as follows:

- To which Microsoft cloud tenant should the report be published?
- To which, Power BI workspace should the report be published?

A Power BI developer can develop reports for multiple different tenants, the decision to what to publish is given by the signed-in user in Power BI Desktop. If the tool is not yet signed-in, a sign-in dialog will be offered automatically just before publishing.

In an organization using Power BI, there is usually already an established structure of workspaces. Part of the publishing procedure is to select the right workspace the report should be published in.

After the report is published, Power BI Desktop can be closed because the subsequent steps are performed in the Power BI service.

Let us now perform this step practically with the report we have developed for Project Wizards, Inc.

Exercise 15: Publishing a report

In this exercise, we are going to publish the report to our tenant, we are working in, and into the "*My Workspace*", a default workspace, which exists automatically for every Power BI user.

Please perform the following steps:

1. Start the Power BI Desktop and close the initial pop-up window.
2. If not signed-in, click on the upper right side on the "`Sign in`" button and sign-in with the cloud credentials you use for the exercises.
3. Click "`File`" and "`Open report`" and select the file "`Project Wizards Analytics.pbix`".

4. Click the button "**Publish**" on the ribbon on the right side.

5. In the workspace selection dialog, click on "**My Workspace**" and confirm with the button "**Select**".

6. Wait a few seconds until the report is published.

7. Close Power BI Desktop.

8. Navigate in your Internet browser in incognito mode to Power BI service, using the URL: **https://app.powerbi.com/**.

9. Sign-in to the Power BI service with your cloud credentials.

10. On the left navigation pane, click on "**My workspace**". You will see a list of two items with the same name, "**Project Wizards Analytics**", according to the following screenshot:

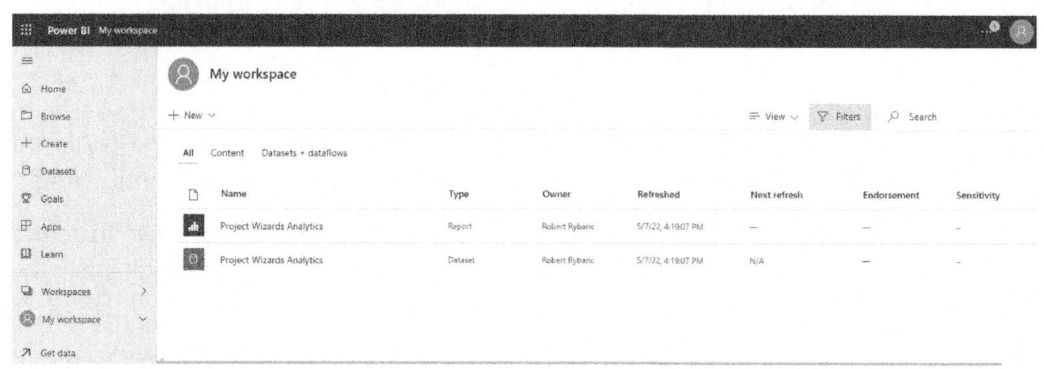

Figure 7.22: Power BI solution components in Power BI service

The two items represent the following Power BI solution components:

- **The Power BI dataset:** The dataset contains the data from one or three data sources we used to build the report.

- **The Power BI report:** The report contains the configuration of the visual representation of the data (two pages with four visualizations each).

As we have used the Import mode in the solutions, the dataset is a physical copy of the data from the originating data sources. For such a dataset, an automated scheduled refresh can be configured to keep the data fresh. For our solution, we will not configure the scheduled refresh since part of the data originates from local, not cloud data sources (local Microsoft SQL Server and local MySQL). In order to enable scheduled refresh for on-premises data sources, the on-premises infrastructure (in this case, your own PC) would need to run permanently, and you would need to establish an On-Premises Data Gateway installation on your PC.

Let us now inspect our creation in the Power BI service. Click on the "**Project Wizards Analytics**" component of type "**Report**", to open the report in the cloud. The report should look like as shown in the following screenshot:

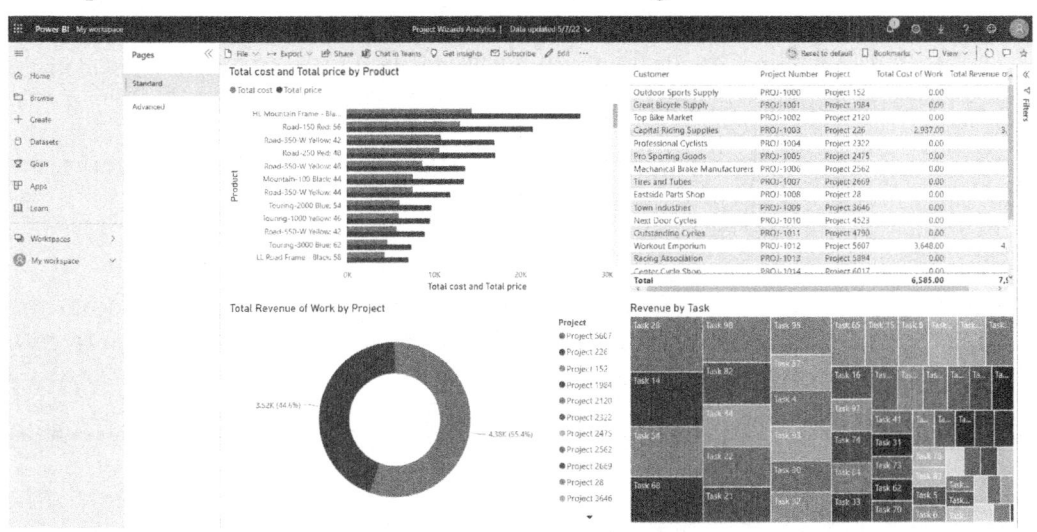

Figure 7.23: Power BI report in Power BI service

You can now try several interesting features like auto-filtering between the visualizations when you click on some data elements in the visualizations, navigation between pages, and the use of the slicers on the second page.

Congratulations! You have created and published an analytical solution for Project Wizards, Inc.

In the next section, you will learn, what are the remaining configuration possibilities that can be performed directly in the Power BI service.

Create Power BI dashboards

The Power BI dashboard is an optional but very important part of a Power BI solution. The dashboard is usually considered as a start screen of the whole solution, presenting the most important or interesting parts of the solution. Imagine a complex solution where the report has 10 pages and, on each page, there are approximately six visualizations, which is a total of 60 visualizations. For a usual end user, it could be not so easy to navigate between all those visualizations and quickly find and understand the content. A dashboard can make this much easier. Dashboards are created in the Power BI service by picking and pinning the most important visualizations from the report and placing them on the dashboard. These visualizations are then called tiles.

The dashboard has the following main features:

- The dashboard has always just one single page.
- Certain capabilities of the report are not available, for example, the drilling down or the filtering of the entire dashboard.
- The tiles on the dashboard can be resized.
- Dashboards support the creation of alerts for specific tiles, for example, the KPI tiles.
- Dashboards contain the natural language query (Q & A) capability.

The practical creation of a dashboard is very simple—it is needed to locate the required visualizations on the report pages and pin them on a dashboard. In case there is no dashboard yet, it can be created on the fly.

In the following exercise, you will have the possibility to create a dashboard based on the published report from the previous exercise.

Exercise 16: Creating a dashboard

In this exercise, we are going to create a new dashboard with the published Power BI solution.

Please perform the following steps:

1. Navigate to the Power BI website: **https://app.powerbi.com/**.
2. Sign-in with your cloud credentials.
3. Navigate to "**My workspace**" and open the "**Project Wizards Analytics**" report.
4. Hover with the mouse over the visualization "**Total cost and Total price by Product**"—in the upper right corner of the visualization, and there are some small buttons; select the "**Pin**" button, like as shown in the following screenshot:

Integrate Analytics with Power BI ■ 201

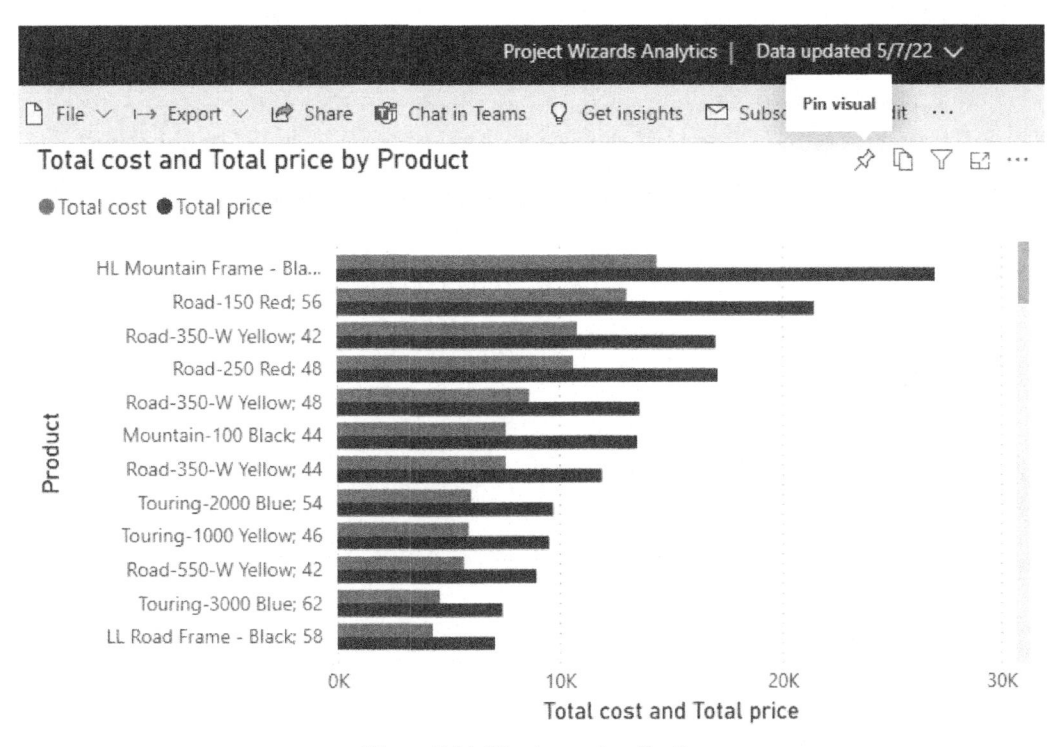

Figure 7.24: Pinning a visualization

5. When you click on the "**Pin**" button, a visualization pinning dialog will show up. Since there is not yet any dashboard in the workspace, you need to create a new one. Give the dashboard the name "**Project Wizards Analytics**", according to the following screenshot. Confirm by clicking on the yellow button "**Pin**":

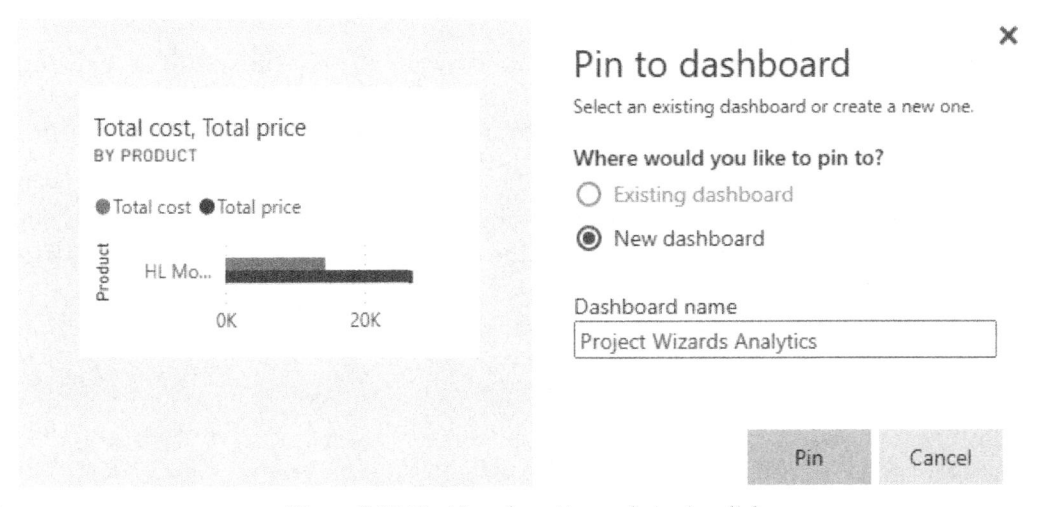

Figure 7.25: Dashboard creation and pinning dialog

6. After clicking on the yellow button "**Pin**", the dashboard is immediately created. To see the dashboard, navigate back to "**My workspace**" in the main navigation. In the list of components, there will be a third component with the same name, "**Project Wizards Analytics**" of type "**Dashboard**".

7. Click on the dashboard to open it, and you will see the first visualization placed in the upper left corner as a tile.

8. Navigate back to "**My workspace**" and open the report.

9. Pin the visualization "**Total Revenue of Work by Project**" to the existing dashboard.

10. Navigate again to the dashboard to see that the two visualizations are placed in the first row of the dashboard as tiles. Now, you can try to resize the tiles to find the proper size for each.

Congratulations! Your Power BI solution looks even better now since you have enhanced it with a dashboard.

In the next section, we will present an interesting feature, making it possible to retrieve analytical results from Power BI ad-hoc by formulating a query using a natural language.

Use Natural language query

Natural language query, or Q&A, is an AI-driven Power BI capability where a user can get the required insight into the data in the Power BI solution by simply formulating a question in a natural language. The Power BI engine will try to understand the question, understand which data elements are requested, and answer with the best suitable visualization.

The visualization returned by Power BI can be immediately pinned to an existing or new dashboard. This capability gives the creators an option to enhance the dashboards with tiles, not inherited from any existing report visualizations but created ad-hoc. Such tiles will stay on the dashboards permanently.

The practical use of this capability is very simple. The right place to start is a Power BI dashboard, where, in the upper part of the dashboard, there is a link area "**Ask a question about your data**", as illustrated in the following screenshot:

Figure 7.26: Natural language query link

Clicking on the link navigates to the Q & A part, where a user can formulate the question. An example of this capability is illustrated in the following screenshot:

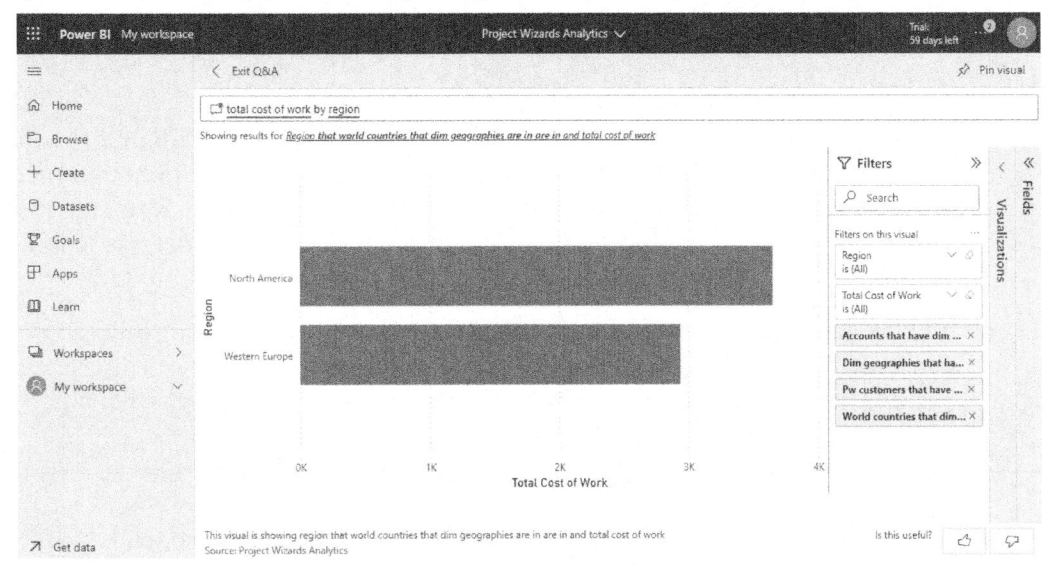

Figure 7.27: Result of a natural language query

As you can see in *figure 7.27*, the query **"total cost of work by region"** leads to a bar chart showing an analytical view of the labor cost grouped by the regions of the respective project customers.

When the visualization is interesting and should become part of a dashboard, it can be easily pinned using the "**Pin visual**" button in the upper right corner.

Feel free to experiment with this helpful feature and pin some additional interesting visualizations on the dashboard we created in the previous exercise.

In the last section of this chapter, we will investigate the possibilities to integrate a Power BI solution with the other parts of the Power Platform.

Integrate analytics with apps and flows

One of the last questions which need to be answered when building analytical solutions with Power BI is how the end users will consume the content. There are multiple ways how to do it:

- **Power BI service:** The end user can always navigate to the Power BI service URL **https://app.powerbi.com/**, sign-in with their cloud credentials, and consume the content made available for them.

- **Power BI mobile:** The end user can use the possibility to consume Power BI content on the go by installing and using the Power BI mobile application. The principle with this mobile app is the same as for Power Apps mobile or Power Automate mobile. The user needs to sign-in and get access to the content.

- **Power App model-driven app:** A Power BI dashboard or a single tile can be made part of a model-driven app. There is a possibility to either embed a Power BI component into the model-driven app for all users or to give the users the possibility to add a Power BI component as a personal dashboard for use by that particular user only.

- **Power App canvas app:** A Power BI tile can be embedded on a canvas app. Since canvas apps are primarily dedicated for mobile devices with small screens, the whole dashboard cannot be embedded, only a single tile.

- **Power App portal app:** A Power BI component can be also embedded in a portal app to enhance the functionality of the portal.

Another interesting integration capability is the integration between Power BI and Power Automate. This integration can cover the following scenario:

- A Power BI dashboard is equipped with alerts. Alerts is a capability to notify the users when certain values are reached in the Power BI tiles—this is possible for numerical tiles, like KPIs or gauges.

- The users would like to be notified about the alerts using additional channels, for example, with an e-mail message.

The solution for the preceding scenario is to build a Power Automate cloud flow with the Power BI trigger, responding to an alert event. The flow could then notify the users with an e-mail message.

In the last exercise of this chapter, you will integrate the Power BI dashboard into the "**Project Management**" model-driven application as a personal dashboard.

Exercise 17: Integrating a dashboard

In order to integrate an external dashboard into a model-driven application, a modification of the site map needs to be performed first. For this, you will need to refresh your knowledge gained in *Chapter 2, Building Enterprise Solutions with Power Apps*.

Please perform the following steps:

1. Open to the Maker Portal, navigate to "**Solutions**", and select the solution "**Project Management**".

2. Locate the model-driven application "**Project Management**", select it, and click on the "**Edit**" button in the command bar, to open the application for configuration changes. Depending on the time of reading this book, there might be the need to use the "**Edit in preview**" instead of "**Edit**" to open the app in the modern app designer.

3. On the left navigation side of the app designer switch from "**Pages**" to "**Navigation**".

4. Select the "**Projects**" node and click on "**+ Add page**" in the command bar.

5. In the page configuration, select "**Dashboard**" as page type and click "**Next**".

6. Select the "**Microsoft Dynamics 365 Overview**" dashboard and click "**Add**". A new navigation subarea will be added to the site map.

7. Click on the ellipsis (three dots) right from the name of the subarea "**Dashboard**" and select "**Move up**" to make the "**Dashboard**" navigation subarea the first in the whole app.

8. Click on "**Save**" on the right side of the upper command bar.

9. Click "**<- Back**" on the left side of the upper command bar. This will return back to the solution overview.

10. Click "**Publish all customizations**" and wait until the publishing finish.

11. Click "**<- Back to solutions**".

This was the last step in the preparation phase for the dashboard embedding. The next task will be to embed our dashboard as a personal dashboard into the model-driven app.

Please perform the following steps:

1. In the Maker Portal, navigate to "**Apps**" and open the model-driven app "**Project Management**".

2. You will notice the change in the site map and the fact that the first navigation element is now "**Dashboards**". The selected dashboard, "**Microsoft Dynamics 365 Overview**", will automatically open; however, the content of that dashboard is not relevant to us.

3. Click "**+ New**" and then "**Power BI Dashboard**".

Note: Should there be no option to add a new Power BI dashboard, you need to change the setting for your environment in the Power Platform Admin Center. You need to locate the settings area "Features" and switch on the feature "Power BI visualization embedding".

4. By default, you should be presented with the selected Power BI workspace "**My workspace**" and with the dashboard "**Project Wizards Analytics**". Click "**Save**" to save this dashboard reference to the model-driven app.

5. The previously created dashboard from Power BI is now embedded into the model-driven app. You can click on the button "**Set as Default**" on the upper command bar so that this dashboard will always be automatically populated.

6. The model-driven application "**Project Management**" should now look like as shown in the following screenshot:

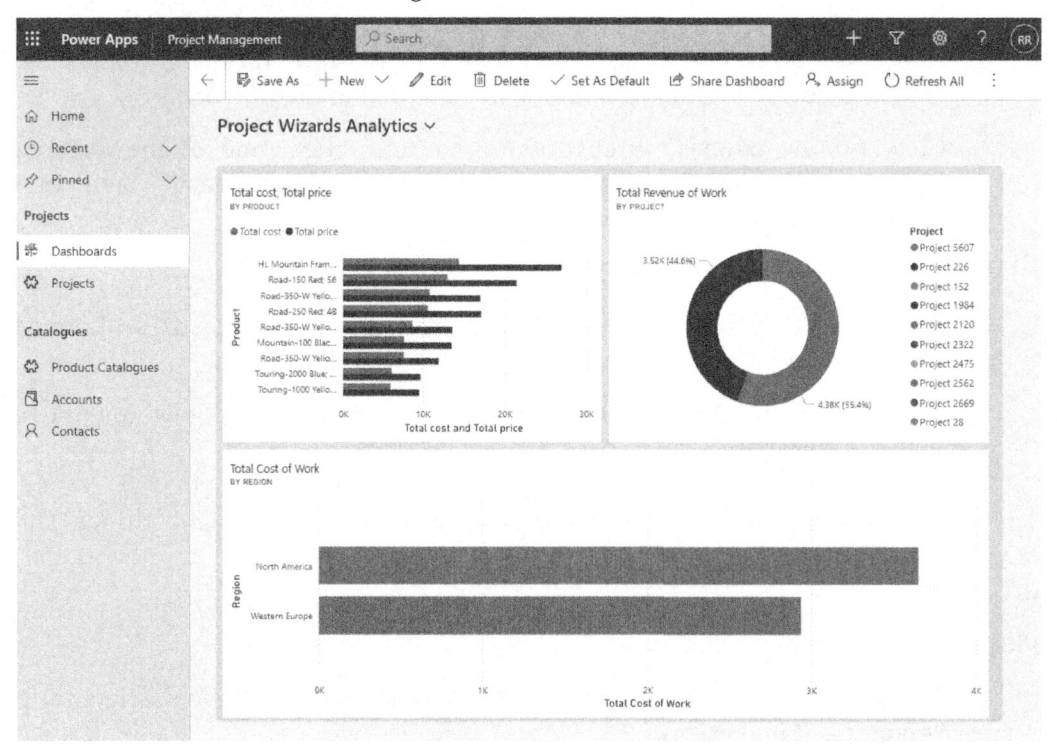

Figure 7.28: Power BI dashboard embedded into a model-driven app

This was the last step in this exercise.

Congratulations! You have successfully embedded the Power BI dashboard into your model-driven application *"Project Management"*. From now on, the users of the application will always have an analytical view of the most important project management data.

Conclusion

In this chapter, you have continued learning the various capabilities of Power BI. You have made yourself familiar with the visualizations, which are a key component for building analytical solutions. You have seen what the typical steps are when creating a Power BI report and how to place and configure visualization on the report. Next, you have learned how to publish a report on the Power BI service and what are the additional capabilities of that cloud service. You have seen what is a dashboard and how to use the natural language query. In the end, we have presented the options for integrating Power BI solutions with other Power Platform components. In the practical part of this chapter, you have created a report, published the report to Power BI service, created a dashboard, and finally embedded the dashboard into the Project Management model-driven app for Project Wizards, Inc.

In the upcoming chapter, we will fully focus on the next Power Platform component, the Power Virtual Agents. You will learn what are the typical scenarios for using chatbots in business applications and how can Power Virtual Agents help create them. We will present the fundaments of this product, the concept of bots, topics, and conversation nodes. You will learn about entities and how to integrate a chatbot with other surrounding IT systems and solutions. Finally, we will work together through the possibilities to integrate a chatbot into various hosting environments.

Questions

1. What is the purpose of Power BI visualizations?
2. What types of visualizations do you know?
3. What is the structure of a Power BI report?
4. What are the steps to fully configure a visualization?
5. What is the purpose of publishing a Power BI report?
6. What is a Power BI dashboard?
7. What are the benefits of natural language queries in Power BI?
8. How can a Power BI solution be integrated with other Power Platform components?

CHAPTER 8
Chat with Power Virtual Agents

Introduction

The relevance of chatbots in different business scenarios is growing rapidly, and companies are concerned about how to easily build them without deep software development and AI knowledge. Power Virtual Agents is the ideal solution for these requirements because it provides an easy-to-use graphical designer for building bots. In this chapter, you will learn how to build a chatbot and what are the options and possibilities. You will see how to integrate a chatbot with the rest of your business applications. Finally, we will provide you with an overview of the options, how and where a chatbot can be hosted, and what analytics you can expect from operating Power Virtual Agents chatbots.

Structure

In this chapter, we will discuss the following topics:

- Use cases for Power Virtual Agents
- Power Virtual Agents fundamentals
- Create a bot
- Create topics and conversation nodes

- Integrate your bot with other IT systems
- Test and publish your bot
- Host your bot on a website and in Microsoft Teams

Objectives

After reading this chapter, you will be able to understand what are chatbots and what are typical scenarios where chatbots can be used to replace human workers. You will learn the fundamentals of the Power Virtual Agents cloud service, which is a low-code/no-code service for building chatbots. You will further see what the topics are, how are they used, and why are they so important for building chatbots. Next, you will learn how the conversation structure can be configured in a topic and what are the possible components in the conversation. After that, you will dive deeper into the possibilities to connect and integrate a chatbot with other IT systems to retrieve information or trigger processes. You will also learn how to test and publish a chatbot and what are the possibilities to integrate a chatbot into a hosting environment. As always, the chapter is accompanied by some interesting practical examples.

Use cases for Power Virtual Agents

Before we dive into the matter, we need to clarify certain basic terms and understand the use cases for chatbots. First, what is actually a chatbot? To understand this, we need to first define the *"chat"* in the given context. A *"chat"* is an instant, remote, text-based conversation between two or more individuals. Many of us know this type of interaction very well from all those modern chatting applications such as Messenger, WhatsApp, Signal, and so on, just to mention a few of them. It is not a surprise that this type of communication, originally intended purely for private use, has found its way into the business. Chat, as an additional communication channel, is used today, for example, in customer service, and in some other scenarios. Chat, however, requires human beings to be involved on a permanent base to serve the other side, let it be customers, citizens, or whoever. Many of the scenarios where a chat channel is being used, however, represent repeated routine procedures, where the human workforce is not necessarily used in the best way.

With the rise of **artificial intelligence** (**AI**), the idea of chatbots came as a replacement for the human workforce in all scenarios, where a machine can provide better and easier service than a human. So, what are the typical scenarios where a chatbot can be used? Let us examine a few of them:

- **Customer service:** Customer service is the most traditional area, where a chat communication channel was offered with the intention to improve customer satisfaction. A partial replacement with chatbots is a natural evolution of this scenario. A chatbot can serve as first-level support, catching the initial communication from the customers and trying to help resolve known, typical, and repeated issues the customers might have. In case the chatbot is not able to resolve the issue, an escalation to a human customer service agent needs to be offered.

- **Sales support:** Another area where a chatbot is increasingly used is sales support, specifically in online shops. The chatbot can clarify typical customer questions about product features, guide through the selection of the right products, and also help answer after-sales questions, such as the status of the order, the payment, the delivery, and so on.

- **Employee support:** A chatbot can also help inside the organization, providing support for the employees. A typical scenario is employee onboarding, where a chatbot can answer known repeating questions regarding the structure of the organization, internal processes, procedures, and many more.

There is no doubt that chatbots are increasingly important, and more and more organizations understand the added value of implementing chatbots in some of the described or any other suitable scenarios. The question is, however, how a chatbot can be technically implemented. Surprisingly, it is not easy because a chatbot needs to use artificial intelligence to be able to recognize and understand human input. And implementing a technical solution using AI is a complex undertaking, requiring a lot of deep expertise. Here comes Microsoft Power Platform with its service Power Virtual Agents, which is a pure low-code/no-code cloud solution were building a chatbot is a matter of configuration combined with a graphical design.

Let us now dive into the fundamentals of this service.

Power Virtual Agents fundamentals

Power Virtual Agents (PVA), as a member of the Power Platform family, lives inside of a Power Platform environment. When you decide to use this service, corresponding data structures in the Microsoft Dataverse are created, and you can start building your first chatbot. For the configuration of the chatbots, a specific cloud designer is used. This designer is started directly from the Maker Portal, from the area called *"Chatbots"*. It is possible to create one or multiple chatbots in one single Power Platform environment. The questions, whether one or multiple are needed, must be answered based on the individual needs and certain main product features of Power Virtual Agents. One of the key features influencing this decision is the language of the conversation, since an individual PVA chatbot supports only one single language.

The process of creating a chatbot with PVA consists of certain main steps:

1. Create a bot.
2. Create topics and conversation nodes.
3. Optionally, create, and use entities.
4. Integrate the bot with other IT systems.
5. Test and publish a bot.
6. Host the bot in the appropriate environment.
7. Analyze the performance of the bot and refine it if necessary.

In the following sections, you will learn the necessary information about the previous steps.

Create a bot

Before the configuration of the chatbot can start, a bot object needs to be created in a Power Platform environment. The environment needs to have Microsoft Dataverse deployed and needs to be in one of the supported Power Platform regions.

> **Note:** The Power Virtual Agents service is not available in every Power Platform region. Please refer to the product documentation https://docs.microsoft.com/en-us/power-virtual-agents/data-location to learn which regions are supported.

In the bot creation dialog, the following are the required settings:

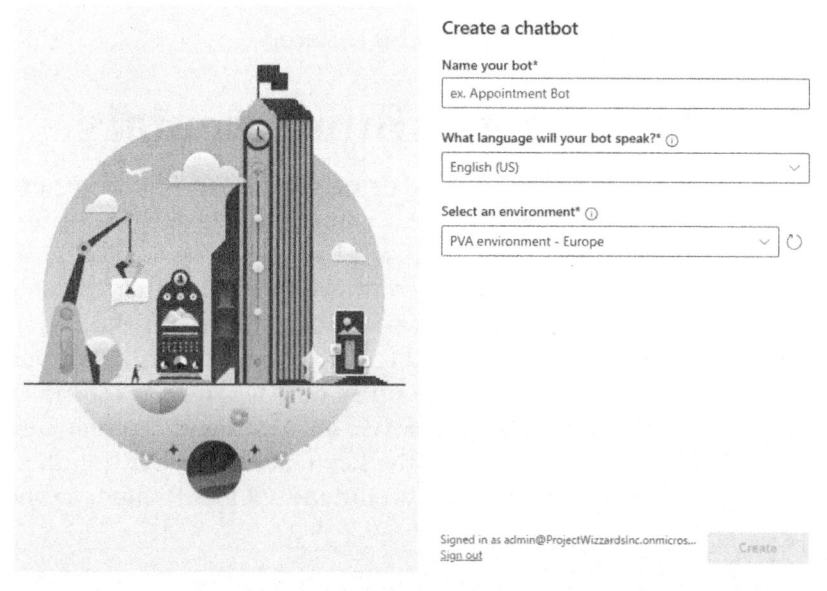

Figure 8.1: Bot creation dialog

As we can see in *figure 8.1*, it is required to choose a *name* for the bot, the supported *language*, and the Power Platform *environment* in which the bot object will be created. As of writing this book, there are around 20 languages that can be used for building a bot.

Create topics and conversation nodes

After the bot is created, the next step is to create the topics. The topic is the most important item in a chatbot, and it can be described as a specific discussion item around which a certain conversation capability is configured. To better understand the purpose of the topics, let us discuss a few examples:

- **Order status:** The main purpose of an order status topic would be to help the customer figure out what is right now happening with their order.

- **Product selection:** The main purpose of a product selection topic would be to assist the customer who is browsing a complex Web shop to find the most suitable product based on their needs.

- **Employee onboarding**: This topic can answer the most typical questions of a new employee.

A PVA topic consists of the following main parts:

- **Topic name:** Every topic needs to have a name explaining the main purpose of the topic. The name, however, does not have any impact on the functionality of the topic.

- **Topic trigger phrases:** The trigger phrases are the most important part of the topic since they "*teach*" the AI in the background of PVA to correctly recognize the human input. It is imperative to prepare and configure quality trigger phrases representing various human formulations of the essence of the topic. It is recommended to have more than 10 trigger phrases in a single topic, but the more, the better.

- **Topic conversation nodes:** The conversation nodes represent the conversation flow required for the topic. The nodes are configured in a graphical designer, similar to a flow diagram designer.

How do the trigger phrases actually work? PVA is driven in the background by Microsoft Azure **Artificial Intelligence** (**AI**) components, which are able to recognize the human language. Those components need to have some input first to train themselves on the specifics of a certain topic. And the trigger phrases are exactly that input. You need to think about possible typical formulations a human can express when asking for something specific. And then, you need to put all those different formulations as trigger phrases into the topic specification. This will ensure that the

AI has enough material to recognize any similar human expression and select the corresponding topic.

In the following screenshot, you can find a topic example. This is one of the out-of-the-box topics, which are generated automatically in every PVA bot and serve learning purposes:

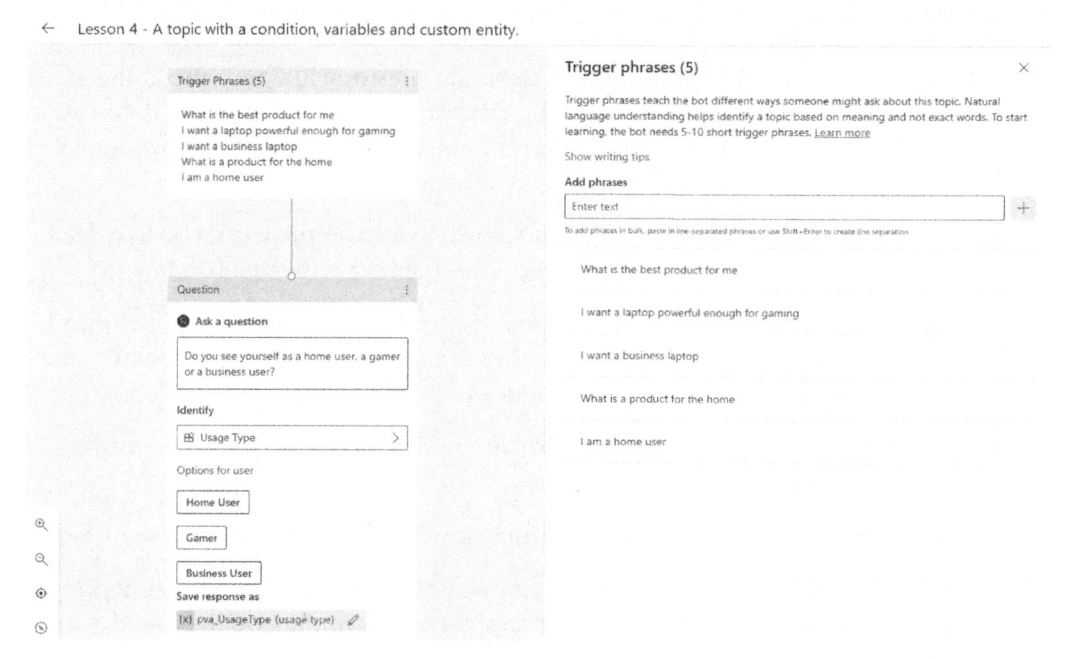

Figure 8.2: Topic example

As you can see in *figure 8.2*, there is a topic with the name "*Lesson 4—A topic with a condition, variables and custom entity*" equipped with five trigger phrases (which is usually not enough). On the right side of the screenshot, there are the five trigger phrases; on the left side, the first part of the conversation nodes.

The conversation nodes are used to configure the whole flow of the conversation, which should happen when the chatbot identifies the topic. The conversation nodes can contain any of the following node types:

- **Show a message:** This node represents showing a text block of static or static + dynamic text, which the chatbot shows to the human user. The dynamics part of a message can be implemented by inserting a variable into the message text. The message does not expect any response from the human user.

- **Ask a question:** This node represents showing a question to the human user and expecting an answer to that question. It is possible to configure many different answer types to the question. Every question node automatically creates a PVA variable, which stores the answer of the human user.

- **Call an action:** This node is used to communicate with other IT systems. The node implements a Power Automate cloud flow with a specific PVA trigger and action. The purpose is to talk to an external IT system to either retrieve some data (for example, the status of a certain sales order) or to perform an action (for example, to create a ticket in a ticketing system). It is possible to submit input parameters to the flow and receive output parameters from the flow.

- **Redirect to another topic:** This node type is used to explicitly switch from the current topic to another topic. Switching between topics is usually driven by the AI in the background, but a chatbot designer can force the switch by using this node type.

- **End the conversation:** This node implements a successful or unsuccessful termination of the conversation. A successful termination means the chatbot was able to satisfy the human user's requirements, and it is represented by a short one-question customer satisfaction survey. An unsuccessful termination is implemented as an escalation; in other words, the communication should be handed over from the chatbot to the human agent.

Before we proceed to the next section, let us quickly explain another PVA component, the entity. An entity is a term from the world of AI. It represents a defined piece of information of a specific type. An entity can be, for example, *"city"*, *"country"*, *"color"*, *"money"*, and so on. Entities are used in PVA to make the recognition of the human language easier to interpret and consolidate into a machine-understandable form. As an example, let us consider a PVA question *"In which country are you living?"*. Possible human answers can be: *"United States"* or *"USA"* or *"U.S."*. In order for PVA to always recognize a consolidated answer value, it is possible to configure the answer type on the question as a "**Country or region**" prebuilt entity, according to the following screenshot:

Figure 8.3: Question example

As you can see in *figure 8.3*, the answer type for the question (the *"Identity"*) is configured as *"Country or region"*. This will help PVA to easier recognize the answer as a country or region, regardless of the formulation of the human user.

Integrate your bot with other IT systems

The next very important concept of PVA is the integration capability with other IT systems. As described earlier in this chapter, a chatbot must almost always perform certain communication with other IT systems in order to fulfill the requirements of the human user. In PVA, the direct integration with Power Automate is used to connect and communicate with other systems. This has a huge benefit due to the fact that Power Automate can communicate with so many different IT systems using data connectors.

An example scenario, how to practically use this integration can be as follows:

- The chatbot should provide information about the status of a customer order.

- The conversation nodes will first ask the human user for the order number. This will be implemented using the *"Ask a question"* node type. The answer of the human user will be automatically saved in a PVA variable.

- The next step will be a node type *"Call an action"*. This step will call a Power Automate flow with one input parameter. This parameter will be the value of the order number.

- The Power Automate flow will use the respective data connector to the order management system used in the organization to retrieve the order details based on the order number.

- The Power Automate flow will finally return back to the PVA conversation with the defined values of the retrieved order, like the order date, payment date, ship date, and so on.

- The chatbot will finally use the node type *"Show a message"* to inform the human user about the details of the order.

Now is the right time to start the next exercise, where we implement a PVA chatbot for Project Wizards, Inc.

Exercise 18: Creating a chatbot

In this exercise, we configure a Power Virtual Agents chatbot to be able to provide the values *"Total Work Cost"* and *"Total Work Price"* of a given project from our *"Project Management"* solution.

In order to fulfill this requirement, we will need to configure a new topic with the corresponding trigger phrases and conversation nodes.

Please perform the following steps:

1. Open to the Maker Portal, select the correct environment, navigate to "**Chatbots**", and select "**Create**".

2. Click on "**+ New chatbot**"; this will open a new browser tab with Power Virtual Agents. Since PVA has a separate licensing, you will need to first go through the steps of activating the trial license. Perform the same steps as you have already used earlier for activating the other Power Platform licenses.

3. After you have performed all the license activation steps, you will be redirected to the PVA portal and need to configure the chatbot creation details. Please provide the following details in the bot creation dialog:

    o **Name your bot:** "Project Wizards Bot".

    o **What language will your bot speak?:** Select **English (US)**.

    o **Select an environment:** Select the same environment you are working in the whole time.

4. Click "**Create**" to start the bot creation. Allow for a few seconds for the bot to be created. There will be a message in the upper part of the PVA designer portal saying that the bot is ready after a short time. The designer should look like as shown in the following screenshot:

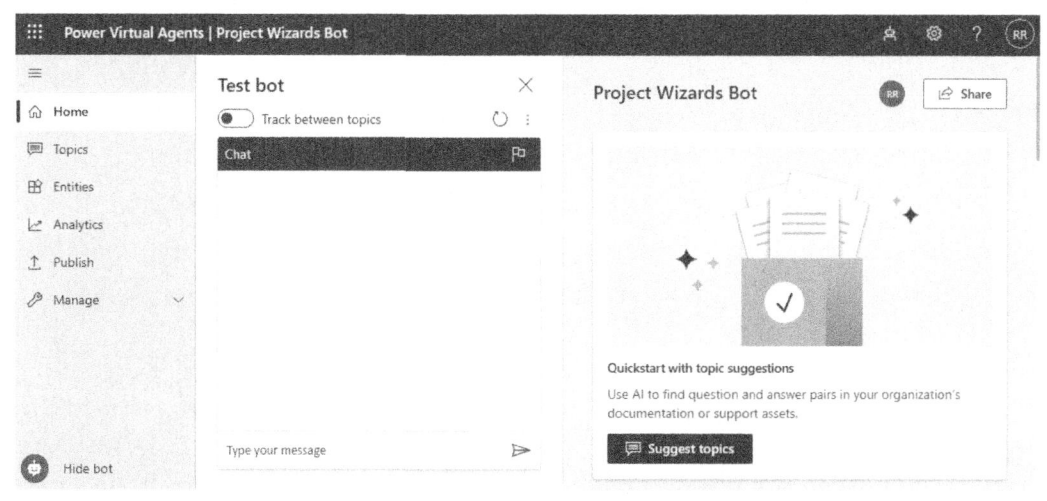

Figure 8.4: Power Virtual Agents designer portal

218 ■ Microsoft Power Platform Up and Running

5. The next task will be to create the mentioned topic. Within the portal, navigate to "**Topics**" and click on "**+ New topic**" and then "**From blank**".

6. Give the topic a name – in the upper part just below the command bar, replace "**Untitled**" with "**Return project status**".

7. On the right side, there is a trigger phrases configuration pane. Always enter the trigger phrase and click on the "+" sign to add a new phrase to the list. Add the following trigger phrases:

    o What is the status of my project?

    o Give me the project status.

    o What status has my project?

    o Project cost and price overview.

    o What are the total cost and total price of my project?

8. In real-life scenarios, it would be helpful to add more trigger phrases, but for the purpose of this exercise, five phrases are enough. The topic's main area should look like as shown in the following screenshot:

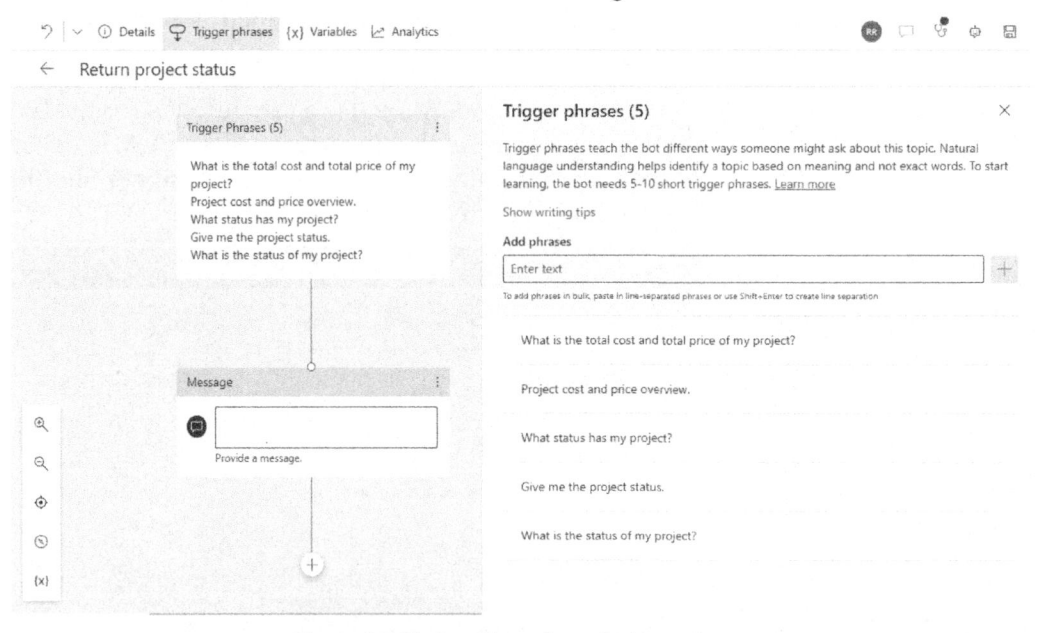

Figure 8.5: Topic with configured trigger phrases

9. The next step will be to configure the conversation nodes in the left part of the topic designer. Click on the first empty message box and enter the following text: "**I will be happy to provide you with the financial details of your project.**"

10. Click on the "**+**" sign below the message and select "**Ask a question**". Enter the following text into the question field: "**Please provide the project number**"

11. Select the answer type (called *"Identify"*) as "**User's entire response**".

12. Click on the automatically created variable "**Var**", on the command bar, select "**{x} Variables**" and rename the variable to "**ProjectNumber**".

Note: Use either the zoom capability of the designer canvas (the "+" and "−" signs on the small left vertical command bar) or move the canvas area with the mouse to get access to the hidden parts of the conversation nodes.

13. Click on the "**+**" sign below the question and select "**Call an action**", and from the selection of possibilities, select "**Create a flow**". This will launch Power Automate in an additional browser tab. In the Power Automate portal, you should find a template flow for communicating with PVA. The template consists of a PVA trigger and a PVA action. It is your responsibility to configure everything in between those elements.

14. First, rename the flow's template-based name *"Power Virtual Agents Flow Template"* in the upper left area of the Power Automate portal to *"PVA retrieve project details"*.

15. Click on the trigger with the name "**Power Virtual Agents**" and then click on the "**+ Add an input**".

16. Select the data type of the input parameter "**Text**". Rename the input parameter as "**ProjectNumber**".

17. Move the mouse between the trigger and the action. You will see a "+" sign on the connecting line; click the "**+**" sign and select "**Add an action**".

18. From the "**Choose an operation**" dialog, search for "**variable**" and select the "**Initialize variable**" action. Configure the action as follows:

    o **Name of the action**: "Initialize TotalCost"

    o **Name field**: TotalCost

    o **Type field**: Float

    o **Value field**: 0

According to the following screenshot:

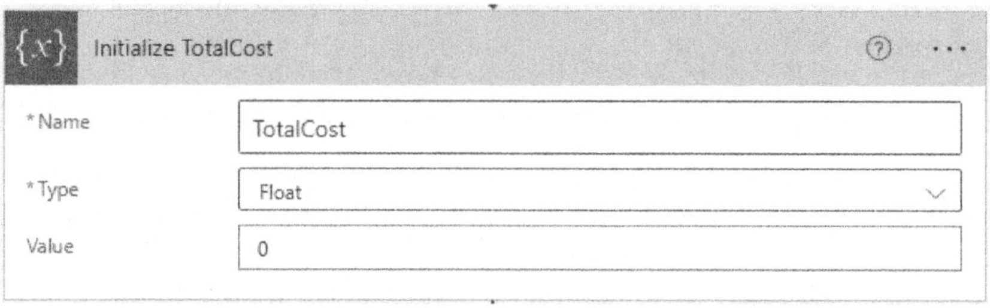

Figure 8.6: Configuration of a variable initialization

19. Below the previous action, click the "+" sign on the connecting line and add another "Initialize variable" action. Configure this action similar to the previous one with the following values:
    - **Name of the action**: "Initialize TotalPrice"
    - **Name field**: TotalPrice
    - **Type field**: Float
    - **Value field**: 0

20. Below the previous action, click the "+" sign on the connecting line and add a new action. From the "**Choose an operation**" dialog, select the "**Microsoft Dataverse**" connector (the one with the green icon) and then select the action "**List rows**".

21. Rename the action from "List rows" to "Retrieve a project".

22. Select the table "**Projects**" from the "**Table name**" selector.

23. Click "**Show advanced options**".

24. In the field "**Filter rows**", enter the following formula: "**pw_number eq**" and stay with the mouse cursor at the end of the entered text.

25. Click on the "**Add dynamic content**" link to display the dynamic content pane to the right. Select the dynamic value "**ProjectNumber**" from the flow trigger.

26. After the dynamics value-added, insert a space and finally add the following string: '

27. There is BEFORE and AFTER the dynamic value always a single apostrophe character (').

28. The configuration of the action should look like as shown in the following screenshot:

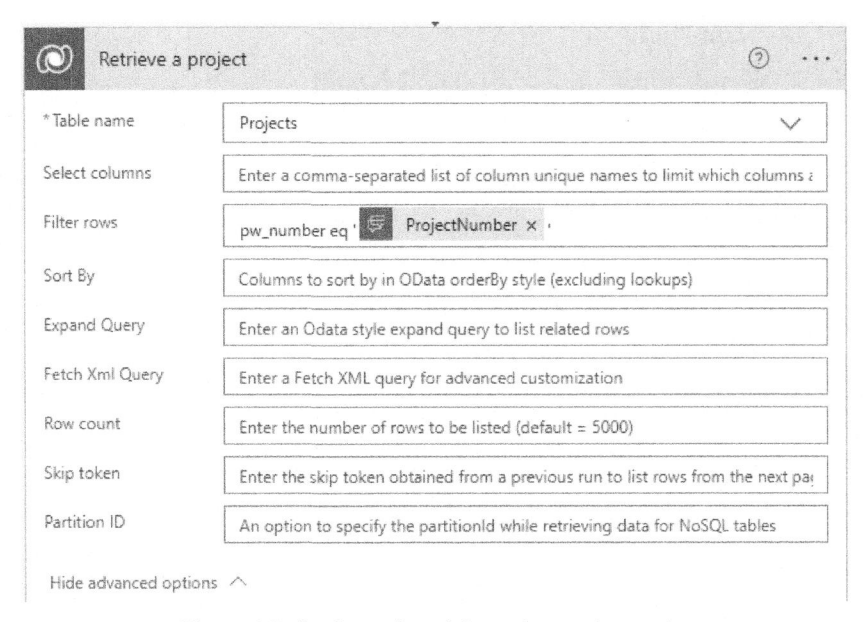

Figure 8.7: Configuration of the project retrieve action

29. Below the previous action, click the "**+**" sign on the connecting line, select "**Control**", and then select "**Apply to each**" from the selection of possible actions.

30. In the "**Apply to each**" looping action, click on the field "**Select an output from previous steps**". This will open the dynamic content pane. Select the dynamic value "**value**" from the group "**Retrieve a project**".

31. Click *inside* the "**Apply to each**" loop control on "**Add an action**", search for "**variable**" and select "**Set variable**" from the selection of possible actions.

32. Configure the action as follows:
    - **Name of the action**: "Set TotalCost"
    - **Name field**: TotalCost
    - **Value field**: dynamic value "Total Work Cost" from the group "Retrieve a project"

33. Click *inside* the "**Apply to each**" loop control on "**Add an action**" below the previous action, search for "**variable**", and select "**Set variable**" from the selection of possible actions.

34. Configure the action as follows:
    - **Name of the action**: "Set TotalPrice"

o **Name field**: TotalPrice

o **Value field**: dynamic value "Total Work Price" from the group "Retrieve a project"

35. The whole "`Apply for each`" loop action should look like as shown in the following screenshot:

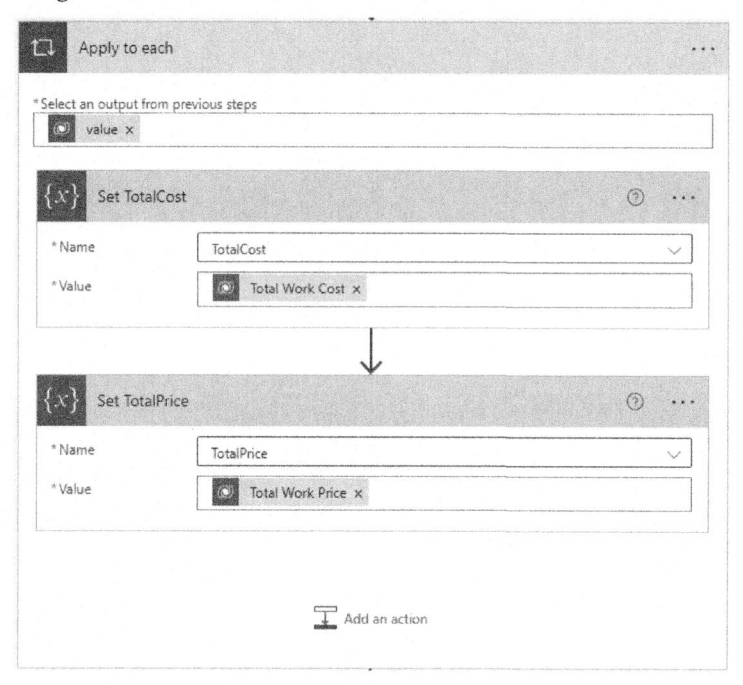

Figure 8.8: Configuration of the loop action

36. Finally, configure the PVA action (the last action in the flow) with the name "`Return value(s) to Power Virtual Agents`" by adding two output parameters of the "Number" data type. Configure the two output parameters according to the following screenshot—use the two variables as dynamic content to define the values for the two output parameters:

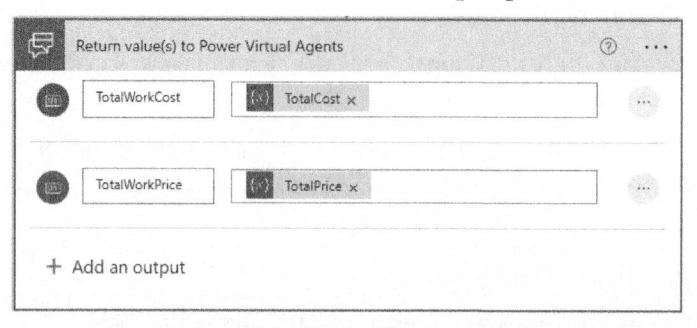

Figure 8.9: Configuration of the output parameters

37. The whole structure of the Power Automate flow should look like as shown in the following screenshot:

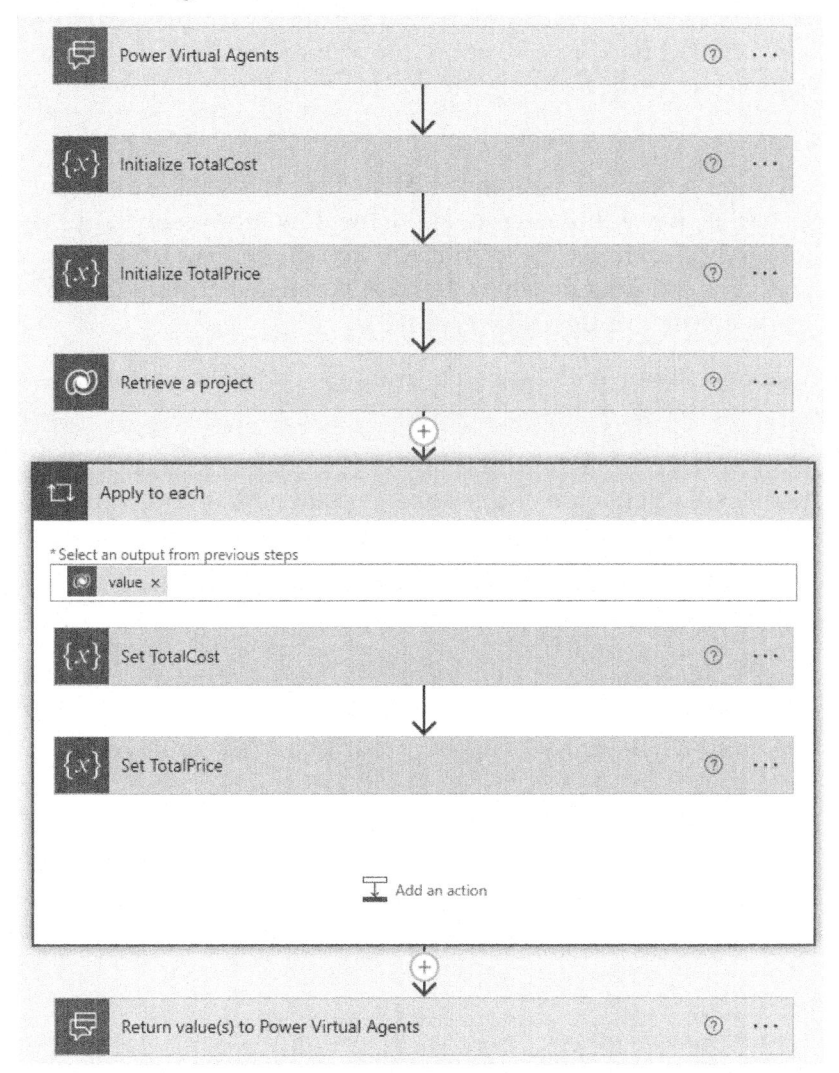

Figure 8.10: Configuration of the whole flow

The flow implements the following logic: the flow execution is triggered by the PVA topic conversation. After the start, the input parameter gets the value of the project number entered by the human user in the PVA chatbot. Next, two Power Automate variables are initialized to accommodate the two numerical values of total project cost and price. Then, the flow retrieves the project from the Dataverse table and, in a loop, works through the result. The two variables get assigned the values from the project record. Finally, the PVA action at the end of the flow gets assigned the numerical values to the two created output parameters.

You may be wondering about the "**Apply for each**" loop. This is necessary because the Dataverse action "**List rows**" can retrieve multiple rows and must be processed in a loop. In our case, we know that the action will always return just one single row; that is why we do not need to care about the values assigned to the variable; they will always be correct as soon as a correct project number is entered by the human user.

> **Note: The Power Automate flow is simplified for the purpose of this book. In real-life scenarios, we would need to make the flow more robust, by catching all possible anomaly situations, for example, when the human user enters a project number that does not exist or when there is, by mistake, more than one project with the same number in the Dataverse table.**

Now, we need to continue with the configuration, and please perform the following next steps:

- After you have configured the Power Automate flow, click on the "**Save**" button on the right side of the upper command bar and wait until the flow is saved.

- Now you can close the Power Automate portal and return back to the PVA designer portal.

- In the PVA designer portal, click again on the "**+**" sign after the "**Question**" conversation node and select "**Call an action**". Now, your Power Automate flow will be available for selection, according to the following screenshot:

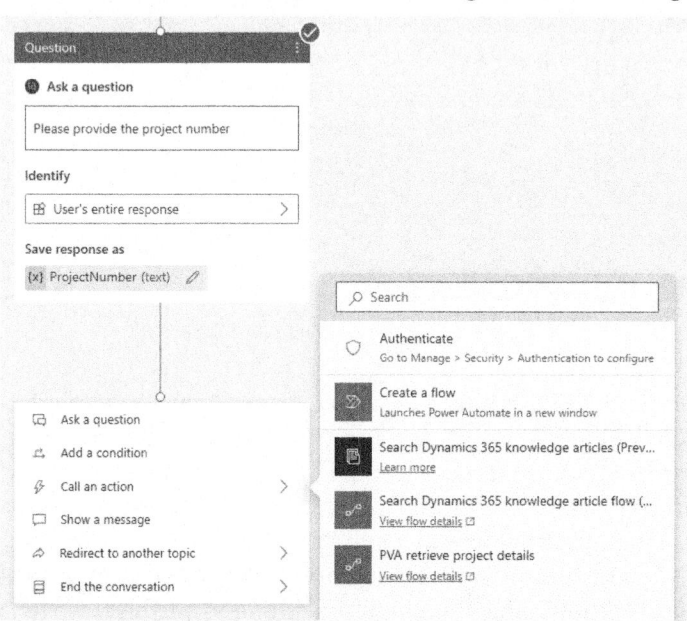

Figure 8.11: Select a Power Automate flow

- Select the flow "**PVA retrieve project details**", which we have created in the previous steps.

- Select the PVA variable "**ProjectNumber**" as the input variable for the flow. The "**Call an action**" node will automatically recognize that the Power Automate flow returns two output values and will create corresponding PVA variables for those. Verify that the node is configured according to the following screenshot:

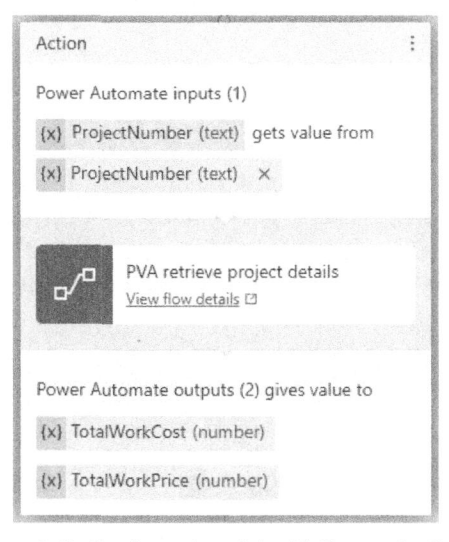

Figure 8.12: Configuration of the "Call an action" node

- The last step in the configuration of the topic conversation nodes will be to inform the human user about the retrieved project information. Click on the "**+**" sign after the "**Action**" node and select "**Show a message**". We need to configure the message to contain not just static text but also dynamic values from the PVA variables. Selecting a variable can be performed by clicking on the "**{x}**" button within the "**Message**" text content in the right place where you want the variable to be used. Configure the "**Message**" according to the following screenshot:

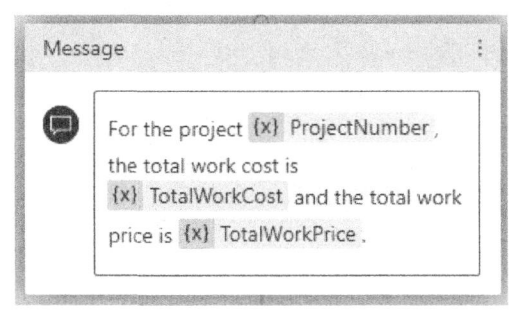

Figure 8.13: Configuration of the last "Message" node

- As you can see in *figure 8.13*, you can enter any of the available PVA variables at any place in the message text. The message text can also be formatted using simple formatting capabilities.

- Click on the "**Save**" button on the right side of the command bar to save the topic.

Congratulations! You have just successfully created your first Power Virtual Agents chatbot. In the next section, you will learn how to test and publish the chatbot.

Test and publish your bot

A chatbot needs to be thoroughly tested before it can be integrated into a host environment. Continuous testing can be easily performed at any time during the chatbot configuration using the test panel named "Test bot", which is part of the PVA designer portal. It is recommended to switch on the setting "`Track between topics`" to see the chatbot behavior of jumping from one topic to another during testing, as documented in the following screenshot:

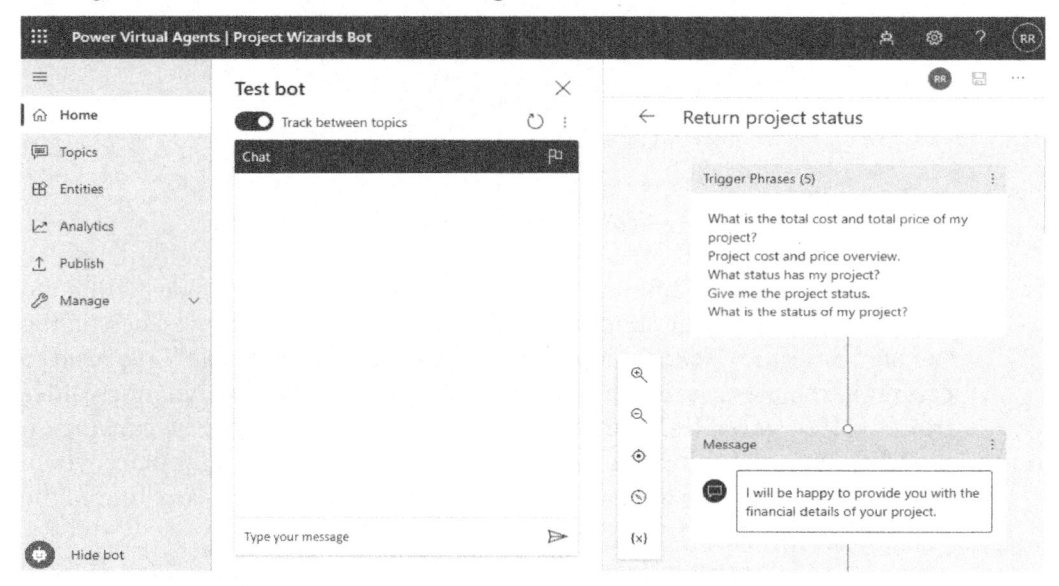

Figure 8.14: Power Virtual Agent test pane

You can now easily test your chatbot using the following three messages entered into the test input field in the lower part of the test pane (after each message, click on the "**Send**" button):

```
Hi
Project status
PROJ-1000
```

The three messages represent the *greeting* to the chatbot to start the conversation, the *project status inquiry*, and finally, entering a *project number*. The result should look like as shown in the following screenshot:

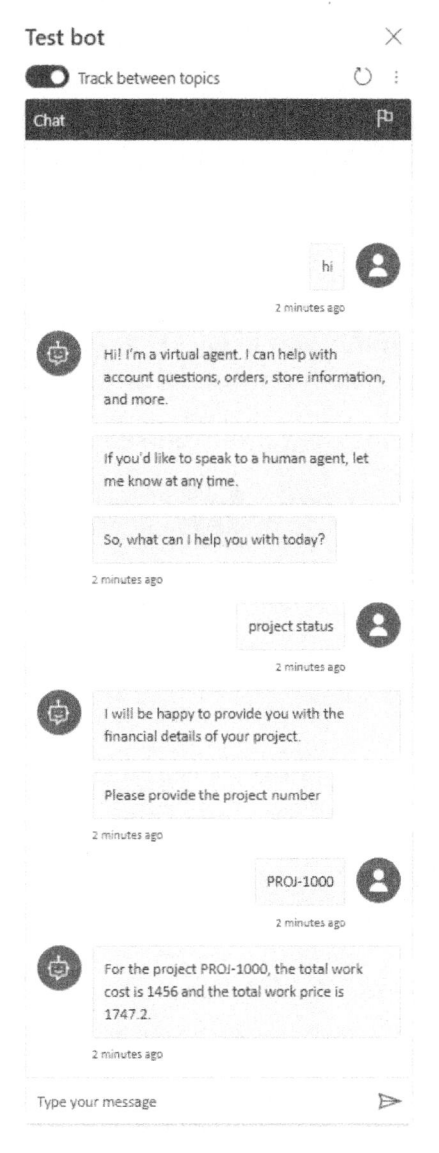

Figure 8.15: Power Virtual Agent testing

As you can see in *figure 8.15*, the chatbot correctly identified an existing project from the "Project Management" solution and responded with the financial values of total work cost and price. The first messages are coming from the built-in "Greeting" topic. The texts of the messages can be modified as well to better serve the purpose of the chatbot.

Now, when the chatbot is tested and works correctly, it must be published. Publishing is a simple step consisting of just one single click. You need to navigate to "**Publish**" in the PVA designer portal, click the "**Publish**" button and confirm publishing.

Finally, we need to learn how can a published topic be integrated into a certain hosting environment, where it will serve the human users.

Host your bot on a website and in Microsoft Teams

A Power Virtual Agents chatbot can be hosted in multiple different hosting environments. The available environments can be inspected when you navigate to "**Publish**" and then click on "**Go to channels**". As of the writing of this book, there are fifteen supported hosting environments, according to the following screenshot:

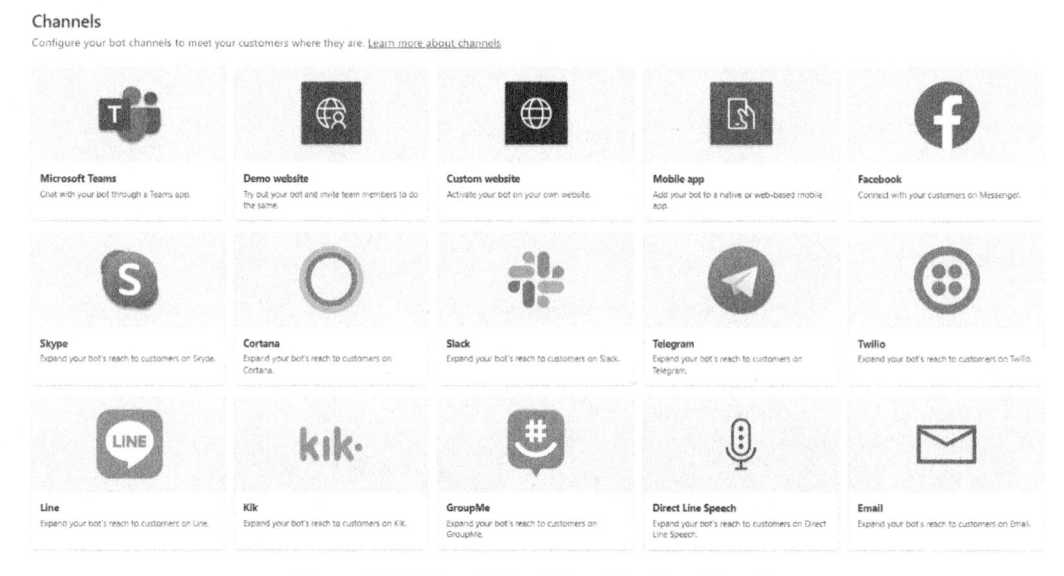

Figure 8.16: Power Virtual Agent hosting channels

As you can see in *figure 8.16*, there are the typical hosting environments like a custom website or Microsoft Teams, but mobile apps and third-party applications are available. The hosting configuration depends on the channel used and can be very simple but also quite complex. To illustrate the hosting capabilities, we will perform integration into the Power Apps portal in the following exercise.

Exercise 19: Integrating a chatbot into a Power Apps portal

In this exercise, we will return back to the Power Apps portal configured for Project Wizards Inc. and configure the portal to host our Power Virtual Agents chatbot.

Please perform the following steps:

1. Open to the Maker Portal, select the correct environment, navigate to "**Apps**", select the portal app "**Project Wizards Customer Portal**", and click on "**Edit**" in the upper command bar. The Power Apps Portals Studio will open the portal.

2. Click on the "**+**" button on the left vertical navigation and select "**Chatbot**". A chatbot component will be placed on the surface of the portal on the lower right side.

3. On the properties pane of the chatbot, select the chatbot "**Project Wizards Bot**" and keep the setting "**Chatbot visibility**" to "**All pages**". The configuration should look like as shown in the following screenshot:

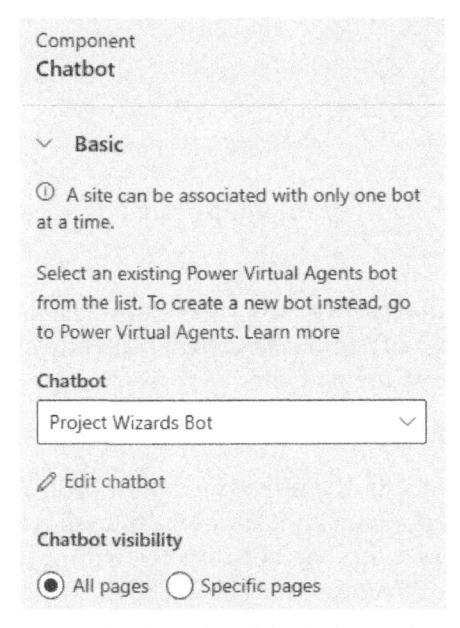

Figure 8.17: Configuration of the chatbot on the portal

4. Click on the "**Sync**" button on the upper command bar to save the change in the portal configuration.

5. Click on the "**Preview**" button on the upper command bar and select "**Desktop**".

230 ■ *Microsoft Power Platform Up and Running*

6. The portal will open, and in the lower right corner, there will be a **chatbot icon**. Clicking on the icon will open the chatbot window, where you can enter messages the same way as during the testing in the PVA designer portal. The chatbot will be rendered according to the following screenshot:

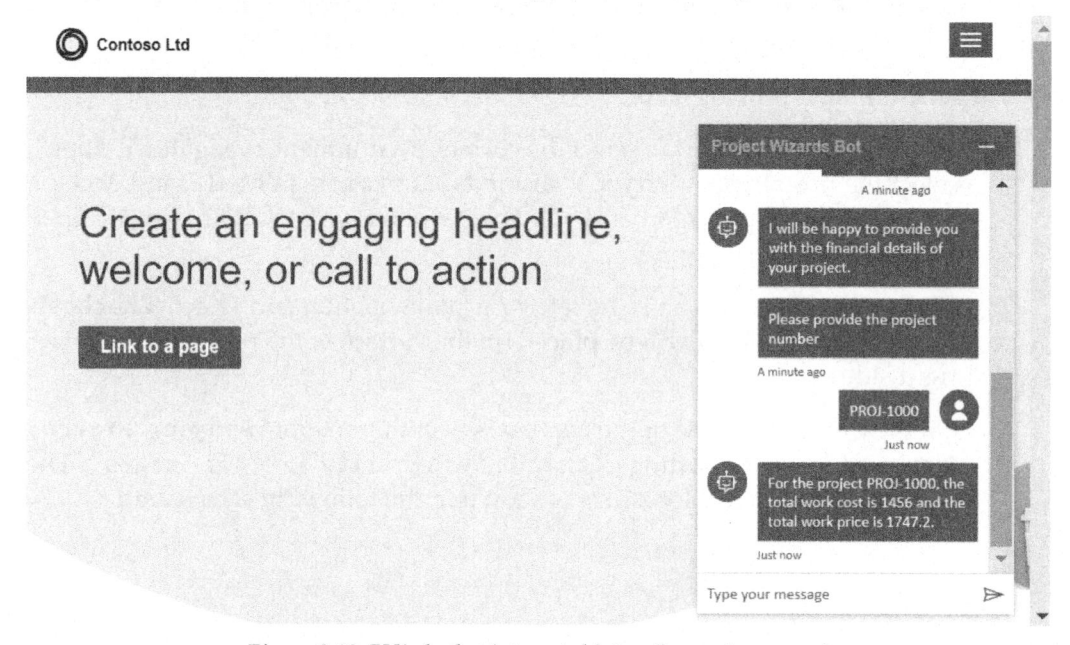

Figure 8.18: PVA chatbot integrated into a Power Apps portal

Congratulations! You have successfully integrated a Power Virtual Agents chatbot into a Power Apps portal.

> **Note: Integration into another website that is not based on Power Apps Portals is not that simple; PVA will generate an HTML code snippet, which must be integrated into the code of the website.**

A Power Virtual Agents chatbot can be integrated into any of the mentioned channels.

After a while, when the chatbot is already used in production environments, and a larger number of conversations with different human users are collected, we can analyze the performance of the chatbot directly within the PVA designer portal. The analytical part of the PVA designer portal provides a comprehensive analytical overview that can give us an indication of how well the chatbot works in real life. An example of such analytics is provided in the following screenshot:

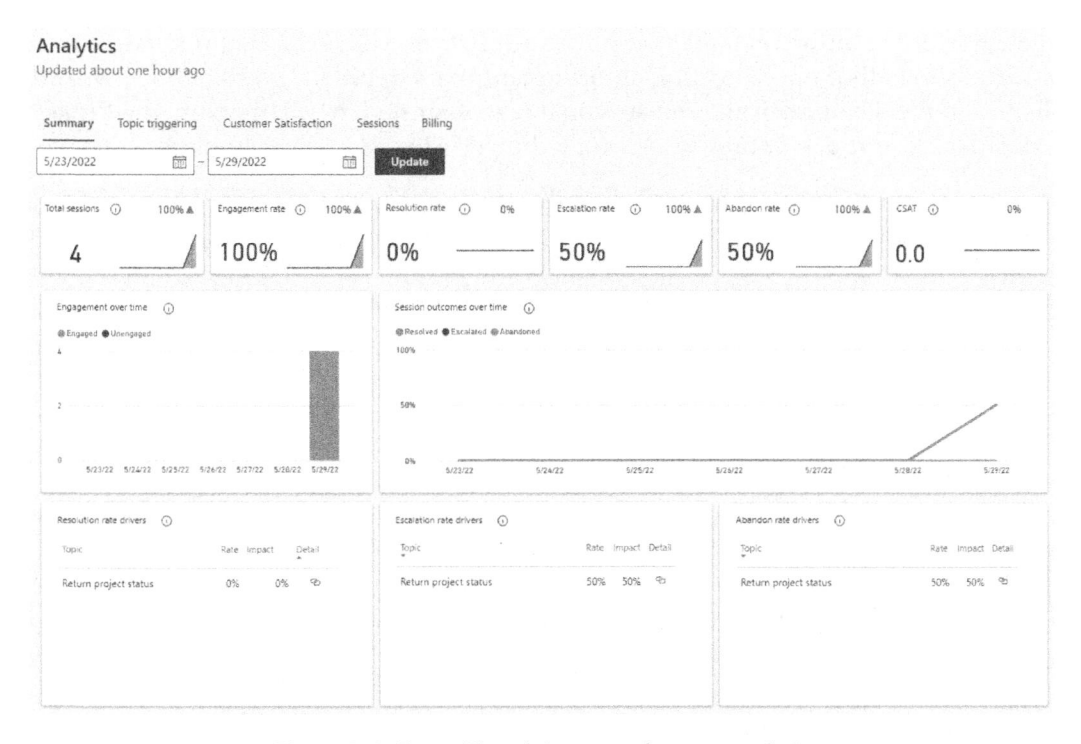

Figure 8.19: Power Virtual Agents performance analytics

As you can see in *figure 8.19*, the analytics provides KPIs like total sessions, engagement rate, resolution rate, escalation rate, abandon rate, or the overall **customer satisfaction (CSAT)** value. Based on those values, refinement and improvement of the chatbot might be necessary.

Conclusion

In this chapter, you have learned a new Power Platform cloud service, the Power Virtual Agents service, which represents a low-code/no-code service for building chatbots. You have seen multiple scenarios and use cases where a chatbot can be used in modern IT systems. You have learned the fundamentals of Power Virtual Agents and the main building blocks of a chatbot. You have specifically seen the importance of the topics and how they are used in a chatbot to recognize human input. You have seen how a topic can be created and why are the topic trigger phrases so important. In the next part, we have discussed the structure of the conversation nodes, what node types are available, and how they can be used to configure the flow of the chatbot's conversation. Next, you have learned how the integration of a chatbot with the surrounding IT systems can be implemented using a connected Power Automate flow. In the practical exercise, you have built your own chatbot to answer a basic question about the financial status of the projects in the Project

Management solution. Finally, you have seen how to test a chatbot, publish it, and integrate a chatbot into a hosting environment, for example, a website or Microsoft Teams. In the next practical exercise, you have integrated the chatbot into the Project Wizards, Inc. portal solution based on the Power Apps Portals technology.

In the upcoming chapter, we will dive deeper into the last Power Platform cloud service we have not seen yet, the AI Builder. As usual, you will see, what are the typical scenarios and use cases for AI integration in business applications. You will learn the fundamentals of AI Builder and gain an overview of the currently available AI models supported by the service. Next, you will see what the necessary steps are to prepare an AI model for integration and use within a Power Platform-based business solution. In the last part of the chapter, you will learn the technical implementation methods to integrate an AI Builder model with a model-driven app, a canvas app, or a Power Automate cloud flow.

Questions

1. What is a chatbot, and why is it important to use chatbots?
2. What are the typical use cases for using chatbots?
3. What is the Power Virtual Agents cloud service?
4. What are the main parts of Power Virtual Agents?
5. What is a topic, and why is it the most important part of Power Virtual Agents?
6. Why are good trigger phrases so important?
7. How can a conversation flow be configured within a topic?
8. What are entities, and how are they used within Power Virtual Agents?
9. How can a chatbot be integrated with other IT systems for retrieving information or triggering processes?
10. How can a chatbot be tested?
11. In which types of hosting environments can a Power Virtual Agents chatbot be integrated?

CHAPTER 9
Bring Intelligence with AI Builder

Introduction

Artificial intelligence is today finding its way into various areas of human life, including business applications. There are many interesting scenarios of how AI can help make business applications more productive and automate areas where, in the past, the human workforce was necessary. In this chapter, you will learn how to easily build AI models with AI Builder. This cloud service contains multiple AI models tailored for use in business scenarios. After you have built your AI models, you will see how these models can be integrated into Power Apps and Power Automate.

Structure

In this chapter, we will discuss the following topics:

- Use cases for AI Builder
- AI Builder fundamentals
- Overview of the AI Builder models
- Configure and test a custom model
- Integrate your model with model-driven apps

- Integrate your model with canvas apps
- Integrate your model with Power Automate

Objectives

After reading this chapter, you will be able to understand what are the typical use cases for integrating an AI capability into business applications. You will make yourself familiar with the AI Builder as the last Power Platform component we are going to present in this book, a component bringing low-code/no-code experience into the world of AI. You will see, which AI models are currently supported by this service, and what they are used for. Next, you will learn the steps to prepare, configure, train, and publish an AI model with AI Builder. Finally, you will see what the possibilities are to integrate an AI Builder model with model-driven apps, canvas apps, or Power Automate flows. As part of this chapter, you will get the possibility for hands-on examples to completely prepare an AI model and then to make a test on how to integrate the model using Power Automate.

Use cases for AI Builder

The first question that needs to be clarified is whether there is a need to include artificial intelligence in business applications at all. Traditionally, a business application made no use of AI and was dedicated to completely different domains. But in today's modern business world, AI found a way into business applications and can serve in many business scenarios to make the life of a business user easier and to bring added value to business applications.

Let us highlight a few of the most typical business scenarios where AI plays an important role.

Document processing

A typical scenario is to be able to automatically process documents, for example, vendor invoices or sales orders, receipts, business cards, or identity documents. The automated processing of all those types of documents can significantly increase the processing speed and reduce manpower since cumbersome manual data entry can be replaced with an automated machine-based solution. Practically, documents would need to be prepared as digital files (image file types, PDF, and so on) and then processed with an AI-driven solution to extract the required blocks of information from the documents.

If you remember *Example 1* in *Chapter 4, Automate Processes with Power Automate*, we have already touched on the possibility of automatically processing vendor invoices for Project Wizards, Inc. In this chapter, we will go a step further and present AI-driven document processing as a practical example.

Products recognition

Imagine a typical scenario called store checking that is widely used by manufacturers of retail goods. Employees visit stores to check whether the products are properly placed in the contractually binding positions within the store. This is manual work, where the employee needs to count the number of products on the shelves and enter this information into paper-based forms. An AI-based solution can reduce the effort of just taking a few photos using the mobile phone and sending the photos to an AI model for analysis. The AI model would be able to recognize all products on the photos and return the respective metadata for digital processing. This scenario can be easily extended to any automated product recognition requirement, which can arise in production, logistics, or anywhere else.

Automated text analysis

There are numerous scenarios where text could be analyzed automatically instead of manually. Let us highlight some of them:

- Incoming e-mail messages in a customer service scenario should be evaluated on their *sentiment*, which means how positive or negative is the tone of the message. Based on the sentiment, the message can be processed with different priorities or by different customer service teams.

- In the same scenario as previously, the e-mail messages should get an automated *category classification* or *key phrase* extraction, which can also help better route the messages to proper customer service teams.

- The *language* of business-related texts should be automatically recognized, or an automated *translation* from one language into another should be performed.

For all those scenarios, AI-driven automated processing is required.

But AI is generally very complex, and building AI-based solutions using traditional tools requires deep AI expertise as well as programming skills. Here comes the Power Platform cloud service called AI Builder, which removes this barrier and makes it possible to prepare and integrate an AI model into a business solution just by using a low-code/no-code approach.

AI Builder fundamentals

The AI Builder is a cloud service and is used as part of the Power Platform to configure and integrate AI models into business applications using just configuration procedures, completely hiding the AI complexity behind the curtains.

AI Builder offers a growing number of selected AI models falling into one of the following categories:

- **Prebuilt models:** The prebuilt models do not require any training with their own data; they are pre-trained with generic data so that they can be used immediately.

- **Custom models:** The custom models are not pre-trained with any data, so a training step needs to be part of the model configuration. The benefit of these models is that they can be tailored exactly to the needs of the customer with their own data.

The preparation of a final AI-based solution can be broken down into typical steps, as illustrated in *figure 9.1*:

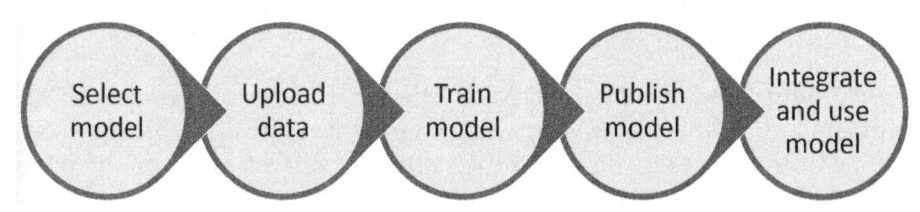

Figure 9.1: AI Builder model creation steps

As we can see in *figure 9.1*, there are five basic steps, which need to be performed, some of them, however, are only for the custom models:

- **Select model:** It is important to understand which AI models are available in AI Builder and whether there is any model suitable for the given requirements. The number of AI models available in the service is constantly growing, so it makes sense to check the possibilities regularly. Should there be no suitable AI model available, there is still the possibility to look in Microsoft Azure and into the AI services such as Cognitive Services or Machine Learning.

- **Upload data:** This step is only required for the custom models. A more detailed overview of all AI Builder models follows in the next section. In the overview, you will learn which are the custom models and what data is required to upload so that the model can use them for training.

- **Train model:** This step is only required for the custom models. For training the model, it is required to highlight the necessary information we need the model to process for us. This is a manual step and is also called tagging. We must give AI Builder the information about the important parts of a document to extract the text content from, which objects we are interested in for the model to detect, and so on. After the tagging is finished, the training procedure is just a click on the respective button. The training procedure can take some time, depending on the amount of training data provided.

- **Publish model:** After a custom model is trained, we can quickly test the performance of the model by providing some test data and evaluating the results. In case the performance of the model is satisfying, the model can be published. Pre-trained models can be published immediately. The publishing is just a click on the respective button.

- **Integrate and use model:** After a model is published, it can be integrated into the Power Platform business solution either directly into a model-driven app or a canvas app or by using Power Automate. Details about the integration capabilities follow in the subsequent sections of this chapter.

Now, when we already have the first idea about AI Builder, let us dive deeper into the available AI models.

Overview of the AI Builder models

As of writing the book, there are *seventeen* AI models available for us in AI Builder, as illustrated in the following screenshot:

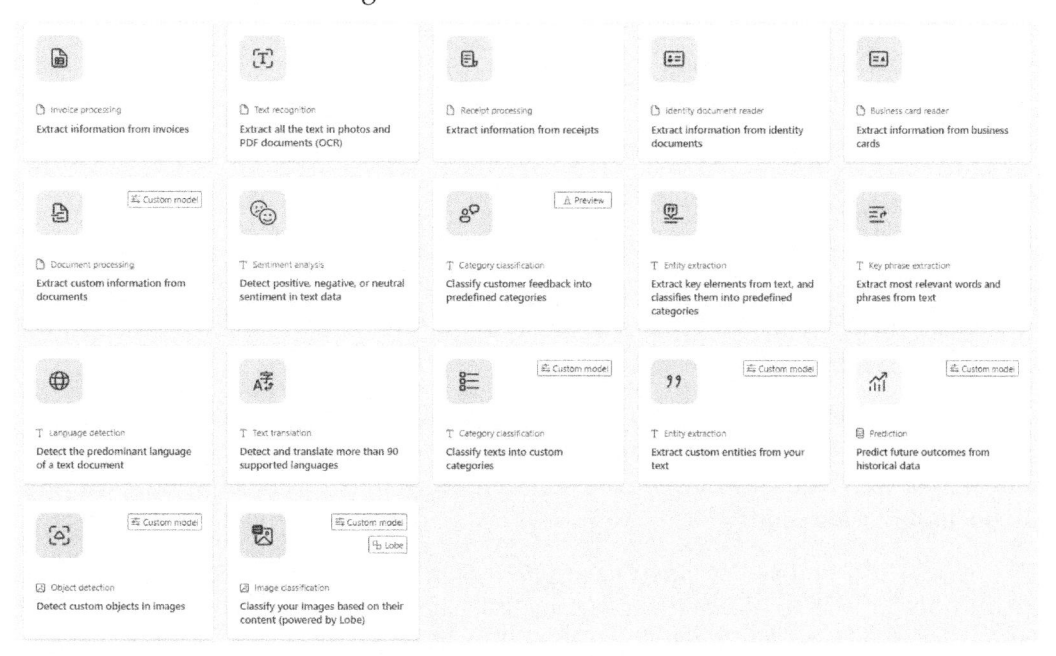

Figure 9.2: AI Builder overview of the models

The models are not just of the two mentioned categories (prebuilt and custom); there is also another categorization based on what type of data the model is processing. Based on these criteria, there are the following three model categories:

(1) **Text-processing models:** The models from this category use text input for the processing.

(2) **Image-processing models:** The models from this category use images for processing.

(3) **Data-processing models:** The models from this category use data of any kind, for example, some data structures from relational databases for processing.

In the following, we are going to describe the available models in each of these three categories.

Text-processing models

AI Builder currently contains **six** text-processing models.

Sentiment analysis

This AI model takes a block of text consisting of one of the multiple sentences and returns one of the values:

- Positive
- Negative
- Neutral
- Mixed

What is sentiment?

It is the overall tone of the text, whether the text sounds positive or negative. A positive tone contains appreciations, positive wording, and so on; a negative tone contains criticism, bad wording, and so on. If nothing of them is mentioned in the text, then the tone is neutral.

The value of "`Mixed`" is used for a text block, which consists of multiple sentences, and there are sentences with different sentiments. Besides the sentiment value, the model also returns a confidence score ranging from 0 to 1 indicating how sure the model is about the sentiment.

This model can be used to analyze any text in situations we need to understand the attitude of the customers or other actors. The model currently supports eight languages and is available only as a prebuilt model.

Category classification

This AI model takes a block of text and returns categories useful for the intended purpose. This model exists as a prebuilt as well as a custom model. As of writing this book, the prebuilt model has a classification structure based on customer feedback, and additional classification models are expected to come soon. The custom model allows you to configure your own categories to better tailor the model to the needs of a customer. The model currently supports seven languages.

The custom category classification model requires to use of Microsoft Dataverse for storing the training data. The training procedure requires preparing text blocks/ sentences and equipping each block or sentence with one or more tags. It is recommended to have at least **ten** text elements for every tag. After the manual data preparation is done, the model can be trained.

Entity extraction

This AI model takes a block of text and extracts the data considered as entities. We have touched on the term *"entities"* in *Chapter 8, Chat with Power Virtual Agents*, where they are used to better recognize the human input inside a chatbot. In AI Builder, the entities are used for the same purpose, for the AI to better structure important information contained in the provided text. Just to remember, an entity can be anything like a color, a city, a country, a monetary value, and so on. This model also exists as a prebuilt as well as a custom model. The model currently supports seven languages.

The custom entity extraction model requires to use of Microsoft Dataverse for storing the training data. The training procedure requires preparing text blocks/sentences and defining the entities within the text. It is recommended to have at least **five** text elements for every entity. After the manual data preparation is done, the model can be trained.

Key phrase extraction

This AI model takes a block of text and extracts the data considered as key phrases. It might sound similar to the previous model, but there is a subtle difference. Although an entity is a structured and predefined piece of information, as explained previously, a key phrase is not predefined, and it is always an individual piece of information contained in a sentence, which represents the essence of the sentence. Key phrases are basically what remains from a sentence, when we remove everything not primarily relevant. The model currently supports seven languages and is available only as a prebuilt model.

Language detection

This AI model is very easily explained; it takes a block of text and returns the predominant language used in the text. Along with the detected language, the model also returns a **confidence score** ranging from 0 to 1 indicating how sure the model is about the language. In contrast to the previous model, the language detection model supports a large number of languages used across the globe. As of the writing of this book, the model is supporting 115 languages and is available only as a prebuilt model.

Text translation

This AI model is also very easy to understand because it provides the capability to translate text from one language to another one. The model is available only as a prebuilt model and currently supports *five* languages.

Image-processing models

AI Builder currently contains *eight* image-processing models:

Invoice processing

This AI model takes an image containing a scan or photo of an invoice document and returns a predefined set of information blocks retrieved from the input file. As of the writing of this book, the model is rather limited as it can process only invoices in the English language and with the typical United States invoice content. The model is prebuilt, which means it cannot be tailored using its own invoice structures.

Text recognition

This AI model takes an image containing texts, for example, photos from books, busy streets with a lot of stores, traffic signs, car plates, and so on, and extracts all recognized text elements into text blocks, which can be used for further processing. It is a prebuilt model and does not require any training.

Receipt processing

This AI model is similar to invoice processing; it takes a scan or photo of a receipt and extracts the relevant information. The model is a prebuilt model, processing currently only English receipts from Australia, Canada, the United States, Great Britain, and India.

Identity document reader

This AI model is able to process **identity document** (**ID**) like passports or US driver's licenses. It is a prebuilt model, returning a predefined set of personal information retrieved from the document. As of the writing of this book, the model supports only documents using the Latin character sets.

Business card reader

This is another prebuilt AI model being able to extract relevant information from business cards. Since it is prebuilt, it returns a predefined set of information from the analyzed business card image.

Document processing

This AI model is a custom model, and the purpose is to process document images and extract the relevant information from them. The model must be trained with its own document images. The model supports a broad variety of languages.

The training procedure requires uploading training image files. After uploading the images, it is necessary to define the information elements to extract from the images. The last step before the training can start is manual tagging of the document images by drawing a rectangle around the part of the image representing an information element and assigning the right tag to the rectangle.

Object detection

This AI model is also a custom model, and its purpose is to recognize objects in provided images. The model must be trained with its own sets of training images first.

The training procedure requires uploading training image files and performing manual tagging of the objects of interest on the images. It is important to have enough images per detected object, and the images must represent the best possible diversity in terms of background, size, light, or camera angles. After the images are uploaded, it is required to create a set of tags and then perform manual tagging by drawing a rectangle around the object of interest on the image and using a tag to inform the AI builder which object was tagged. After the manual data preparation is done, the model can be trained. The model requires at least *fifteen* images for every object of interest.

Image classification

This AI model takes images and creates categories of the images by assigning labels. This is also a custom model, which means it is required to provide training images and perform the labeling.

Data-processing models

AI Builder contains currently only *one* model—the Prediction.

Prediction

The Prediction AI model takes historical data and learns to create associations between the data elements to be able to predict some required values. The model is able to give three different types of predictions:

- **A binary prediction:** This model type answers a given question with a yes or no.

- **Multiple outcome prediction:** This model type answers a question, which can have multiple possible answers.

- **Numerical Prediction:** This model type answers a question with a numerical answer.

This AI model requires the analyzed data to be stored in Microsoft Dataverse, and you need to have a certain volume of training data to make the model reliability high enough. Even though the official minimal requirements are rather low, it is recommended to provide at least 1.000 records of historical data.

Configure and test a custom model

Now, after we have learned the capabilities and features of the AI Builder service, let us jump into the practical part of this chapter by implementing an example AI model. This model will enhance *Example 1* presented in *Chapter 4, Automate Processes with Power Automate* of this book. Part of this example was to use the capabilities of AI Builder to automatically extract the required information from incoming vendor invoices to be able to process this information in the subsequent steps of the automation.

Example 3: Extract information from vendor invoices

In this example, you will see how to prepare an AI solution for extracting required information from vendor invoices. As the Invoice Processing AI model is currently limited to US invoices only and is prebuilt, we use the Document Processing AI model instead, which makes it possible to train the model with its own data.

> Note: Even though this is an example and not an exercise for Project Wizards, Inc., you are encouraged to perform the described steps on your own to make hands-on experiences with AI Builder.

For this example, we use a sample data collection from Microsoft, which can be downloaded by using the following URL: **https://go.microsoft.com/fwlink/?linkid=2128080**

For the example, please perform the following steps:

1. Use the preceding URL to download the sample data package. It is a ZIP file containing two folders: "**Invoices**" and "**Rental Agreements**". Unzip the file to your favorite file location.

2. Navigate to the Maker Portal and select the correct environment.

3. Navigate to "**AI Builder**" and then "**Explore**". You will find the collection of available AI models.

4. Select the "**Document Processing**" AI model. You will need to eventually activate the trial license for AI Builder at this point.

5. On the model overview, click on "**Get started**". This will start a guided dialog in which you provide all the required information for AI Builder to be able to train itself.

6. In the first step of the guided dialog, you need to select one of the two types of documents. The "**Structured and semi-structured documents**" are used for documents having a unified structure, for example, sales orders, invoices, delivery slips, and so on; the other option "**Unstructured and free-form documents**" is used for documents not having any unified structure, for example, e-mails, letters, and so on.

7. For our example, select "**Structured and semi-structured documents**" and click "**Next**".

8. The next step of the guided dialog is to specify which information should be extracted from the documents. As we are going to use the sample data from Microsoft, we must define the information, available in the sample files. For the specification of the information, you need to always click on "**+ Add**" and

244 ■ *Microsoft Power Platform Up and Running*

select the type of information. In the first step, we add information elements of the type "`Field`" according to the following screenshot:

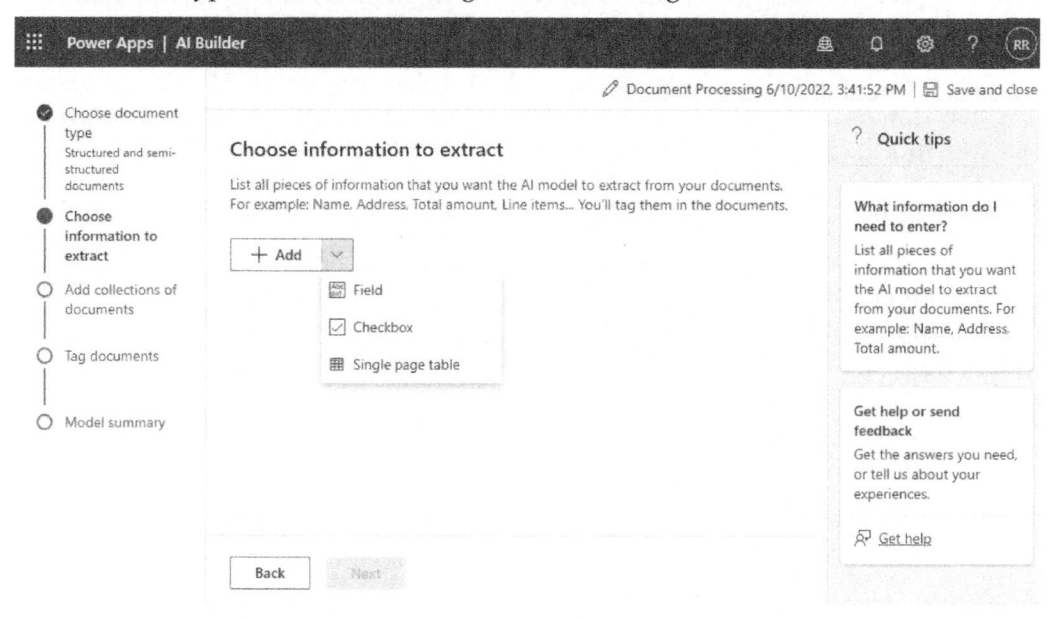

Figure 9.3: Adding information elements of type "Field"

9. As you can see in *figure 9.3*, there are three different types of information. First, we create the following information elements of type "`Field`":

- `Invoice Date`
- `Due Date`
- `Invoice Number`
- `Customer ID`
- `Customer Name`
- `Subtotal`
- `Sales Tax`
- `Shipping`
- `Total`

10. Verify that the group you created contains information elements of type "**Field**" according to the following screenshot:

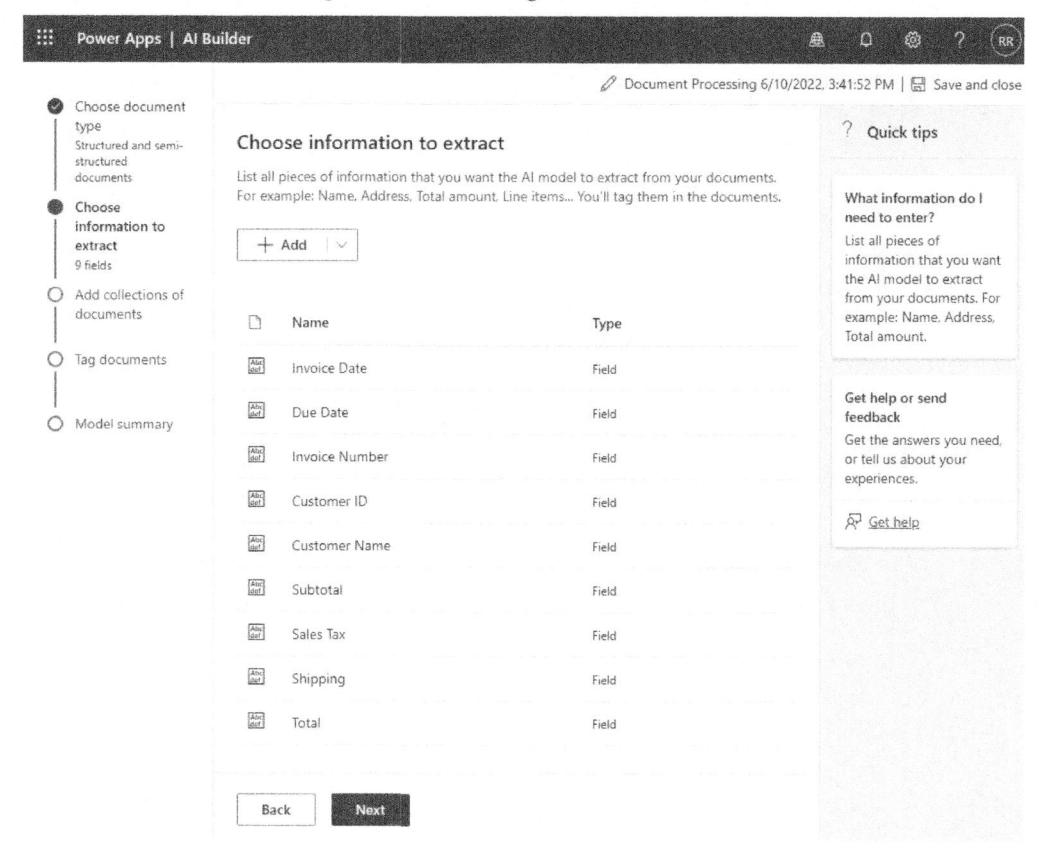

Figure 9.4: Added information elements

11. Next, we create an information element of type "**Single page table**" to accommodate the invoice line items. Click on "**+ Add**" and then "**Single page table**". Give the table the name "**Line Items**".

12. Now, we need to create table columns for the important line-item columns we want to capture. Click on the first column, "**Column 1**" and rename it to "**Item description**".

13. Click on the "**+**" sign right to the first column. To create another column, give the new column the name "**Item value**".

14. Verify that the single-page table is configured according to the following screenshot:

← **Single page table**   ×

Give your table a name and define the columns you want the AI model to extract. This capability is currently in preview.

| Line Items |

Item description	Item value	+

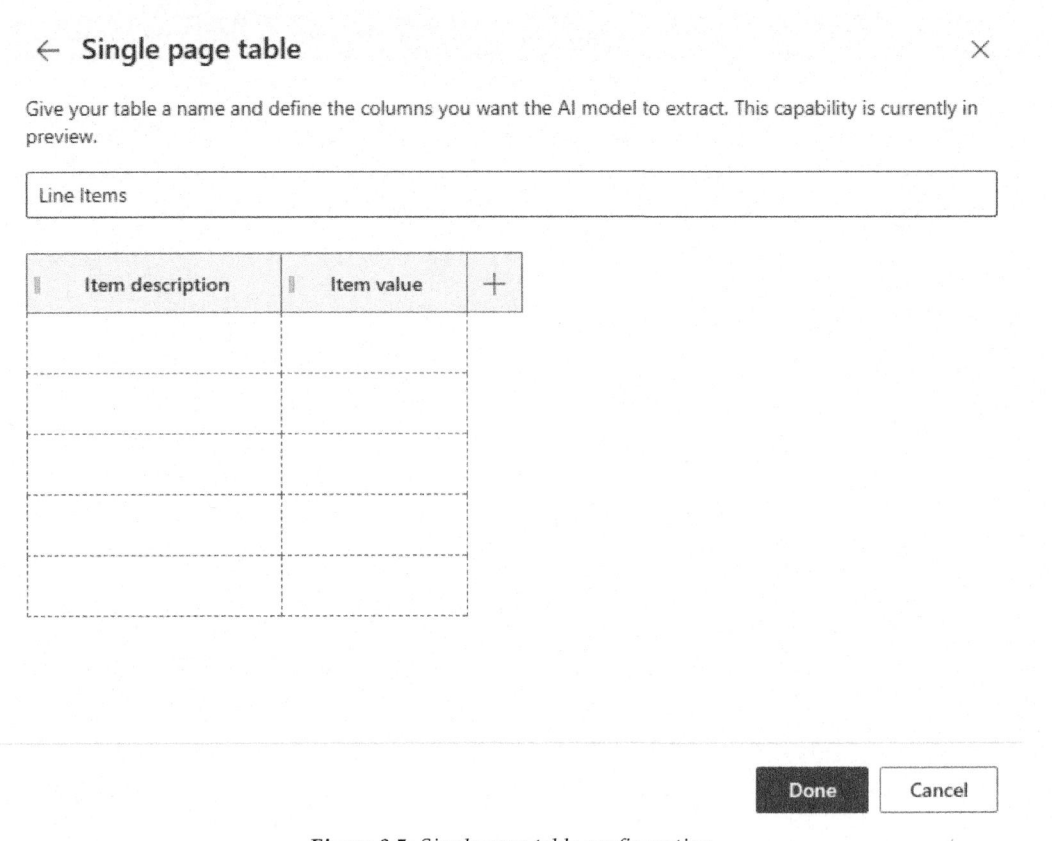

Done Cancel

Figure 9.5: Single page table configuration

15. Click "**Done**" to save the table definition.
16. Click "**Next**" to proceed to the next step of the guided dialog.
17. In this step, we need to first create a separate collection for every document type. Because in the sample data from Microsoft, there are two different

templates for the fictitious companies "*Adatum*" and "*Contoso*", we create two collections with the respective names, according to the following screenshot:

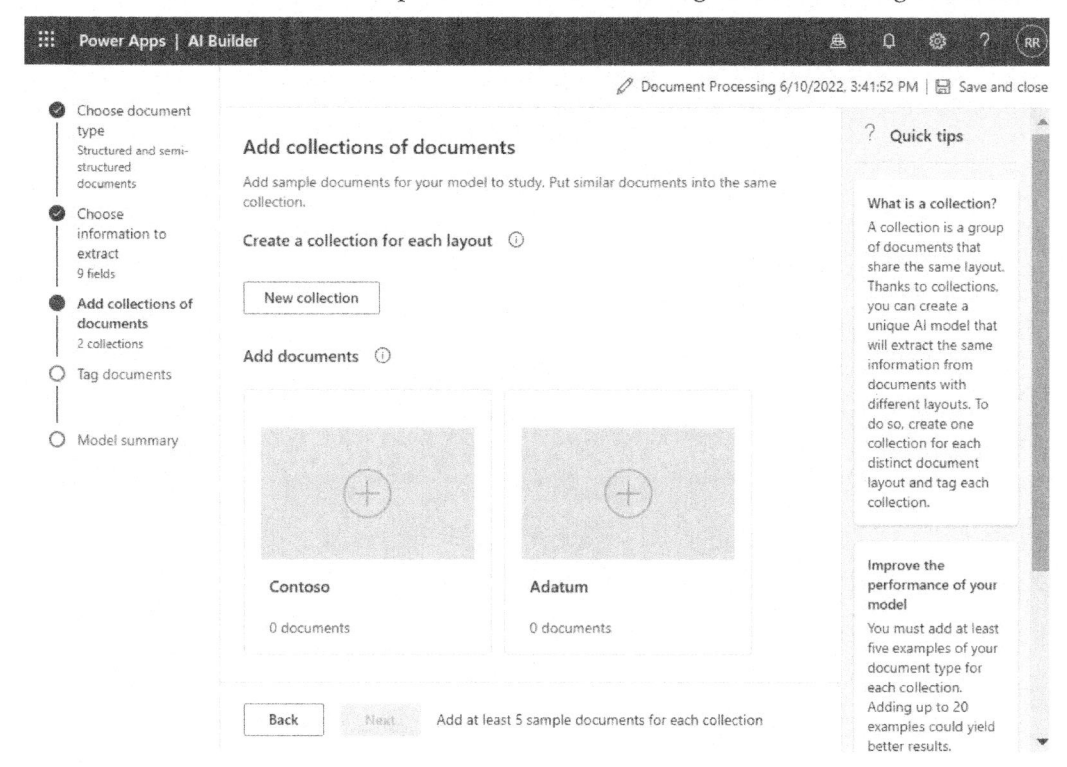

Figure 9.6: Document collections

18. Now, we need to upload the sample data for the two fictitious companies into the two created collections. In each of the two folders of the downloaded data for "*Adatum*" and "*Contoso*", there are two sub-folders, "**Test**" and "**Train**". We always upload the files found in the sub-folder "**Train**". For the upload, click first on the "**+**" sign in the middle of the collection, then click on "**Add documents**", and finally select "**My device**" as the source of

the files. In the respective folder, select all the five files and click "**Open**". This will upload the files according to the following screenshot:

Upload documents

These documents will be used to train your model.

		Name	Size	Status
✓	📄	Adatum 1.pdf	46.7 KB	
✓	📄	Adatum 2.pdf	45.9 KB	
✓	📄	Adatum 3.pdf	46.1 KB	
✓	📄	Adatum 4.pdf	45.9 KB	
✓	📄	Adatum 5.pdf	46.6 KB	

[Upload 5 documents] [Cancel]

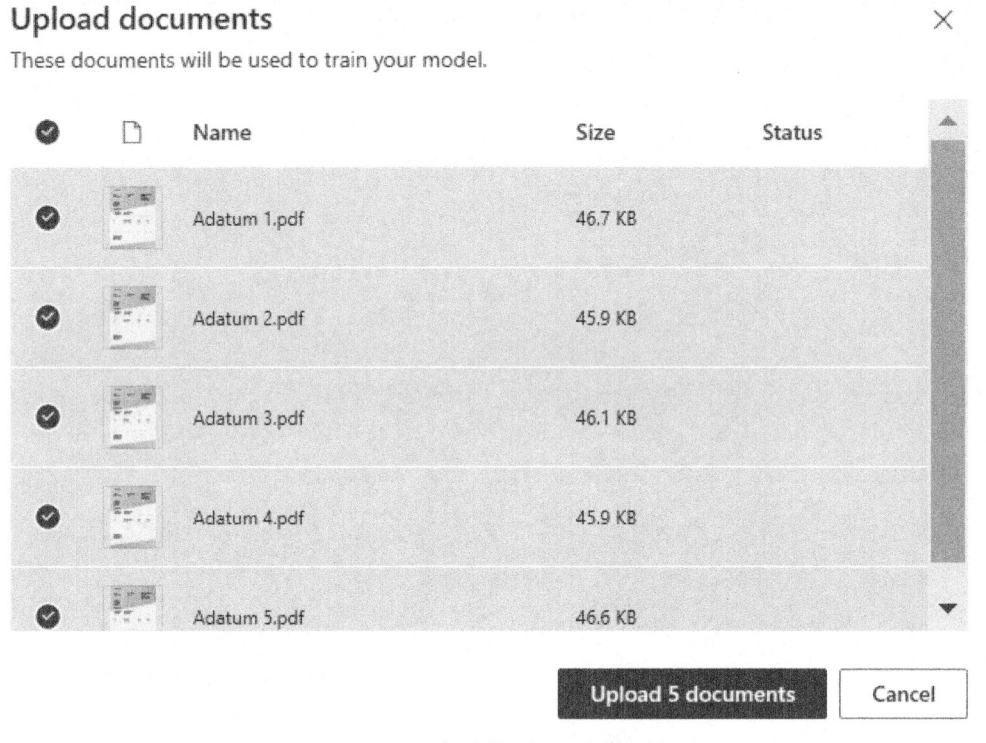

Figure 9.7: Upload files into a collection

19. Confirm the upload by clicking on "`Upload 5 documents`". Repeat the procedure for both collections "`Adatum`" and "`Contoso`".

20. Now comes the most important but also the most labor-intense part of the training procedure, the tagging of the training files. First, click on "**Next**" to proceed to the next step in the guided dialog.

21. Select the collection "`Adatum`", and this will open the tagging dialog for the files in the collection. On the top right side, you will find the *previews* of the five uploaded files, in the lower right side the *information elements*, and in the middle, the *first of the documents prepared for tagging*. The tagging consists of selecting the correct area on the document with a rectangle and assigning a tag to the area. For individual pieces of text, it is sufficient to click on the text; if a longer area with multiple words needs to be selected, you need to draw a rectangle around that area (for example, for the Customer Name). If any of the information elements is not on the document, you need to select

those elements and, using the local three-dot menu, select "**Not available in document**".

22. Next, we need to also tag the line items table. Draw a larger rectangle around the whole table with the line items and select the table information element "**Line Items**". Ensure that the "**Advanced tagging mode**" is on. Select the first cell from the right pane with the name "**Item description**", and in the invoice line items table, select a cell in the first line under the column "**DESCRIPTION**". Then select the second cell with the name "**Item value**" from the right pane, and in the invoice, the line-items table selects a cell in the first line under the column "**LINE TOTAL**" according to the following screenshot:

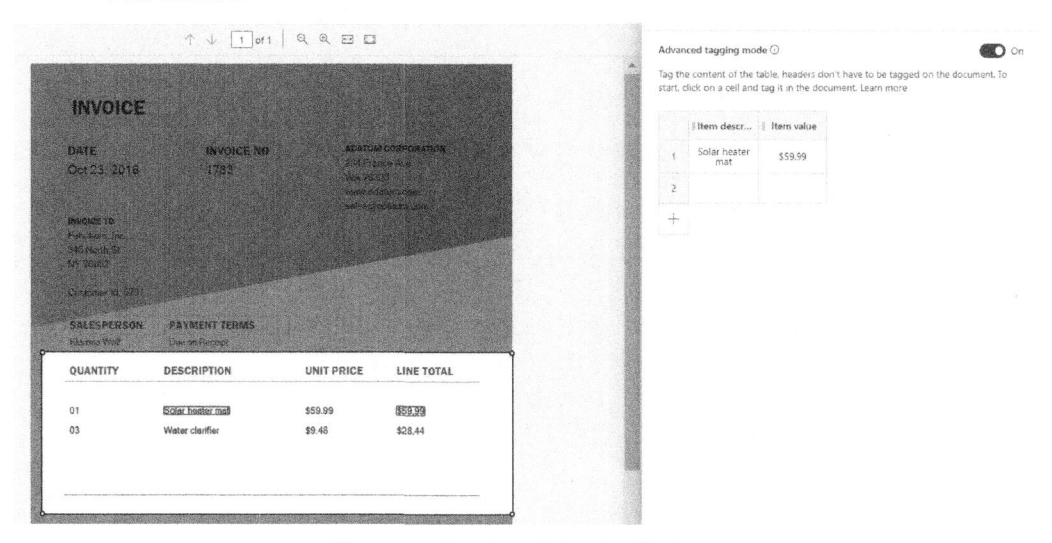

Figure 9.8: Tagging the invoice line items

23. Click "**Done**" to finish the configuration of the line items table.

24. After you have processed all information elements, the document is flagged as completely tagged, according to the following screenshot—verify that you have tagged all available fields on the document as well as the line items

table correctly and excluded the two not available elements "**Due Date**" and "**Shipping**":

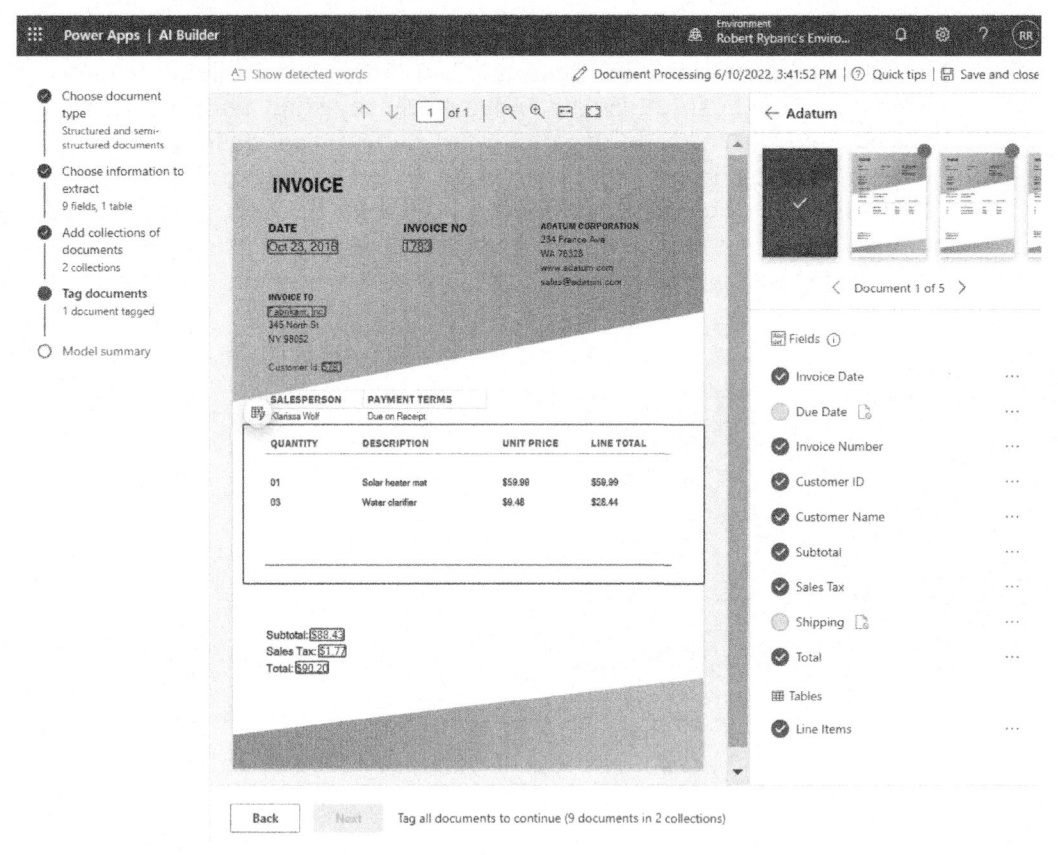

Figure 9.9: Fully tagged document from the "Adatum" collection

25. Perform the tagging procedure for all four remaining invoice documents from the "**Adatum**" collection.

26. Click on the "**<- Adatum**" to return back from the "**Adatum**" collection and select the "**Contoso**" collection, where the same tagging needs to be performed. You will see that the training files for the "**Contoso**" collection are not so sharp and rectangular but rather a bit blurry and skewed, representing documents received, for example, via fax or by scanning paper documents.

27. Repeat the whole tagging procedure for all five documents from the "**Contoso**" collection. You will find certain differences in the content, and certain fields are not available; others which were not on the "**Adatum**" invoices are present on the "**Contoso**" invoices. This is a typical real-life scenario where you need to find the best way to accommodate data from various sources.

Bring Intelligence with AI Builder ■ 251

28. Verify that the tagging of the "**Contoso**" invoices corresponds to the following screenshot:

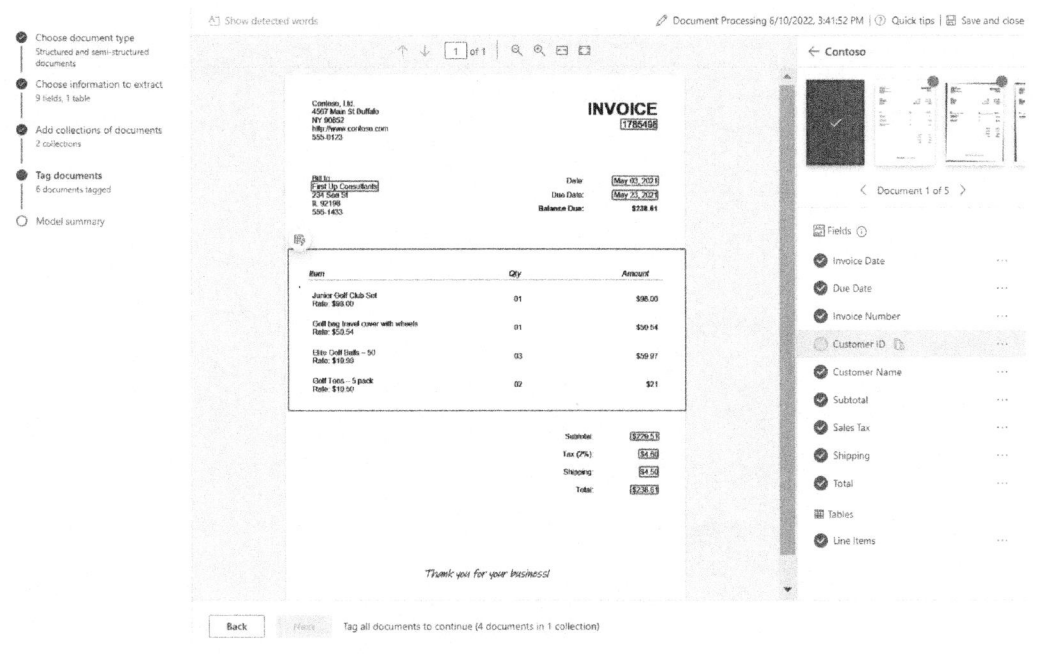

Figure 9.10: Fully tagged document from the "Contoso" collection

29. You may notice the differences between the content of the two collections by comparing the finished tagging between *figure 9.9* and *figure 9.10*.

30. Perform the tagging procedure for all four remaining invoice documents from the "**Contoso**" collection.

31. Click on "**Next**" in the guided dialog to see the last step in the dialog with the model summary. Now, AI Builder has everything it needs to train itself so that we can click on the "**Train**" button and then wait until the training process finishes. The training may take some time to conclude.

32. After the training is finished, click again on the AI model to open the model's dashboard, containing the accuracy score, according to the following screenshot:

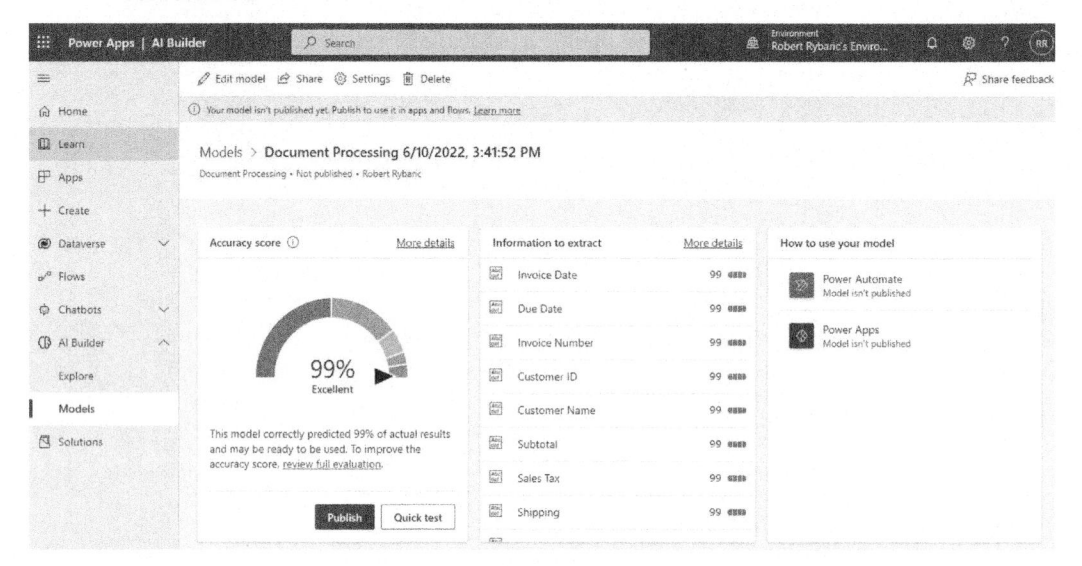

Figure 9.11: AI model's dashboard

33. As you can see in *figure 9.11*, the accuracy of the model is very high, so the model should be able to perform high-quality recognition of real documents.

34. In order to quickly test the functionality of the model, we can use the "**Quick test**" button. Click on the button, and in the following dialog, drop the sample invoice from the sub-folder "**Test**" of the folder "**Adatum**" on the Quick test canvas. After a short analysis, the Quick test canvas should show the recognized areas on the document along with confidence values. Repeat the same test with the sample invoice from the sub-folder "**Test**" of the folder "**Contoso**".

35. The last step in this example is to publish the AI model for use within a Power Platform solution by clicking on the "**Publish**" button.

Congratulations! You have successfully prepared, configured, and trained a custom AI model using the AI Builder. This is not the end; we have another example later in this chapter, demonstrating how can an AI model be integrated within a Power Platform solution.

In the next three sections, you will learn how can be AI Builder models directly integrated with the three possible Power Platform services: the model-driven apps, the canvas apps, and Power Automate flows.

Integrate your model with model-driven apps

As of writing this book, the only AI Builder model that can be directly integrated into the user interface of a model-driven app is the Business Card Reader. Integrating this model requires a multi-step configuration, which is well described in the Microsoft product documentation. The result of the integration is the possibility to use scans or photos of collected business cards to directly create records in Microsoft Dataverse, specifically in the tables containing personal information fields, for example, in the tables "**Contact**" or "**Lead**".

Integrate your model with canvas apps

Direct integration into the user interface of the canvas app is currently supported for the following five AI Builder models, as illustrated in the following screenshot:

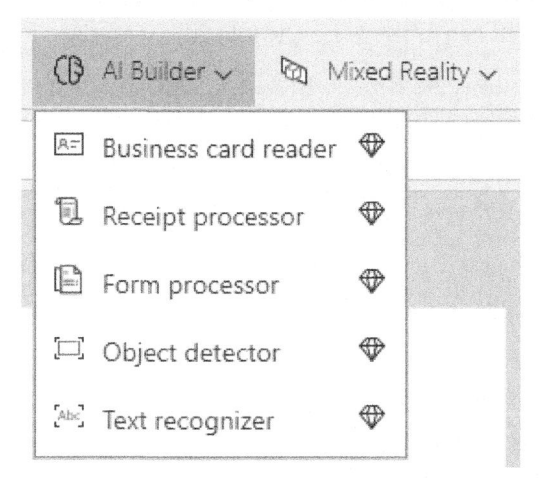

Figure 9.12: AI Builder model integration into canvas apps

All the five models can be placed on a canvas app screen as usual controls and can be directly called from the app by feeding them with the required data. This can be used in a variety of practical scenarios, for example:

- Take photos of the collected business cards, receipts, or forms using the mobile phone camera and directly submit the photos to the business card reader, receipt processor, or form processor models for analysis. As a possible next step, save the received data into a business application.

- Take photos containing objects of interest, for example, products placed on the shelves in supermarkets, and submit these photos to the Object detector model for analysis and processing.

- Take photos of texts of interest, such as book pages, newspapers, and so on, and send those photos to the Text recognizer model for further processing.

Integrate your model with Power Automate

Power Automate is the only Power Platform service that can directly integrate with any of the existing AI Builder models, using a specific AI Builder data connector. The data connector contains a collection of actions to call any of the AI Builder models.

In the following example, we are going to test this approach by building a simple Power Automate flow to call the AI model we created in *Example 3* and evaluate the results.

Example 4: Test vendor invoice processing

In this example, we will build the following logic:

- The Power Automate flow will be equipped with the Button trigger for manual execution.
- The Button flow will contain an input variable of data type File to be able to select a file containing a vendor invoice.
- The flow will call the Document processing AI model we have built in *Example 3* and submit the file as a parameter.
- The flow will receive the recognized content from the AI model and present this within an e-mail sent to ourselves for verification.

Since this example does not belong to the solution built for Project Wizards, Inc., we will create the flow outside of the project solution.

Please perform the following steps:

1. Navigate to the Maker Portal.
2. Navigate to "**Flows**", select "**Cloud flows**", and click on "**+ New flow**". From the options, select "**Instant cloud flow**".

3. In the flow creation dialog, give the flow the name "**Test AI model**" and select the trigger "**Manually trigger a flow**". Confirm with "**Create**"; this will open the Power Automate flow designer.

4. Click on the trigger "**Manually trigger a flow**" and then click on "**+ Add an input**". Select the data type "**File**" and give the input parameter the name "Vendor invoice" according to the following screenshot:

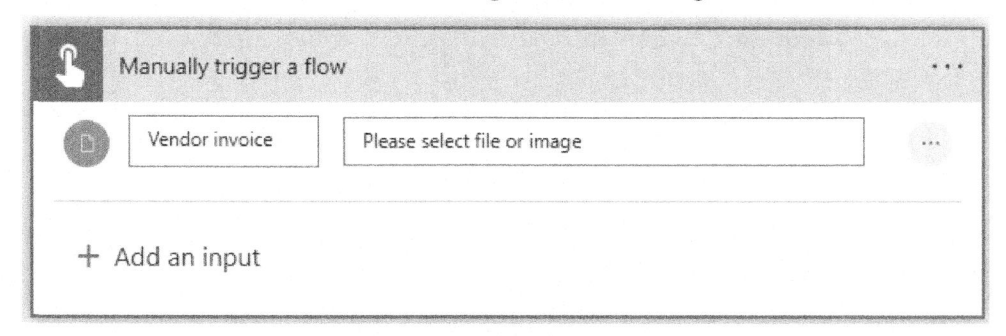

Figure 9.13: Configuration of the trigger

5. Click on "**+ New step**" below the trigger and search for the data connector "**AI Builder**".

6. Select the connector "**AI Builder**" to see the list of available actions. Find and select the action with the name "**Extract information from forms**".

7. Configure the action according to the following screenshot, where the name of the AI model needs to be selected from a list of available models and represents your AI model name:

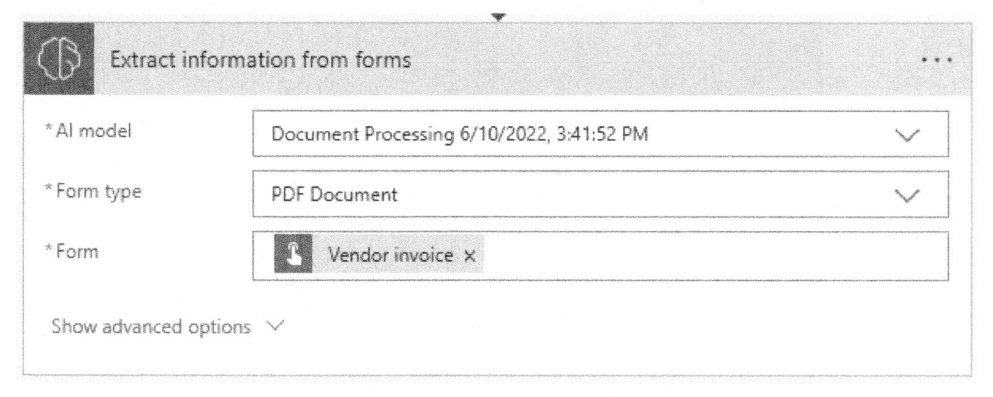

Figure 9.14: Configuration of the AI Builder action

256 ■ *Microsoft Power Platform Up and Running*

8. Click on "**+ New step**" below the AI Builder action and search for the data connector "**Office 365 Outlook**".

9. Select the connector "**Office 365 Outlook**" to see the list of available actions. Find and select the action with the name "**Send an e-mail (V2)**".

10. Configure the action according to the following screenshot. You may experiment with different configurations; just keep in mind that we need to get some information from the analyzed document sent per e-mail to ourselves:

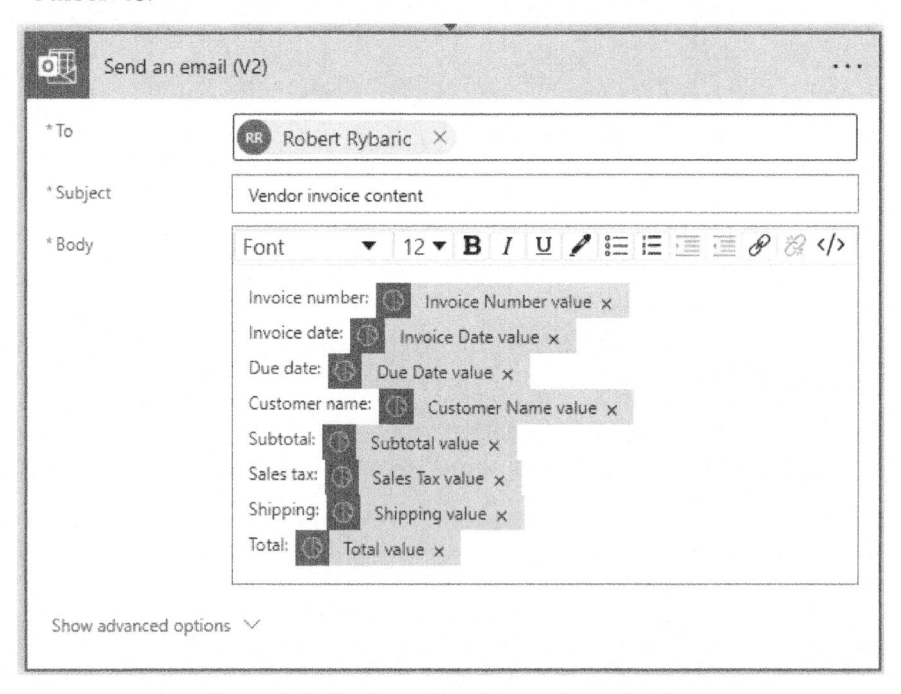

Figure 9.15: Configuration of the send e-mail action

11. The final flow structure should correspond to the following screenshot:

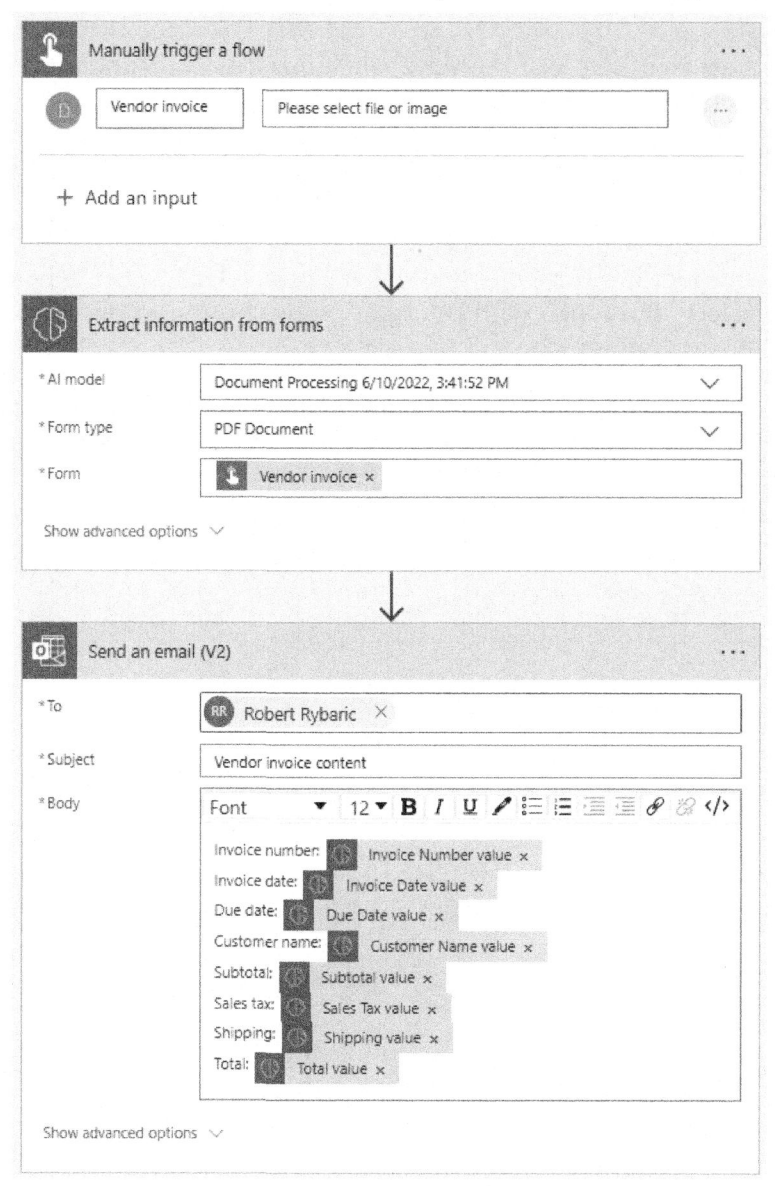

Figure 9.16: Final flow structure

258 ■ *Microsoft Power Platform Up and Running*

12. Click on "**Save**" on the right side of the command bar and wait until the flow is saved.

13. The next step is to test the flow. Click on "**Test**" on the right side of the command bar, confirm "**Manually**", and click "**Test**".

14. In the input parameters dialog, click on "**Import**" and select one of the two "**Test**" invoices from either the "**Adatum**" or "**Contoso**" group of files. Finally, click on "**Run flow**" and wait until the flow run finishes.

15. In the upper left corner of the Maker Portal, click on the "**Apps**" selection and select "**Outlook**" with the right mouse button to open Outlook in an additional browser tab.

16. You should find an e-mail message in your Inbox with the following content:

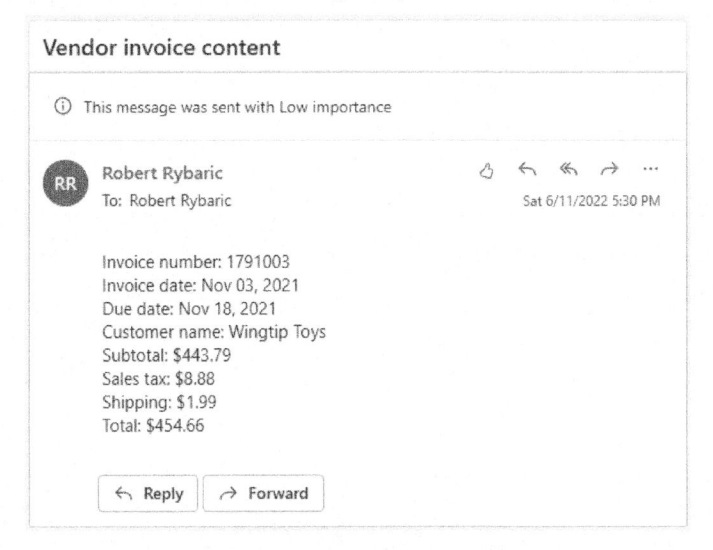

Figure 9.17: Notification e-mail

17. As you can see in *figure 9.17*, the flow sent us some of the fields of the vendor invoice analyzed with AI Builder. When we compare this result with the original source of the test invoice (from the "**Contoso**" group), we can immediately see the true power of AI, which is able to do the hard work of recognizing the content even from a low-quality source and prepare the content for automated machine processing. The AI model was even able to recognize a manually corrected invoice number. Please refer to the following figure:

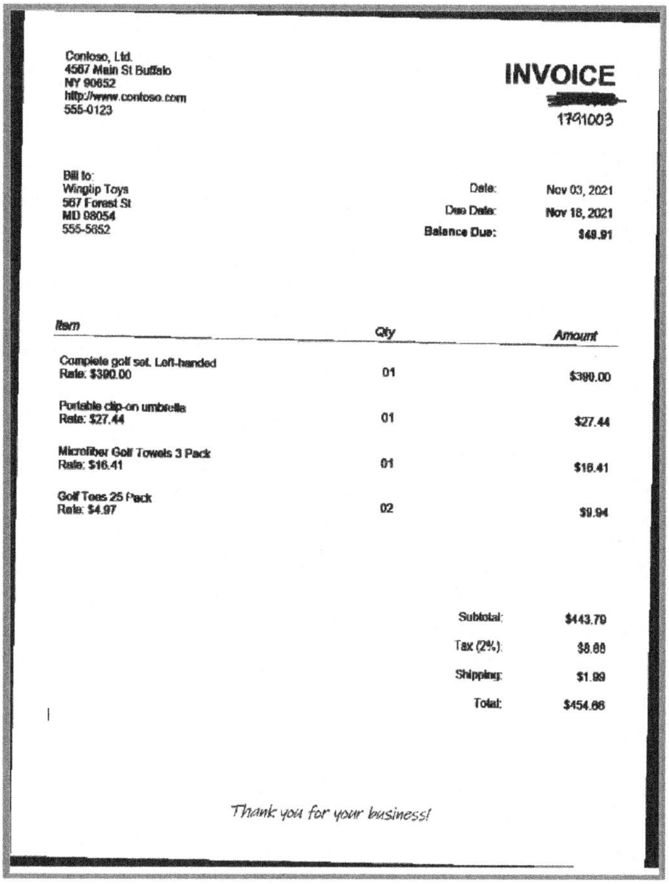

Figure 9.18: *Original invoice document*

Congratulations! You have successfully tested your AI Builder model using Power Automate. You have seen AI in action and the amazing results AI can provide even in the somehow boring world of business applications. When you now refer to *Example 1* in *Chapter 4, Automate Processes with Power Automate*, you can imagine how powerful can be such a solution for Project Wizards, Inc. to automatically process their vendor invoices.

Conclusion

In this chapter, you have learned the last outstanding Power Platform component, the AI Builder. You have understood that in today's world, AI has become a natural extension of business applications, serving the user of the applications to be more productive, automate repetitive tasks, or even replace the human workforce in certain situations. You have seen some of the typical use cases where this can happen. Next, we focused on the foundation overview of the AI Builder service. You have learned which AI models are currently available and what business requirements they can address. You learned the steps necessary to prepare an AI model to use within a Power Platform solution. In the last part of this chapter, you have seen, what are the possibilities to integrate an AI Builder model with the model-driven app, canvas apps, and Power Automate flows. The chapter was enhanced with two interesting examples, where you could learn on your own how can an AI Builder model be prepared, trained, and published. In the second example, you have seen how integration with Power Automate can work.

The upcoming chapter is fully dedicated to the administration of the Power Platform. In the chapter, you will get an overview of the administration possibilities, and you will learn the Power Platform Admin Center a bit more to see what can be done with this portal. Next, we will dive deeper into the world of the Power Platform environments, and you will learn what types of environments are available and what strategies you can consider when planning for smaller or larger Power Platform projects. After that, you will make yourself familiar with the foundation of solution management as the key pillar for **Application Lifecycle Management (ALM)**, or in other words, how to distribute solutions across environments. In the last part of the chapter, you will learn what the possibilities for automating certain Power Platform administration tasks are.

Questions

1. Why is AI important in today's business applications?
2. What are the typical scenarios and use cases where AI can significantly help automate processes, increase productivity, or eliminate manual work?
3. What is the AI Builder?
4. What AI models does AI Builder contain?
5. What is the difference between a prebuilt and a custom AI model?
6. What are the three types of information an AI Builder model can process?
7. How are custom AI models trained?
8. What is the tagging when preparing training data for AI Builder?
9. What is a confidence score of an AI model?
10. Which AI models can be integrated into model-driven apps?
11. Which AI models can be integrated into canvas apps?
12. Which AI models can be integrated with Power Automate?

Chapter 10
Administer the Power Platform

Introduction

This chapter is dedicated to the administration of Power Platform solutions. You will learn the various options and how the whole Power Platform ecosystem in your company can be administered. Power Platform can be administered using multiple approaches, and we will present you with an overview of the available options.

Structure

In this chapter, we will discuss the following topics:

- Overview of the Power Platform administration
- Power Platform environments overview
- The Power Platform admin center
- Power Platform environment strategies
- Solution management fundamentals
- Application lifecycle management fundamentals
- Automate Power Platform Fundamentals

Objectives

After reading this chapter, you will be able to understand the basics of administering the Power Platform and deploying Power Platform solutions across environments. First, you will learn, what are the typical tasks, a Power Platform administrator needs to perform on a daily basis. You will understand, what different types of Power Platform environments exist, and what is the purpose of each of the types. Next, you will make yourself familiar with the main Power Platform administration tool, the Power Platform Admin Center, as well as the Power BI Admin Page for administering Power BI. After that, we will dive deeper into the topic of Power Platform environment strategies, and you will learn on some examples how an environments set-up for large Power Platform projects can look like. In the next part, we will provide you with the fundamentals of solution management within the Power Platform and how solutions are used for deployment processes. You will learn the basics of **Application Lifecycle Management** (**ALM**) for Power Platform, and finally, we will present you with some tools and procedures on how to automate administration and solution deployment within Power Platform.

Overview of the Power Platform administration

Microsoft Power Platform is a collection of complex cloud solutions, and as always, there is a need to configure, administer and maintain the platform. The Power Platform is a **Software as a Service** (**SaaS**) cloud, so the administration and maintenance focus only on a subset of the typical tasks the IT administration usually requires. *Figure 10.1* offers a quick comparison of the responsibilities in an on-premises IT landscape compared with a SaaS cloud landscape:

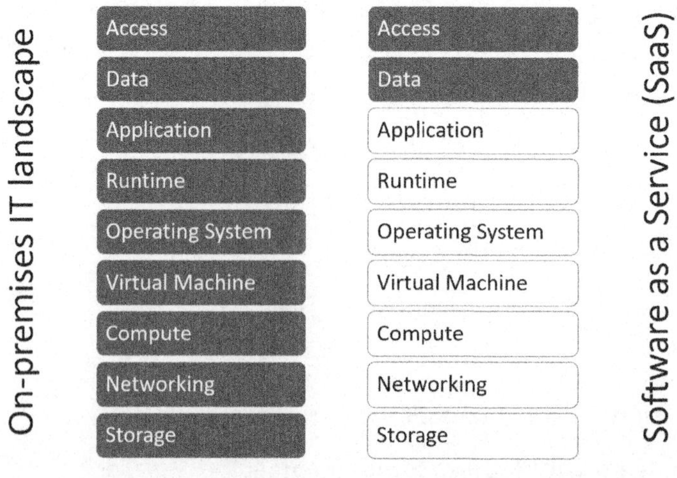

Figure 10.1: *Administration responsibilities comparison*

As you can see in *figure 10.1*, in a cloud landscape, specifically in a SaaS cloud, there is much less to be done in terms of configuration, administration, and maintenance since everything, from hardware (storage, networking, and compute), through virtual machines and operating system, up to the application itself is maintained by Microsoft. The administration of the Power Platform focuses on the following main areas:

- Users and groups administration
- Administration of Power Platform environments
- Configuration settings in Power Platform environments
- Power BI administration

In the following sections, you will learn the most important information about those main areas.

Users and groups administration

The first step that needs to be taken for a user to be able to work with the Power Platform is to provision that user with the Microsoft cloud.

> **Note:** You will learn more about the security aspects of the Power Platform in *Chapter 11, Secure and Govern the Power Platform* of this book. In this chapter, we are focusing only on the administration tasks and procedures.

There are the following main steps required for fully provisioning a user for the Power Platform:

- Every user of any Microsoft cloud service, including the Power Platform, must have a cloud user account created in the tenant, which a cloud customer got from Microsoft with the cloud services subscription. The creation of a user account is not done in any Power Platform tool but rather either in the Microsoft 365 Administration portal (**https://admin.microsoft.com/**) or in the Microsoft Azure portal (**https://portal.azure.com/**).

- After a user is created in the Microsoft cloud, a license needs to be assigned to them to give access to the Power Platform services. As you have learned in *Chapter 1: Introduction* of this book, there are many possible licensing options that can be used. The license assignment to users is performed in the same portals as mentioned previously.

- For Power Platform environments without Microsoft Dataverse, there might be an optional step to assigning one of the existing environment roles to them.

- For Power Platform environments provisioned with Microsoft Dataverse, there is another step required to give the users access to Dataverse. This consists of adding the users into Microsoft Dataverse, assigning them to a business unit, and adding them to one or multiple security roles.

> Note: The whole user administration does not belong directly to the Power Platform administration area, and it is rather a centralized cloud administration within an organization.

After all of the previous steps are finished, new users are able to start using the Power Platform.

Administration of Power Platform environments

The administration of the Power Platform environments consists of the following main tasks:

- Create new environments when required by some users in the organization. Depending on the policies and procedures, new environments can be either created only by the administrators or by a broader community, for example, by the makers.
- Delete existing environments when no more is needed. The deletion of environments should be performed with care to avoid the loss of important solutions and data. Once deleted, there is a grace period during which an environment can be restored.
- Reset the existing environment. The reset transaction recreates the environment into a default state, and any customizations and data will be removed.
- Changing the environment type, when necessary, based on the user's request or for some maintenance or other purposes. The environment of type "**Sandbox**" can be changed to the type "**Production**" and vice versa.
- Create on-demand backups of environments (for certain environment types, a periodic backup is executed automatically).
- Restore environments from previously created backups.
- Copy one environment into another. This is especially useful for establishing a test or training environment as a copy from a production one.
- Install solutions from the "*Dynamics 365 app*" group of solutions. The available solutions to be installed depend on the licenses purchased by the organization.

- Track available storage capacity. Power Platform comes with a defined maximum storage capacity, which depends on the number and type of purchased licenses. The storage capacity is available for the whole tenant, and every new Power Platform environment occupies a certain part of this overall capacity. Not all types of environments count for these capacity limits, as you will learn in the subsequent section of this chapter.

- Set the data loss prevention policies. These policies are used to prevent data leakages by improper use of data connectors. You will learn more about these policies in *Chapter 11:* Secure and Govern the Power Platform of this book.

There are a few more tasks that belong to the basic Power Platform environment administration. Another big area where an administrator needs to work on is the area of configuration settings, as described in the next section.

Configuration settings in Power Platform environments

Power Platform environments provisioned with Microsoft Dataverse have a large set of configuration settings an administrator needs to know. The following are the main setting areas:

- Activating various **product features** such as Power BI embedding, Bing Maps mapping, search options, and more.

- **Business-related settings** such as the currencies, connection roles for connecting records from various tables, queues, or regional formatting for date and time values, and more.

- **Security settings** such as the management of users, business units, security roles, and more.

- Configuration of the **auditing capability**, being able to create an audit log about all changes in data, sign-ins, and even logging the read transactions.

- Configuration of various **templates** used across a model-driven application like templates for Word or Excel documents, for data imports or for e-mail signatures.

- Configuration of the **integration** between Microsoft Dataverse and **Microsoft Exchange**. This is a very typical integration performed in many Power Platform implementations. When used, the users of model-driven applications will be able to send e-mails directly from the app, receive e-mails, and also synchronize appointments, tasks, and contacts between Microsoft Exchange/Microsoft Outlook and the Microsoft Dataverse.

- Configuration of the **integration** between Microsoft Dataverse and Microsoft **SharePoint, Microsoft OneDrive for Business,** or **Microsoft Teams**. All of those integrations bring added value for the end user of the applications by providing an integrated document management capability or integrated workspace within Microsoft Teams by including Power Apps or Power Automate flows.

- Configuration of various **data-related settings** like the bulk deletion jobs for deleting a large number of data records, duplicate detection settings used to prevent the creation of duplicates, settings for data imports, translations, and many more.

In a newly created Power Platform environment with Microsoft Dataverse, most of the settings are configured with default values. It is important to understand the settings to be able to make appropriate changes in the settings and establish some of the most important product features and integrations, as mentioned previously.

Power BI administration

As Power BI is technologically different from the remaining parts of the Power Platform, Power BI has its own administration. The following are the most important administration tasks within Power BI:

- Configure **tenant settings**, like the settings for workspace creation and behavior, information protection settings such as the use of sensitivity labels, the export and sharing settings defining the possibilities to export, download, or publish parts of the Power BI solutions, integration settings to multiple external services, and many more.

- Configuration of **organizational visuals**, which makes it possible to import additional visuals from the Microsoft AppSource or from own developed visual files.

- **Custom branding** makes it possible to set the colors, logo, images, and so on.

There are many smaller settings available in the Power BI administration, such as the configuration settings for workspace creation and use, the information protection settings, or the options for exporting and sharing content.

Power Platform environments overview

Before we dive deeper into some details about the administration, we need to learn some basic information about Power Platform environments. We use one Power Platform environment the whole time for our exercises, but do we really have a good understanding about what are the environments? A Power Platform environment is a unit hosting all Power Platform components we use or create for a solution. There is, however, one exception, and that is Power BI. Power BI is not part of the Power Platform environment; it is a separate small *"cloud"*.

A Power Platform environment can be created either without or with Microsoft Dataverse. When created without Microsoft Dataverse, the possibilities to build solutions are rather limited; only Power Apps canvas apps and Power Automate cloud flows can be created. With Microsoft Dataverse, the Power Platform can be used in its entirety to build solutions containing its own data model in Microsoft Dataverse, any type of Power Apps; Power Automate flows, Power Virtual Agents chatbots, or AI Builder models.

There are multiple types of Power Platform environments with the following features:

- **Default environment:** This type of environment exists automatically in every Microsoft tenant and is used indirectly in multiple situations. For Power Platform solutions, it is not recommended to use this environment because there is no possibility to manage access for users—every user has automatic access.

- **Trial environment:** A trial environment is a free, timely-limited environment, which is typically used to test certain product features before deciding to purchase a license. A trial environment runs for 30 days and is not limited in functionality. The trial environment does not count into the overall storage capacity.

- **Developer environment:** A developer environment is a free and permanent environment with one restriction, that only one user—the creator of the environment can use it. It is typically used for testing various concepts and preparing solution ideas but not for production purposes. The environment can be provisioned using the specific URL **https://powerapps.microsoft.com/en-us/developerplan/** we have also used in *Chapter 1: Introducing Microsoft Power Platform* of this book to provision the environment for our exercises. The developer environment does not count into the overall storage capacity.

- **Sandbox environment:** A sandbox environment is used for any pre-production purposes when building Power Platform solutions, such as the development, testing, training, bug-fixing, and other purposes. A Sandbox environment can be only created with a commercial Power Platform license.

- **Production environment:** A production environment is used for running Power Platform solutions in production. This environment type can also be created with a commercial Power Platform license only.

- **Microsoft Teams environment:** A Microsoft Teams environment is a specific one used for creating and operating Power Platform solution components directly within Microsoft Teams. The solution components like Power Apps or others created here can be used only within Microsoft Teams but not outside. In case a user creates a solution with data, a Microsoft Dataverse for Teams is created within this type of environment. It is a lightweight Dataverse with limited capabilities.

- **Support environment:** A support environment is only created by Microsoft support engineers when they need to resolve a customer issue. They usually create a copy of the customer's environment, identify the issue, and resolve it. Afterward, this environment is deleted.

In the next section, you will learn some more details about the Power Platform Admin Center and some other tools for administering the Power Platform.

The Power Platform Admin Center

Administering the Power Platform can be done using multiple tools and approaches. The simplest approach is to use the Power Platform Admin Center—a Web portal where the administration can be performed interactively. The Power Platform Admin Center can be opened using the following URL: **https://admin.powerplatform.microsoft.com/**. The portal offers a broad range of administration possibilities, as illustrated in the following screenshot (*figure 10.2*):

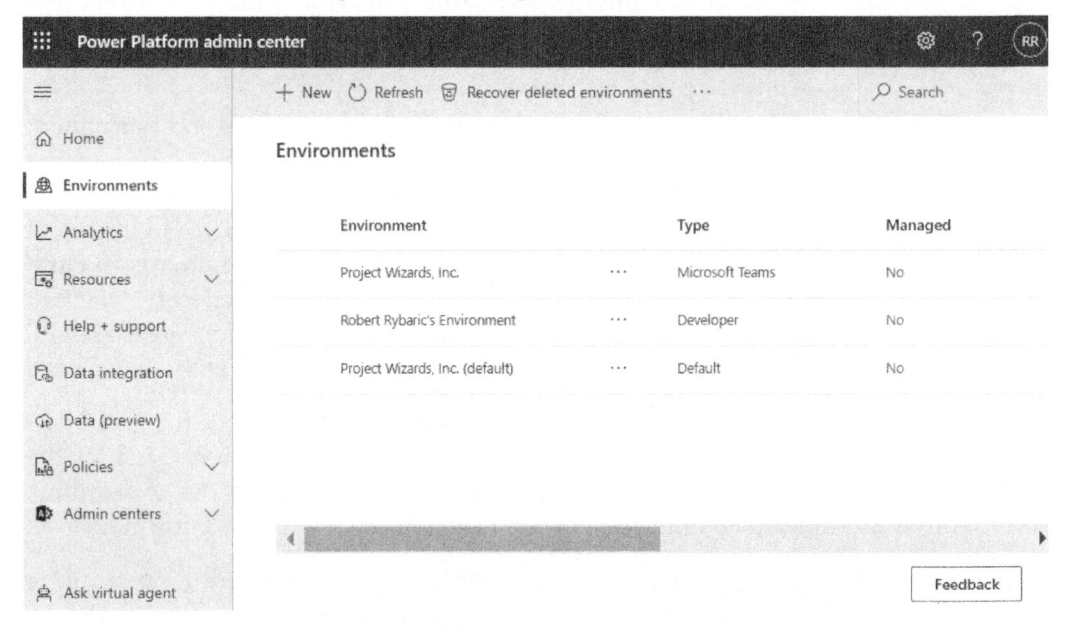

Figure 10.2: Power Platform Admin Center

As we can see in *figure 10.2*, the Power Platform Admin Center supports all administration capabilities with Power Platform environments, technical analytics of Microsoft Dataverse, Power Automate, and Power Apps. Further, you will find the capacity overview, administration, and installation of the Dynamics 365 apps in case there are respective licenses available, administration of the Power Apps Portals, but also the management of the data loss prevention policies, and a link to the other three administration centers—Azure Active Directory, Microsoft 365, and Power BI.

Administering Power Platform is possible also using other approaches such as PowerShell, Power Automate flows using the specific management connectors, or using tools like Microsoft Azure DevOps with the Power Platform Build Tools or even GitHub using the specific Power Platform actions. These approaches are used more in larger organizations within centralized IT administration teams or when building larger Power Platform solutions. You will get an overview of these methods later in this chapter.

Power BI Admin Portal

Power BI has its own administration portal, which can be found using the following URL: **https://app.powerbi.com/admin-portal**. The portal offers all required administration options for Power BI, as described earlier in this chapter. An example of the Power BI Admin Portal is provided in the following screenshot:

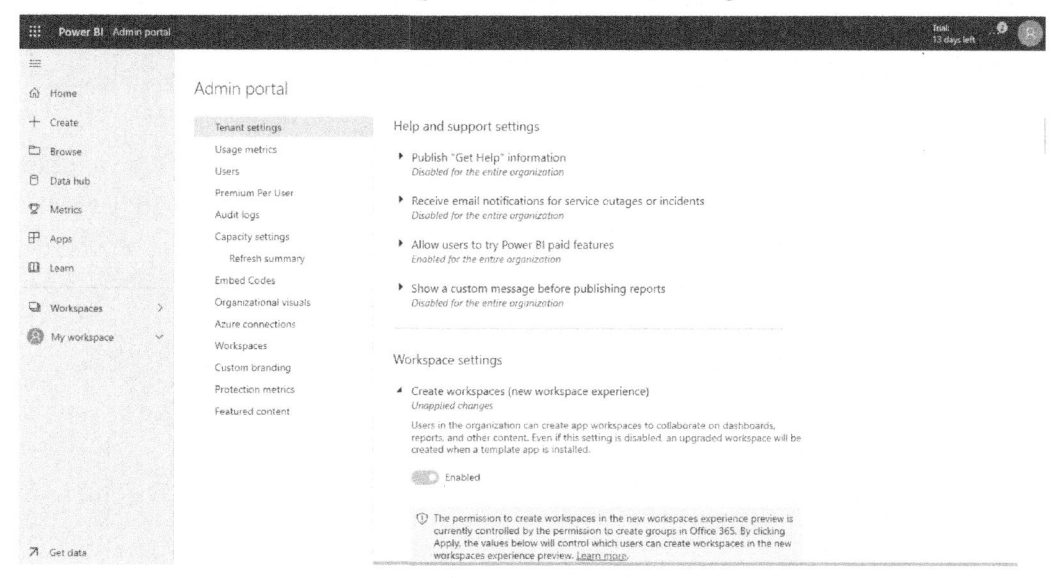

Figure 10.3: Power BI Admin portal

As you can see in *figure 10.3*, the Power BI Admin Portal is integrated into the Power BI website and offers all the described administration features.

In the next section, we will drive our attention to a more project-related area on how to properly set-up environments for different project complexity levels.

Power Platform environment strategies

When setting-up the necessary prerequisites for a smaller or larger Power Platform project, it is necessary to have an understanding of the required Power Platform environments.

Power Platform is a low-code/no-code cloud service where you can build everything from small personal automation or a simple app for a few coworkers to large, complex, and enterprise-wide solutions for thousands or tens of thousands of users.

In the case of personal automation or something similarly small, you do not need to bother with an environmental strategy; you just build and use everything in one single environment. For larger solutions, it is, however, not recommended to think about a single environment for everything from development to production. Instead, you must understand the possibilities for creating a multi-environment set-up to serve the needs of the planned large project.

In this section, you will learn about some best practices for specifying environment strategies for different levels of Power Platform projects, taking the more complex ones into consideration.

Simple project

A simple project can be defined as a project where a Power Platform solution should be built by a single, well-organized team of experts. The typical environment set-up is illustrated in the following diagram:

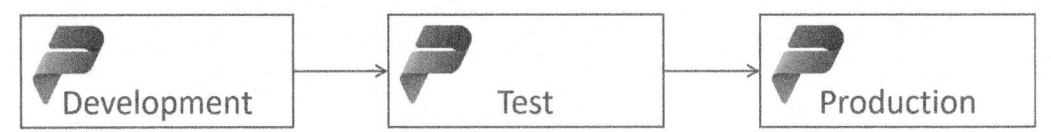

Figure 10.4: Environment set-up for simple projects

As you can see in *figure 10.4*, the set-up consists of three Power Platform environments with the following purposes:

- **Development:** A development environment is used for building the solution by the project team. For this purpose, a Power Platform environment of the type "**Sandbox**" is used.

- **Test:** A test environment is used to test the solution by a team of testers who are independent of the development team. For this purpose, a Power Platform environment of the type "**Sandbox**" is used.

- **Production:** A production environment is used for running the final Power Platform solution by the end users. For this purpose, a Power Platform environment of type "**Production**" is used.

You can see the arrows showing a flow of logic and how a Power Platform solution is built and deployed. This, however, does not exactly represent the technical distribution of the solution artifacts.

Complex project with multiple teams

A complex project with multiple teams belongs to the highest category of complexity, where a very complex solution is built in parallel by multiple development teams, requiring separate working environments. In this case, multiple development Power Platform environments might be necessary, as illustrated in *figure 10.5*:

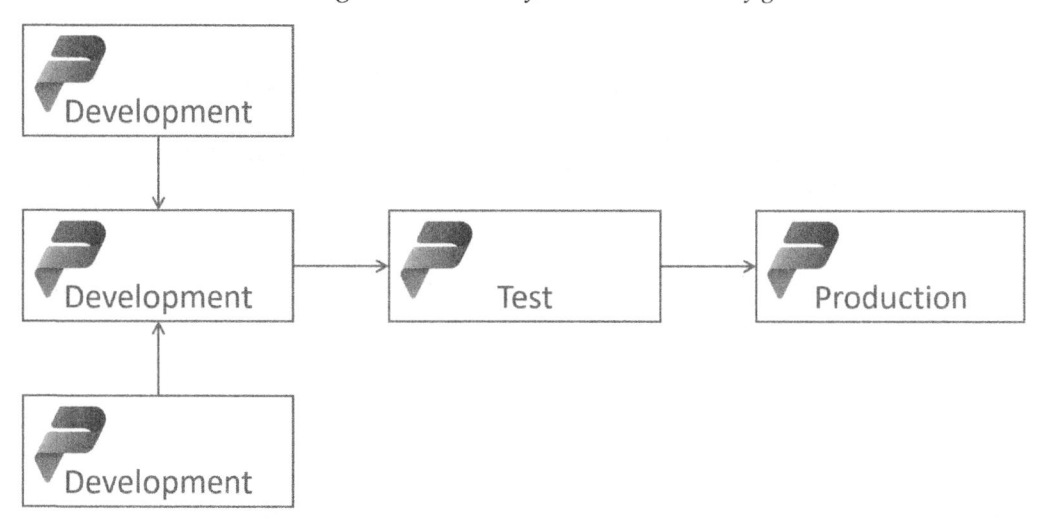

Figure 10.5: Environment set-up for complex projects with multiple teams

As you can see in *figure 10.5*, there are two normal development environments dedicated to two separate development teams, represented by the upper and the lower development environments. In the middle, there is something we call "**Development Master**", an additional environment where all the artifacts from the other two are merged together to form a consolidated overall solution, ready for downstream deployment.

Complex project with multiple releases

There is another example of an environment set-up for complex projects, where the final solution needs to be achieved within multiple releases, and every release is brought into production. In such a case, we need to have at least two parallel streams of environments, one for supporting the current release and another one for developing the next release of the solution, as illustrated in *figure 10.6*.

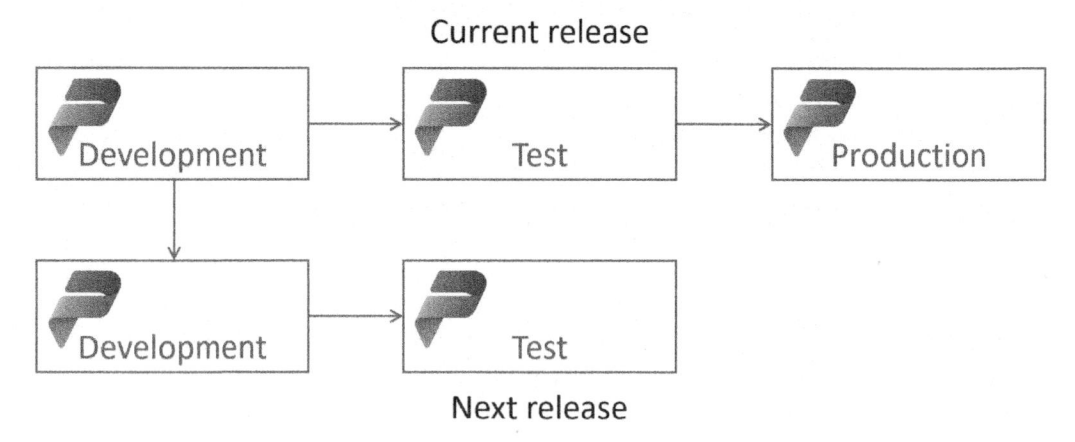

Figure 10.6: Environment set-up for complex projects with multiple releases

As you can see in *figure 10.6*, the upper stream consisting of three environments represents the current release, which must be maintained and bug-fixed until the next release is ready for production. The lower stream of two environments represents the development of the next release. The down-arrow from the upper to the lower development represents a very important capability of reporting all bugs from the current release to the development of the next release so that those bugs do not get propagated into the next release once again.

In this section, we have mentioned just a few possible scenarios where you need to take an environment strategy into account. In the next section, you will learn more about the Power Platform solution management.

Solution management fundamentals

Another important aspect of managing Power Platform is the deployment of solutions across environments. As you have seen in the previous section, for larger Power Platform projects, it is always required to use more than one single environment. But when we say that we develop on one, test on another, and use in production on a third one, how can the solution components be deployed from one environment to another one? For this purpose, we have something called solution management.

Solution management in Power Platform is the capability to pack all solution components, such as the data model extension, the apps, the flows, and so on, into a container and then deploy the container from one environment to another. This container is called a **Power Platform solution.** We created one solution at the beginning of our practical exercises and worked within that the whole time. But how does the deployment look like? The deployment consists of exporting and importing the solution packages. The whole procedure, in its simplest form, consists of the following steps:

- Open the Power Platform solution and perform the *publishing* of all customizations.
- Verify the solution using the *Solution checker* to be sure the solution does not contain any inconsistencies. This does not need to be done for every single deployment, but it is recommended to perform the solution check regularly. The solution checker can be started from the list of Power Platform solutions by selecting the required solution and starting the checker from the command bar, according to *figure 10.7*:

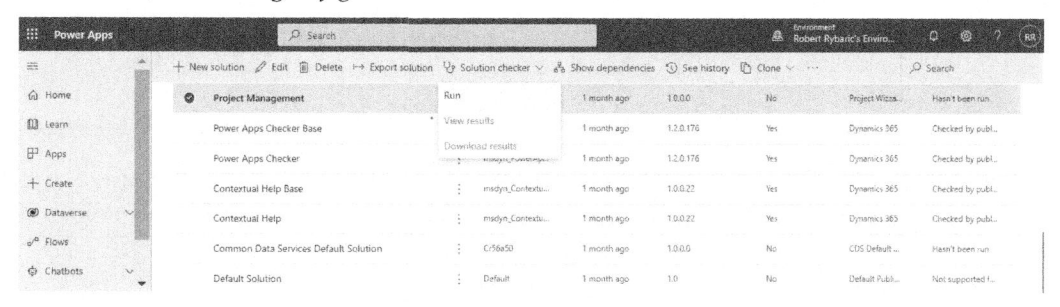

Figure 10.7: Solution checker

- Export the solution, which means that the container is downloaded as a ZIP file to the local PC. The export can be started from the list of Power Platform solutions by selecting the required solution and clicking on "**Export solution**". In the side pane dialog, there will be the possibility for publishing as well as for checking the solution offered on the first page. After you confirm with "**Next**", there will be another dialog for specifying the *version number* of the exported solution (the Maker Portal offers automated version number incrementing, you can, however, also change the version numbers manually) as well as specifying whether the exported solution will be *unmanaged* or *managed*. The solution versioning is another key capability of the overall solution management, and it is important to define the versioning structure as part of the environment strategy. The export dialog is illustrated in *figure 10.8*:

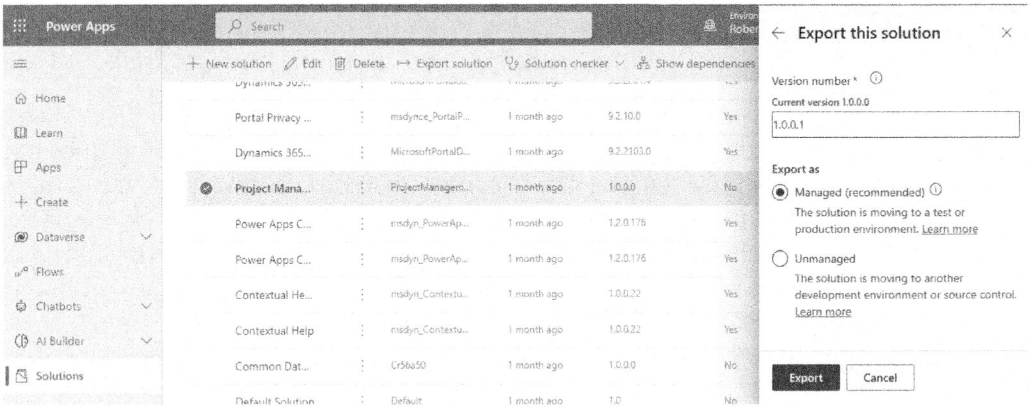

Figure 10.8: Specifying export solution parameters

- After the solution is exported, you will get a ZIP file to be downloaded and saved on the local PC. The name of the file contains the name of the solution and the version number.

- The last step is to *import* the solution into another—target Power Platform environment. During the solution import, you will need to select the ZIP file and, in the subsequent dialog, decide how to import an updated solution package and perform some more configurations.

After the solution is imported, the whole content of the solution package is available in the target environment.

> Note: The solution package can be used for the deployment of all solution artifacts except business data. If a transfer of business data from one environment to another is required, there are other tools and approaches how to achieve it. For more information, please refer to the documentation about the Configuration Migration Tool at https://docs.microsoft.com/en-us/power-platform/admin/manage-configuration-data

There is one more basic concept, which needs to be explained, and that is the type of solution. Power Platform solutions can be of two types, with the following characteristics:

- **Unmanaged**: Every solution which is manually created is always unmanaged. Unmanaged solutions are used to build the solution components and synchronize the customizations between multiple development environments, for example, for such a set-up, as illustrated in *figure 10.5*. Unmanaged solutions lack some of the important features required for professional deployment processes; for example, after you delete an unmanaged solution imported onto a target Power Platform environment, the content of the solution is not deleted; rather, it would need to be removed manually.

- **Managed**: Managed solutions are created when exporting an unmanaged solution from the source environment. Part of the export procedure is to decide whether the exported solution will be unmanaged or managed. It is strongly recommended to use managed solutions when deploying from development to the downstream environments (test, production, and so on). Managed solutions offer the required capabilities for professional deployment, for example, the possibility to remove the solution from the target environment with all its components, the possibility for upgrading and patching, and so on.

After we have now learned so much about the Power Platform administration and solution deployment, let us work through a small exercise and practice the solution exporting.

Exercise 20: Exporting a Power Platform solution

In this exercise, we will practice the preceding procedure. Please perform the following steps:

1. Open the Maker Portal and navigate to the list of solutions.

2. Check the solution "`Project Management`", and on the command bar, select the command "`Solution checker`" and then "`Run`". This will start the solution checker. The check will take some time; wait for the check to complete.

3. Once completed, select the command "`Solution checker`" and then "`View results`". You might see some issues found by the checker in the list, similar to the following screenshot:

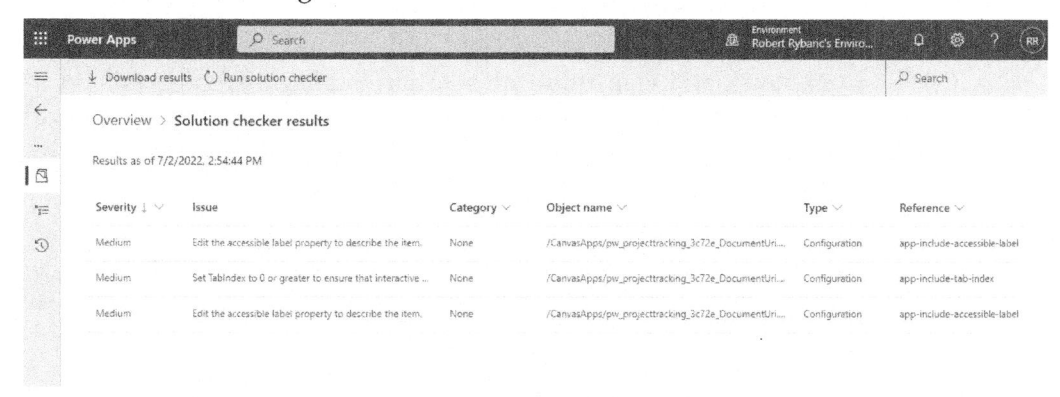

Figure 10.9: Solution checker results overview

4. As you can see on the results overview in *figure 10.9*, there are some findings from the canvas apps, specifically some accessibility settings missing. This is a typical finding because the canvas app designer does not require to configure the accessibility settings, but the solution checker will find them and present them in the report.

5. Return back to the list of the solutions and check the solution "**Project Management**" again.

6. Click on "**Export solution**" in the command bar. Click "**Next**" to access the versioning and solution type dialog. Keep the automatically generated version number and select "**Unmanaged**" first, according to the following screenshot:

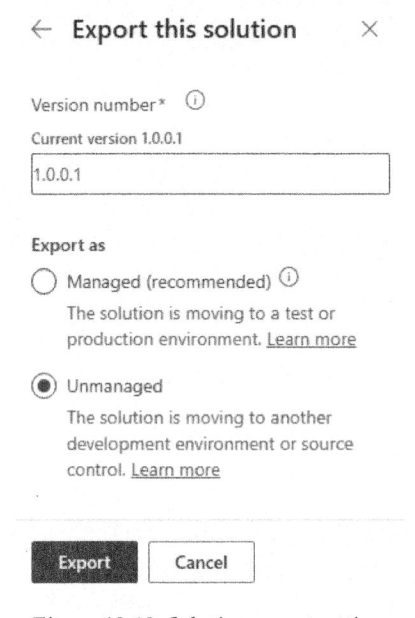

Figure 10.10: Solution export settings

7. Click on "**Export**" and wait until the solution is available to download in your browser. The solution export is an asynchronous process, so you will not see any progress indicator, just a notification when the solution is ready to download, as shown in the following screenshot:

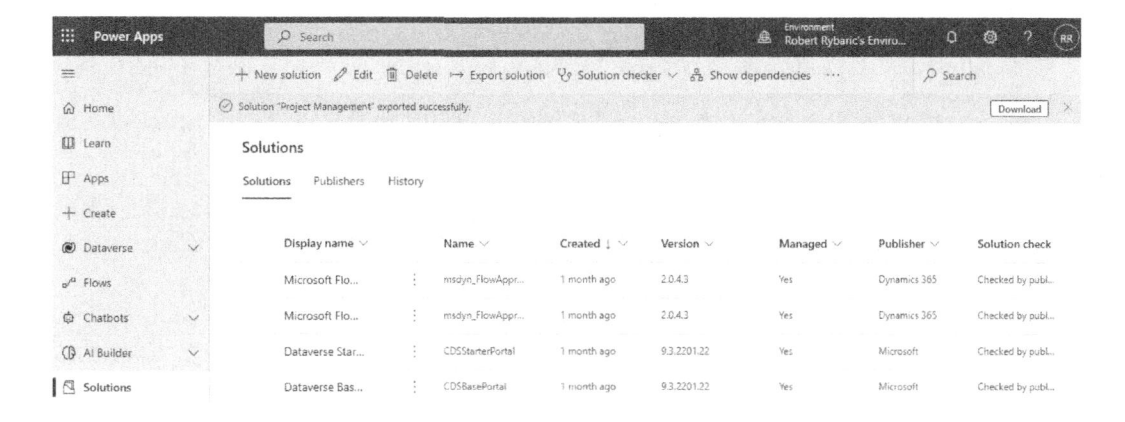

Figure 10.11: Solution ready for download

8. Depending on the browser type used, download the file to your local PC.

9. Observe the file name of the downloaded solution. The name should be like "`ProjectManagement_1_0_0_1.zip`".

10. Repeat the same procedure once again but now select "**Managed**" in the "**Export as**" setting to obtain the managed solution package. The name of the managed solution should be "`ProjectManagement_1_0_0_2_managed.zip`".

11. The files could be used to import the solution into another environment; however, we do not have any additional environment right now, so this procedure will not be practiced.

The deployment processes are a very important part of every Power Platform project. While for smaller and simpler projects, those processes can be performed manually, for complex projects, we need to use automation. It would not be reasonable anymore for a human to handle the deployment complexity without errors. In the next section, you will learn the fundamentals of ALM, in other words, how to handle the deployments in an automated way.

Application lifecycle management (ALM) fundamentals

As described in the previous section, the deployment of a solution from the source environment (for example, **Development**) to a target environment (for example, **Test**) requires certain steps to be performed in a certain order. In fact, the deployment processes can contain some other steps not yet described, for example:

- Unpacking the solution package and checking-in into a source control system such as GIT, GitHub, or Azure DevOps repository.
- Deployment of not just one but multiple solution packages in a predefined order.
- Deployment is not just from a single source to a single target environment, but rather a series of exports and imports in a multi-environment configuration.
- Import of data into the target environment, and many more.

It is hardly possible to think about performing these deployments manually, specifically in cases when they need to run daily. In order to automate deployment processes, Microsoft provides certain products and capabilities to automate them. In the next section, you will learn about the typical tools and approaches for automating the administration in Power Platform and the deployment of Power Platform solutions.

Automate Power Platform fundamentals

We have learned in the previous sections of this chapter that administering the Power Platform and performing professional solution deployments are complex tasks, and in larger organizations with thousands of licensed Power Platform users and citizen developers, it is almost impossible to handle them manually. As mentioned in the previous section, Microsoft offers certain tools and possibilities to automate all those tasks.

The following are the most used tools and methods:

- **Azure DevOps with the Power Platform Build Tools:** Azure DevOps is a widely used cloud solution for managing big software projects. For automating Power Platform administration and deployment tasks, the Add-On "`Power Platform Build Tools`" need to be installed on Azure DevOps. This package makes it possible to automate the typical tasks of creating/deleting/copying environments, publishing customizations, setting solution version numbers, exporting, and importing solutions, unpacking, packing solutions, and so on.

> Note: For more information, please refer to the product documentation: https://docs.microsoft.com/en-us/power-platform/alm/devops-build-tools

- **GitHub with the Power Platform actions:** GitHub is a very popular platform for software developers and is primarily used as a repository for software development artifacts. With the Add-On actions for Power Platform, you can configure the same automation as with Azure DevOps.

> Note: For more information, please refer to the product documentation: https://docs.microsoft.com/en-us/power-platform/alm/devops-github-actions

- **PowerShell with the Power Platform cmdlets:** PowerShell is a widely popular technology used by Microsoft administrators to administer every aspect of Microsoft software products. When extended with the proper cmdlets for Power Platform administrators and makers, it can be used to automate the processes described previously as well.

> Note: For more information, please refer to the product documentation: https://docs.microsoft.com/en-us/power-platform/admin/powerapps-powershell

- Other methods, like using Power Automate with the managed connectors and some more.

Power BI, as a technologically different part of the Power Platform, offers similar tools and methods for automation as described previously.

Conclusion

In this chapter, you have learned the fundamentals of the Power Platform administration and solution management. You have seen what the most important areas are, where an administrator needs to support the citizen developers and the users to achieve their goals. You have gained an overview of the administration portals used for interactive administration of the Power Platform and Power BI. In the next part, you have learned the basic information about Power Platform environments, what they are and what types of environments exist in the Power Platform. Further, we have presented some best practices about environment strategies when planning for a large Power Platform project. In the second part of this chapter, we have focused on solution management as the deployment approach within the Power Platform. You have learned what the solutions are and what types of solutions can be created and used in which situations. Finally, we have discussed the application lifecycle management within the Power Platform and how can be some administration and solution deployment tasks be automated using the most popular tools and approaches. Part of this chapter was a small practical exercise to practice solution export using the Maker Portal.

In the last chapter of this book, we will focus on a very important aspect of every business solution, and that is security. Business solutions are many times handling internal and confidential data of an organization so that their protection is imperative. In the upcoming chapter, you will learn the fundaments of IT security and how the security is implemented in the Microsoft cloud and specifically in the Power Platform. You will learn about authentication, generally in every Microsoft cloud solution. Next, we will focus on the authorization for granting access to data and functionality. You will see how authorization is implemented in Microsoft Dataverse, Power Apps, Power Automate, and Power BI. In the second part of the chapter, we will drive our attention to the Power Platform governance. You will also learn why governance is specifically important within Power Platform and how are data loss prevention policies and the Power Platform Center of Excellence Starter Kit supporting you to build a healthy governance structure within your Power Platform ecosystem.

Questions

1. What is the Power Platform administration, and which are the most important activities when administering the Power Platform?
2. What capabilities are providing the Power Platform Admin Center and the Power BI Admin Portal?
3. What are the Power Platform environments?
4. What types of Power Platform environments exist?
5. What typical environment strategies can be used when planning for large Power Platform projects?
6. What is the Power Platform solution management?
7. What types of Power Platform solutions exist, and what is their typical use?
8. What is the Application Lifecycle Management (ALM) in the context of the Power Platform?
9. What are the methods to automate Power Platform administration and solution deployment tasks?

Chapter 11
Secure and Govern the Power Platform

Introduction

This chapter focuses on the security and governance of Power Platform solutions. Business applications often manage business-critical data and security, and protection of this data is imperative. We will present you with the security features of Power Platform and how to leverage the different options to make your solutions safe. In the next part of this chapter, you will see what are the possibilities to make your Power Platform not just easy to use but also completely governed and managed.

Structure

In this chapter, we will discuss the following topics:

- IT security fundamentals
- Authentication in the Microsoft cloud
- Authorization in Microsoft Dataverse
- Authorization in Power Apps
- Authorization in Power Automate
- Authorization in Power BI

- Build secure Power Platform solutions
- Power Platform governance fundamentals
- Data policies
- The Center of Excellence Starter Kit

Objectives

After reading this chapter, you will be able to understand two main topics about the Power Platform—security and governance. In the first part of this chapter, we start diving deeper into all important aspects of the Power Platform security. We will provide a general overview of the security fundamentals and then the implementation of those general principles in the Power Platform. You will learn how the authentication works across all Microsoft clouds, including the Power Platform. Next, we will dive pretty deep into the very complex Microsoft Dataverse authorization possibilities; you will learn about business units, security roles, record ownership, and how these principles build up the basic hierarchical authorization scheme. You will also see how the optional authorization features can help implement a very detailed and complex authorization setup in Microsoft Dataverse. In the following sections, we will guide you through the authorization specifics of Power Apps, Power Automate, and Power BI and present several useful best practices for building secure business applications with the Power Platform. In the second part of this chapter, we will handle governance as a very important principle when deploying the Power Platform across the organization. You will learn about the two major governance solutions—the data loss prevention policies and the Power Platform Center of Excellence Starter Kit.

IT security fundamentals

Microsoft Power Platform is used for building business applications that manage business data, which is a critical asset in every organization. Another important aspect is that the Power Platform is a cloud, and we need to take care of the cloud specifics as opposite to on-premises IT systems. That is why it is imperative to carefully think about security in the context of the Power Platform and the solutions we build with it.

The ultimate goal of IT security is to protect your data against stealing or tampering and to protect your IT systems against attacks that might break them. But how do the attacks happen in most of the cases? They happen because of compromised security credentials; the attackers get the credentials and use them for their malicious activities. That is why is protecting access to the IT systems one of the fundamental security measures you need to implement. There are two concepts that will help you with this, which are as follows:

(1) **Authentication:** The authentication procedure verifies the identity of the user or a service account. There are multiple methods of authentication, from no authentication, where the IT system does not verify the identity, to most complex authentication procedures requiring multi-factor authentication, and so on. A successful authentication means that the IT system has verified that the person or service is really the one it claimed to be.

(2) **Authorization**: The authorization is usually the second security concept, coming after the successful authentication. Authorization means that based on the user's authenticated identity, certain permissions within the IT system are granted, for example, access to certain data or certain services.

When you implement strong authentication and authorization, your IT systems are much less vulnerable to any kind of attacks, your data is safe, and you have peace of mind.

In the next sections of this chapter, you will learn more about both authentication and authorization within the Microsoft Power Platform.

Authentication in the Microsoft cloud

The authentication in the Microsoft cloud ecosystem is implemented using a unified concept across all clouds (Power Platform, Dynamics 365, Microsoft 365, and Azure). The key component implementing authentication is called **Azure Active Directory**. It supports the following main features:

- **User management**: User management is fundamental for authentication. Every user, whether an interactive human user or a service account used for communicating with an interface, must be first created as a user in the Azure Active Directory. The creation can be either manual, using the administration portals, or automated when integration between the Azure Active Directory and an on-premises active directory is established.

- **Group management**: The groups are used for various purposes within the Power Platform, so it is important to understand the concept. An Azure Active Directory security group can contain members—usually users, and can be used instead of a user in scenarios such as sharing Power Apps, Power Automate flows, and so on.

- **License management**: License management is very important because only after a user is assigned some of the Microsoft cloud services licenses they can start using the services. As we have learned in *Chapter 1, Introducing Microsoft Power Platform*, there are multiple types of Power Platform licenses; the licenses purchased by the organization can be assigned to the users either interactively in the administration portals or programmatically, using the Azure Active Directory API.

Now, let us discuss the practical steps needed to provision a new cloud user to fully use the Microsoft Power Platform. A typical series of steps are depicted in the following diagram:

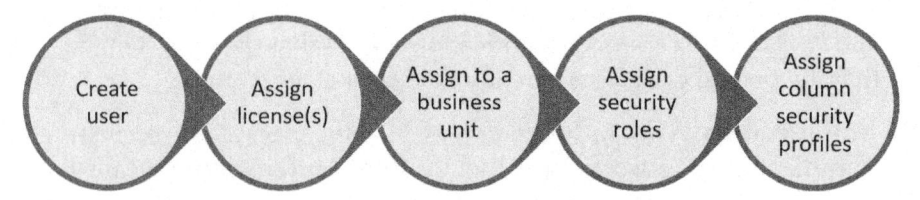

Figure 11.1: Provisioning user access in the Power Platform

As you can see in *figure 11.1*, there are multiple steps needed to be performed before a new user can start using the Power Platform. The steps are as follows:

1. **Create user**: As described previously, the first step for a new user is a user account created in the Azure Active Directory.

2. **Assign license(s)**: After the user is created, the respective licenses (Power Apps, Power Automate, and Dynamics 365) need to be assigned to the user. In case you do not plan to use Microsoft Dataverse in an environment, the subsequent steps are not necessary. It might be, however, necessary to assign some of the environment roles to the user. More about environment roles will be explained later in this chapter.

3. **Assign a business unit**: In case you are going to use Microsoft Dataverse, you need to ensure the user is first inserted into the Microsoft Dataverse, and then you need to assign them to the proper business unit. More about business units will be explained later in this chapter.

4. **Assign security roles**: After assigning a user to a business unit, you need to assign one or more security roles to them. More about security roles will be explained later in this chapter.

5. **Assign column security profiles**: The last optional step is to assign the user to one or more column security profiles in case the column security is actively used in Microsoft Dataverse. More about column security profiles will be explained later in this chapter.

Let us now get deeper into more advanced authentication concepts, which an organization can implement using the Microsoft cloud and on-premises components.

Advanced authentication concepts

The basic authentication using Azure Active Directory supports authentication with username and password only. For higher levels of security, the following concepts can be implemented.

Multi-factor authentication (MFA)

The MFA means that the authentication consists of at least two of the three following authentication elements:

- **Something you know:** This is usually the username, password, PIN code, and so on.

- **Something you have:** This is usually a source of additional secrets such as a grid card, an authentication token generating random numbers, an identity smart card, or the Microsoft Authenticator app on your mobile device.

- **Something you are:** This is usually some biometric information such as fingerprint, iris scan, or face recognition.

The combination of two or even three of the preceding elements represents a very high level of security. MFA is supported by Azure Active Directory.

Integration between on-premises active directory and Azure Active Directory

Some organizations which invested heavily into internal security within their own on-premises active directory structures prefer to continue using this secured environment even with the migration into the Microsoft cloud. Azure Active Directory supports multiple integration scenarios, giving the customer the best option of their preference. With this integration, you get either a simplified user authentication within the cloud or a federated environment, where the authentication happens in the highly secured on-premises AD rather than in the cloud.

Conditional access

With conditional access, you can implement an AI-driven authentication service, which can recognize the authentication situation and decide whether to grant or revoke access or to grant access only after an additional MFA is successfully performed. This capability looks for factors, such as the location of the user, the type of device, and the type of application, to decide what level of security needs to be applied. This capability is also fully supported with Azure Active Directory.

Authorization in Microsoft Dataverse

Before we dive deeper into the very complex Microsoft Dataverse authorization, let us have a look into the authorization available in a Power Platform environment without Microsoft Dataverse. As mentioned earlier in this chapter, without Microsoft Dataverse, you can only assign one of the built-in environment roles to a user:

- **Environment administrator**: A user equipped with this role has administration privileges within the environment, can add new users, remove users, and assign the environment roles to users. The environment administrator can also decide to add Microsoft Dataverse to the environment or manage the data loss prevention policies within that environment. You will learn more about the data loss prevention policies later in this chapter.
- **Environment maker**: A user equipped with this role has the privileges to build apps and flows and share those with other users.

If a user does not get any of the preceding environment roles assigned, then they can just use apps and flows assigned to them.

The privileges of the two environment roles cannot be modified, and neither can other environment roles be created.

The authorization system changes dramatically when we have a Power Platform environment with Microsoft Dataverse. With Microsoft Dataverse, you get a complex authorization system, being able to fulfill even the most complex security requirements. Let us now dive deeper into this authorization system.

The Microsoft Dataverse authorization consists of the following seven pillars:

(1) The Microsoft Dataverse users

(2) The ownership of records

(3) The business units

(4) The security roles

(5) The teams (optional)

(6) The hierarchy security (optional)

(7) The column-level security (optional)

As you can see in the list, the last three components are optional, while the first four are mandatory. In the following sections, you will learn about all those pillars.

The Microsoft Dataverse users

Simply said, every user who should use any application based on Microsoft Dataverse needs to be provisioned in a specific table called "**systemuser**". As described earlier in this chapter, provisioning a user into Microsoft Dataverse is part of the standard onboarding procedure. You can find the Microsoft Dataverse users in the Power Platform Admin Center; when you select an environment, go to "**Settings**", then "**Users + permissions**", and finally "**Users**", according to the following screenshot:

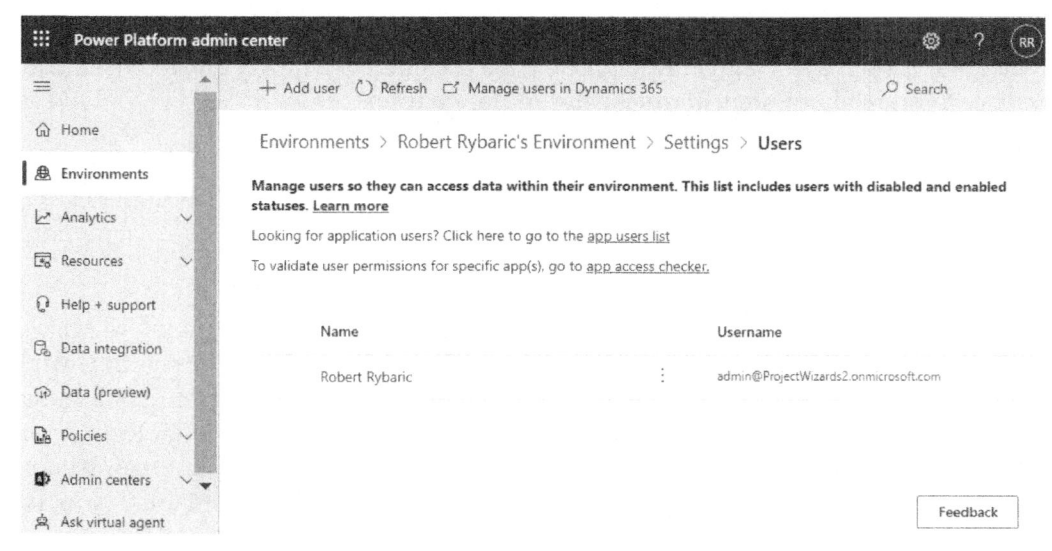

Figure 11.2: List of users in the Power Platform Admin Center

As you can see in *figure 11.2*, there is a list of users; in the case of our environment, only one single user is listed, which is the limitation of the Power Platform environment type "Developer".

In other environment types, you can add new users by clicking on "`+ Add user`". In the subsequent dialog, you can then select any Azure Active Directory user equipped with the proper license to be added to Microsoft Dataverse. In the next step, you can assign one or multiple security roles to the added user, as illustrated in the following screenshot:

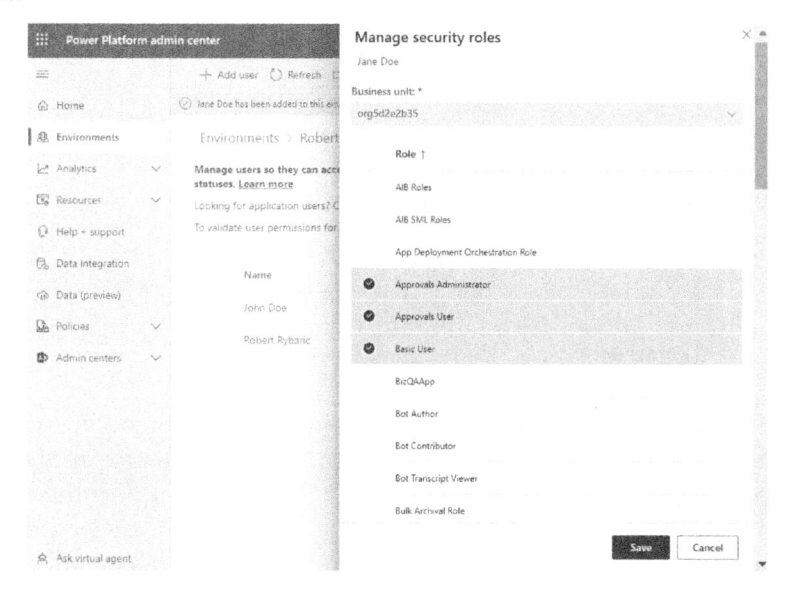

Figure 11.3: Adding security roles to a new Microsoft Dataverse user

As you can see in *figure 11.3*, there is a large number of out-of-the-box security roles available in Microsoft Dataverse, which can be assigned to a newly created user. You will learn more about security roles later in this chapter.

When the user is fully created and equipped with security roles, they can start using the Microsoft Dataverse-based applications, for example, model-driven apps, canvas apps, or Power Automate flows.

The ownership of records

Another very important concept to understand is the ownership of records. Most of the Microsoft Dataverse tables containing business data has specific columns to manage ownership. Ownership means that every record on those tables has an owner. The owner can be either a user or a team. You will learn about teams later in this chapter. The column for ownership is usually placed on the table forms in model-driven apps, as illustrated in the following screenshot:

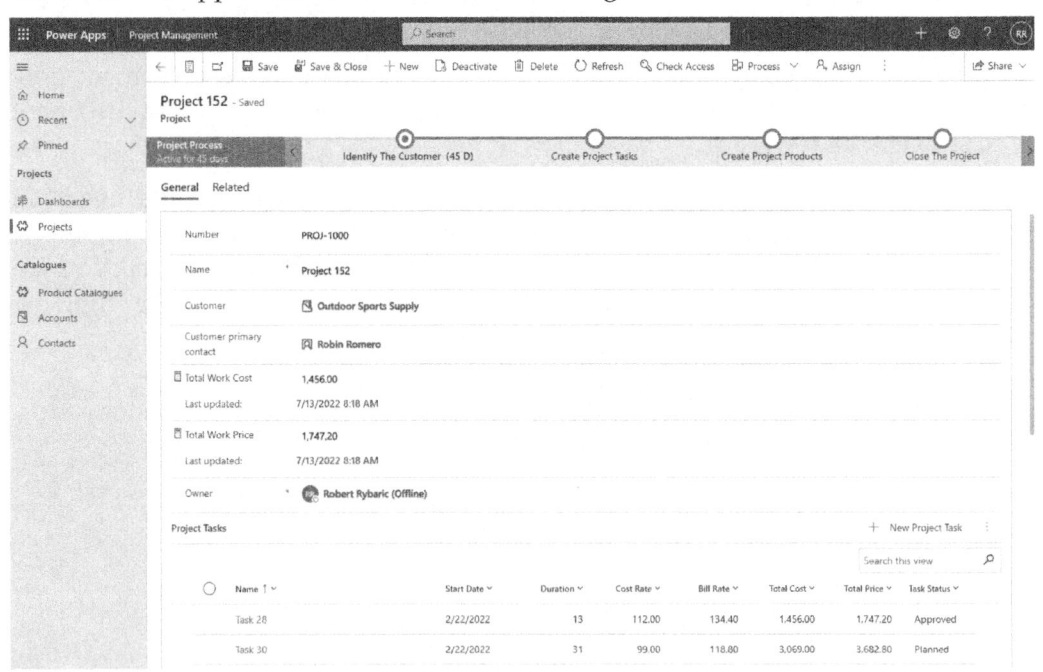

Figure 11.4: Model-driven form containing the owner column

As you can see in *figure 11.4*, which is a screenshot from our own model-driven app, "**Project Management**", there is a column called "**Owner**", representing the ownership of the record. In our app, the owner of each record in the tables is the same, but in real-life solutions with hundreds or thousands of users, the owner is different from one record to another. The ownership has a major influence on the overall authorization concept within Microsoft Dataverse, as you will learn later in this chapter.

The business units

The next very important concept is called business units. Simply said, this is a component used to represent the hierarchical nature of every organization. The main purpose of creating a business unit hierarchy in Microsoft Dataverse is to support a hierarchical view of business data. Usually, the requirement in every organization is that the higher in the hierarchy an employee is, the more data in a business application they should see. Let us take an example: a sales representative might need to see just their own sales opportunities. The sales manager managing a team of sales representatives should see all opportunities of all their team members, whereas the vice president of sales should certainly have access to all opportunities in the business application, regardless of the owner of the opportunity.

Practically, we use it to create a simplified structure of the business units, just for the purpose of the described hierarchical visibility. When the business unit hierarchy is created, the next important step is to *assign the users to the corresponding business units* so that the users become parts of the hierarchy.

The business units can be found in the Power Platform Admin Center; when you select an environment, go to "**Settings**", then "**Users + permissions**", and finally "**Business units**", according to the following screenshot:

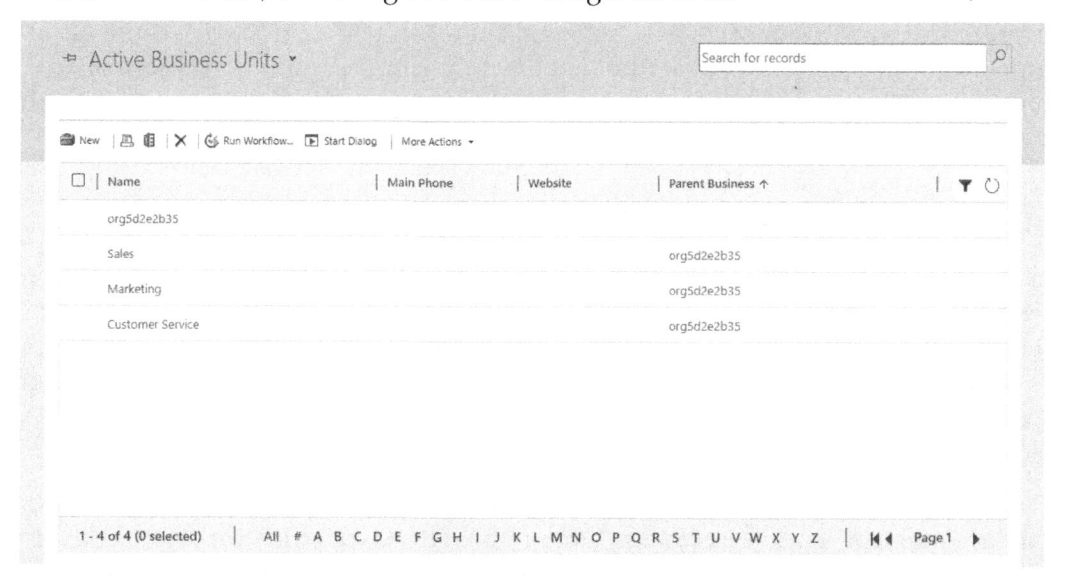

Figure 11.5: Business units in Microsoft Dataverse

As you can see in *figure 11.5*, there are some sample business units created below the root business unit with the cryptic name. The root business unit is always created automatically and cannot be deleted. Should the cryptic name of the root business unit be disturbing, there is a way how to rename it.

Following is an example of a structure of the business units you can imagine in a real-world scenario:

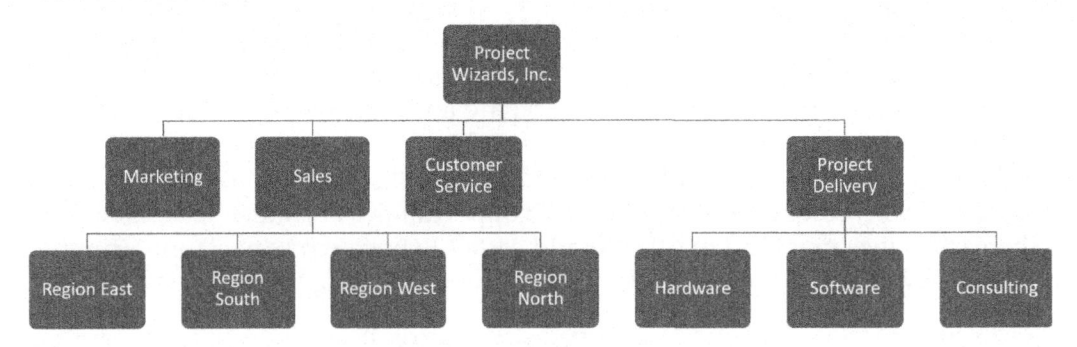

Figure 11.6: Example business unit hierarchy

As you can see in *figure 11.6*, there is a simple example of a business unit hierarchy, being able to support the hierarchical view on data in various tables in Microsoft Dataverse. For example, a salesperson assigned to the business unit *"Region East"* could see just their own opportunities, whereas the sales manager in the same region could see the opportunities of all users in the same region but not outside of that region. The vice president of sales, assigned to the business unit *"Sales"*, could see all opportunities of all salespersons, but not the data from marketing, customer service, or project delivery. The COE of the organization, assigned to the root business unit *"Project Wizards, Inc."* could see all records in the whole business application.

The security roles

The security roles are undoubtedly the most important part of the whole authorization concept in Microsoft Dataverse. The security roles define the individual permissions to everything within Microsoft Dataverse to record in all tables as well as to a multitude of table-independent capabilities. Microsoft Dataverse comes with a lot of ready-to-use security roles, but you can create any number of your own custom security roles.

You can find the security roles in the Power Platform Admin Center; when you select an environment, go to "**Settings**", then "**Users + permissions**", and finally "**Security roles**", according to the following screenshot:

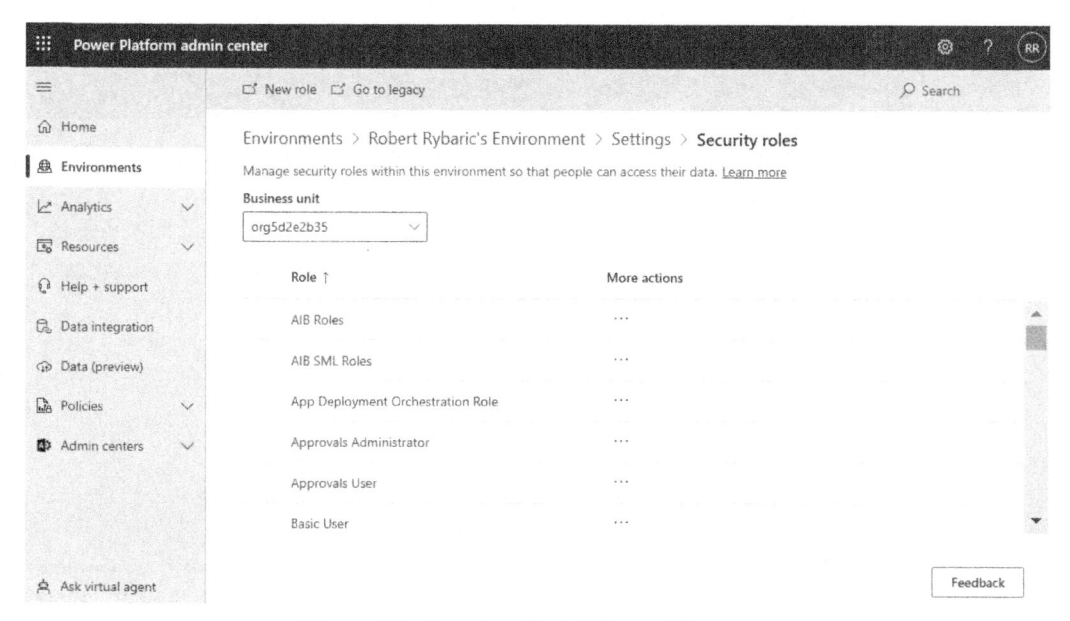

Figure 11.7: Security roles in Microsoft Dataverse

As you can see in *figure 11.7*, there are multiple security roles available in Microsoft Dataverse, even though we have not created any roles yet. Let us now learn what permissions are configured in a security role. Basically, there are two types of permissions:

- **Table-related permissions:** These permissions specify access rights to records in a particular table in Microsoft Dataverse. There are eight different transaction types for which the permissions can be specified individually, and for each of those, you can specify one of the five permission levels. More details about how this concept works will follow later in this chapter.

- **Table-independent permissions:** These permissions specify access rights to various table-independent functionalities in Microsoft Dataverse, such as creating bulk delete jobs, viewing audit history, exporting data to Excel, and many more.

The following screenshot illustrates the settings available in a security role:

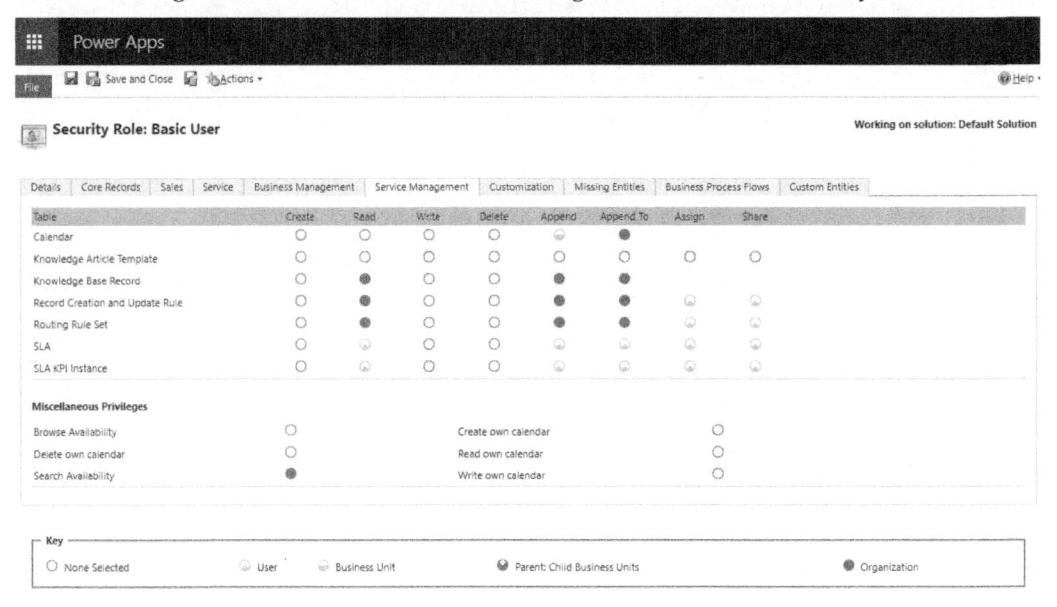

Figure 11.8: Security role example

As you can see in *figure 11.7*, there are table-related permissions in the upper part of the form and table-independent permissions in the lower part—they are called "`Miscellaneous Privileges`".

For every Microsoft Dataverse table, we can define individual permissions for the following transactions:

- **Create:** Gives permission to create new records in the table.

- **Read:** Gives permission to read records in the table. This is the basic permission type; without this, the user has no access to records in the table.

- **Write:** Gives permission to update existing records in the table.

- **Delete:** Gives permission to delete records in the table.

- **Append:** Gives permission to associate records in the table with records in other tables.

- **Append to:** Gives permission to associate records in other tables with records in the table.

- **Assign:** Gives permission to assign records in the table to different owners.

- **Share:** Gives permission to share records in the table with other users or teams.

To make it even more complex, the permissions to perform the transactions mentioned in the previous list have permission levels, defining the number of records for which the permissions are granted. There are five different permission levels:

(1) **None Selected:** This permission level does not grant any access.

(2) **User:** This permission level grants access only to records, where the owner equals the singed-in user.

(3) **Business Unit:** This permission level grants access to records owned by the signed-in user, as well as owned by any other user assigned to the same business unit as the signed-in user.

(4) **Parent: Child Business Units:** This permission level represents the true power of the hierarchical access to data. It gives permission to records owned by the signed-in user, owned by any other user, assigned to the same business unit as the signed-in user, and in addition, owned by any user who is below in the hierarchy of the business unit of the signed-in user.

(5) **Organization:** This permission level grants access to all records in the table, regardless of the owner.

Everything described so far about the Microsoft Dataverse authorization is quite complex and hard to digest, but in the following section, we are going to illustrate the whole concept with easy-to-understand examples.

Basic authorization model explained

Let us imagine the following situation: John is a Microsoft Dataverse user assigned to the *"Sales"* business unit, together with Nancy. There is also Amanda, assigned to the root business unit *"Project Wizards, Inc."* and Jim, assigned to the *"Region North"* business unit, as illustrated in the following figure:

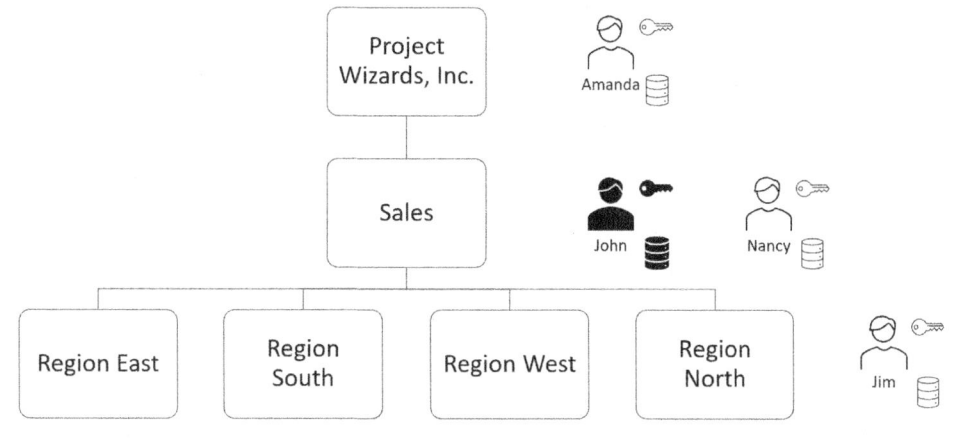

Figure 11.9: Basic authorization model explained I.

As you can see in *figure 11.9*, each of the four users has a security role assigned (represented by the small lock image) and is the owner of a certain number of records from a given Microsoft Dataverse table, for example, opportunities (represented by the small database image). Now, we will analyze the impact on the overall number of opportunity records available to John based on the permission level assigned to him.

First, we grant the permission level *"None Selected"* to John. In this case, he will have no permission to see any opportunities and work with them. In fact, with this permission level, John would not be able to be the owner of any opportunities at all.

Next, we grant John the permission level *"User"*. The result will be that John will get access to those opportunities where he is the owner, as illustrated in the following figure:

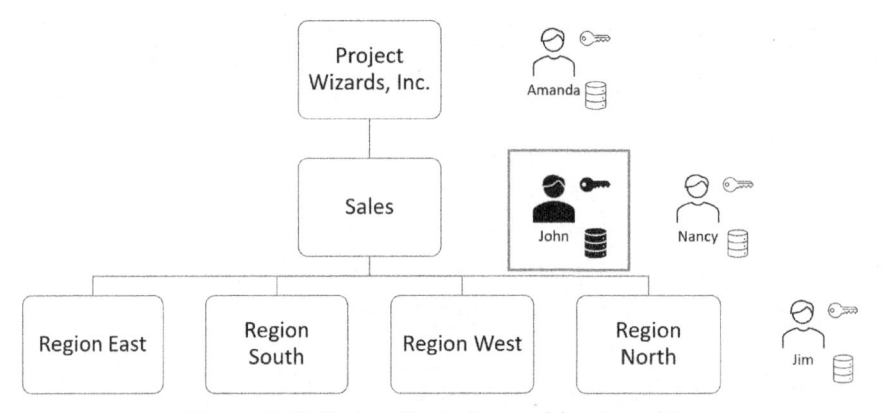

Figure 11.10: Basic authorization model explained II.

Next, we grant John the permission level *"Business Unit"*. The result will be that John will get access to those opportunities where he is the owner, as well as to those where Nancy is the owner because Nancy is in the same business unit as John. The situation is illustrated in the following figure:

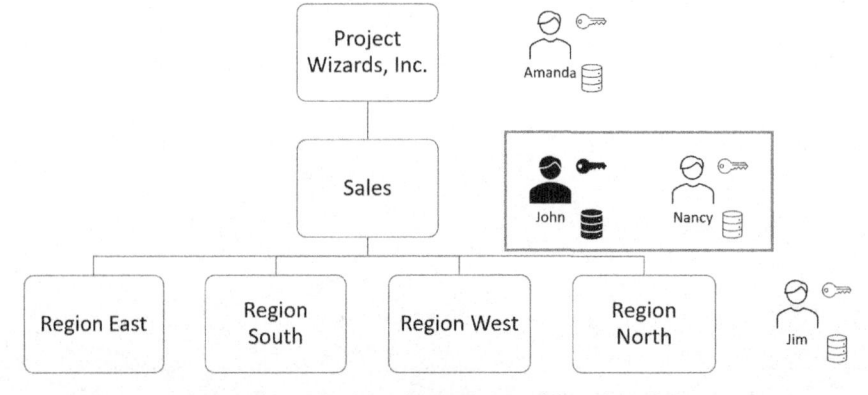

Figure 11.11: Basic authorization model explained III

Now, we continue and grant John the permission level *"Parent: Child Business Units"*. The result will be that John will get access to those opportunities where he is the owner, to those where Nancy is the owner because Nancy is in the same business unit as John and in addition to those where Jim is the owner because Jim is in the business unit hierarchy below John's business unit. The situation is illustrated in *figure 11.12*:

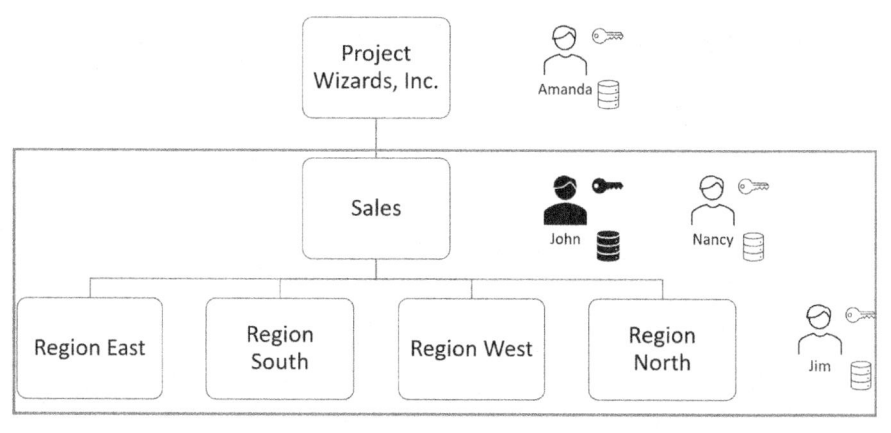

Figure 11.12: Basic authorization model explained IV.

Finally, we grant John the permission level *"Organization"*. This permission level ensures that John has access to all opportunities, regardless of the owner, so that he has access to his own opportunities and to those owed by Nancy, Jim, and Amanda, as illustrated in the following figure:

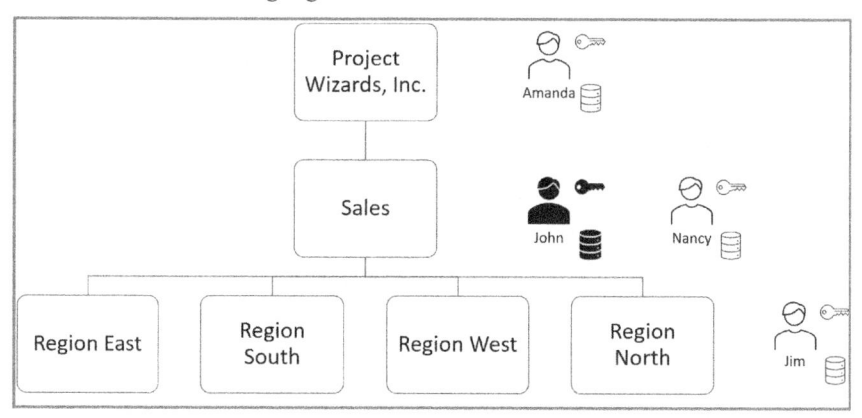

Figure 11.13: Basic authorization model explained V.

The examples in this section explain the essence of the hierarchical authorization model and are key for the overall understanding of how this authorization works.

Now, let us drive our attention to the optional authorization components in Microsoft Dataverse.

The Teams

Teams are structures in Microsoft Dataverse, being able to have assigned users as members. The Teams are used for granting access to records outside of the standard hierarchical model described in the previous section. There are two different team types in Microsoft Dataverse:

- **Owner teams:** These team types are almost as capable as the users—they can have security roles assigned and can be owners of business records.

- **Access teams:** These team types are lightweight, cannot have security roles assigned, and cannot own records; they are rather used for granting ad-hoc access to records.

Let us now illustrate the use of both team types as examples.

Owner Teams

Let us imagine the following situation: In the customer support department, there is regularly the need to involve experts from the project delivery department in order to resolve customer cases. However, the standard hierarchy authorization would not allow access to records from both the customer service and project delivery departments unless everybody would obtain organization-level permission. Project Wizards, Inc., however, wants to restrict permissions and does not want to grant organization-level permissions to the users from the two departments. The solution for this situation is the use of the owner teams. An example of a possible setup is illustrated in the following figure:

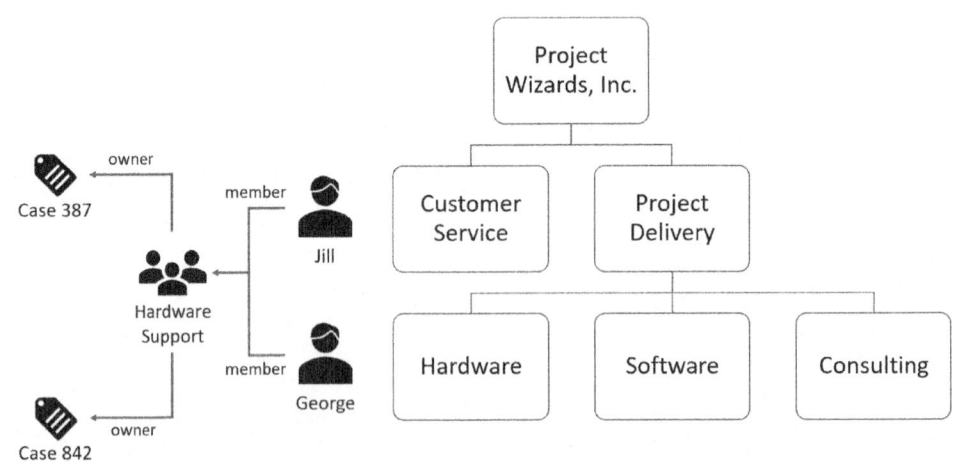

Figure 11.14: Owner team example

As you can see in *figure 11.14*, there is a customer service representative, Jill, assigned to the business unit *"Customer Service"* and a hardware specialist, George, assigned to the business unit *"Hardware"* from the project delivery department. To give both access to cases without compromising the standard authorization, we can create an owner team, *"Hardware Support"*, and make it the owner of all required cases—in our example, there are cases with the numbers 387 and 842. Finally, we make both Jill and George members of the owner team, *"Hardware Support"*. This configuration will give both users access to the required cases.

Access teams

Let us now examine a different situation in the sales management area. Occasionally, the salesperson responsible for creating a complex offer to the customer might need temporary help from experts from different parts of the organization, for example, to perform a complex product configuration. In this case, again, the standard hierarchical authorization will not allow access without granting the organizational level permission, which is prohibited in Project Wizards, Inc. The solution for this situation can be the use of access teams, as illustrated in the following example:

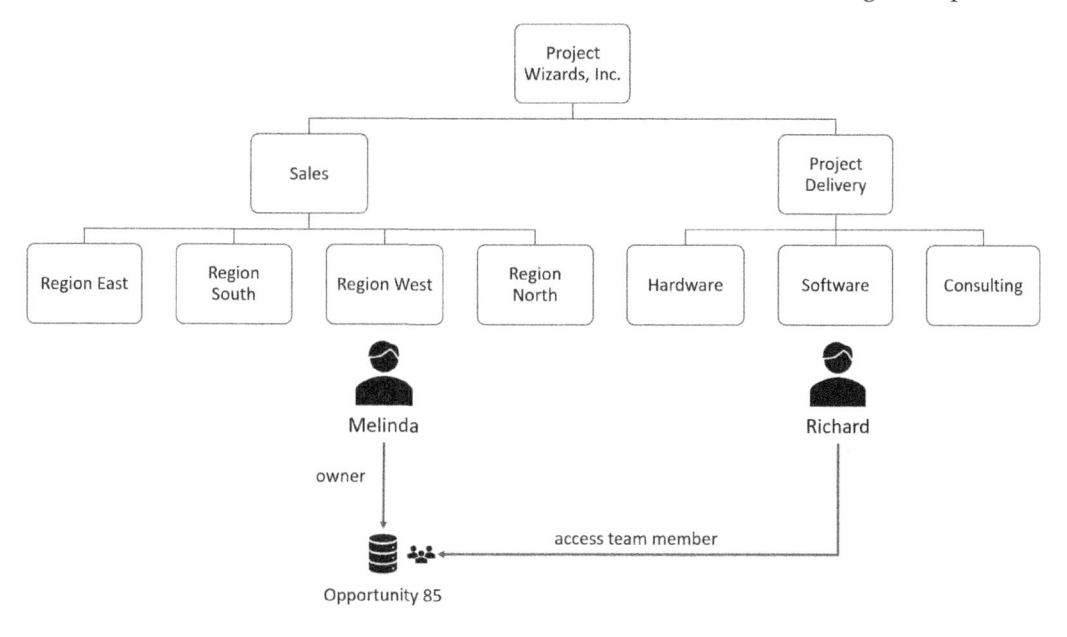

Figure 11.15: Access team example

As you can see in *figure 11.15*, there is a salesperson Melinda from the business unit *"Region West"* from the sales department, working on a complex opportunity number 85 for a customer. At some point, Melinda needs help from Richard from the business unit *"Software"* from the project delivery department. Richard is an expert on software products, and Melinda needs him to prepare a detailed description of the product for the customer. To cover scenarios like this, we need to establish the *"access teams"* capability for the Microsoft Dataverse table "Opportunity" (in fact, the access teams are already configured for this table in Dynamics 365 Sales). After this is done, Melinda or any other user can just add another user, in this case, Richard, to the access team of the respective opportunity record. By adding him, he will immediately get access to the opportunity. After he is done with the work for Melinda, she can remove him from the access team, and he will lose access to the record.

The Hierarchy Security

Another optional authorization concept in Microsoft Dataverse is called *"Hierarchy security"*. Please do not be confused with the naming, and the standard business unit hierarchy is something different from this hierarchy security. Although the business unit hierarchy belongs to the mandatory authorization configuration, the hierarchy security is a fully optional extension. The main purpose of the hierarchy security is to provide another hierarchical dimension to the authorization possibilities of Microsoft Dataverse. This capability is seldom used but is well suitable for matrix-structured organizations, for example, an organization from the professional services industry. In professional services, the majority of employees work on projects and, as such, have beside their line manager also a temporary secondary manager—for example, a project manager, program manager, and so on. Those temporary managers might have a legitimate interest in having access to some data of their subordinate employees for the duration of the project. And exactly this type of scenario can be covered with the hierarchy security.

The Column-Level Security

Another optional but often used capability is called column-level security. When we look back into all the Microsoft Dataverse authorization concepts so far, they all implement access rights to records. The column-level security, however, goes a step deeper and provides the possibility to protect individual columns. This capability works as follows:

- First, we need to identify the columns in some Microsoft Dataverse tables which require additional protection. These are usually columns containing sensitive information, which should not be available to all users having access to the respective records. Examples are SSN, credit card numbers, data about the wealth of bank customers, and so on.

- For the identified columns, the flag "`Enable column security`" needs to be set, according to the following screenshot:

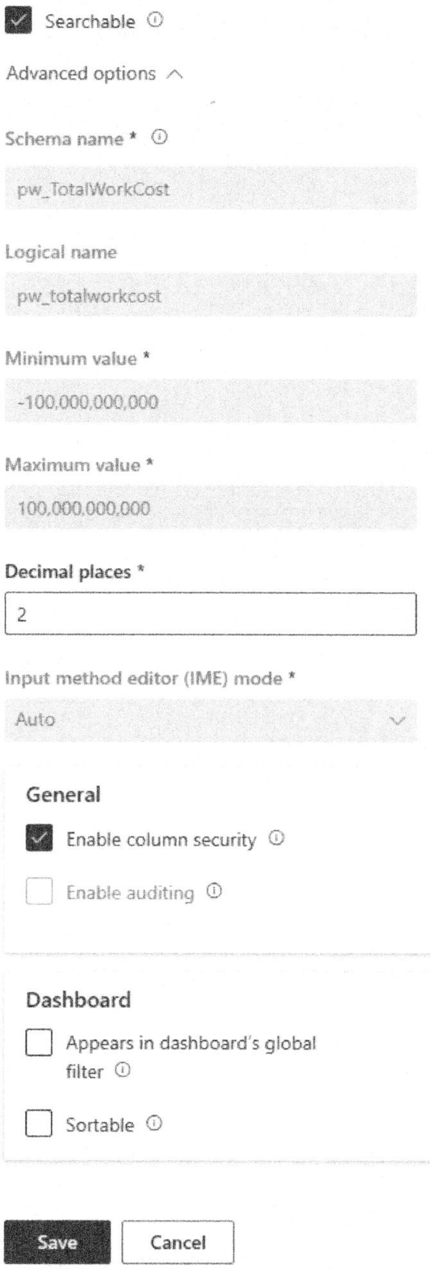

☑ Searchable ⓘ

Advanced options ∧

Schema name * ⓘ

pw_TotalWorkCost

Logical name

pw_totalworkcost

Minimum value *

-100,000,000,000

Maximum value *

100,000,000,000

Decimal places *

2

Input method editor (IME) mode *

Auto

General

☑ Enable column security ⓘ

☐ Enable auditing ⓘ

Dashboard

☐ Appears in dashboard's global filter ⓘ

☐ Sortable ⓘ

Save Cancel

Figure 11.16: Enable column security

- To be able to grant access to those protected columns, "**Column security profiles**" need to be created next. In each profile, the access rights to the protected columns need to be specified, according to the following screenshot:

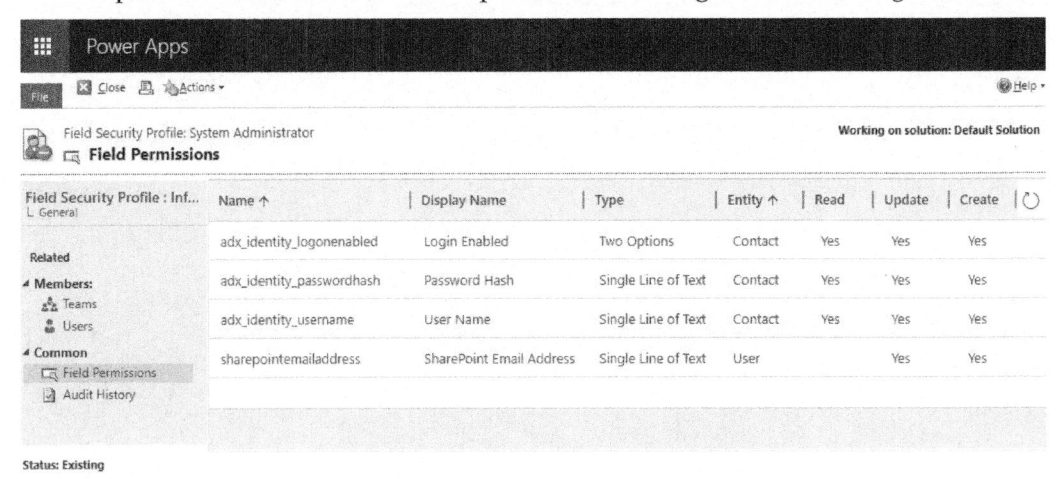

Figure 11.17: Column security profile

- For every column, it is possible to enable read access, create access or update access.

- The last step is to include selected users as members of the column security profile. The members will get the permissions to the columns defined in the profile. Users not included in any profile will have no access to the protected columns.

With this last capability, we have concluded the Microsoft Dataverse authorization and can now move forward to the authorization concepts in Power Apps and the other Power Platform components.

Authorization in Power Apps

As we already learned in *Chapter 1, Introducing Microsoft Power Platform*, there are three different types of Power Apps, and the authorization of these three Power Apps types is also different. Let us briefly describe the capabilities in the next sections.

Model-driven apps authorization

Access to model-driven apps can be granted using one of the two available options:

- **Direct assignment of security roles:** This is the traditional method for granting access to model-driven apps. You need to assign one or multiple security roles to the model-driven app, and every user holding some of those security roles will get access to the app. You can find this option by opening the model-driven app and then clicking on the name of the app. This opens a pop-up window showing all model-driven apps in the environment. Clicking the ellipsis on the respective app opens a dialog with two options. One of the options is called "**Manage Roles**", as illustrated in the following screenshot:

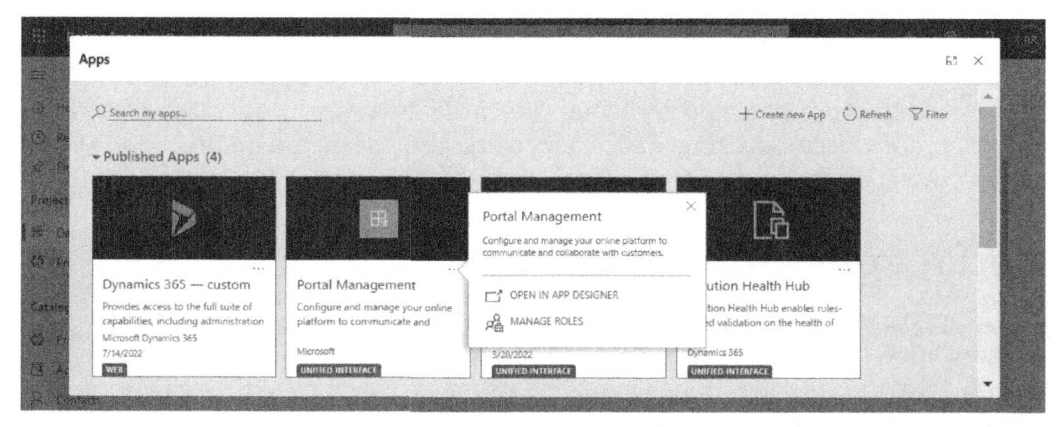

Figure 11.18: Assigning security roles to a model-driven app

You just need to click on the option and then select the Microsoft Dataverse security roles which you plan to assign to the app.

- **Sharing:** Sharing is a new method for granting access to model-driven apps; you need to select this option from the Maker Portal from the list of all apps. Selecting the ellipsis for the respective app opens a local menu with multiple options, one of which is the option to share the app. Selecting this option opens an app-sharing dialog, which serves the same purpose as the previous method.

Granting access to a model-driven app alone does not provide access without assigning proper security roles to the users.

Canvas apps authorization

Canvas apps are independent of Microsoft Dataverse, and that is why granting access to the apps is easier and does not require working with Microsoft Dataverse security roles unless you use the Microsoft Dataverse data connector.

Access to the canvas app is granted using sharing. The sharing capability has the following main features:

- You can share the app either with individual users, with security groups, or even with *"Everyone"*, which means the app will be available for every licensed user in the organization.

- Sharing is also possible with guest users in your Microsoft tenant.
- Sharing is possible in a *"user"* mode or in a *"co-owner"* mode. The latter means that the other users will be able to modify the app the same way as you as the owner can.
- The Power Platform can send an invitation Email message to all users to inform them that a new app was shared with them.

Part of the authorization must always be also a consideration of how to authorize the data connectors the app is using. You need to keep in mind also licensing considerations because using data connectors also means an indirect use of the underlying IT systems and solutions.

Portal apps authorization

Portal apps are quite complex, and so is also the authorization. We had touched the authorization already when we configured the portal app for Project Wizards, Inc. Simply said, the authorization is managed using a concept called *"web roles"*. Every authenticated portal user needs to be assigned at least one web role, which grants the user certain permissions on the portal. In detail, the *web role* contains underlying structures specifying the following permissions:

- **Access permissions to web pages in the portal:** This is important because we need to hide certain web pages from the anonymous access available to everybody. Such protected Web pages can be only accessed when an authenticated user with proper permission levels visits the portal app. As an example, a Web page showing the list of open tickets of a particular customer needs to be hidden from anonymous visitors and only revealed to authenticated users with proper permission.

- **Access permissions to records in Microsoft Dataverse tables:** These permissions define the number of records an authenticated user of the portal app can create, modify, or delete. For example, an authenticated user visits the Web page with the list of tickets but can only see the tickets they created or can see the tickets created by any other portal user belonging to the same customer.

The portal apps authorization concept is similar to the Microsoft Dataverse authorization and needs a well-thought design to work properly and avoid information leakages.

Authorization in Power Automate

The authorization in Power Automate is relatively simple and is based on the same sharing concept as for the canvas apps. There are two main scenarios where we need to care about authorization in Power Automate:

- **Button flows:** Button flows are the only flows used by human users, and that is why we need to ensure the flows are distributed to the respective user population. In this scenario, the sharing works exactly as with canvas apps. We decided to share a button flow either with selected users, with security groups, or with everyone.

- **Team flows:** Flows of other types (scheduled flows and event-driven flows) do not need to be shared with users since they run in the background. However, there might be a need to share the flows with co-workers so that they can also work on the flows. In this case, we perform sharing in the "*co-owner*" mode, and the other users will get the ability to modify the flows as we can.

Equally, as with canvas apps, for Power Automate flows, we need to care about the authorization of the data connectors and also the proper licensing of the underlying IT systems.

Authorization in Power BI

As we mentioned multiple times in this book, Power BI is technologically different from the other Power Platform components, and so is the authorization as well. We have touched on this topic in *Chapter 6, Start with Power BI* of this book already; here is just a summary.

With Power BI, we can use two fundamentally different data handling modes, the Import mode and the DirectQuery mode. Although with the DirectQuery mode against Microsoft Dataverse, we do not need to care about authorization because the Microsoft Dataverse authorization is fully honored, with the Import mode, we need to build a separate authorization. Power BI has its own authorization feature called **Row-Level Security** (**RLS**). With RLS, you can achieve the following:

- Define *roles*, and for each role, define data *restrictions (filters)* filtering the data in Microsoft Dataverse (or any other data source) based on given criteria. For example, you could create multiple roles for sales analytics, and in each role, you could filter all relevant data based on a selected sales territory. The creation of roles is performed in the Power BI Desktop so that they become part of the report.

- *Assign* roles to individual Power BI users. Doing so will limit the amount of data available to the individual users; for example, a user with the assigned role "*Sales territory west*" would only see records in the visualizations where the sales territory is "*West*".

With this section, we have concluded the overview of the various methods for authorizing access to data, functionality, and applications with the Power Platform; in the next section, you will learn some best practices for building secured solutions.

Build secure Power Platform solutions

As mentioned at the beginning of this chapter, the Power Platform is used for building business applications, and they manage business data, which is one of the critical assets an organization needs to carefully protect. So, what is the take on all those security features you just learned?

- Security of the final business application needs to be incorporated into the architecture and design from the very beginning. It is not appropriate to start thinking about security just shortly before going live.

- Power Platform is a cloud platform type Software as a Service, which means that most of the security aspects are in the hands of Microsoft, and we need to rely on the highly professional skills of the Microsoft staff and the appropriate security measures they take to fully protect, what is in their responsibility. What remains is our responsibility, and we need to take this responsibility seriously enough.

- Never assume things are safe by default; the opposite is true, and nothing is safe by default. Incorporate strict security measures for authentication (use multi-factor authentication, and so on) and authorization (restrict access to least necessary).

- Security needs to be strict but not block productive work. Think carefully and select the best possible options.

- Use Microsoft Dataverse whenever you decide to build a brand-new business application. The security concepts in Microsoft Dataverse are strong enough to cover even the most complex security requirements.

- Use the security concepts as they are designed. Use standard security (business units and security roles) for most of the cases and advanced concepts (teams, hierarchy security, and column-level security) just for the exceptions.

Now, we are at the end of the security part of this chapter and continue with the second part, dedicated to governance.

Power Platform governance fundamentals

Microsoft Power Platform clearly promotes the modern low-code/now-code approach and the role of a citizen developer, simply said, the idea of making *"everyone"* in the organization an active creator of IT solutions. This idea is great and can bring a whole bunch of benefits to the organization, specifically in terms of the cost of building IT solutions and a lot of agility leading to better time-to-market and higher value-for-money. But we need to look at both sides of the coin. The dark side is represented by things like shadow IT, no clear responsibility and ownership, no clear lifecycle of the solutions, breaking the IT policies and rules, not respecting general laws such as the GDPR, and many more. It can even lead to very harmful consequences in case of sensitive data leakages and other violations of essential internal policies and regulations. That is why we need something called governance. The IT department needs to stay in control of what happens in its own IT cloud landscape, setup and enforce policies and ensure the great idea of low-code/no-code brings real benefits but no issues and problems.

The Microsoft Power Platform is equipped with tools and add-ons, which give the organization's own IT the necessary control so that the previous goals can be achieved. The major governance components are the following:

- The data loss prevention policies (data policies)
- The Power Platform Center of Excellence Starter Kit

In the following sections, you will learn about both of these two governance components.

Data policies

The data policies are addressing one specific but potentially very dangerous situation, which can arise, when improperly or even maliciously using the Power Platform data connectors. The data connectors are a great feature, making the connection to every possible IT system from the Power Apps or Power Automate flows really easy. But what if some user configures an app or flow, which inadvertently or even intentionally releases some sensitive internal information to the public? The harm can be millions, not even mentioning the reputation damage for the organization. In order to prevent data leakages of this type, the Power Platform contains a concept called **data loss prevention policies** (data policies).

The data policies are based on a very simple idea: the data connectors within the customer's tenant can be categorized into three categories:

- **Blocked**: The connectors assigned to this category will be not available for the makers in the organization; they will be not able to use them at all.

- **Non-business**: The connectors assigned to this category will be available for the makers and will represent connectors to IT systems, where no business-critical data is stored.
- **Business**: The connectors assigned to this category will be available for the makers and will represent connectors to IT systems containing business-critical data.

The IT administration in the organization using Power Platform will need to decide how to distribute the connectors into the three categories. Once the categorization is done, the makers will not be able to use connectors placed into the *"blocked"* category and will be able to use in their apps or flows only connectors from either the *"business"* or the *"non-business"* category, but never from both categories in the same app or flow. This would eliminate the situation for a malicious user to configure a flow publishing details about all new sales opportunities directly on *Twitter*, just as an example.

The data policies can be set either on the *tenant level* or on an *environment level*. On the tenant level, the following are the possible scopes of the policies:

- Policy valid for *all* Power Platform environments
- Policy valid for *selected* Power Platform environments
- Policy valid for *all except selected* Power Platform environments

The tenant-level policies can be created and maintained in the Power Platform Admin Center under **Policies | Data policies**, according to the following screenshot:

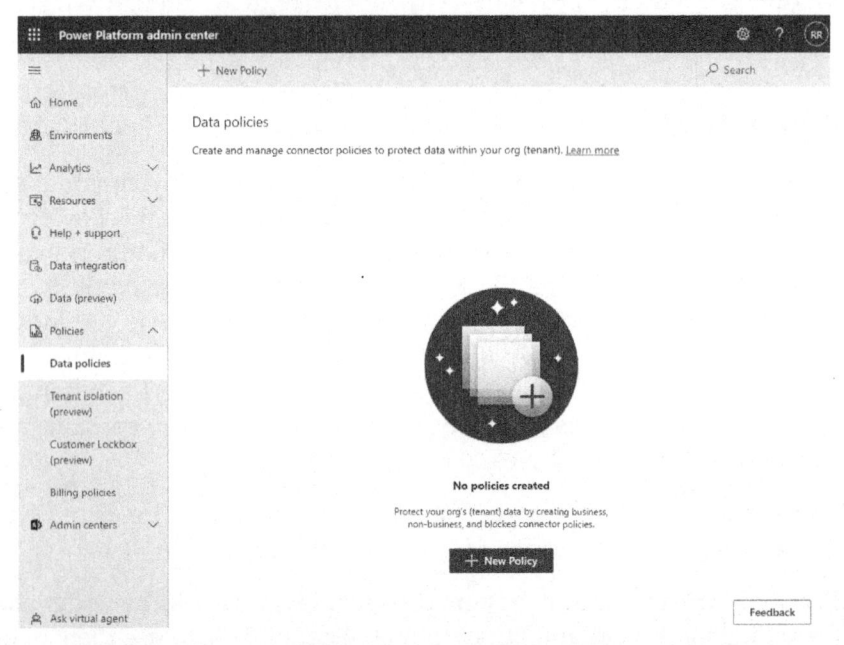

Figure 11.19: Tenant-level data policies in the Power Platform Admin Center

You can directly start creating a new policy by clicking the "**+ New Policy**" button. The policy will be created in an assistant-like fashion, following the required steps. Let us create a new policy for Project Wizards, Inc. in the following exercise.

Exercise 21: Creating a data policy

In this exercise, we will practice the procedure of creating a tenant-level data policy. Please perform the following steps:

1. Navigate to the Power Platform Admin Center (aka.ms/ppac) and sign-in with your cloud credentials.

2. Within the admin center, navigate to `Policies` | `Data policies`.

3. Click "**+ New Policy**". A guided dialog will appear.

4. In the first step in the guided dialog, give the policy the name "`Project Wizards Standard Policy`" according to the following screenshot:

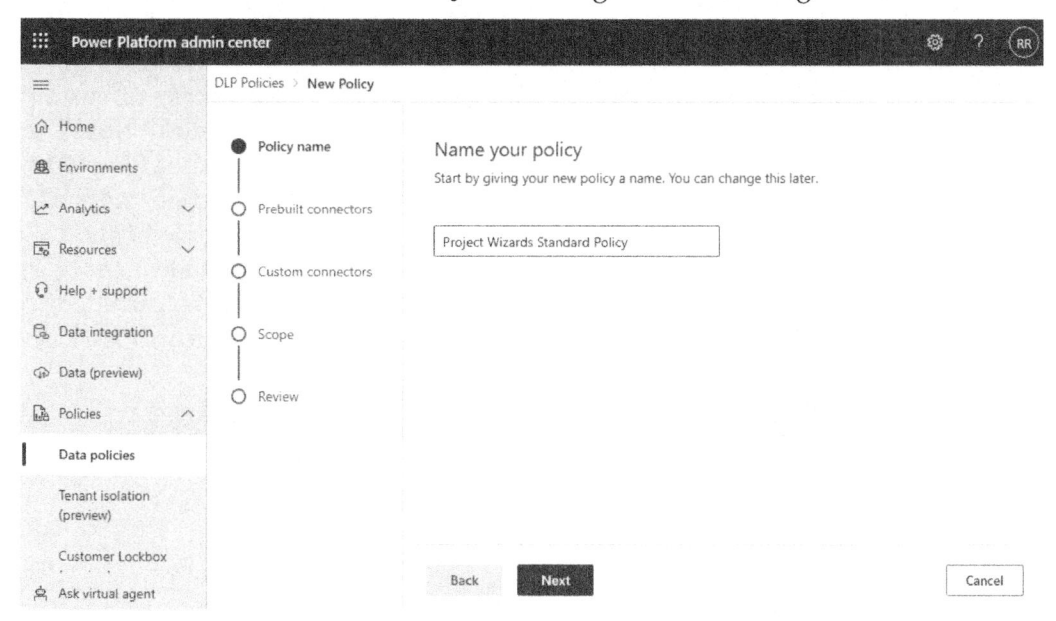

Figure 11.20: Creation of a tenant-level data policy, Step I.

5. Click "**Next**". In the second step, you need to assign the Power Platform data connectors into the three groups, as explained earlier in this section. For the sake of simplicity, search for both Microsoft Dataverse data connectors

and move them into the "**Business**" group, according to the following screenshot:

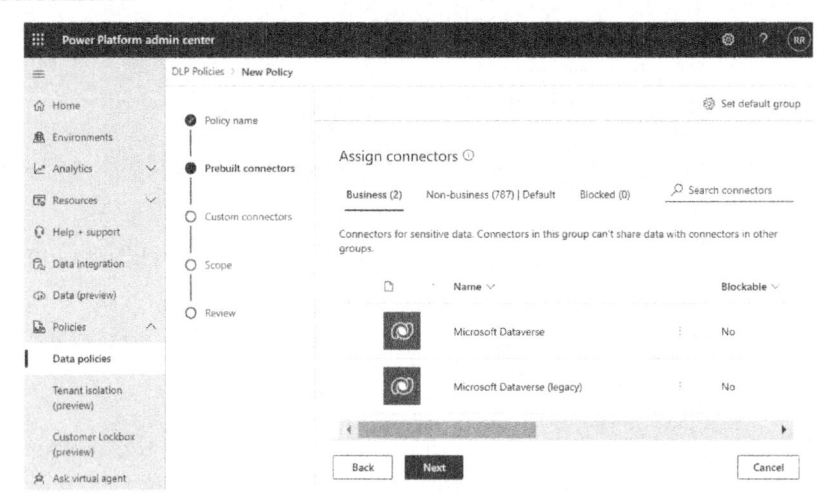

Figure 11.21: Creation of a tenant-level data policy, Step II.

6. Click "**Next**". In this step, you could set rules to limit access to custom connectors. Since we have no custom connectors created, click "**Next**" to move to the next step. In this step, you can define the scope of the policy, as explained earlier in this section. By default, there is the scope "**Add all environments**" selected. When you change the scope to some of the two other options ("**Add multiple environments**" or "**Exclude certain environments**"), you will see that an additional step will be included in the guided dialog. Select "**Add multiple environment**" according to the following screenshot:

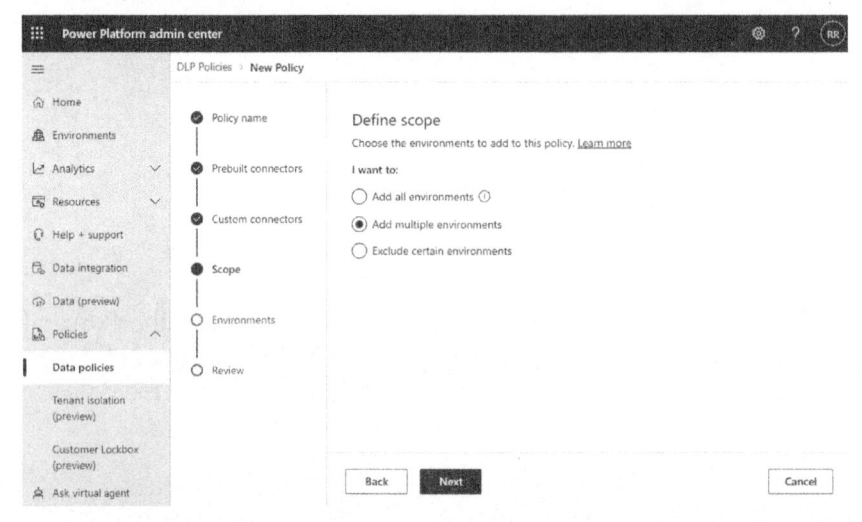

Figure 11.22: Creation of a tenant-level data policy, Step III

7. Click "**Next**" this will open a list of environments in the tenant, and you can select one or multiple environments for which the policy will apply. Select the default environment with the name "`Project Wizards, Inc. (default)`" only and click on the button "`+ Add to policy`" according to the following screenshot:

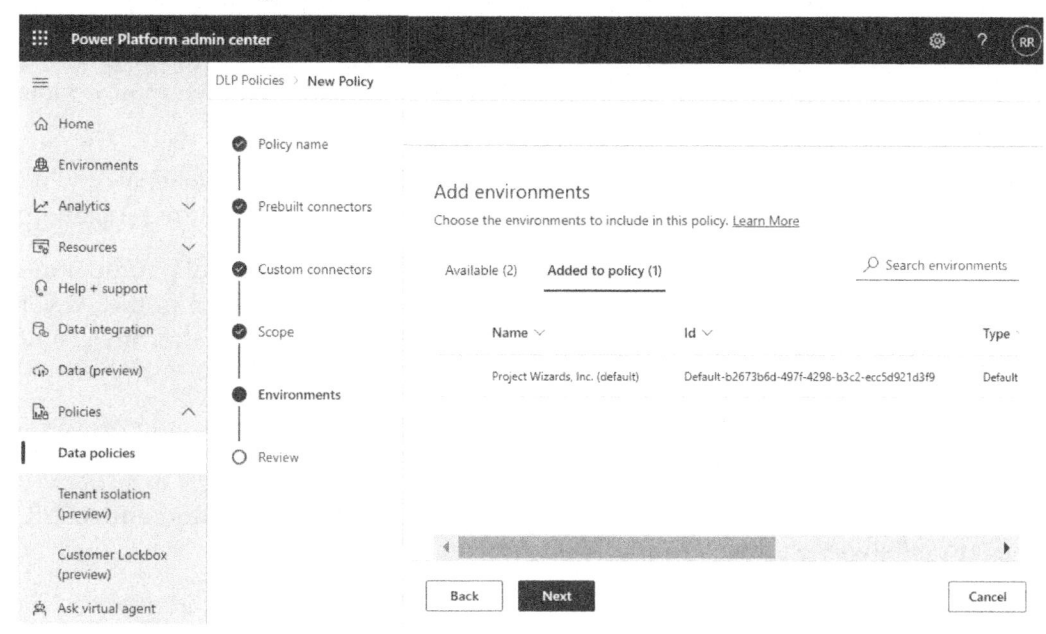

Figure 11.23: Creation of a tenant-level data policy, Step IV

8. Click "**Next**" for the last time to see the summary of the policy, and then click "`Create policy`". The policy will be created and will be visible in the list of data policies.

Note: Do not select the environment of type "Developer", you are working on in the exercises because the policy will restrict the functionality of the Power Automate flow we have created in *Chapter 4, Automate Processes with Power Automate.*

Congratulations! You have created a data policy for Project Wizards, Inc.

In fact, the data policies have more to offer, for the data connectors, you can select which actions are allowed and which are blocked, and for certain connectors, you can even restrict the endpoints to which the connectors can connect. This makes the capability really useful for governance purposes in an organization heavily using many data connectors.

The second governance component you will learn is the Power Platform Center of Excellence Starter Kit.

The Center of Excellence Starter Kit

Compared with the data policies, the Power Platform **Center of Excellence Starter Kit** (**CoE Starter Kit**) is not part of the Power Platform ecosystem but must be installed separately. The CoE Starter Kit is a collection of useful governance tools providing:

- A Power BI report provides a detailed and always current overview of what exists in the Power Platform ecosystem in the cloud tenant of the organization.
- A collection of Power Automate flows performing the necessary automation for collecting inventory information about what was created in the Power Platform, for implementing governance processes and procedures, and many more.
- A collection of Power Apps for the Power Platform administrators, makers, and users.

The CoE Starter Kit can be found under the following URL: **https://docs.microsoft.com/en-us/power-platform/guidance/coe/starter-kit**

The link provides detailed documentation on the installation of the toolkit and on the content. It is a matter of fact that the installation of the toolkit is not trivial and takes considerable time; however, the documentation describes the installation steps very well.

Let us take a closer look at the most important parts of the toolkit.

Power BI CoE starter kit report

The toolkit provides a very comprehensive Power BI report that gives an analytical insight into the Power Platform content present on the cloud tenant. The report has more than 35 pages, and on each page, you can find unique analytics about the Power Platform environment, apps, flows, connectors, and many more. An example of the content is illustrated in the following two screenshots:

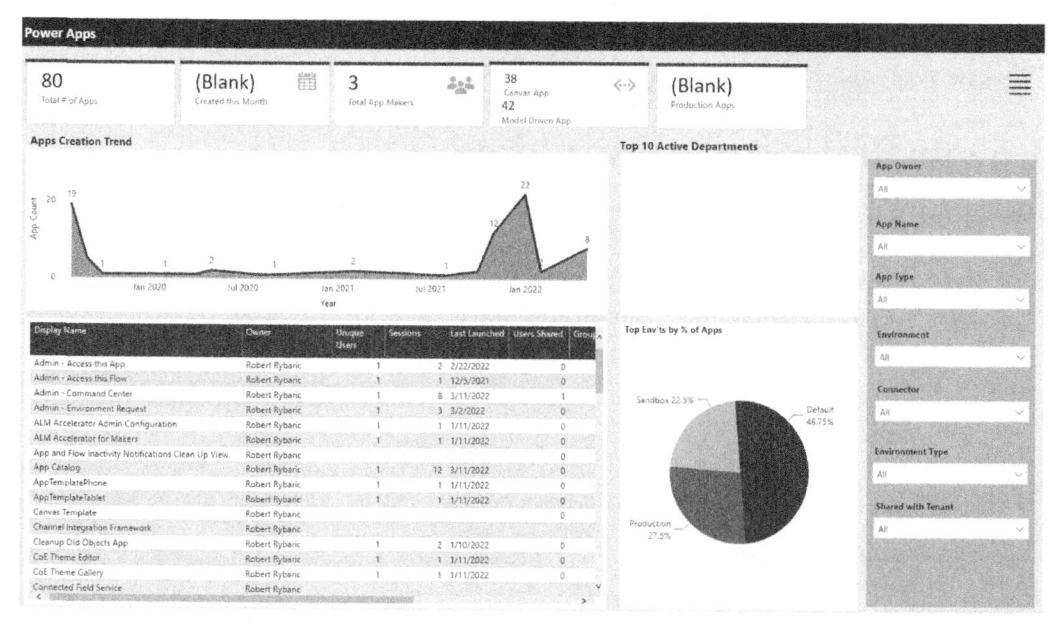

Figure 11.24: CoE Starter Kit Power BI Report example—Power Apps overview

As you can see in *figure 11.24*, there is a detailed analytical overview of all Power Apps found in the tenant. The analytics provides a time-based app creation trend, a list of all apps, and a chart showing the number of apps per Power Platform environment.

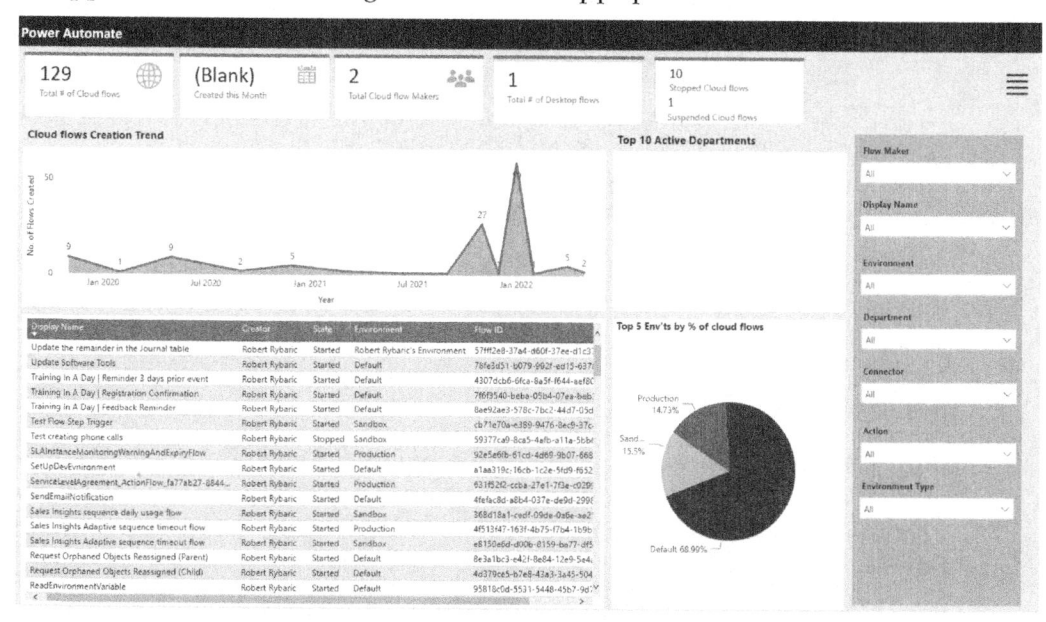

Figure 11.25: CoE Starter Kit Power BI Report example—Power Automate overview

As you can see in *figure 11.25*, a similar analytical overview is also presented for Power Automate flows.

Power Platform admin view

Part of the toolkit is a model-driven app with the name "**Power Platform Admin View**". The app is dedicated to the administrators and provides an overview of all Power Platform objects as they are collected by the Power Automate flows and stored in Microsoft Dataverse. When you start the app, it will show an overview dashboard, according to the following screenshot:

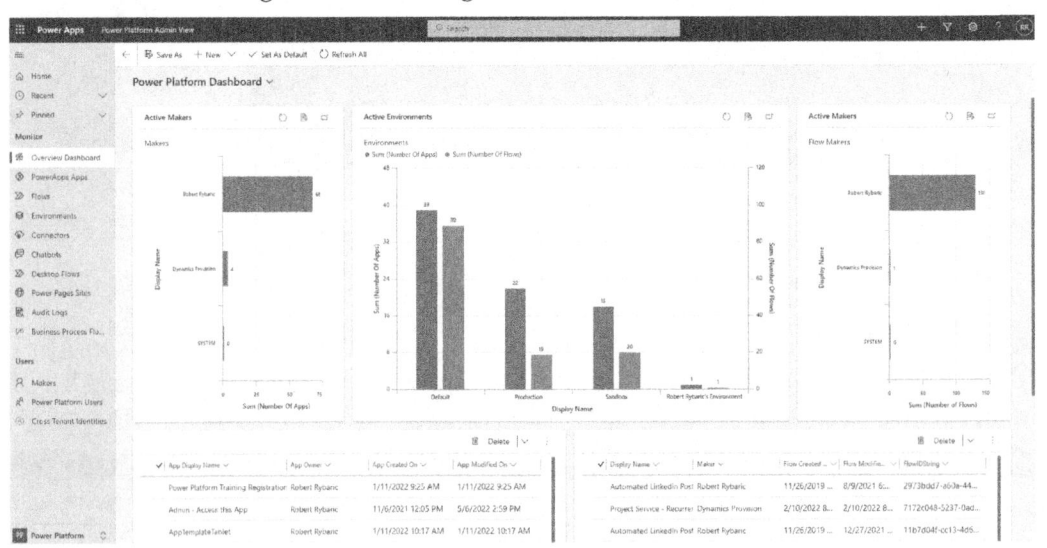

Figure 11.26: CoE Starter Kit Power Platform Admin View

Further, the app provides an overview of the following:

- **Power Apps:** This capability provides a list of all model-driven apps and canvas apps. By opening a record, you will find a lot of details about the apps, including the list of user data connectors and sharing information, auditing information about the apps such as the justification of the app, the business impact, the admin app categorization, and many more.

- **Power Automate flows:** This capability provides a similar detailed overview of the Power Automate flows as the previous capability. You will find the details about the used connectors and even a list of the actions used in the flows.

- **Power Platform environments:** This capability provides a detailed overview of the Power Platform environments in the cloud tenant. You will find the main details about the environment, the storage capacity overview, the auditing information, and lists of all apps, flows, custom connectors, desktop flows, and chatbots created in the environment.

- **Connectors:** This capability provides a list of all currently existing Power Platform data connectors. When you open a record, you will find details about the usage of the connector, in which apps and flows are the connector used, and the usual auditing information.

- **Chatbots:** This capability gives you an overview of all existing Power Virtual Agents chatbots created in the cloud tenant. For every chatbot, you will find the internal details, like the list of all existing topics and their details.

- **Desktop flows:** This capability provides you with the list of Power Automate Desktop flows with some details and the auditing information.

- **Power Page Sites:** As of writing this book, Microsoft introduced new technology as an evolution to the Power Apps Portals under the name *Power Pages*. In this part of the app, there is an overview of portal apps, providing a lot of details about the portal apps, including the auditing details.

Besides that most important information, the app provides insight into the audit logs, the business process flows, and an overview of the makers and the users.

Admin—Command Center

This is a canvas app dedicated to the Power Platform administrators.

After starting the app, you will get the possibility to start any other of the apps belonging to the toolkit, according to the following screenshot:

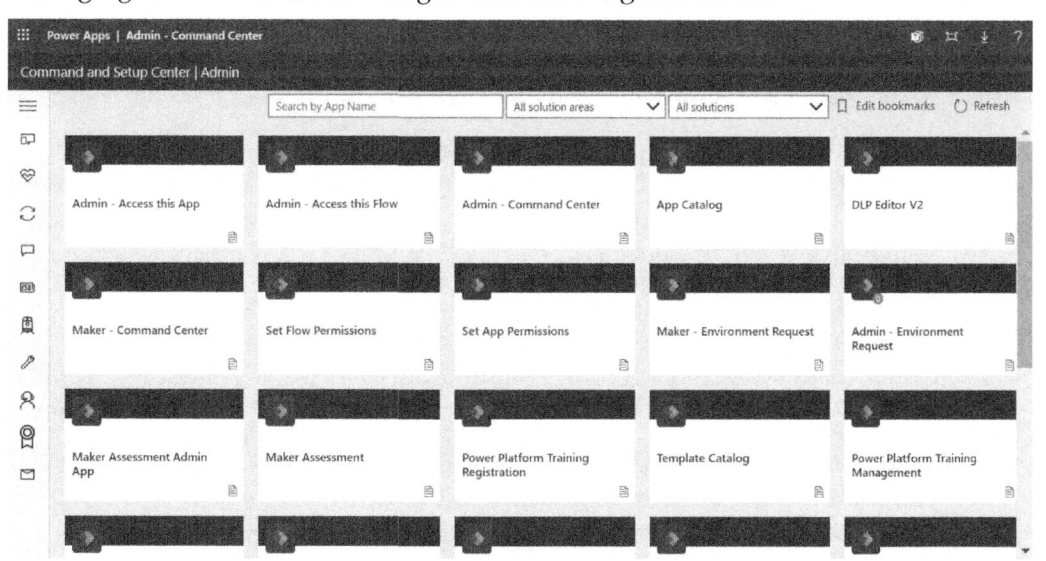

Figure 11.27: CoE Starter Kit Power Platform Admin view

It can be further used for the following purposes:

- Overview of the health of the Power Automate flows running as part of the CoE Starter Kit.
- Overview of the administration messages provided by Microsoft regarding the Power Platform.
- Power Platform news coming from the various Microsoft blogs.
- Release wave news coming from the Microsoft information sources.
- Possibility to create and submit issues discovered in the toolkit via GitHub.
- Link to the selected Microsoft Learn contents.
- Possibility to configure certain settings of the toolkit.

Other apps

Besides the most important apps mentioned previously, the toolkit contains the following other important apps:

- **Apps and flows for the environment request functionality:** The apps implement a process when a maker can request the creation of a new Power Platform environment. This request is then routed to the Power Platform administrators, which can approve or reject the request. Approved requests automatically create the environments. The capability makes it possible to request temporary environments with a time-limited lifecycle.
- **App Catalog app:** This app is intended to be used by all users in the organization. The purpose is that every user can verify whether an app or a flow with a certain business capability already exists in the organization. If so, the user can request access to the app or flow.
- **DLP Editor app:** This app extends the basic capability of creating data policies with impact analysis. This analysis gives the administrator information about what happens with the existing apps and flows when a change in the data policy is performed.
- **Apps for setting permissions of apps and flows:** These apps address the situation when an employee who created some apps and flows retires from the organization without assigning the ownership to another user. An administrator can navigate to such orphan apps or flows and set new owners.
- **Apps for implementing the auditing capability:** Part of the toolkit is the possibility to implement an auditing procedure, where apps and flow can be audited by the Power Platform administrators to verify the purpose and justify the business relevance.

- **Innovation Backlog app:** The app is dedicated to users having an idea about future apps or flows which need to be built. The users can provide details such as the process, the personas, the current tools used, and so on. The idea can then be evaluated, an ROI of the future app or flow can be calculated, and based on that, a decision to build the app or flow can be taken.

With this, we have finished also the second part of this chapter dedicated to the governance possibilities of the Power Platform.

Conclusion

In this last chapter, you have learned about two important areas of interest in the Power Platform: security and governance. You have learned the fundamentals of IT security in general and in the Power Platform in particular. Next, we have presented you the concept and the possibilities of the authentication in the Microsoft clouds with the specifics available in the Power Platform. In the subsequent long section, you have learned a lot of details about the Microsoft Dataverse authorization possibilities. You have seen that Microsoft Dataverse offers a lot of deep concepts for implementing complex authorization scenarios. You have made yourself familiar with business units, security roles, and record ownership as the main pillars of the hierarchical type of security. These concepts were further explained in a series of examples to better understand how they really work. After that, we have also presented the optional Microsoft Dataverse authorization features such as the teams, the hierarchy security, or the column-level security. In the next part of the chapter, we have made an overview of the authorization possibilities available for Power Apps, Power Automate flows, and Power BI. The first part of the chapter was concluded with some best practices on how to build secure business applications with the Power Platform. In the second part of this chapter, we have presented the relevance of governance in the Power Platform to avoid certain risks of the low-code/no-code idea and the idea of the citizen developer. You have learned about the data loss prevention policies, what they are, and how they can help prevent data leakages and another misuse of the data connectors. Finally, we have presented the Power Platform Center of Excellence Starter Kit as a toolkit, providing a lot of useful capabilities to ensure full governance in the Power Platform.

This is the last chapter of this book. We sincerely hope that this book was useful to you, dear reader, and brought you a lot of interesting content about the Power Platform. We wish you a lot of success with implementing the Power Platform in your organization and a lot of business benefits by building business applications with this innovative platform.

Questions

1. What are authentication and authorization in IT security, and what is the difference between them?
2. How is the authentication implemented in the Microsoft cloud systems?
3. What are the steps required to fully provision a new user in the Power Platform?
4. What are the seven pillars of Microsoft Dataverse authentication?
5. What is the main purpose of the business units?
6. What is the main purpose of the security roles?
7. How does the standard security with business units, security roles, and record ownership work?
8. What are teams, and how are they used?
9. What is the optional hierarchy security, and in which scenarios can it be used?
10. What is the column-level security, and in which scenarios can it be used?
11. How does the authorization work for Power Apps?
12. How does the authorization work for Power Automate?
13. How does the authorization work for Power BI?
14. What is the Power Platform governance, and why is it important?
15. What are the data loss prevention policies, and what scenario in the governance do they cover?
16. What is the Power Platform Center of Excellence Starter Kit, and what features does it offer?

Index

A

admin command center 313
advanced authentication 284
  conditional access 285
  Multi-factor authentication (MFA) 285
  on-premises active directory, integrating with Azure Active Directory 285
AI Builder 9, 233
  fundamentals 236, 237
  use cases 234
AI Builder models
  custom model, configuring 242
  custom model, testing 242
  data-processing models 242
  image-processing models 240
  integrating, with canvas apps 253
  integrating, with model-driven apps 253
  integrating, with Power Automate 254
  overview 237, 238
  text-processing models 238
  vendor invoice processing, testing 254-259
AI Builder scenarios
  automated text analysis 235
  document processing 234
  products recognition 235
analytical solutions
  integrating, with apps and flows 203, 204
App Catalog app 314
application lifecycle management (ALM) fundamentals 277, 278

approval workflow
  analysis and preparations 102
  creating 102
  practical implementation 103-112
area chart 178, 179
artificial intelligence (AI) 210
authentication in Microsoft cloud 283, 284
  advanced authentication 284
authorization in Microsoft Dataverse 285, 286
  basic authorization model 293-295
  business units 289, 290
  Column-Level security 298, 300
  Hierarchy security 298
  Microsoft Dataverse users 286-288
  ownership of records 288
  security roles 290-293
  Teams 296
authorization in Power Apps
  canvas apps authorization 301, 302
  model-driven apps authorization 300, 301
  portal apps authorization 302
authorization in Power Automate
  button flows 303
  Team flows 303
authorization in Power BI 303, 304
automated cloud flows
  approval workflow, creating 102
  configurations example 101
  examples 100
Automate Power Platform fundamentals 278, 279
Azure Active Directory 283

group management 283
license management 283
user management 283
Azure DevOps 278

B

backend automations 145
bar chart 176-178
bubble chart 182
bubble map 184
business IT
  in 21st century 2
Business Process Flows (BPF)
  analysis and preparation 130, 131
  capabilities 130
  creating 130
  fundamentals 129
  practical implementation 131-136
business rules
  analysis and preparations 137
  creating 137
  practical implementation 137-140
business units 289
button cloud flows fundamentals 120-124
button flows, for personal automation
  Azure Active Directory user, creating 128, 129
  files, uploading SharePoint or OneDrive 126, 127
  using 125
  vacation request 125, 126

C

canvas apps 62
  connecting, to data 65, 66

creating 63-68
employee mobility, enabling 79
example 31
features 31
fundamentals 62, 63
publishing 79
sharing 79
testing 79
canvas apps user interface
　application header, configuring 70, 71
　building 68, 69
　buttons, configuring 74-76
　gallery, configuring 72-74
　screen, designing 70
　toggle control, configuring 71
Center of Excellence Starter Kit (CoE Starter Kit) 310
　Admin-Command Center 313, 314
　Power BI CoE starter kit report 310, 311
　Power Platform admin view 312, 313
chatbot 209
　conversation nodes, creating 214, 215
　creating 212, 213, 216-226
　customer service 210, 211
　employee support 211
　hosting, in Microsoft Teams 228
　hosting, in website 228
　integrating, into Power Apps portal 229-31
　integrating, with IT systems 216
　publishing 227
　sales support 211
　testing 226, 227
　topics, creating 213, 214

classic custom actions 140
classic workflows 140
cloud flows
　action types 95, 96
　actions 94
　automated cloud flows 100
　desktop flows 113
　example 94
　expressions 97-100
　fundamentals 94
　logic 94-97
　scheduled cloud flows 112, 113
　trigger 94
cloud flows, in Power Apps
　event-based automations 141
　on-demand automations 141
　scheduled automations 141
　using 140
column chart 176-178
Column-Level security 298-300
conversation nodes 214
customer portal
　creating 82, 83
　model-driven view and form, preparing 83, 84
　portals solution, configuring 84-89
custom model, AI Builder
　configuring 242
　information, extracting from vendor invoices 242-252
　testing 242

D

dashboard
　integrating 204-206
data connectors 9

data loss prevention policies (data policies) 305-307
data modeling exercise, Power Query 167-171
data model, Microsoft Dataverse
　analysis and preparations 35, 36
　calculated and rollup columns, configuring 46-48
　column data type Autonumber, configuring 50
　columns, configuring with choice data type 49, 50
　columns, creating in custom tables 43-45
　creating 35
　custom tables, creating 40, 41
　existing tables, adding to solution 39
　Power Platform solution, creating 36-38
　practical implementation 36
　relationships between tables, creating 41-43
data model, Power Query
　building 165
　calculated columns, creating 166, 167
　measures, creating 167
　relationship between tables, creating 165, 166
data-processing models
　prediction 242
Dataverse automations
　business rules 136, 137
　fundamentals 136
Dataverse automations, in Power Apps
　backend automations 145
　frontend automations 143, 144

　on-demand automations 144, 145
　using 143
decomposition tree 186
default environment 267
desktop flow
　fundamentals 113, 114
developer environment 267
Development Master 271
DirectQuery mode, Power BI 151, 152
　features 153
DLP Editor app 314
donut chart 183
dynamic content 97
Dynamics 365 considerations 58
　Dynamics 365 Customer Service 59
　Dynamics 365 Field Service 59
　Dynamics 365 licensing 13
　Dynamics 365 Marketing 59
　Dynamics 365 Project Operations 60
　Dynamics 365 Sales 59

E

enterprise-ready model-driven apps
　building 56, 57
　sample data, importing 57, 58
event-based automations 141

F

filled map 184
frontend automations 143, 144
funnel chart 180, 181

G

gauges 185
GitHub 278

H

Hierarchy security 298
hyper-automated solutions
  building 114, 115

I

identity document (ID) 241
image-processing models
  business card reader 241
  document processing 241
  identity document reader 241
  image classification 241
  invoice processing 240
  object detection 241
  receipt processing 240
  text recognition 240
Import mode, Power BI 151
  features 153
  versus DirectQuery mode 151, 152
IT industry
  in 21st century 2
IT security fundamentals 282, 283

K

key influencer chart 186
KPIs 186

L

line chart 178, 179
low-code development platform (LCDP) 3
low-code/no-code paradigm 3
  benefits 3, 4
  examples 4, 5

M

Maker Portal 17
  URL 17
maps 183
  bubble map 184
  filled map 184
  shape map 184
matrices 185
Microsoft 365/Office 365 licensing 11, 12
Microsoft cloud tenant
  provision 20-23
Microsoft Dataverse 7, 30
  features 7
Microsoft Dataverse fundamentals 33
  data model, creating 35
  simplified data model 34
Microsoft Power Platform 1
Microsoft SQL Server 18
Microsoft Teams environment 267, 268
model-driven app
  analysis and preparations 51
  autogenerated main forms, updating 52-54
  autogenerated views, updating 54, 55
  creating 51, 55, 56
  example 30
  features 29, 30
  fundamentals 50, 51
  practical implementation 51
multi-factor authentication (MFA) 285
MySQL 19

N

natural language query
  using 202, 203
no-code development platform (NCDPs) 3

O

on-demand automations 141
   creating 141-143
on-premises data gateway 9, 16
   usage 10

P

pie chart 183
portal apps 62
   customers, integrating with 89, 90
   example 32
   features 32
   fundamentals 80
   user authentication 89
   user authorization 90
Portal Management app 81
Power Apps 7
   canvas apps 7, 31
   for Project Wizards, Inc. 33
   model-driven apps 7, 29
   portal apps 7, 32
   types 29
   use cases 28, 62
Power Apps Mobile application 15
Power Apps Portals Studio 80
Power Automate 8, 91
   business process flow 8
   business process flows 93
   cloud flows 8, 93
   desktop flows 8, 93
   types of automations 93
   use cases 92, 93, 120
Power Automate Desktop tool 16
Power Automate portal 17
   URL 17

Power BI 8
   fundamentals 149
   Power BI Desktop 150
   Power BI Mobile 150
   Power BI Report 150
   Power BI Service 150
   requirements 150, 151
   use cases 148, 149
Power BI administration 266
Power BI Admin Portal 269
Power BI CoE starter kit report 310, 311
Power BI dashboard 199
   creating 199-202
Power BI Desktop 16, 18
   connecting, to Dataverse 157-163
   data, connecting 155, 156
   overview 154, 155
Power BI licensing 13, 14
   Power BI Free 13
   Power BI Premium per capacity 13
   Power BI Premium per user 13
   Power BI Pro 13
Power BI report
   building 186-197
   publishing 197-199
Power BI visualizations
   area chart 178, 179
   bar chart 176-178
   column chart 176-178
   decomposition tree 186
   donut chart 183
   funnel chart 180, 181
   gauges 185
   key influencer chart 186
   KPIs 186

line chart 178, 179
maps 183
matrices 185
overview 176
pie chart 183
ribbon chart 180
scatter chart 181, 182
slicers 185
tables 185
treemaps 185
waterfall chart 180
Power Fx 31, 76
  app functionality, configuring 77, 78
  fundamentals 76, 77
Power Platform
  fundamentals 5, 6
  starting 16
  system requirements 15, 16
Power Platform admin center 17, 268, 269
  URL 17
Power Platform administration
  overview 262, 263
  users and groups administration 263, 264
Power Platform admin view 312, 313
Power Platform components 6
  AI Builder 9
  data connectors 9
  fusion development 10
  Microsoft Dataverse 7
  on-premises data gateway 9, 10
  Power Apps 7
  Power Automate 8
  Power BI 8
  Power Virtual Agents 8, 9
Power Platform developer plan 14
Power Platform environment administration
  configuration settings 265, 266
  overview 266, 267
  tasks 264, 265
Power Platform environments
  default 267, 268
  developer 267
  Microsoft cloud tenant 20-23
  Microsoft Teams environment 267, 268
  Power Platform developer plan license, activating 23-25
  preparing 19, 20
  production 267
  sandbox 267
  trial 267
Power Platform environment strategies
  complex project, with multiple releases 271, 272
  complex project, with multiple teams 271
  setting up 270
  simple project 270, 271
Power Platform governance
  fundamentals 305
  data policies 305, 306
Power Platform licensing overview 10, 11
  Dynamics 365 licensing 13
  Microsoft 365/Office 365 licensing 11, 12
  Power BI licensing 13, 14
  Power Platform developer plan 14
  Power Platform pay-as-you-go

324 ■ Microsoft Power Platform Up and Running

licensing 14, 15
Power Platform standalone
   licensing 12
Power Platform trials 14
Power Platform mobile 19
Power Platform solution 272
   exporting 275-277
   managed 275
   unmanaged 274
Power Platform standalone licensing
   options 12
   Power Apps per app plan 12
   Power Apps per user plan 12
   Power Automate per flow plan 12
   Power Automate per user plan 12
Power Platform tools 16
   Maker Portal 17
   Microsoft SQL Server 18
   MySQL 19
   Power Automate portal 17
   Power BI Desktop 18
   Power Platform admin center 17
Power Platform trials 14
Power Query 163, 164
   data model, building 165
   data modeling exercise 167-171
   data transforming with 163, 164
PowerShell 279
Power Virtual Agents (PVA) 8, 9
   chatbot, creating 212
   fundamentals 211
   use cases 210
Prediction AI model 242
   binary prediction 242
   multiple outcome prediction 242

numerical prediction 242
production environment 267
Project Tracking app
   creating 66
   designing 64, 65
   table views, creating 66, 67
Project Wizards customer portal
   creating 81
Project Wizards, Inc. case study 28, 29

R

ribbon chart 180
Robotic Process Automation (RPA) 8, 93
Row-level security (RLS) 153

S

sample vendor invoice processing
   solution
   creating 115-117
sandbox environment 267
scatter chart 181, 182
scheduled automations 141
scheduled cloud flows 112, 113
secure Power Platform solutions
   building 304
security roles 290
shape map 184
simple portal apps
   configuring 81, 82
simplified data model
   columns 34
   database tables 34
   example 34
   relationships, between tables 34
slicers 185
Software as a Service (SaaS) type 10

solution management
  fundamentals 272-275
standard data connectors 11

T
tables 185
Teams 296
  access teams 296, 297
  owner teams 296
tenant-level data policy
  creating 307, 308, 309
text-processing models
  category classification 239
  entity extraction 239
  key phrase extraction 239
  language detection 240
  sentiment analysis 238

  text translation 240
tiles 199
treemaps 185
trial environment 267

U
user management, ADD 283

V
vendor invoice processing
  testing 254-259

W
waterfall chart 180

Printed in Great Britain
by Amazon